The Montmorency River has its source high up in the Laurentides.
Further down it eventually joins the Saint Lawrence River after a
drop of about 250 feet (75m). This mighty waterfall, which formerly
dropped directly into the Saint Lawrence, now ends about 1600 feet
(480m) from the edge of the riverbank. In winter, the dense mists at
the base of the waterfall freeze to form a massive cone of ice, which
is known as 'sugar loaf' by the Quebecois.

Photograph c.1876

'You have told us such beautiful things, said a Huron to the Jesuit Father Brébeuf in the early 1640s, and everything you have taught us may be true, but these truths are the truths of your people who have come from beyond the sea. Can you not see that we live in a world altogether different from yours, with our own Paradise and our own ways of arriving there?'
François-Xavier Charlevoix (1774)

Photograph c.1890

Snow in January: dazzling whiteness
everywhere, the air bitingly cold and
a muffled silence all around. High
winds and storms are also common
in the frozen winter months. Before
Montreal had an underground system,
and before the invention of the snow
plough, the extreme winter conditions
were an ordeal for the inhabitants.

Photograph c.1901

**This is a Borzoi Book
published by Alfred A. Knopf**

www.aaknopf.com

First American Edition

ISBN 0-375-71107-4

Originally published in France by Nouveaux-Loisirs, a subsidiary of Editions Gallimard, Paris, 1995. Copyright © 1995 by Editions Nouveaux-Loisirs.

Series editors
Shelley Wanger and Clémence Jacquinet

Translated by
Clive Unger-Hamilton and Matthew Clarke

Typeset by
Adrian McLaughlin

Edited by
Grapevine Publishing Services Ltd, London

Printed and bound in Italy by
Editoriale Lloyd

QUEBEC
Original French-language edition
COORDINATION: Virginie Maubourguet
EDITORS: Denis Béliveau, Céline Bouchard, Anne Cauquetoux, Sophie Mastelinck, Sabine Rousselet (Practical Information)
NATURE: Alban Larousse
ARCHITECTURE: Domitille Héron
LAYOUT: Benoît Giguère and Anne Thomas
ILLUSTRATIONS: Margaux Ouimet
COMMUNICATIONS: Chantal Périé
UPDATES: Michèle Delagneau, Denis Béliveau, Soraya Khalidy

Authors
IDENTITY: Claude Meinau
NATURE: Serge Courville, Kateri Lescop-Sinclair, Jean-Luc DesGranges, Pierre Fradette
HISTORY AND LANGUAGE: Paul-André Linteau, Daniel Arsenault, Laurier Turgeon, Thomas Wien, Claire Gourdeau, Brian Young, Nive Voisine, Michel Noel, Gaston Dulong, Henri Dorion, André Bolduc
ARTS AND TRADITIONS: Jocelyne Mathieu, René Hardy, Lucie K. Morisset, Eileen Marcil, Jean-Claude Dupont, Paul-Louis Martin, Donald Guay, Bernard Genest, Sophie-Laurence Lamontagne, Isabelle Tanguay, Aline Gélinas, Stéphane Lépine, Pierre Véronneau
ARCHITECTURE: Lucie K. Morisset, Jean Simard
QUEBEC AS SEEN BY PAINTERS: François-Marc Gagnon
QUEBEC AS SEEN BY WRITERS: Jean-François Chassay
ITINERARIES: Yves Beauregard, Jean-Paul Bernard, Hélène Bouchard, Russel Bouchard, Dinu Bumbaru, Dimitri Christozov, Normand David, Eric Fournier, Pierre Fradette, David B. Hanna, Fernard Harvey, Marc Lafarance, Serge Laurin, Jean-Marie Lebel, Paul-André Linteau, Paul-Louis Martin, Louis Messely, André Michel, Cristian Morissonneau, Museum of Civilization, Michel Noel, Pierre Rastoul, Bernard Saladin d'Anglure, Michel Savard, Louise Trottier, Bernard Vallée, Réal Viens, Claude Villeneuve, Odette Vincent, Nive Voisine

Illustrators:
NATURE: Jacqueline Candiard, Jean Chevallier, François Desbordes, Claire Felloni, Domitille Héron, Gilbert Houbre, Alban Larousse, Dominique Mansion, Patrick Mérienne, Serge Nicolle, François Place, Pascal Robin
HYDROELECTRICITY: Domitille Héron, Jean-Olivier Héron
ARTS AND TRADITIONS: Frédéric Back, Domitille Héron
THE SEASONS: Frédéric Back
ARCHITECTURE: Domitille Héron, Jean-Benoit Héron, Donald Lavoie, Josée Morin
ITINERARIES: Frédéric Back, François Desbordes, Domitille Héron, Alban Larousse
PRACTICAL INFORMATION: Justine Fournier, Maurice Pommier
MAPS AND COMPUTER GRAPHICS: Saintongé Vision Design

Cartographers
Saintonge Vision Design, Édigraphie

Photographers:
Pierre Lahoud, Sylvain Majeau, Brigitte Ostiguy, Pascal Quittemelle, Francois Rivard, Maxime St-Amour

With special thanks to:
Frédéric Back, Denis Béliveau, Roselyne Hébert, Paul-Louis Martin, Roanne Moktar, Lucie K. Morisset, Marie-Claude Saia, Nathalie Thibault and most particularly Paul-André Linteau for his clever advice.

We should also like to thank the Fonds de Solidarité des Travailleurs du Québec (FTQ) without whose support this book could never have been completed. The FTQ is an investment fund which calls publicly upon the savings – and the economic solidarity – of the 450,000 members of the Quebec Workers' Federation, as well as the entire population of the region in helping to create and conserve jobs in Quebec, especially with regard to small businesses.

In addition it is also a fund which seeks to be cost-effective and manage the accounts of its 430,000 shareholders. On June 30, 1998 the net assets of the fund were 3.8 billion dollars. Together with other associated funds, it held shares in more than 1,000 businesses in Quebec.

Quebec

KNOPF GUIDES

CONTENTS
Encyclopedia section

NATURE, *17*

Landscapes modeled by man, *18*
The land, *20*
The Saint Lawrence: fluvial section, *22*
The Saint Lawrence Estuary, *24*
Marine animals, *26*
Fishing methods, *28*
Tundra, *30*
Taiga, *32*
Temperate forest, *34*
Maple syrup, *36*

HISTORY AND LANGUAGE, *37*

History, *38*
Native Americans and Europeans in
the 16th century, *46*
The fur trade, *48*
The colonization of Nouvelle-France, *50*
The English influence, *52*
Catholic dominance from 1840 to 1960, *54*
The Quiet Revolution, *56*
Native Americans: the awakening, *58*
The Quebecois language, *60*
Place names in Quebec, *62*
FROM WATERMILLS TO HYDROELECTRIC POWER, *65*

ARTS AND TRADITION, *73*

Traditional dress, *74*
Forestry, *76*
Furniture, *78*
Transport on the Saint Lawrence, *80*
Maple sugar time, *82*
Hunting, *84*
Fishing, *86*
Sport, *88*
Preserving tradition, *90*
Songs and singers, *92*
Theater, *94*
Cinema and television, *96*
Food: *cipaille*, *98*
Quebec specialties, *100*
QUEBEC THROUGH THE SEASONS, *101*

ARCHITECTURE, *109*

The classical style in Nouvelle-France, *110*
Canadian architecture in the 18th century, *112*
British classicism (1780–1825), *114*
Neoclassicism (1825–60), *116*
Historical styles of the 19th century (1825–1914), *118*
19th-century church architecture, *120*
RELIGIOUS HERITAGE IN THE COUNTRYSIDE, *122*
From tradition to modernism (1900–40), *124*
Architecture of the Quiet Revolution (1950–75), *126*
Postmodernism (1975 to present), *128*
The way ahead, *130*

QUEBEC AS SEEN BY PAINTERS, *131*

QUEBEC AS SEEN BY WRITERS, *141*

CONTENTS
Itineraries in Quebec

MONTREAL, *163*

THE UNDERGROUND CITY, *176*
MONT ROYAL, *182*
'THE MAIN', *188*
BRIDGES AND ISLANDS, *198*
Montérégie, *204*
THE REBELLIONS OF 1837–8, *206*
Estrie, *210*
The Laurentides, *216*
From Montreal to Hull, *222*

MONTREAL

OTTAWA AND HULL, *225*

Abitibi–Témiscamingue, *230*
THE CARIBOU OR 'TUKTU', *232*
Radisson, *234*

TROIS-RIVIÈRES, *235*

OTTAWA AND HULL

Saint-Maurice Valley, *240*
THE BEAVER, *242*
Around les Bois-Francs, *244*
On the banks of Lake Saint-Pierre, *248*

QUEBEC, *251*

TROIS-RIVIÈRES

THE MUSEUM OF CIVILIZATION, *256*
THE FORTIFICATIONS, *262*
Chaudière River–Beauce, *274*
Côte-de-Beaupré and Charlevoix, *276*
DEVOTIONS TO SAINT ANNE, *278*
CAP TOURMENTE, *282*
CHARLEVOIX: BETWEEN SEA AND MOUNTAIN, *286*
South Shore and Lower Saint Lawrence, *288*
'THE RIVER WITH GREAT WATERS', *294*

QUEBEC

GASPÉSIE AND ÎLES-DE-LA-MADELEINE, *297*

FORILLON PARK, *304*
A CHAIN OF ISLANDS IN THE GULF
OF SAINT LAWRENCE, *310*
Îles-de-la-Madeleine, *312*

GASPÉSIE AND–
ÎLES-DE-LA-MADELEINE

SAGUENAY-LAC-SAINT-JEAN, *317*

SAGUENAY FJORD, *324*

NORTH SHORE, *327*

SAGUENAY-–
LAC-SAINT-JEAN

ANTICOSTI ISLAND, *332*
Lower North Shore, *334*

NUNAVIK, *335*

Inuit history, *336*
INUIT TRADITIONS, *338*
INUIT MYTHS, RITUALS AND BELIEFS, *340*
INUIT ART, *342*
The Inuits of Nunavik today, *344*

NORTH SHORE AND
LOWER NORTH SHORE

PRACTICAL INFORMATION, *345*

INDEX, *398*

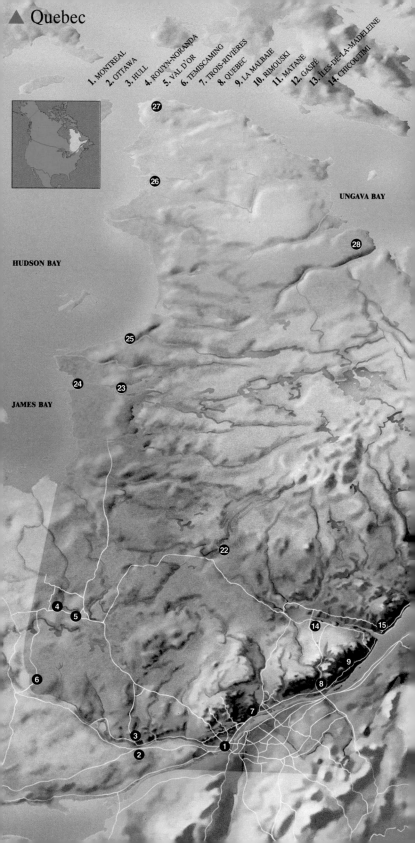

▲ Quebec

1. MONTREAL
2. OTTAWA
3. HULL
4. ROUYN-NORANDA
5. VAL D'OR
6. TEMISCAMING
7. TROIS-RIVIÈRES
8. QUEBEC
9. LA MALBAIE
10. RIMOUSKI
11. MATANE
12. GASPÉ
13. ÎLES-DE-LA-MADELEINE
14. CHICOUTIMI

HUDSON BAY

UNGAVA BAY

JAMES BAY

15. TADOUSSAC
16. BAIE-COMEAU
17. SEPT-ÎLES
18. HAVRE-SAINT-PIERRE
19. ANTICOSTI ISLAND
20. BLANC-SABLON
21. FERMONT
22. CHIBOUGAMAU
23. RADISSON
24. CHISASIBI
25. KUUJJUARAPIK
26. PIVIRNITUK
27. IVUJIVIK
28. KUUJJUAQ

ATLANTIC OCEAN

SAINT LAWRENCE RIVER

● The province of Quebec

INDUSTRY
The industrialization of Quebec has always been linked to hydroelectricity ● 65, an inexpensive and readily available source of power. The growth of industries such as aluminum production and paper manufacture, which require a lot of power, depended on hydroelectricity.

Quebec is also one of the richest mineral regions in the world, with mines producing gold, iron ore, copper, zinc and asbestos. Communications, pharmaceuticals and aeronautics are also growth industries in the province.

QUEBEC IN FIGURES

Surface area:
594,534 sq. mi.
(1,667,926 sq. km)
(15.5% of Canada)
Population:
7,372,000
(24.75% of Canada)
Provincial capital:
Quebec
Official language:
French
19 tourist regions
1. Îles-de-la-
   Madeleine
2. Gaspésie
3. Bas-Saint-Laurent
4. Quebec
5. Charlevoix
6. Chaudière-
   Appalaches
7. Mauricie
8. Estrie
9. Montérégie
10. Lanaudière
11. Laurentides
12. Montreal
13. Outaouais
14. Abitibi-
    Témiscamingue
15. Saguenay-Lac-
    Saint-Jean
16. Manicouagan
17. Duplessis
18. Nouveau-Quebec-
    Baie-James
19. Laval

TOURISM
This is an increasingly important part of the province's economy. Apart from the US market, which provides a regular influx of visitors, tourism has more than doubled in the last 15 years. Today Quebec attracts more than seven million visitors per year, a larger figure than the population of the entire province.

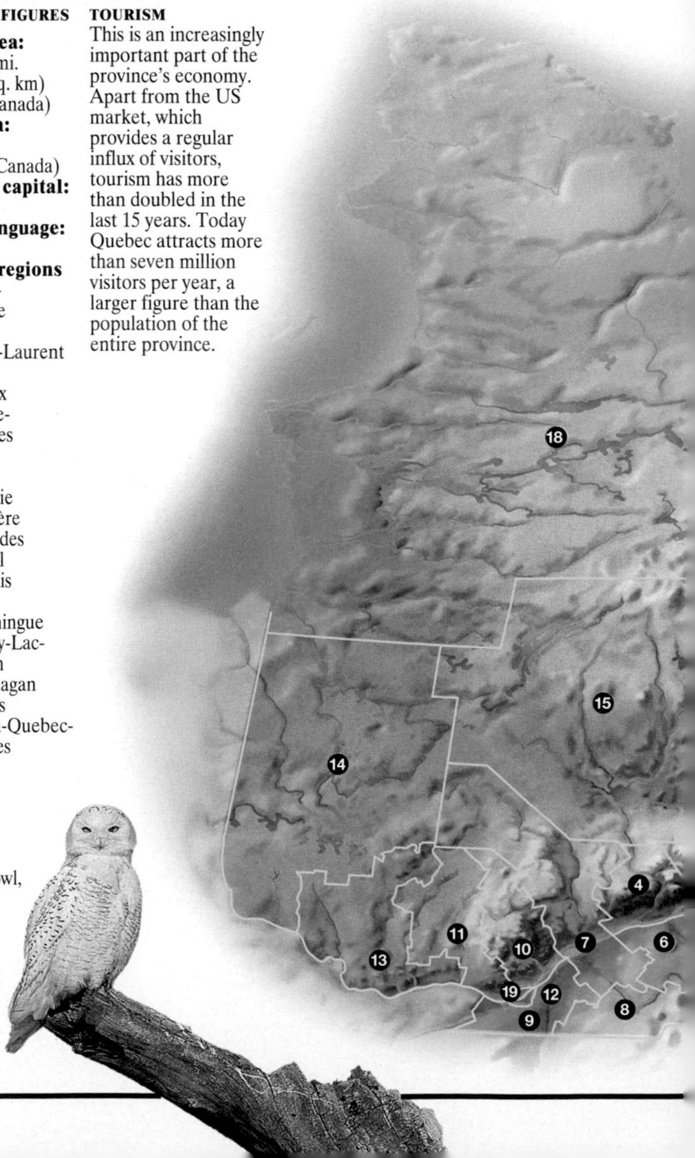

EMBLEM
The snowy owl, a large, white, nocturnal bird of prey, was adopted as Quebec's official emblem in 1987.

14

AGRICULTURE
The Quebec countryside is divided into distinctive narrow parcels of land called *rangs*, a relic of the old seigneurial system ● *50*. Dairy farming predominates, accounting for almost one-third of Quebec's total agricultural production. After hay, which is grown to feed livestock, sugar beet is one of the most important crops.

POPULATION AND LANGUAGE
Around 82 percent of the population are French-speaking, 10 percent English-speaking and 1 percent aboriginal, leaving roughly 7 percent of people known as 'allophone', in other words speaking languages other than those mentioned above. A bill (Law 101) was passed in 1977, making French the official language of Quebec.

FOREST
Almost two-thirds of the province is covered by forest, and about half of that is commercially farmed. The northern part is mainly coniferous, supplying the paper, pulp and construction industries. In mixed forest with both conifers and broad-leaved trees, oils of spruce and pine are extracted on a commercial basis.

'JE ME SOUVIENS'
The slogan 'I remember' became a byword of the new Quebec Parliament, for which a new building was erected between 1877 and 1886. It was officially adopted by the province in 1883, as part of the struggle to preserve the French way of life and urge people to remember their Gallic heritage in the face of British conquest.

15

How to use this guide

The symbols at the top of the page refer to the different sections of the guide.

- ■ Nature
- ● Encyclopedia section
- ▲ Itineraries
- ◆ Practical information

The itinerary map shows the main sites and enables you to refer to a road map.

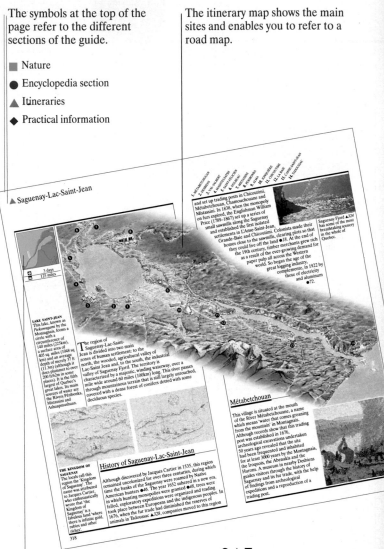

▲ Saguenay-Lac-Saint-Jean

3 days
125 miles

LAKE SAINT-JEAN
This lake, known as Piekowagami by the Montagnais, forms a circle with a circumference of 140 miles (225km), a surface area of 405 sq. miles (1048 sq. km) and an average depth of the nearly 37 ft (11.3m) (although it does plummet to over 200 ft/63.2m in some places). It is the fifth largest of Quebec's great lakes. Its main sources of water are the Rivers Péribonka, Mistassini and Ashuapmushuan.

The region of Saguenay-Lac-Saint-Jean is divided into two main zones of human settlement: to the north, the wooded, agricultural valley of Lac-Saint Jean and, to the south, the industrial valley of Saguenay Fjord. The territory is characterized by a majestic, winding waterway, over a mile wide around 60 miles (100km) long. This river passes through mountainous terrain that is still largely untouched, covered with a dense forest of conifers dotted with some deciduous species.

THE KINGDOM OF SAGUENAY
The locals call this region the Kingdom of Saguenay. The name was attributed to Jacques Cartier, who enthusiastically wrote that 'the Kingdom of Saguenay' is a fabulous land 'where there is infinite gold, rubies and other riches'.

History of Saguenay-Lac-Saint-Jean

Although discovered by Jacques Cartier in 1535, this region remained uncolonized for over three centuries, during which time the banks of the Saguenay were roamed by Native American hunters ●46. The year 1652 ushered in a new era, in which hunting monopolies were organized and trading took place between Europeans and the indigenous peoples. In 1676, when the fur trade had diminished the reserves of animals in Tadoussac ▲228, companies moved to this region

1. MÉTABETCHOUAN
2. DESBIENS
3. VAL-JALBERT
4. ROBERVAL
5. SAINT-FÉLICIEN
6. DOLBEAU
7. MISTASSINI
8. PÉRIBONKA
9. ALMA
10. JONQUIÈRE
11. CHICOUTIMI
12. LA BAIE
13. L'ANSE-SAINT-JEAN
14. TADOUSSAC

and set up trading posts in Chicoutimi, Métabetchouan, Chamouchouane and Mistassini. In 1838, when the monopoly on furs expired, the Englishman William Price (1789–1867) set up a series of small sawmills along the Saguenay and established the first isolated settlements in L'Anse-Saint-Jean, Grande-Baie and Chicoutimi. Colonists made their homes close to the sawmills, clearing plots so that they could live off the land ●18. At the end of the 19th century, timber merchants grew rich as a result of the ever-growing demand for paper pulp all across the Western world. So began the age of the great logging industry, complemented, in 1922 by those of electricity and aluminum ●72.

Saguenay Fjord ▲324 has some of the most breathtaking scenery in the whole of Quebec.

Métabetchouan

This village is situated at the mouth of the River Métabetchouane, a name which means 'water that comes groaning from the mountain' in Montagnais. Although records show that this trading post was established in 1676, archeological excavations undertaken 50 years ago revealed that the site had been frequented and inhabited for at least 3000 years by the Montagnais, the Iroquois, the Abenakis and the Hurons. A museum in nearby Desbiens guides visitors through the history of Saguenay and its fur trade, with the help of findings from archeological expeditions and a reproduction of a trading post.

318

In the itineraries, all the sites of interest are given a map reference.

The mini-map pinpoints the itinerary within the wider area covered by the guide and there is an indication of how long it would take to cover the route by different methods.

- 🚗 By car
- 🚶 On foot
- 🚲 By bicycle
- ⏱ Duration

● ▲ ■
The above symbols within the text provide cross-references to a place or a theme discussed elsewhere in the guide.

★
The star symbol indicates sites of outstanding beauty, atmosphere or cultural interest.

Nature

Landscapes modeled by man, *18*
The land, *20*
The Saint Lawrence: fluvial section, *22*
The Saint Lawrence Estuary, *24*
Marine animals, *26*
Fishing methods, *28*
Tundra, *30*
Taiga, *32*
Temperate forest, *34*
Maple syrup, *36*

■ Landscapes modeled by man

'It is a totally new world ... a land almost 1800 leagues in length, traversed by the mighty Saint Lawrence River, the jewel in its crown,' wrote the French traveler Samuel de Champlain in 1619 about the land he was exploring. Formed by shifting ice in the Quaternary, Quebec boasts a variety of different landscapes: lakes, rivers, mountains, prairie and high plains.

Mankind settled here gradually, in a series of expeditions that formed the history of the province. From the first Native American villages to the great hydroelectric schemes in James Bay, Quebec's history is an astonishing tale of change and survival in the face of remorseless but abundant nature.

THE SEIGNEURIES OF THE PLAIN
Following some tentative but fruitless attempts at colonization, the first 'seigneuries' ● *50* were established on the banks of the Saint Lawrence in the early 17th century. Thanks to the use of the river as a line of communication and the rich alluvial soil of the plain, the early French colonists prospered. Land management worked on the old French seigneurial principle: whether they were nobles or not, seigneurs were given a piece of land which they divided into narrow strips extending inland from a river frontage such as the Saint Lawrence. This unique patterning of the Quebec landscape into *rangs* is still evident today.

EASTERN TOWNSHIPS
Once the banks of the Saint Lawrence were settled, subsequent waves of immigrants had no choice but to move further afield. In the late 18th century, English colonists opposed to American independence (so-called 'loyalists') migrated north to Canada where they set up a cadastral system of land on territory known as the Cantons de l'Est (Eastern Townships) ▲ *210* – a different system to *rangs*.

NEW FRONTIERS
Since World War 2, the exploitation of natural resources, such as forests, minerals and hydroelectric power, has extended the limits of workable territory to the very edges of the province (in regions such as the North Shore ▲ *328*). Consequently, several new townships have sprung up which are dependent upon a single industry for their survival.

FIRST OCCUPANTS
The first Native Americans crossed the ocean from Asia and settled in Canada about 10,000 years ago, toward the end of the last ice age. A few thousand years later, different groups ● *44* were able to settle in other parts of Quebec, thanks to the retreating glaciers.

REGIONS TO CONQUER
In the 19th century Quebec underwent much migratory movement, which was linked to the exploitation of its natural resources – in particular, timber and farmland. In spite of the poor quality of much of the land, colonists worked tirelessly to develop underpopulated regions such as Gaspésie ▲ *298*, Mauricie ▲ *240* and the Laurentides ▲ *216*. The economic crisis of 1930 also brought another influx of colonists, especially to Abitibi ▲ *230*.

GROWTH OF URBANIZATION
While streams of colonists were heading out to occupy virgin territory, others preferred to settle in established townships in hope of finding work there. Montreal underwent a huge demographic increase in the 19th century but the population of Quebec remained predominantly rural until 1921.

■ The land

FIELD OF FLOWERS IN GASPÉSIE
In late summer, a profuse blooming
of wild flowers brings the brief season
of growth to an end.

A relief map of Quebec does not
reveal any marked contrasts.
The seasons, on the other hand, are extremely diverse, under
the influence of the cold Labrador current. A long, harsh winter
gives place to a much-awaited spring, followed by a hot summer
and a richly tinted fall. Three phytogeographic zones, their limits
defined by temperature, the nature of the ground, the growing
season and the prevailing winds, make
up the landscape: tundra in the north,
boreal forest in the center, and
temperate forest in the south.

Arctic zone

Boreal zone

Temperate zone

Extent of ice on Jan 1

Extent of ice at end of Jan

Extent of ice on Feb 26

Extent of ice on April 1

Ocean

Boreal forest grows
on a base formed of
crystalline
Pre-Cambrian rock
■ 32.

Phases of last glaciation
(no. of years ago in relation
to the present day)

0 to −7000   −10000 to −13000
−7000 to −10000   −13000 or more

Snow (average no. of days per year)
more than 280   160 to 200
240 to 280   120 to 160
200 to 240   80 to 120
                 less than 80

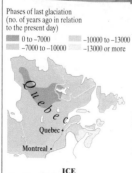

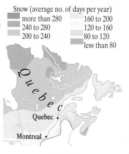

January (average temperature in degrees F)
−13 or lower   5 to 23
−13 to 23   above 23

ICE
Wisconsinian glaciation struck
Quebec 20,000 years ago. The
advance and retreat of the
glacier were responsible for
shaping the Quebec landscape.
Today, the ice formation on
the river and in the gulf is at
its lowest in early May.

SNOW
The south of Quebec has
snow on the ground for the
fewest days per year. In the
northern tundra, snow
remains almost until June. In
certain places the landscape is
dotted with snow-filled valleys
in early summer.

TEMPERATURE
The lowest annual temperatures
are recorded in January.
Even in the south of Quebec
temperatures commonly drop
below −22°F (−30°C).

INDIAN SUMMER
This brief spell of warm weather occurs in mid-fall, after several frosts. Its name derives from Native Americans who thought this period came as a gift from a benevolent god who lived in the south-west.

In the north, the tundra is covered by low vegetation ■ *30*. Snow is on the ground for about nine months of the year, and the low rate of evaporation gives this region a dry climate.

HARSH WINTER
The first snow falls begin early in the fall and continue to blow in until late April. During this period the Saint Lawrence freezes over ■ *22*. Quebec is also situated in the path of severe storms.

The icy Labrador current follows a path between Baffin Island and Greenland. It makes the Quebec climate even colder as it passes along the Labrador coastline.

Temperate forest is found chiefly in the low-lying lands of the Saint Lawrence Valley and in the Appalachian region ■ *34*. This area enjoys the province's longest growing season.

SHELTER FOR LICHEN
A spruce forest in the taiga, or boreal zone. In winter it is covered by a thick layer of snow that offers protection to vegetation and refuge for animals who make it their winter home.

BARNACLE GOOSE
This familiar bird nests in the boreal forest and tundra of Quebec and other northern parts of Canada, flying down to the US to escape the freezing winter. The geese migrate in noisy groups, which fly in a V formation, and return north in March when the snow begins to melt. The barnacle goose is also known as the Canada goose.

■ The Saint Lawrence: fluvial section

TYPHA. These aquatic plants grow abundantly on the fertile organic waste of the riverbed, and are largely responsible for the densely reeded banks of the river.

The richest biological environment on the Saint Lawrence is the wetland region around Lake Saint-Pierre. Large expanses of grassy bog and clumps of floating vegetation cover much of this shallow river tributary, fringed by water meadows, forest and marshland shrubs. All kinds of invertebrate life here provide a valuable source of food for other animals, and in addition the area is an ideal place for migrating birds to rest.

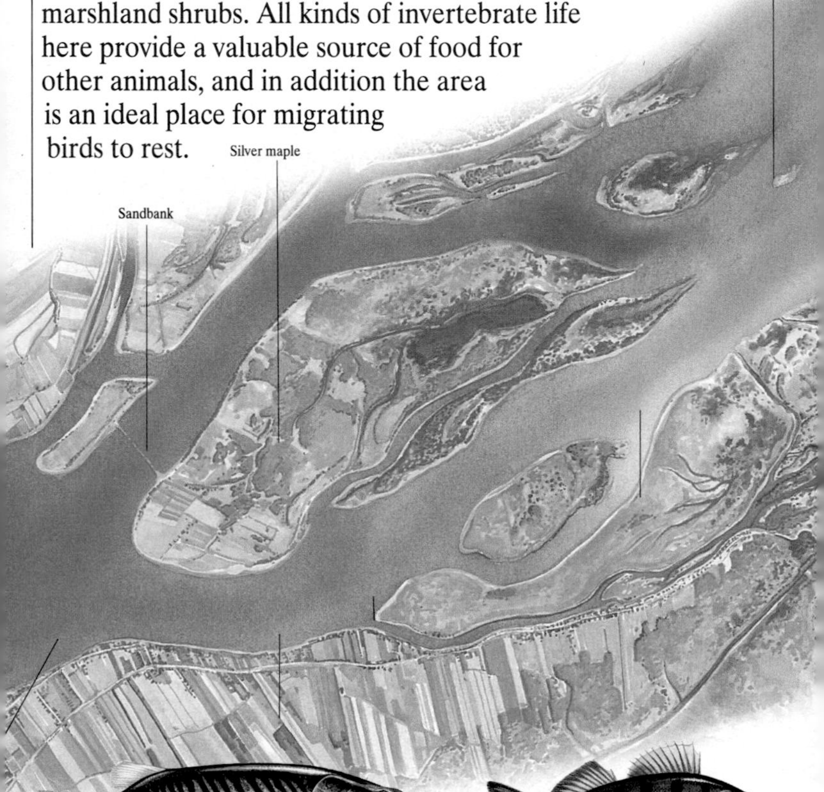

Spillway

Silver maple

Sandbank

PIKE
This large freshwater fish lives in the still and densely weeded lakes that border the fluvial section of the Saint Lawrence.

YELLOW PERCH
A common prey of larger fish, as well as some fish-eating birds.

Deposits from Lake Champlain (sand and silt) up to 300 feet (90m.) deep.

Sedimentary layer on the low-lying lands around the Saint Lawrence (schist, limestone and shale).

Extent of the fluvial section of the Saint Lawrence

THE SAINT LAWRENCE IN WINTER
A navigable channel, sections of which have to be dredged or de-iced, gives water traffic access to the Great Lakes.

Alluvial deposits

Typha marsh
Richelieu River

St Francis River

HERON
One island in the Lake St Peter archipelago has a heronry with almost 1000 nesting pairs.

MARSH WREN
This bird's nest is a ball of woven grass attached to the stem of an aquatic plant.

WOOD DUCK (CAROLIN)
It normally nests in the hollows of trees, but the wood duck can easily be persuaded to settle in an artificial nest, which helps to ensure its survival.

Maritime channel

The Saint Lawrence Estuary

The spartina saltmarsh produces three times as much vegetable matter as a well-fertilized field of corn.

The south bank of the maritime St Lawrence Estuary consists of alluvial marine mudflats which are gradually replaced by coastal cliffs overhanging the rocky beaches. Here and there along the coast at the back of bays and coves are tussocky salt marshes. Chiefly composed of spartina, they provide a rich source of nutrition: millions of migrating coastal birds stop here to feed and rest, while other aquatic birds find it an ideal environment in which to live and rear their young.

ESTUARY AND GULF OF SAINT LAWRENCE
These are the gateway to an international navigation route 2,400 miles (3,700 km) long.

Gulf of St Lawrence
Estuarial zone

BLACK DUCK
A wading duck that is found in tidal waters as well as in marshy freshwater habitats.

EIDER DUCK
A marine duck covered with a dense, soft down, from which the eiderdown derives its name.

Winter plumage

BLACK GUILLEMOT
This tiny auk nests in small colonies, in clifftop crevasses or on slopes of scree.

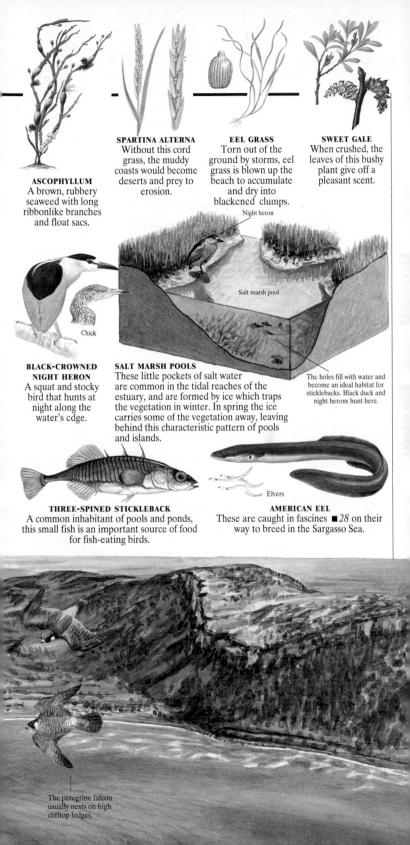

ASCOPHYLLUM
A brown, rubbery seaweed with long ribbonlike branches and float sacs.

SPARTINA ALTERNA
Without this cord grass, the muddy coasts would become deserts and prey to erosion.

EEL GRASS
Torn out of the ground by storms, eel grass is blown up the beach to accumulate and dry into blackened clumps.

SWEET GALE
When crushed, the leaves of this bushy plant give off a pleasant scent.

Night heron

Salt marsh pool

Chick

BLACK-CROWNED NIGHT HERON
A squat and stocky bird that hunts at night along the water's edge.

SALT MARSH POOLS
These little pockets of salt water are common in the tidal reaches of the estuary, and are formed by ice which traps the vegetation in winter. In spring the ice carries some of the vegetation away, leaving behind this characteristic pattern of pools and islands.

The holes fill with water and become an ideal habitat for sticklebacks. Black duck and night herons hunt here.

Elvers

THREE-SPINED STICKLEBACK
A common inhabitant of pools and ponds, this small fish is an important source of food for fish-eating birds.

AMERICAN EEL
These are caught in fascines ■*28* on their way to breed in the Sargasso Sea.

The peregrine falcon usually nests on high clifftop ledges.

Marine animals

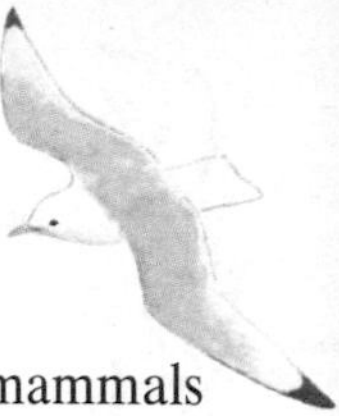

THREE-TOED GULL
These seabirds nest in
colonies on cliffs and
catch food in the sea.

Numerous marine mammals
visit this arm of the Atlantic
Ocean, the gulf and the estuary
of the Saint Lawrence River. The
mineral-rich water rising from
the ocean depths to the upper
reaches of the maritime estuary and around Mingan on the north
coast creates ideal conditions for an abundant population of
phytoplankton, small fish and crustaceans. Such a seemingly
endless supply of food attracts seals and whales in vast numbers:
the population of beluga whales alone may be as many as 500.

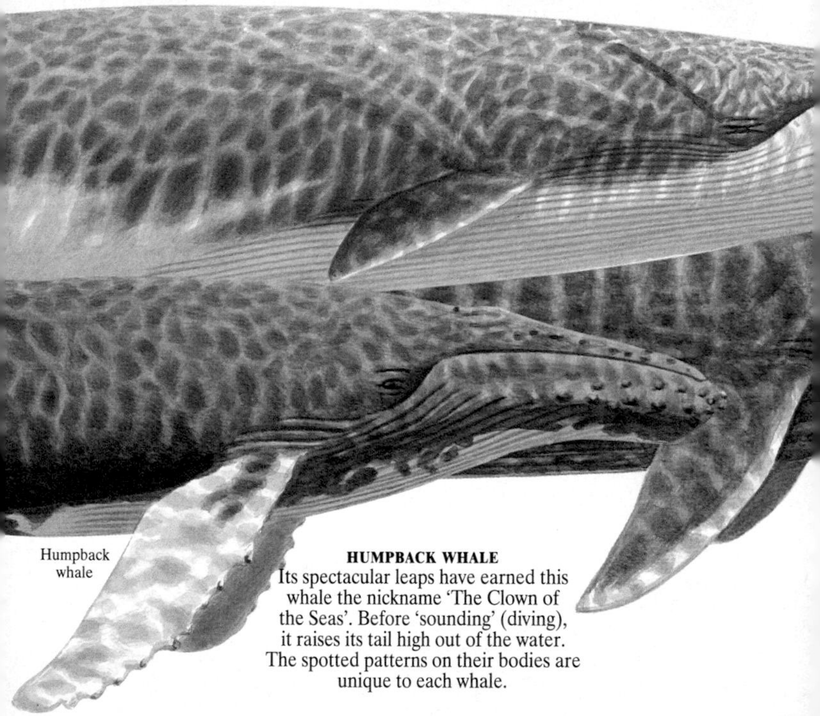

Humpback
whale

HUMPBACK WHALE
Its spectacular leaps have earned this
whale the nickname 'The Clown of
the Seas'. Before 'sounding' (diving),
it raises its tail high out of the water.
The spotted patterns on their bodies are
unique to each whale.

DIVING SEQUENCE OF FOUR WHALES

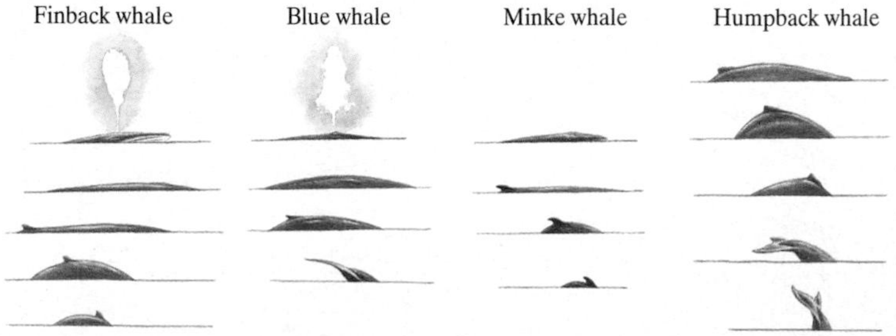

| Finback whale | Blue whale | Minke whale | Humpback whale |

PARASITIC JAEGER
When migrating, these birds chase seagulls, forcing them to regurgitate their food, which the jaegers catch in mid-air.

BONAPARTE'S GULL
This seabird feeds on fish that the whales fail to ingest.

Common seal

Gray seal

FINBACK WHALE
When feeding, it rolls on its right side, opens its mouth and swims in circles to catch shoals of tiny fish trying to escape.

COMMON SEAL AND GRAY SEAL
These animals are widely distributed in the oceans and seas, but small colonies of common seals are found in some lakes in northern Quebec. Both species are often seen basking on rocks around the coast. In the water they are hunted by killer whales and sharks.

Finback whale

Blue whale

BLUE WHALE
A blue whale will feed up to six times per day, consuming four or five tons of krill that it has filtered through its baleen plates. Its stomach can hold about a ton of food at a time.

MINKE WHALE
After breathing and just before diving, it arches its back and shows its dorsal fin, but not its tail.

COMMON PORPOISE
The smallest of the cetaceans (less than 7 feet/2.1 m long), this porpoise swims on the surface, not far offshore, in schools of 10 or 15.

Common porpoise

Beluga

Atlantic white-sided dolphin

ATLANTIC WHITE-SIDED DOLPHIN
Between dives, a school of dolphins will swim along the ocean surface in close formation at around 15 knots. They can often be seen leaping out of the water.

BELUGA
The so-called 'sea canary' sings almost constantly, emitting clicks, squeals and whistles. It uses echo-location to find holes in the ice to enable it to breathe during the freezing winters. While other whales migrate and only come to the Quebec waters to feed, the beluga whale lives and breeds in the Saint Lawrence area.

■ Fishing methods

FASCINE FISHING. The fascine is a barrier of vertical sticks planted close together near the shore; it traps fish, such as herring, which swim in but cannot get out again.

The fishing ports found all along the estuary and the Gulf of Saint Lawrence reflect the wide variety of fishing methods used by coastal and deep-sea fishermen. Some of the most famous specialties of the region are the shellfish, such as lobster, crab, prawns and shrimp, and deep-sea fish such as cod and sea bream. Herring and capelin (a small fish related to the smelt) are caught in their breeding grounds close to the shore.

CHIEF FISHING PORTS
Lobster is the specialty of ports in Gaspésie and the Îles-de-la-Madeleine, Nordic prawns come from Matane, and dragging for gapers is the main occupation of Rivière-Portneuf. Crabbing is the chief industry in the ports on the north side of the estuary.

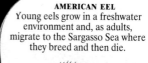

AMERICAN EEL
Young eels grow in a freshwater environment and, as adults, migrate to the Sargasso Sea where they breed and then die.

SEA BREAM
Two species of sea bream, virtually identical in appearance, live in the deep waters of the Saint Lawrence. Their growth is slow, and they can reach 35 years of age.

ATLANTIC SALMON
After some years at sea, adult salmon swim back upriver to spawn. This is where they become the keenly sought prey of fly-fishermen ●86.

GREENLAND HALIBUT
Also, and confusingly, known as the Greenland turbot, this flatfish likes deep, cold water. It is caught using longlines or gillnets.

COD
Cod glide amongst rocks on the seabed, foraging ceaselessly for food.

MOLLUSCS. The gaper (1) lives buried in mud and feeds by filtering seawater. Scallops (2) live on the shifting sandy seabed. Clams (3) are found chiefly in tidal areas, while blue mussels (4) attach themselves to solid objects such as rocks.

HERRING.
Herring feed exclusively on plankton, which they catch at night when it rises to the surface.

CRABBING. Crabs are harvested by inshore and deep-sea fishing fleets. The boats range from 45 to 80 feet (14 to 24m) in length.

SHRIMP BOAT. Its net generally trails out from the stern of the boat. Once sorted, the catch is packed in ice in the hold.

PINK SHRIMP
Pink shrimps are hermaphrodite. They are born male and metamorphize to female at about three years old. They are fished with nets and, in contrast to crabs, it's preferable to eat the females.

LOBSTER POT
Semi-cylindrical or rectangular, the baited pots have a small entrance through which the lobsters are unable to escape.

POT FOR SNOW CRAB
Snow crab are trapped in large, conical steel-mesh traps that are usually baited with chopped herring and sit on the ocean bed at depths of between 30 to 1500 feet (9 to 450m).

SNOW CRAB
Soft-shelled, so-called 'white crabs' appear in crab-pots in the molting season, indicating the start of the short fishing season.

AMERICAN LOBSTER
Like all crustaceans, the lobster sheds its shell as it grows. After molting, it will eat its own cast-off shell. Males molt every year, while hen lobsters molt every two years, as they spend every other year carrying eggs in their abdomens. It takes between six and eight years for a lobster to reach a commercial size.

Tundra

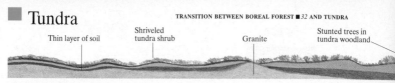

Thin layer of soil | Shriveled tundra shrub | Granite | Stunted trees in tundra woodland

Tundra occurs in the far north of Quebec, where the prevailing climate is harsh, with low temperatures and strong winds. Permafrost (permanently frozen ground) covers a large part of the region. The countryside is made up of patches of tundra overlaid with low, scrubby vegetation. Various lichens are a feature where the ground is dry, along with dwarf willows and heathers. In spring and summer, both of which are short at these latitudes, plants have to complete their annual life cycle quickly. To the south of the region, in valleys and sheltered places, are low, dense growths of spruce (*krummholz* trees).

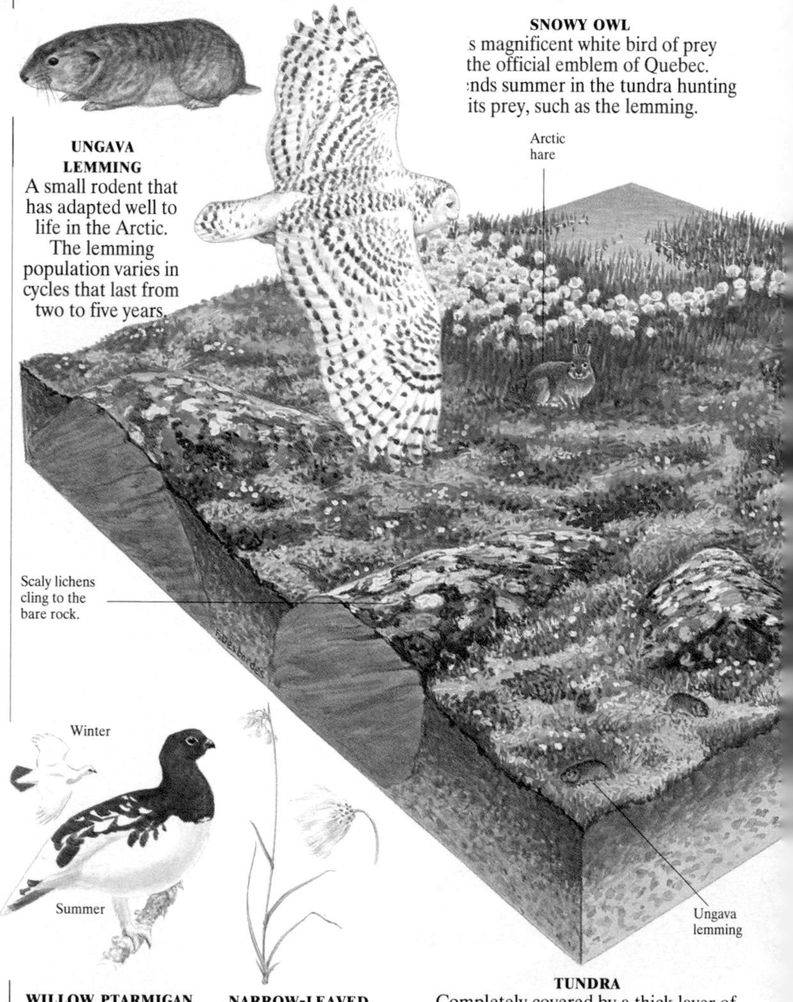

SNOWY OWL
s magnificent white bird of prey
the official emblem of Quebec.
:nds summer in the tundra hunting
its prey, such as the lemming.

Arctic hare

UNGAVA LEMMING
A small rodent that has adapted well to life in the Arctic. The lemming population varies in cycles that last from two to five years.

Scaly lichens cling to the bare rock.

Winter

Summer

Ungava lemming

WILLOW PTARMIGAN
This bird lives among the dwarf willows. Feathered feet help protect it from cold.

NARROW-LEAVED COTTON GRASS
A plant with fluffy white flowers that thrives in damp soil.

TUNDRA
Completely covered by a thick layer of snow for most of the year, tundra erupts into a blaze of color during the short summer season ■ 20.

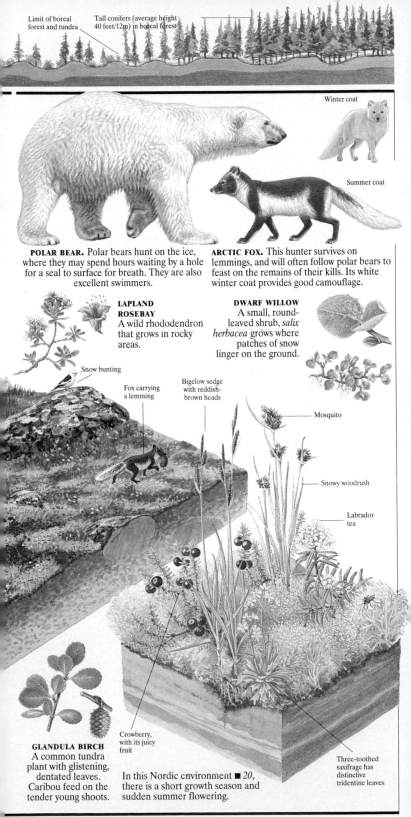

Limit of boreal forest and tundra

Tall conifers (average height 40 feet/12m) in boreal forest

Winter coat

Summer coat

POLAR BEAR. Polar bears hunt on the ice, where they may spend hours waiting by a hole for a seal to surface for breath. They are also excellent swimmers.

ARCTIC FOX. This hunter survives on lemmings, and will often follow polar bears to feast on the remains of their kills. Its white winter coat provides good camouflage.

LAPLAND ROSEBAY A wild rhododendron that grows in rocky areas.

DWARF WILLOW A small, round-leaved shrub, *salix herbacea* grows where patches of snow linger on the ground.

Snow bunting

Fox carrying a lemming

Bigelow sedge with reddish-brown heads

Mosquito

Snowy woodrush

Labrador tea

GLANDULA BIRCH A common tundra plant with glistening, dentated leaves. Caribou feed on the tender young shoots.

Crowberry, with its juicy fruit

In this Nordic environment ■ 20, there is a short growth season and sudden summer flowering.

Three-toothed saxifrage has distinctive tridentine leaves

Taiga

The taiga, or boreal forest, which consists largely of balsam fir and black spruce trees with the occasional paper birch, covers a large part of the province of Quebec. Dense in the south but more scattered in the north, it has sparse undergrowth and the trees rarely live long, due to frequent forest fires. The soil is acid, and the land is broken up by peat bogs, lakes and rivers. It is a harsh ecosystem with freezing winters and short, hot summers, but some mammals, such as the American marten and red squirrel, have managed to thrive.

FORESTRY. Cutting trees in a checkerboard pattern helps to conserve the habitat of many animal species in the forest.

MOOSE (ELK)
An excellent swimmer, this giant deer (6 feet/1.8m at the shoulder) lives near lakes in summer, where it grazes on aquatic plants.

Female

Male

WHITE-WINGED CROSSBILL
Its curious beak allows it to peel the conifer seeds which form the mainstay of its diet.

LABRADOR TEA
Its leaves have a refreshing smell, and are used to make a popular herbal tea.

CLADONIA RANGIFERNIA
A gray-green lichen, known as caribou moss, this is common in well-drained, open environments.

COW PARSNIP
Common in maple groves, and mixed and coniferous forests, this plant is also known as wild lily-of-the-valley.

Burnt forest

BALSAM FIR. Its symmetrical shape makes it the ideal Christmas tree. The flat needles have white undersides.

BLACK SPRUCE. Black spruce trees dominate the landscape of the northern boreal forests. Their elongated shape and four-sided needles make them easy to recognize.

GRAY PINE. It favors sandy or shingly ground. Its cones only open if exposed to the intense heat of fire.

PAPER BIRCH
Its white bark peels away in long strips, which Native Americans once used to make canoes and domestic containers.

Lightning starts forest fires.

Fire spreads from one treetop to another.

Dead trunks remain standing for years while the forest grows again.

Contrary to popular belief, forest fires are a vital part of conserving boreal forest: some tree species only spread their seeds when their cones reach a high temperature.

Boreal owl (Tengmalm's owl)

The American red squirrel feeds on seeds from the cones of the black spruce.

Temperate forest

Raccoon

In southern Quebec, tundra and boreal forests give way to temperate forest. Maple groves, cultivated for the production of maple syrup, dominate the warmest regions, while at higher altitudes or further north they are interspersed with yellow birch and conifers, such as eastern hemlock and white pine. Temperate forest has dense undergrowth, thick with ferns and vibernum. There is a wide variety of animal life, including beavers and deer, and numerous birds, such as nuthatches, warblers and thrush.

RACCOON
The black and white masked face and ringed tail are the raccoon's most prominent, trademark features.

VIRGINIA DEER
Also known as the white-tailed deer, it lives among young trees, but spends winter in thick coniferous forest, where the snow is thinner.

AUTUMN COLORS
In fall, the trees take on magnificent red and gold tints, which vary according to the acidity of the soil and the temperature.

TREE FROG
In spring, the incessant nocturnal calling of these tree-dwellers sounds like a peal of tiny bells.

WHITE PINE
A majestic conifer that is now rare, as a result of over-expoitation by foresters in the 19th century.

Woodpecker

R. Desbordes

The Blackpoll warbler visits Canadian forests in spring, on its way north to breed.

RED-BACKED SALAMANDER
This reptile hunts for insects in the leaves on the ground at night.

SUGAR MAPLE ■ *36* ● *82*
Perhaps the most familiar tree in temperate forests, the sugar maple likes a shady environment and can live for 300 or 400 years. In fall its colors are particularly spectacular.

RUFFED GROUSE
When courting, the male beats its wings so loudly it sounds like an automobile engine starting up.

SCARLET TANAGER
A forest dweller, this attractive bird migrates to Colombia and Bolivia in winter.

BLACK-CAPPED CHICKADEE
This bird is common in suburban areas as well as in deep forest.

PILEATED WOODPECKER
Nests in woodland and drills holes in tree trunks in search of insects. It has a distinctive two-note song.

YELLOW BIRCH
Its bark peels off in thin strips, and has a strong smell.

ADDER'S TONGUE
Erythronium Americanum is one of the first forest flowers to bloom in spring.

WHORLED ASTER
Whorled leaves and purplish flowers characterize this plant, which grows on wooded hillsides.

GRAND TRILLIUM
This flower is found in large patches in the maple groves of southern Quebec.

■ Maple syrup

In spring, maple groves are the setting for many colorful traditions ● 82.

The sugar maple is the most important tree in the temperate Quebec forest. In the fall it displays a beautiful range of colors, from purple through to gold. In spring it is tapped for its abundant sap, which is collected by producers using buckets or pipes and then boiled down to thicken into the delicious sweet syrup that is the specialty of the region.

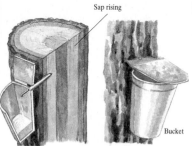

Sap rising

Bucket

A cut is made and a small pipe or *chalumeau* is inserted to collect the sap.

FROM SAP TO SYRUP
The sap, which circulates within the tree, liquefies during the daytime and descends toward the roots. Its transit is stopped by a pipe, which directs the sap into a container. When it has been collected, the sap is poured into a barrel and traditionally transported on a horse-drawn wagon. The liquid, which has a high sugar content, is heated to boiling point and reduced into maple syrup.

Optimum flow of sap requires frosty nights and daytime temperatures above freezing.

Summer

MAPLE LEAF
The five points make it easily identifiable. Its chlorophyll dies in the fall, creating the marvelous red, gold and orange colors. The leaf then drifts to the ground and is buried in snow.

Fall

LEAF AND KEYS
Maple seeds, borne on the air by 'keys' which disperse them, will eventually be transformed, after a dormant period, into new, young shoots.

Winter

History and language

History, *38*
Native Americans and Europeans
in the 16th century, *46*
The fur trade, *48*
The colonization of Nouvelle-France, *50*
The English influence, *52*
Catholic dominance from 1840 to 1960, *54*
The Quiet Revolution, *56*
Native Americans: the awakening, *58*
The Quebecois language, *60*
Place names in Quebec, *62*

1492 Christopher Columbus lands in America

1515–47 Francis I King of France

1562–98 French Religious Wars

1607 Founding of Jamestown, Virginia

Arrival of Native Americans

1534 Jacques Cartier lands in Canada

Beginning of the fur trade

1608 Champlain founds Quebec

Prehistory

Around 8000 BC Asian nomads crossed into Alaska and settled in what is now Quebec. Initially concentrated in the south, they gradually moved northward as the glaciers retreated. Over the next millennia they were followed by other prehistoric settlers. When Europeans first arrived in the 16th century, they found the indigenous peoples divided into three large linguistic groups. The Algonquins, hunter-gatherers who moved around according to the seasons, had the lion's share of the territory. The Iroquois, who stayed in one place and practiced farming, lived on the banks of the Saint Lawrence. The north was occupied by Inuits ● 44. Their ways of life were profoundly affected by contact with Europeans ● 46, and their numbers dwindled when they caught diseases from the newcomers to which they had no innate immunity.

Sauvage Iroquois

The French colony

AN EMPIRE FOUNDED ON FUR

On his three voyages between 1534 and 1542, Jacques Cartier explored the Saint Lawrence as far as Montreal and took possession of the territory in the name of the French king. During the 16th century French and Basque fishermen spent the summers in the estuary and began to trade furs with the Native Americans. In 1608 Samuel de Champlain founded a trading station, the first permanent French settlement on the Saint Lawrence. For years the fur trade remained the colony's chief commercial activity, creating alliances with the Native Americans and provoking the hostility of the

Iroquois, who sided with the English until the Peace of Montreal (1701). From Saint Lawrence Valley the French explored inland and set up trading posts around the Great Lakes. Quebec and Montreal became head of a vast commercial empire whose subjects were trappers and woodsmen ● 48.

1643–1715	1689–97 War of		1701–14	1755	1763	1776	1789
Louis XIV	the League of		War of the	Deportation	Treaty of	American	French
King of	Augsburg		Spanish	of Acadians	Paris	Independence	Revolution
France			Succession				
		1700					1800

1642	1689–97 First war		1701 Peace	1760 England	1774	1791
Maisonneuve	between French and		of Montreal	conquers	Quebec	Constitutional
founds Montreal	British colonists			Canada	Act	Act

NOUVELLE-FRANCE

After it had been exploited by commercial enterprise, Canada became a colony of the French Crown in 1663. Its territory corresponded to present-day southern Quebec and the Great Lakes. Encouraged by the authorities who administered the colony, between 1608 and 1760 ● *50* some 10,000 French immigrants settled in the Saint Lawrence Valley. The Catholic Church enjoyed a religious monopoly and became very powerful. The new colonists, who were in regular contact with the Americans to the south and with Native Americans, soon developed their own individual way of dealing with the diverse seasons and adapting to life in the colony. Colonization continued in succeeding years, but remained slow; in 1760 there were only 65,000 settlers of French origin in Canada, most of them centered round the cities of Quebec and Montreal.

COLONIAL RIVALRY

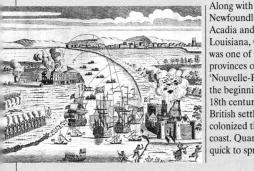

Along with Newfoundland, Acadia and Louisiana, Canada was one of the provinces of 'Nouvelle-France' at the beginning of the 18th century, while British settlers colonized the Atlantic coast. Quarrels were quick to spring up between the two factions: there were disputes over fishing rights, access to fur-producing regions and other territorial matters. The eventual war, the War of the Conquest (1754–60) resulted in France capitulating, and the colony became British in 1763.

The British colony

NEW SETTLERS

For 20 years the only British settlers were colonial administrators and merchants but after the American War of Independence (1775–83), thousands of loyalist immigrants arrived and settled in Quebec and what would later become Ontario. The end of the Napoleonic Wars in 1815 brought a new wave of British colonists, and thousands of Irish settlers arrived in 1846–7, fleeing the Potato Famine in their native land. Quebec was no longer exclusively French.

By the mid-19th century, the British made up one-quarter of the population and even outnumbered the French in Montreal, the Eastern townships and Outaouais. Fortunately French-speakers enjoyed a high birth rate, which assured their demographic growth. Early in the 19th century the fur trade, which had passed into the hands of the Scots, was supplanted by the lumber industry as the province's principal export. Most of the population were farmers, and after the War of the Conquest their produce supplied the capital and other cities of the province. But early in the 19th century there was an agricultural crisis, brought about by overpopulation of the rural areas and the resulting poor quality of the soil.

1803 The Louisiana Purchase	1815 Defeat of Napoleon at Waterloo	1837–1901 Victoria Queen of England
1800	1820	1840
1812–14 Anglo-American War	1826 Patriot Party founded	1837–8 Patriots' Rebellion	1840 Union of Upper and Lower Canada

TOWARD A POLITICAL STRUCTURE

After the Conquest, the Royal Proclamation of 1763 established the first civil government in the province of Quebec, the new name of Canada. London favored British immigration to the province and the assimilation of French-Canadians. French laws were abolished and Catholics excluded from holding public office. Along with growing agitation in the other American colonies, the consequent unrest led to the passing of the 1774 Quebec Act, re-establishing French civil law and restoring the rights of the Catholic Church. In 1791 the Canada Act created the first parliamentary institutions and divided the province into two colonies: Upper Canada (Ontario), which was predominantly British, and Lower

Canada (Quebec), whose population was mainly of French origin.

POLITICAL UNREST

Parliamentary government led to the emergence of an

exclusive French-Canadian political faction that made vehement national demands. Intolerant of British control over executive power, they demanded that control be returned to the province, a request that Britain refused. Political unrest increased under the leadership of Louis-Joseph Papineau, exploding into open rebellion in 1837–8, which was subsequently suppressed by British troops ▲ 206. The dream of a French-Canadian republic lay in ruins, and Lord Durham was despatched from London to look into the situation. He recommended that steps be taken to ensure that the French-Canadians remained a minority by uniting Upper and Lower Canada into a single colony. This was achieved through the Act of Union in 1840. The Catholic Church wisely chose to remain loyal to the British Crown, and emerged stronger than ever from this crisis, while the secular élite were left seriously weakened by the Act of Union.

POLITICAL UNION

Under the terms of the Act of Union, French-speaking political leaders petitioned for the recognition of French as an official language in Parliament and in courts of law, which was finally granted in 1848. This effectively made for a two-headed government, jointly led by English- and French-speakers. Many reforms were undertaken: the seigneurial system was abolished in 1854, and French civil laws were updated. The Catholic Church proliferated, keeping the faithful close to heel, enlarging the religious community, and controlling education and social services ● 54. Construction of the railroad and growing industrialization resulted in an economic boom but the agricultural crisis deepened, and many French-Canadians migrated to the United States. In politics, ministerial irresolution led the administration to propose a federal regime which would reunite the British colonies of North America, a vision that became reality with the 1867 Confederation.

	1861–65 American Civil War	**1870** Franco- Prussian War	**1876** Invention of the telephone		**1899–1902** Boer War	
	1860			**1880**		**1900**
1848 Responsible government	**1854** Reciprocity Treaty		**1867** Canadian Confederation	**1885** Execution of Métis leader Louis Riel	**1897–1936** Liberal Party in power	

Confederation

A FEDERAL PROVINCE

The Confederation separated the two regions that had been united in 1840. Quebec became one of the four provinces of the new federation, along with Ontario, New Brunswick and Nova Scotia. It had a French-speaking majority in Parliament, which passed some important reforms regarding its own culture, including those affecting education and civil law. But in the country as a whole, the position of the French-speaking minority was exacerbated by the addition of the newly formed maritime provinces, which were mainly English-speaking.

YEARS OF CHANGE

By the end of the 19th century agriculture was emerging from its depression, thanks to an upsurge in dairy farming. The overpopulation of rural areas led many to move to the towns and cities of New England, and then on to those in

Quebec as well. Industrialization gathered momentum after 1867. Organized by English-Canadians, working together with the big American industrialists, a large semi-skilled French-Canadian workforce was mobilized at little cost. The workers settled at first in the big cities, but in the 20th century natural resources such as hydroelectricity and the pulp and paper industry extended industrial regions to outlying areas such as Saguenay, Mauricie and Outaouais. World War 2 further stimulated production and Quebec soon became urbanized, resulting in major social and cultural changes, which included proletarianization, a lower birth rate and the development of a new urban culture.

TRAVAIL PRÉCIS·
·RIPOSTE À L'ENNEMI

1914–18	1929	1939–45
World War 1	Start of global economic crisis	World War 2

1900	1915	1930	1945

1900 Canada's first bank set up by Desjardins

1917 Conscription crisis

1936–39 & 1944–59 Maurice Duplessis Prime Minister of Quebec

1948 Fleur-de-lys becomes the flag of Quebec

SURVIVAL

Amid all these changes, the Catholic Church ● *54* continued to promote the traditionalist vision of a society that idealized rural life. It urged families to have more children to counter the effects that immigration was having on the French-speaking community. During the 20th century its authority was undermined by more progressive attitudes. The desire to preserve French culture, however, remained at the heart of the nationalist movement and is a vital part of the Quebecois identity, even today.

Modern Quebec

THE QUIET REVOLUTION

In spite of much progress made by society in the early 20th century, the establishment inherited from the 19th century adjusted slowly to the changes around it. The Conservative regime of Maurice Duplessis, who was in power from 1936 to 1939 and from 1944 to 1959, put the brakes on reform. From 1960 to 1966 the Liberal Party, led by Jean Lesage, ushered in a period of rapid change known as the Quiet Revolution ●*56*. Government was modernized and increasingly centralized, adopting the principles of the welfare state. It also intervened in the economic sector, creating nationalized electricity companies as suggested in the 1940s. These reforms were accompanied by an increased secularization of institutions and sweeping reforms in the fields of education, health and welfare.

NATIONAL DEMANDS

The Quiet Revolution was the result of a new and unashamedly modern nationalism, which determined to make Quebec an independent state, an ideal which was soon abandoned in favor of more moderate and realistic aims. Culture was playing an increasingly important role, led by a new generation of artists ●*92*. Quebec was exploiting its French heritage in many ways, and a law was passed putting the French language on an equal footing with English. Successive Quebec governments decentralized federal powers, leading to greater provincial autonomy. One faction struggled to obtain sovereignty for Quebec, leading to the formation of the Parti Québécois, led by René Lévesque in 1968. The question of independence from the rest of Canada has been debated ceaselessly since 1960, and in 1980 and 1995 there were two sovereignty referenda, the second of which was lost by a mere 50,000 votes.

1955	1969	1989	1991	1992 North
Warsaw Pact	First Moon landing	Fall of the	USSR	American Free
		Berlin Wall	dismantled	Trade Agreement

| 1960 | 1975 | 1990 | 2000 |

1960 Start of	1976–1985 Parti	1977 French	1980	1982 New	1995 Second
the Quiet	Québécois in power	Language	Sovereignty	Canadian	sovereignty
Revolution	under René Lévesque	Charter passed	referendum	constitution	referendum

A NEW SOCIETY

AMERICAN INFLUENCE

In the course of the 20th century, the influence of the US grew increasingly strong, and transformed the Canadian way of life. New technology revolutionized industry and daily life as well. The products of huge US corporations with their accompanying marketing poured onto the market. Translated into French, American culture flooded the media. Four northeastern US states border Quebec to the south, and the Florida sunshine seems to be irresistible to the Quebecois in winter.

As it has in most Western countries since World War 2, society in Quebec has continued to evolve at an ever-increasing pace. Religious belief and the authority of the Church are at their lowest ebb, replaced by secular, individualist values. In this consumer-driven age, the standard of living and the school-leaving age have both risen. The French Quebecois have been the first to benefit from these new measures; with a thriving economy they are able to make the most of their heritage and culture, and the French language is once again on an upswing in all walks of life. Native Americans have also become increasingly aware of their national identity, and ethnic balances are shifting: Quebecois of British origin have declined, while immigration from every continent in the world is increasing. At the same time as it is successfully opening the way to diversity and a genuine multiculturalism in the 21st century, Quebec has managed to retain the dominance of its French heritage and encourage the widespread use of the French language.

NATIONALISM

French-Canadian nationalism gradually evolved during the early years of the 20th century. Nationalists called for Canadian independence from Britain, and for the French language to be established on an equal footing with English. The eventual failure of this Pan-Canadian movement resulted in a concentration of nationalist demands for an autonomous Quebec. Since 1960 there have been repeated calls for the province to gain its independence.

By the time the first Europeans set foot in Quebec, several Native American groups were already well established there. Unevenly distributed over this vast territory, they formed a population of about 40,000, belonging mainly to three different tribes: Algonquins, Iroquois and Inuits. Each tribe had its own language, religion, culture, traditions and highly organized society.

RELIGIOUS BELIEFS

Shamanism was and still is at the heart of Native American ritual. Singing, dancing, funeral rites and sacrifice are part of a rich mythology featuring fantastic gods and ancestral spirits. Shamans communicate with spirits through dreams and in trances, by smoking pipes, with sacrificial offerings or through kabbalistic symbols.

NOMADS OR SETTLERS?

Living by hunting, fishing and gathering wild fruit, the Inuit and Algonquin tribes were nomadic, moving around according to the seasons. The Iroquois, however, were relatively settled and farmed the Saint Lawrence Valley.

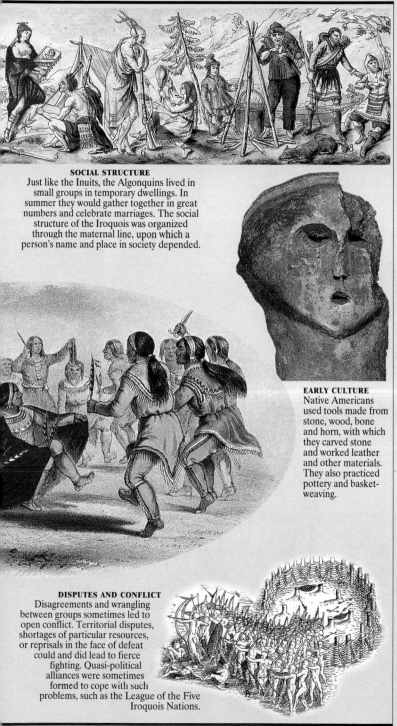

'Pierre Pastedechouan told us that his grandmother loved talking about the savages' surprise when they saw a French ship ... They thought it was a moving island.'

Père Paul Lejeune (1633)

SOCIAL STRUCTURE

Just like the Inuits, the Algonquins lived in small groups in temporary dwellings. In summer they would gather together in great numbers and celebrate marriages. The social structure of the Iroquois was organized through the maternal line, upon which a person's name and place in society depended.

EARLY CULTURE

Native Americans used tools made from stone, wood, bone and horn, with which they carved stone and worked leather and other materials. They also practiced pottery and basket-weaving.

DISPUTES AND CONFLICT

Disagreements and wrangling between groups sometimes led to open conflict. Territorial disputes, shortages of particular resources, or reprisals in the face of defeat could and did lead to fierce fighting. Quasi-political alliances were sometimes formed to cope with such problems, such as the League of the Five Iroquois Nations.

45

● Native Americans and Europeans in the 16th century

In the early 16th century, English, Portuguese, French and Spanish fishermen took advantage of the well-stocked waters of the Gulf of Saint Lawrence. The French, in particular, sent hundreds of boats to the Gulf and were the first to trade furs with the Native Americans, exchanging them for European goods from the time of Jacques Cartier's first voyage in 1534 onwards. The trade became more organized in the second half of the 16th century, becoming quite separate from fishing, and it eventually led to French colonization of the territory at the beginning of the 17th century.

CULTURAL EXCHANGE
As well as trading goods, Europeans and Native Americans also exchanged skills and foreign words. By the early 17th century, for example, the Micmacs of Acadia spoke French and Basque and knew how to sail a boat. Accounts from various journeys tell how the Native Americans helped the Basques to melt whale blubber in exchange for 'a mouthful of cider and a hunk of bread'. This sort of contact explains how the Native Americans contracted the diseases that wiped them out in great numbers. By the time Samuel de Champlain (c.1567–1635) had set up a permanent colony at Quebec in 1608, the Iroquois had vanished from the Saint Lawrence Valley.

NATIVE AMERICAN LEGACIES
From the Native Americans, the French learned how to make canoes, sleds and snowshoes, which helped them adapt to the terrain of their new land. They also began to wear moccasins, and added corn and squash to their diets. Winter fishing techniques were another important lesson learned.

THE FIRST EUROPEANS

Cod was the first natural resource exploited by the Europeans. Between June and September a fleet of 500 or 600 fishing boats (about half of which were French) were at work around the coast and on the banks of Newfoundland, and along the coasts of Nova Scotia and Gaspésie. Most of the catch was salted and dried in small huts built on shore ▲ *303*. Whaling became an important activity towards the middle of the 16th century. The Basques undertook the lion's share of this work, and every year about 20 ships and boats would appear off the Labrador coast, near North Shore and in the Saint Lawrence Estuary ▲ *293*. There are many different whale species found in these waters in the summer months.

JACQUES CARTIER (c.1491–1557)

Cartier took possession of the land in the name of the French King Francis I in 1534, while prospecting for gold and searching for a passage to Asia. He returned to France with two sons of an Iroquois chief from Stadaconé in Quebec. Back again in 1535 he traced the Saint Lawrence as far as Hochelaga (Montreal) and passed the following winter at Stadaconé. 'The snow is four feet deep,' he wrote, 'well above the gunwales of our ships.' He tried to found a colony at Quebec, but his efforts were fruitless, possibly because of the hostility of the Native Americans.

FURS FOR COPPER

Between 1580 and 1600 about 20 Basque ships were regularly involved in the fur trade. The French exchanged copper bowls, axes, knives and glass beads for beaver, mink and otter skins. These European goods spread rapidly in the new territory, as the Native Americans continued to barter with them, and are often found today on the Acadian coast, at Saguenay, Lac-St-Jean, the Ohio Valley and around the Great Lakes. The native Americans were especially fond of the red copper bowls, which they buried in graves or melted down into pieces of jewelry.

● The fur trade

Metal crown made by a
Montreal silversmith

The transatlantic fur trade began about 1500 and remained the principal economic activity of the young French colony until the late 17th century. The exchange of animal skins had long been a common form of barter between Native Americans. It increased with the arrival of the Europeans who, supplied by the Montagnais and the Algonquins, began to trade at Tadoussac. Soon, encouraged by competition between the merchants, there was a vast network of trading posts throughout the territory, extending through the whole of the Saint Lawrence Valley and the Great Lakes region, and finally reaching the Pacific in the 19th century.

FOREST TRAPPERS
In the mid-17th century colonists and traders were in hot dispute with each other over the fur brought by the Native Americans. The Franco-Iroquois Peace Agreement of 1667 drove soldiers, traders and settlers toward the Great Lakes, in order to trade directly with the Native Americans. Soon hundreds of settlers were living in the forest, to the great displeasure of the authorities. Between 1670 and 1720 various methods were tried to get the colonists back to their lands, and soon the fur trade was under proper control. Thereafter, only men with an official permit could trade in fur, and the French term *coureurs de bois* was used to designate those who trapped illegally in the forest.

TRADING POSTS

In the 16th century the first trading posts were established by the Saint Lawrence, near the mouths of its key tributaries. Relations between traders and their suppliers laid the foundations of a complex system of alliances with the Native Americans. Trading posts were of all sizes, the largest having several buildings protected by a stockade.

FURS FROM THE WOODS

In exchange for fur, Native Americans were usually paid in iron and copper goods, cloth and alcohol, sometimes in large quantities if the competition was stiff. The skins they supplied were sent to Europe. Until the 19th century, when the beaver hat went out of fashion, milliners were the fur trade's best customers. They used the softest beaver fur for felt. The skins of other animals, such as marten, otter, lynx and deer also found a ready market in Europe.

RIVALS AND MONOPOLIES

Under the French system, the authorities gave the monopoly of the fur trade, and then that of exporting beaver pelts, to different companies. Founded in 1783, the Compagnie du Nord-Ouest finally included all the important Montreal traders, before it passed into the control of its main rival, the Hudson's Bay Company, in 1821.

● The colonization of Nouvelle-France

To ensure colonization of the territory of Nouvelle-France, the French government introduced the seigneurial system. Large tracts of land called seigneuries were granted to officials who recruited and settled colonists. The new immigrants were young and mostly Catholic. They initially arrived at a rate of a few dozen per year until the 1660s, when numbers increased with the arrival of the military and *les filles du roi*. These were young, single French women given a small dowry and lured to Canada with a promise of adventure, money and marriage. By 1760 – the end of French rule – about 7,000 land grants had been made to immigrants, chiefly from Normandy, around Paris, and the Atlantic coast.

CITY LIFE
In the late 17th century, one quarter of the population were town-dwellers, and most were tradesmen, craftsmen and apprentices. The authorities prized craftsmen highly, and after six years' work they had the right to run their own businesses. Officials, religious communities, merchants and the militia also made their homes in the colony's towns and cities.

LAND DIVISION
Each seigneury was divided into *censives*, one *censive* being the land allotted to one settler. Each one had three *arpents* (roughly three acres) of river frontage and ran back from the river for 30 *arpents*. Once the banks were settled, a second line parallel to the first, called a *rang*, was made available to incoming colonists. A public highway separated the rangs and led to the river, the main source of communication.

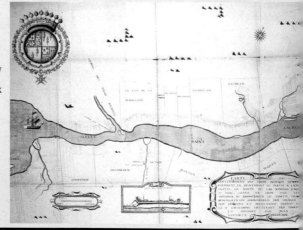

THE SEIGNEURIAL SYSTEM

A seigneur in Nouvelle-France enjoyed certain rights, such as tax collection from tenants; if he built a mill he could charge them to grind their corn. Unlike the feudal system, *seigneuries* encouraged colonization and government by a central authority.

THE FIRST SETTLERS

The young colonists were given parcels of land, in return for which they owed three days' work per year to their seigneur or to a religious community. Around 400 French soldiers, who were brought in in 1665 to defend the colony against the Iroquois, stayed behind and became settlers, many of them marrying *filles du roi*. King Louis XIV bribed between 700 and 800 young girls or young widows to colonize Nouvelle-France during his reign.

RELIGIOUS COMMUNITIES

An order of monks known as Récollets arrived first in 1615, joined 10 years later by the Jesuits, who worked as missionaries, teachers and priests until Quebec Seminary was created by Monseigneur de Laval, the first bishop, in 1663 ▲ *265*. Ursuline nuns came in 1639 to educate girls, and in 1657 the nursing order Sisters of Charity arrived ▲ *268*. Montreal welcomed the first Suplician missionaries in 1657.

● The English influence

Following the Conquest in 1760, the French colony along the banks of the Saint Lawrence came under the direct rule of Britain. English-born merchants and administrators arrived in Canada, and the English-speaking community found itself with new recruits in the form of loyal colonists fleeing from the American Revolution (1776–83), and in the 19th century, Irish immigrants taking refuge from the Potato Famine in their native land. Next came those of Jewish and Italian origin. Britain's economic strength and rich heritage gave it a key role in the economic, social and cultural development of Quebec.

NATIVE AMERICANS AND EUROPEAN RIVALS
The Mohawk tribe formed part of the Iroquois Confederation. In the 18th century, after the Anglo-French War, the Mohawks sided with the British and learned their language. Below: Mohawks camping at Pointe-St-Charles ▲ *200* where they had come to fish (19th century).

MERCHANTS, MAGNATES AND BANKERS
After 1760, many Scotsmen made their fortunes in the fur trade. The English-speaking community in Montreal ▲ *165* became increasingly important in business and industry. It has been estimated that at the end of the 19th century 70 percent of Canada's wealth belonged to a few Montreal families, such as the Molsons and the McGills.

WIELDING THE SHOVEL

After 1820 the colonial authorities, keen to encourage both the development of the English-speaking community and industrial expansion, worked to promote the growth of an English workforce. Between 1845 and 1848 almost 100,000 Irishmen and women arrived, fleeing the famine back home. They helped to build some vast engineering schemes, such as the Lachine Canal ▲ 201 (*left*).

RELIGIOUS SCHOOLS

Under the terms of the 1867 constitution ● 41, education and health came under the jurisdiction of the two provinces. Nevertheless, schools and hospitals in Quebec continued to be run by religious communities. Protestants quickly set up their own institutions and soon had access to a first-class educational system with primary and high schools as well as two universities. One of them, McGill, was founded in Montreal ▲ 179, thanks to a bequest from a rich fur trader James McGill (*above*).

ENGLISH-SPEAKING ARTISTS

Quebec has produced some famous names in the arts from its English-speaking community, including Leonard Cohen (*below*) and Oscar Peterson ▲ 200

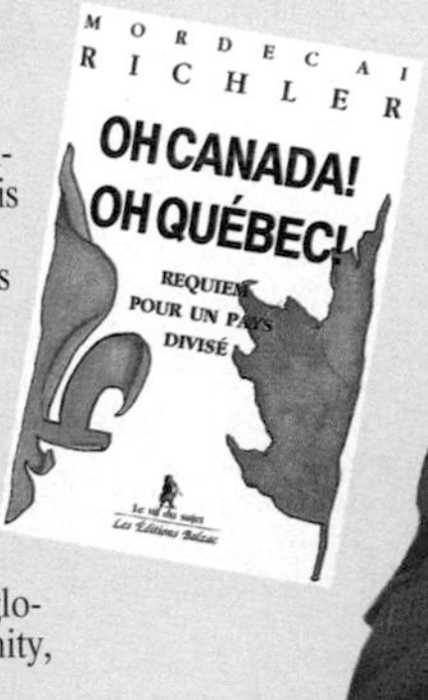

'TWO SOLITUDES'

Today, the English-speaking Quebecois live mainly in the great urban centers and the regions bordering the province of Ontario and the US, such as Estrie ▲ 210 and Outaouais ▲ 222. As part of the Anglo-Canadian community, they are generally opposed to Quebec nationalism and separatism. Some French-Canadian writers, such as Mordecai Richler, have expressed themselves in no uncertain terms on this point.

MORDECAI RICHLER

OH CANADA! OH QUÉBEC!

REQUIEM POUR UN PAYS DIVISÉ

53

● Catholic dominance from 1840 to 1960

LE PAPE
THE POPE

From 1840 the Catholic Church occupied a dominant position in Quebec society. It supervised the lives of individuals, influenced opinion on the political scene and controlled the areas of welfare and education. Seated high on their thrones, the mighty bishops spoke 'long, loud and sharply', wrote Jean Hamelin. They exalted the ideal of a Catholic, French and pastoral utopia, a refuge from the wicked world beyond, and of a mission to convert the whole of North America. But in the 1930s plans for a dramatic secularization of the province were already afoot.

FEAR OF CHANGE
Catholic leaders modeled their actions on the Church's social doctrine, laid down by the Jesuits and the École Social Populaire, an influential pressure group. The Church regarded all change with deep mistrust, intensified by its fear of Communism.

SEPARATION OF CHURCH AND STATE AT THE INSTITUT CANADIEN, MONTREAL
Founded in 1844 as a library and center of debate, the Institut Canadien was a liberal establishment that proposed a split between church and state. Such ideas were condemned by Monseigneur Bourget (*below:* his tomb), who declared war on the Institut in 1858. Those who became members were risking excommunication and, in 1875, the Institut was forced to cease all of its activities.

ANTICLERICAL MOVEMENTS
Between 1840 and 1960, clerical ideology aroused much opposition, even within the Church, but above all in secular society. Opposition grew thanks to the support of such groups as the Institut Canadien de Montreal (1844–75), the Freemasons in the late 19th century, and the world of the Arts: 'Damn the holy water and the French-Canadian toque,' said *Le Refus Global* (*Total Refusal*) ● *140*. But in the 1950s a spirit of openness and freedom was in the air, encouraged by a group of vociferous dissenters centred at the University of Laval and supported by English-speakers in Quebec who were marginalized by Catholicism – especially in Montreal.

EDUCATION AND THE CHURCH
With its army of priests, monks and nuns, the Church succeeded in monopolizing education in the French language, from nursery school through to university. After 1875 it also gained control of the Board of Public Education, after the Ministry of Education, established seven years earlier, had been abolished. Using the possibility of state interference as an excuse, the clergy opposed the concept of free, compulsory schooling up until the 1940s.

TOWARD A THEOCRACY

Ultramontanism, a movement that unquestioningly favors the Pope's absolute power, was insisted on by the clergy from the 1840s ● *40*. This gave them complete freedom to run a kind of 'theocracy'. At the instigation of two bishops of Montreal, Mgr Lartigue (1777–1840) and Mgr Bourget (1799–1885) ▲ *175*, the Church detached itself from all government supervision, and took advantage of a weak government to seize control of public education and welfare, which were to be run by priests and religious communities thereafter. Openly sympathetic and with a caring attitude toward people's needs, ultramontane Catholicism won many followers.

The Quiet Revolution is the name given to a period of rapid change in Quebec under the Liberal government of Jean Lesage (1960–6) and his so-called 'team of thunder' (*équipe du tonnerre*). Putting modernization first, the state of Quebec undertook to reform institutions such as the civil service, education, health and welfare from top to bottom. This new nationalism, openness towards the rest of the world, belief in the welfare state and cultural explosion against the fizzing backdrop of the 1960s meant that the Quiet Revolution created a state of mind that continued well beyond 1966. In addition it subtly shifted the relationship between Quebec and the rest of Canada.

EDUCATION AND LANGUAGE

In 1960, in *Les Insolences*, a teaching friar denounced the deficiencies of the Quebecois educational system, which threw the entire institution into question. Achievement and modernization were given priority in a system of reform that was aimed at all levels, from kindergarten through to college. The choice of English as the prime language for teaching, however, sparked off another battle. The Charter of the French Language (Bill 101) ● 61, aimed to establish French as a key language in Quebec.

SECULARIZATION

With an improved standard of living, the 'baby boom' children

safe at school, and fewer people entering holy orders, the Church found its authority weakened. It no longer controlled education and welfare, which were secularized; schools and hospitals were state-run. Church attendance diminished, and the authority held for more than a century was at an end ● 54.

CULTURAL REVOLUTION

There was a new creative impulse in the air. Poets, writers, painters and sculptors, musicians and singers ● 92 felt freer than ever before. For the first time Quebec felt it had its own, home-grown culture.

poèmes et chansons de la resistance

Pauline Julien

CANADA

expo67 5

ECONOMIC REFORM

The nationalization of electricity by Jean Lesage (*below*) in 1963 was a symbol of the desire to end English-speaking dominance of Quebec's economy. Thenceforth, the state chose to work with native French-speakers.

OU JAMAIS!

TRES NOUS

NATIONALIST REVIVAL

There was a powerful movement dedicated to making Quebec the sovereign state of all French-Canadians, and affirming its importance on the international scene. Canada's identity was thrown into question: some wanted decentralization with increased autonomy for the separate provinces, while more radical voices called for Quebec's independence. So began a lengthy period of debate at all levels, punctuated by referendums, which remains unresolved to this day.

57

● Native Americans: the awakening

After a long period of silence, the Native Americans of Quebec have, in recent years, been searching for their roots, directing their energies toward their cultural and spiritual heritage and demanding their rights at every level – rights that were never voluntarily surrendered in the first place. Their aim is to eradicate the deprivations of more than 400 years of European supremacy, and to regain self-government for the vast lands of their forefathers.

EXODUS
In recent years a growing number of Native Americans (mostly those of younger generations) have moved to the big cities (Montreal alone has over 15,000). They have left their communities to come and study, to work, or simply to feel free of the claustrophobic environment in their home villages. The effects that this exodus will have on the Native American culture are still unknown.

NATIVE-AMERICAN SETTLEMENTS
Today there are around 60,000 Native Americans and 7,000 Inuits, living mainly in some 50 separate communities (*left*). The eleven Native-American nations of which they consist are, for the most part, settled, and they have adapted to the modern way of life.

Ivujivik
Salluit
Kangiqsujuaq
Akulivik
Quaqtaq
Puvirnituq
Kangirsuk
Aupaluk
Inukjuak
Kangiqsualujjuaq
Tasiujaq
Umiujaq
Kuujjuarapik
Whapmagoostui
Kawawachikamach
Matimekosh
Chisasibi
Wemindji
Eastmain
Nemiscau
Waskaganish
Pakuashipi
Mistissini
Uashat
La Romaine
Oujé-Bougoumou
Mingan
Natashquan
Maliotenam
Waswanipi
Pikogan
Obedjiwan
Betsiamites
Gaspé
Lac-Simon
Mashteuiatsh
Gesgapegiag
Témiscamingue
Kitcisakik
Les Escoumins
Listuguj (Restigouche)
Winneway
Weymontachie
Hunter's Point
Manouane
Wendake
Lac Rapide
Kebaowek
Kitigan Zibi
Wôlinak
Kanesatake
Odanak
Akwesasne
Kahnawake

NATIONS

▲ CREE
  ALGONQUINS
▲ ATTIKAMEKS
▲ MOHAWKS
▲ ABÉNAKIS
▲ HURONS-WENDAT
▲ MICMACS
▲ MONTAGNAIS
▲ NASKAPIS
▲ INUIT

IDENTITY CRISIS

The Native-American Rights Movement has proked some dissent among the tribes involved. The illustration (*right*) rebukes some of them for acting like 'apples' – in other words, white beneath a red skin.

ACTIVISM

Native Americans have made many demands at local levels as well as on the national and international scene. In March 1990, Mohawks from Kanesatake near Montreal (Oka) built barricades to protect a stretch of forest that developers had planned to make into a golf course. This dispute became a lengthy confrontation (*left*) that has left its mark on relations between Native Americans and Europeanized Quebecois.

WHAT NEXT?

Those under 25 years of age make up 60 percent of the Native-American population of Quebec. This generation will be the one to decide the fate of their traditional way of life. More headstrong than their elders, many are choosing to pursue a cultural and spiritual revival and to turn to wise men from the tribes to learn all they can about the old ways.

CULTURAL RENAISSANCE

The last 25 years has witnessed a significant cultural revival among people of Native-American origin, in the fields of music (particularly the rock group Kashtin), cinema, dance, painting and sculpture. Figures such as singer and film director Alanis Obumsawin (*right*), have helped to create a communal and powerful medium of expression from their shared cultural heritage.

● The Quebecois language

When General Montcalm arrived in 1756, he was surprised to find that the peasants of the Beaupré Coast could speak French. The settlers had mainly come from Normandy, the region round Paris and western France, and had created a linguistic unity despite the fact that two-thirds of them spoke no French when in France.

A mixed heritage

SURNAMES
A number of Quebec surnames derive from the nicknames of French soldiers formerly posted here, such as Sansfacon (no manners), Sansouci (no worry), Sansregret (no regret), Laterreur (the terror) and Bellehumeur (good mood). Others reveal their geographical origins in France, such as Anjou, Larochelle, Normand, Picard and Poitevin. Some are religious, such as Cardinal, Chrétien and Larchevêque, while in Quebec Bouchard and Tremblay are the equivalents of Smith and Jones in the English-speaking world.

NATIVE-AMERICANISMS

When they came into contact with the New World, Native Americans had to acquire many new words, but occasionally it worked the other way round and Indian words entered Quebec French. Examples include *Annedda* (a remedy for scurvy), *Tabagane* (a sledge without runners or toboggan – see below), and *Babiche* (a fine strip of eelskin used as sewing thread) ▲ 232.

ARCHAISMS AND DIALECT

Every language that travels away from its native land becomes modified, often preserving syntax and expressions that have become out of date in its country of origin. For example, some words such as *avaricieux* for *avare* (selfish), and *capot* for *manteau* (coat) seem decidedly quaint to French speakers from France. However, on the whole it is surprising how much of the original language has been preserved across the years. Textbook French is perfectly understood by French Canadians throughout the province of Quebec, regardless of dialect and archaisms.

The English influence

ANGLICISMS

Following the Conquest, French ceased to be the dominant language, except in church and in French-speaking families. Once government and trade had passed into British hands, the English language was quick to establish itself. Not surprisingly, the French language was unable to avoid assimilating many anglicisms; for example, gloves were made of 'kid' instead of *chevreau*, while cooking pots were no longer *casseroles* but 'saucepans'. Over the years a sort of bastardized French, replete with anglicisms, evolved into a colorful dialect known as *Joual*. The word *Joual* comes from the familiar pronunciation of *cheval* (horse) in certain regions of Canada. During the Quiet Revolution ● 56, many people (including Michel Tremblay) considered that speaking and even writing *Joual* was a proud symbol of national identity in Quebec.

INDUSTRIALIZATION AND ANGLICIZATION AT WORK

Industry, of which timber was the foremost, initially got off the ground thanks to British investments. There were no American backers before 1914. English remains the main language of most businesses, even though the majority of the workforce speak French. Over the last 20 years, a number of companies have chosen to give French a more prominent role, largely as a result of Bill 101 ● *56*, which was adopted in 1977 under René Lévesque's avowedly Francophile government. Signs written in French have been important in helping to highlight the country's heritage.

Vocabulary and the way of life

SEAFARING TALK

The first colonists settled on the islands and along the banks of the Saint Lawrence River. Before there were proper roads, most passengers and goods were transported by canoe or boat, and nautical terminology soon became familiar to almost everyone. Hundreds of seagoing words and phrases that derive from French have remained in use since the 17th century; for example, children are still *appareillé* (rigged) to get ready for school and people *embarquent* (embark) in their automobiles. Houses and apartments or flats might undergo a *radoub* (refit) and have *prélart* (tarpaulin) laid on the floor. And unemployed people are still said by many to be 'at anchor' (*à l'ancre*).

WINTER

The first settlers found their language inadequate in the face of winters they had never before encountered. French terms were soon coined to cope with different types of snow, such as *poudrerie*, which is dry powdered snow lying on the ground, that can be blown about by the wind. This *poudrerie* and some of its variants would shore up into *bancs* (banks) or *congères* (drifts) of snow (*below*). *Croute* (crust) became the name for snow that had melted and refrozen, which was thick enough to walk on.

SWEARING
It is said that in Quebec people don't swear, they 'sanctify'. Derived from years of Catholic rule, many swear words have their roots in terms of worship, such as *calice* (chalice), *ciboire* (ciborium), *calvaire* (Calvary) and *tabernacle*. They were used on their own, or in combination, as in 'Sacre ciboire!' (holy ciborium) or 'Saint calice!' (blessed chalice) and so forth. While not exactly respectable, such expressions are a familiar part of everyday speech, especially when one is in the grip of strong emotion.

● Place names in Quebec

↑ Rivière-à-Pierre
← Notre-Dame-de-Montauban
← Saint-Ubalde

Quebec has an estimated 800,000 lakes, of which fewer than 10 percent have an official name. There are also more than 300 called Lac Long (Long Lake) and almost as many called Lac Vert (Green Lake). Why are place names so banal and uninspired? Actually, they're not: place names in Quebec are often vivid, picturesque and even mysterious. Names say much about the different periods of settlement, and about different regional characteristics.

Inspiration

SOURCES

The geographical map of Quebec shows four different types of place names: Native-American and/or Inuit; French; English; and one more recent than the others, reflecting the strong French revival in the province. Native-American names were essentially descriptive: Quebec means 'narrowing of the waters'; Chicoutimi, 'up to here, it is deep'; Abitibi 'parting of the waters'; Saguenay 'where the water flows out'; and Téiscouta and Témiscamingue, ('deep lake'). When the French arrived, they brought place names inspired by their own heritage and sometimes dedicatory, such as Belle-Isle, Cap Tourmente, Cap Diamant, Bourg-Royal, Montreal, Carlesbourg and Lac Champlain (named by Champlain himself). After the Conquest (1760), the British scattered the region with commemorative names recalling the people and cities of their homeland: Dorchester, New Liverpool, New Glasgow, Buckingham, Sherbrooke and Warwick. The duality of the two successive occupations is the most characteristic feature of place names in Quebec.

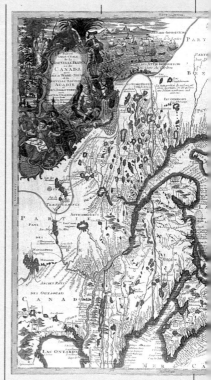

REGIONAL VARIATIONS

The French settlers put their first roots down in the Saint Lawrence Valley, which was the gateway to the colony, with such names as Île d'Orléans, Trois-Rivières and Mont Royal. Place names here are nearly all French. Then came loyalists from across the border bringing their own names for places in Estrie, such as Frelighsburg, Philipsburg and Adamsville. When a wave of Irish immigrants arrived in the mid-19th century, they settled the land round the Canadian Shield, because the flat terrain near the Saint Lawrence was already occupied. This is where names like Rawdon, Kildare and Shannon may still be found. The northern territories tend to have names that are predominantly Native American, like the Koksoak River, Povungnituk (Inuktitut), Opinaca (Cree), Mistassini and Manicouagan (Montagnais). Each region has retained its individual place names, though each also bears the signs of the period and ethnic group of the colonization of the province (French, English and Native American). It is not uncommon to find three adjacent villages each with a name in a different language: Wakeham, Saint-Majorique and Gaspé are all next to each other in Gaspésie.

Holy place names

SAINTS TO CHOOSE FROM

Lakes, rivers, towns and villages are often dedicated to saints. All of the villages on the Île d'Orléans ▲ 277 are named for saints, and two-thirds of the road signs between Montreal and Quebec indicate places whose names have similar holy origins. The movements of the settlers, thanks to the combined efforts of Church and State ▲ 216, were responsible for that. But the concept of instant sanctity had caught the public imagination, and a number of Native American place names underwent holy transformation: Sinsic became Saint-Sixte, Sarosto emerged as Saint-Roustaud and Ashuapmushuan, Saint-Machoine.

SOME HYBRIDS
Sainte-Rose-de-Watford, Saint-Onésime-d'Ixworth, Saint-Roch-de-Mékinac, Grande-Cascapédia, and L'Ascension-de-Patapédia.

NAMES FOR LAKES

Besides more than 200 Lacs Rond (Round Lakes) and 300 Lacs Long (Long Lakes), there are also some named after the trout (*truite*) and beaver (*castor*). Quebec's lakes abound with trout, and in certain parts of the province all the lakes are a long shape. There are so many lakes, it's only a slight exaggeration to say there's one for every citizen of Quebec. It's hardly surprising there is confusion.

REGIONAL FEATURES
Barachois : closed bay;
Batture : foreshore;
Bogue : swamp;
Crique : stream;
Dame : dam;
Echouerie : place where boats or old sea-dogs may run aground;
Platon : high plain;
Plée : plain;
Ruau : straight channel between two islands.

● Place names in Quebec

Place names have . . .

. . . THEIR SECRETS

The apparent simplicity of Quebec place names can at times be deceptive: there's only one river running through the town of Trois-Rivières (Saint-Maurice), although its islands at the mouth of the Saint Lawrence create the illusion that gave the place its name. And the town of Rivière-du-Loup has nothing to do with the French word for 'wolf', but may come either from a type of boat, a Native-American tribe, or even an old sailor. The quaintly named Lac du Spectacle has nothing to do with the view, but its shape resembles a pair of reading glasses! Similarly, the romantic-sounding Havre des Belles-Amours (Sweetheart Harbor) is less soppy than it sounds, its name deriving simply from the corruption of a similar-sounding Basque expression. You can find these and many more tales everywhere in the place names of Quebec.

. . . THEIR POETRY

The map of Quebec is covered in romantic and unlikely sounding place names. For example, a brook or stream which makes a loud noise might be called Rivière Qui-Mène-du-Train (high-life river). A river with spectacular rapids could be called Rapide-Danseur (quick dancer) or, more vividly still, Rapide du Cheval Blanc (white horse rapids). One area of unwelcome, barren land in the province is called Rang Trompe-Souris (Cheat-the-Mouse district), on the assumption that even mice won't be able to find a grain of corn in the place! Some names are all but indecipherable today, like Ha! Ha! Bay, or Lac Trompe-la-Vue (spoil-the-view lake). Bad memories are also preserved in some Quebec place names: during World War 2 one watercourse was named Coulée des Larmes (stream of tears).

. . . AND THEIR CURIOSITIES

Cap d'Espoir (Cape of Hope) in Gaspésie appears on English maps as Cape Despair. Quebec also has ten lakes called Lac Sans-Nom (no-name lake), although there are 700,000 more with no name at all! There are other odd names: Lac Pas d'Eau (no water lake), Lac à Deux-Etages (lake with two floors) and Lac J'En-Peux-Plus (I can't do any more lake)!

From watermills to hydroelectric power

Mills, *66*

Hydroelectric power stations, *68*

How a power station works, *70*

Paper and aluminum, *72*

The kinetic energy generated by water played a large part in the social structure of Nouvelle-France, and watermills set at intervals along the river-bank were central to the life of the first colonists. Mills ground their corn, sawed their lumber and

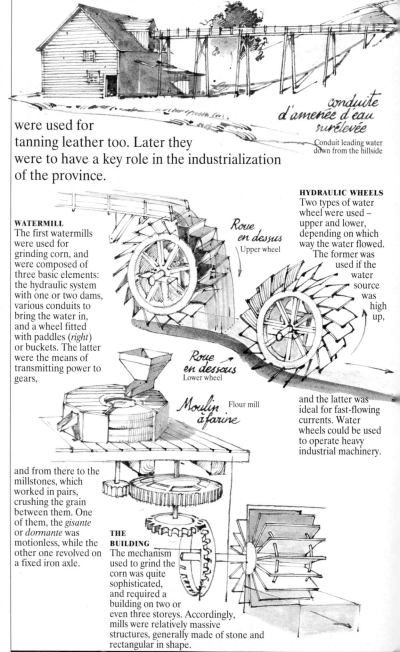

conduite d'amenée d'eau surélevée

Conduit leading water down from the hillside

were used for tanning leather too. Later they were to have a key role in the industrialization of the province.

HYDRAULIC WHEELS
Two types of water wheel were used – upper and lower, depending on which way the water flowed. The former was used if the water source was high up,

WATERMILL
The first watermills were used for grinding corn, and were composed of three basic elements: the hydraulic system with one or two dams, various conduits to bring the water in, and a wheel fitted with paddles (*right*) or buckets. The latter were the means of transmitting power to gears,

Roue en dessus
Upper wheel

Roue en dessous
Lower wheel

Moulin à farine Flour mill

and the latter was ideal for fast-flowing currents. Water wheels could be used to operate heavy industrial machinery.

and from there to the millstones, which worked in pairs, crushing the grain between them. One of them, the *gisante* or *dormante* was motionless, while the other one revolved on a fixed iron axle.

THE BUILDING
The mechanism used to grind the corn was quite sophisticated, and required a building on two or even three storeys. Accordingly, mills were relatively massive structures, generally made of stone and rectangular in shape.

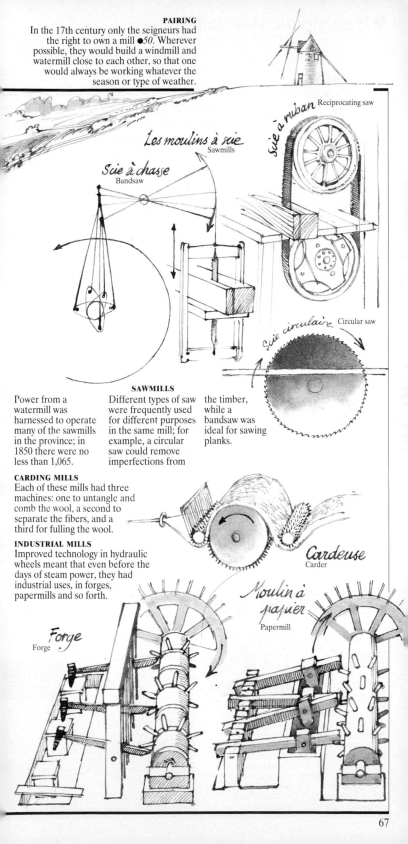

Les moulins à scie
Sawmills

Scie à chasse
Bandsaw

Scie à ruban
Reciprocating saw

Scie circulaire
Circular saw

SAWMILLS

Power from a watermill was harnessed to operate many of the sawmills in the province; in 1850 there were no less than 1,065.

Different types of saw were frequently used for different purposes in the same mill; for example, a circular saw could remove imperfections from the timber, while a bandsaw was ideal for sawing planks.

CARDING MILLS
Each of these mills had three machines: one to untangle and comb the wool, a second to separate the fibers, and a third for fulling the wool.

Cardeuse
Carder

INDUSTRIAL MILLS
Improved technology in hydraulic wheels meant that even before the days of steam power, they had industrial uses, in forges, papermills and so forth.

Forge
Forge

Moulin à papier
Papermill

● Hydroelectric power stations

The exploitation of the immense waterways that are such a feature of Quebec is the result of a series of successful battles against hostile forces: harsh climate, long distances and unusual geological patterns. From modest installations built at the beginning of the 20th century to the powerful modern stations at James Bay, progress has been achieved through the vision and imagination of teams of designers and builders.

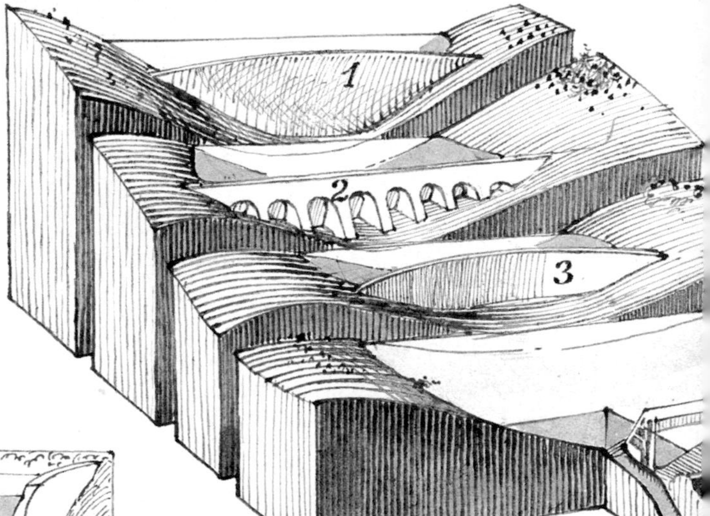

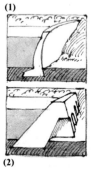

(1)

(2)

(3)

(4)

PIONEERS
In the early 20th century, power from the first hydroelectric stations was used for street lighting and for industrial purposes. In the 1920s, Montreal underwent a massive demographic expansion, and the electricity required for domestic use in homes increased the demand for power. Construction of a power station on the Saint Lawrence River at Beauharnois ● *70*, ▲ *209* met much of this need.

DIFFERENT TYPES OF DAM
In spite of the many different topographical features with which the Quebecois have to cope, it is broadly possible to divide dams into two main types: filled dams, which are packed with materials such as rock, earth and gravel, and concrete dams. Concrete dams can be subdivided again into vaulted dams (3), dams with both vaults and buttresses (2), and then dams with a double curve (1). Above: dam filled with earth and gravel (4).

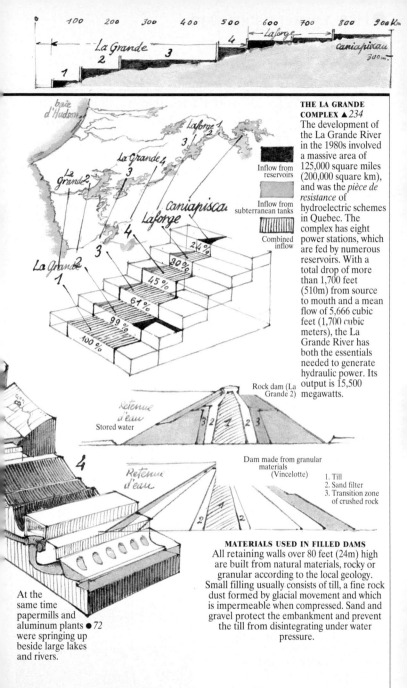

Scale showing 100 to 900 Km, labeled La Grande 1, 2, 3, 4, Laforge, Caniapiscau 300 m.

baie d'Hudson

Laforge 1, 2
La Grande 4, 3
La Grande 2
Caniapisca
Laforge
La Grande 1

Inflow from reservoirs

Inflow from subterranean tanks

Combined inflow

24%
30%
45%
61%
99%
100%

THE LA GRANDE COMPLEX ▲ 234

The development of the La Grande River in the 1980s involved a massive area of 125,000 square miles (200,000 square km), and was the *pièce de resistance* of hydroelectric schemes in Quebec. The complex has eight power stations, which are fed by numerous reservoirs. With a total drop of more than 1,700 feet (510m) from source to mouth and a mean flow of 5,666 cubic feet (1,700 cubic meters), the La Grande River has both the essentials needed to generate hydraulic power. Its output is 15,500 megawatts.

Rock dam (La Grande 2)

Retenue d'eau
Stored water

3 2 1 2 3

Retenue d'eau

Dam made from granular materials (Vincelotte)

1. Till
2. Sand filter
3. Transition zone of crushed rock

MATERIALS USED IN FILLED DAMS

All retaining walls over 80 feet (24m) high are built from natural materials, rocky or granular according to the local geology. Small filling usually consists of till, a fine rock dust formed by glacial movement and which is impermeable when compressed. Sand and gravel protect the embankment and prevent the till from disintegrating under water pressure.

At the same time papermills and aluminum plants ● 72 were springing up beside large lakes and rivers.

THE 1960s

The development of reliable high-tension lines (735,000 volts) made it possible to send vast quantities of power over great distances. This technological breakthrough opened up the rivers of the North Shore ▲ 330, for exploitation, far from the large urban centers. It also provided the means for demographic spread in Quebec. Power stations were then built on the Manicouagan, Aux Outardes and Churchill rivers.

● How a power station works

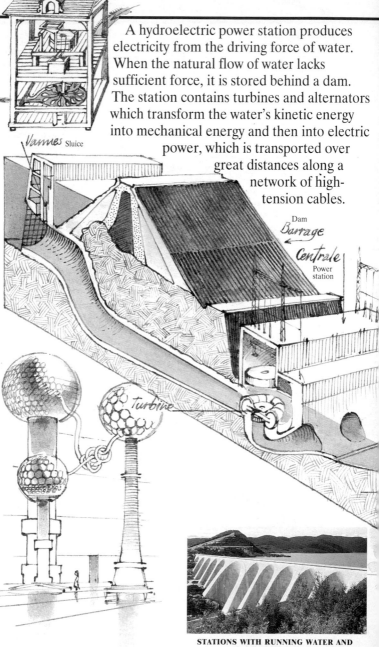

A hydroelectric power station produces electricity from the driving force of water. When the natural flow of water lacks sufficient force, it is stored behind a dam. The station contains turbines and alternators which transform the water's kinetic energy into mechanical energy and then into electric power, which is transported over great distances along a network of high-tension cables.

Vannes Sluice

Dam
Barrage

Centrale
Power station

turbine

LEVIATHANS
The installations at La Grande, built between Latitude 49° and 55° north in the heart of the Quebec taiga, make it one of the largest hydroelectric complexes in the world. In the illustration above, the figure standing between two machines in the high-tension area is the height of an average person, so this gives some idea of the scale of the project.

STATIONS WITH RUNNING WATER AND STATIONS WITH RESERVOIRS
The first power stations were built beside stretches of fast-flowing water, which was impossible to store (Beauharnois ▲ 209). Most of those in Quebec are now powered by reservoirs, so each has a dam behind which water is stored until it is needed. It is then released as a waterfall. (*Above*: Daniel-Johnson Dam ▲ 330).

HOLLOW GRAVITY DAM AT MANIC 2
This is a massive concrete wall (the largest of its kind in the world) built across a valley floor. The dam is the same thickness throughout its length, and resists the water pressure by its sheer bulk. The hollow structure economizes on concrete.

KAPLAN TURBINE
Like a helical turbine, the Kaplan has adjustable blades. Their setting can be changed according to water flow, which changes with the seasons.

HELICAL TURBINE
As its name implies, this turbine takes the form of a helix, allowing it to rotate at high speed. This set-up is ideal where the water flow is weak.

Turbine Kaplan
Kaplan turbine

Turbine Francis
Francis turbine

FRANCIS TURBINE
Looking like a wheel with fitted blades, this turbine is well suited where the fall is less than 700 feet (210m). It is the most widely used turbine in Quebec, and can be found in the Manicouagan station ▲ *330* and in those on James Bay ▲ *234*.

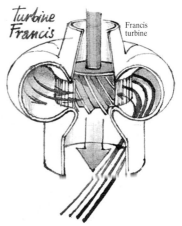

Plan of a turbine/alternator assembly in a hydroelectric station.

HOW A POWER STATION WORKS
Water enters the station through an inlet closed by a sluice and fitted with a grille to prevent foreign bodies penetrating the system. The water is then fed through a long metal pipe down the slope to the turbine spiral. The metal casing surrounding the turbine ensures a constant and regulated flow. Water finally reaches the wheel, the moveable part of the turbine. The shaft to which the wheel is fixed is also attached to the alternator, which in turn produces the electricity. Once past the turbine, the water flows away.

● Paper and aluminum

TIMBER
Tree trunks floating downriver to the mill.

The exploitation of vast areas of forest to make paper and the transformation of bauxite into aluminum were Quebec's dominant industries throughout the 20th century and beyond. Both industries require a lot of water and an abundant and low-cost supply of electricity.

WOOD INTO PAPER

To turn timber into paper pulp, the fibers need to be separated, a process that can be carried out mechanically or chemically. Mechanically, the barked wood billets are crushed with the aid of defibrators. Alternatively, it is possible to heat wood shavings with chemicals in huge autoclaves. Whatever method is used, the resulting pulp is pressed into thin sheets and all of the water squeezed out. The final process involves feeding the product into roller-dryers to obtain the desired thickness.

LEADER

With 12 percent of the world market, Quebec is one of the biggest suppliers of newsprint in the world, outperforming Japan, Sweden and Finland. Their ready supply of trees and highly developed industrial methods make this possible.

1. bauxite
2. broyeur 3. chaux + soude
4. décantat. 5. boues rouges

6. filtre 7. four
8. four 9. électrolyse
10. raffinage (Al. pur à 99,99%)

1. bauxite
2. crushing
3. lime & soda
4. decanter
5. red mud
6. filter
7. oven
8. oven
9. electrolysis
10. refining (99.99% pure aluminum)

BAUXITE INTO ALUMINUM

Aluminum is produced in two stages: the extraction of the metal from bauxite through a chemical process, then the electrolytic separation of oxygen and aluminum oxide. Four tons of bauxite are needed to produce two tons of aluminum oxide, which in turn will yield one ton of aluminum.

Arts and tradition

Traditional dress, *74*
Forestry, *76*
Furniture, *78*
Transport on the Saint Lawrence, *80*
Maple sugar time, *82*
Hunting, *84*
Fishing, *86*
Sport, *88*
Preserving tradition, *90*
Songs and singers, *92*
Theater, *94*
Cinema and television, *96*
Food, *98*
Quebec specialties, *100*

Coping with the harsh winters called for a careful choice of clothing, using a sensible blend of European and Native-American costume. Following the example of the latter, Canadians used animal skins to make clothes for traveling or working in the forest. Native Americans, on the other hand, became used to fabric woven in the ways of the West. During the 19th century, although Canadians continued to borrow features of Native-American dress, the European style was largely prevalent.

ACCESSORIES

In winter, knitted woolen garments, such as hats, scarves, mittens and socks, often in bright colors, are indispensable. In the 19th century, people from the Lanaudière region ▲ 221 used to wear distinctive handwoven belts, which gradually spread west all over the country, becoming a symbol of Canada and its Native Americans.

FUR

Trappers wore mink coats, bearskin hats and deerskin leggings. Along the Saint Lawrence, the settlers had beaver coats with mink sleeves and collars of silver fox, hats of otter fur and sealskin mittens. Then, as now, fur coats were seen as a mark of prestige.

MOCCASINS

Well adapted to local conditions, moccasins were an idea borrowed from Native Americans. They were made of cow- or deerskin and then waterproofed with linseed oil or seal blubber. The *botte sauvage* is an extended moccasin reaching to the knee. Warm and supple, they are often worn with snowshoes.

The *soulier de bœuf* is a moccasin made of oxhide, and is very hard-wearing.

'ETOFFE DU PAYS'

Literally 'cloth of the region', *l'étoffe du pays* is cloth traditionally woven at home from the owner's sheep and used to make trousers, skirts, jackets and coats. After weaving, the grayish woolen fabric could be compressed to make it warmer and more water-resistant.

● Forestry

Exploitation of the forests on a commercial basis began in the 19th century, when Britain decided to import wood from her colonies. The giant pines were the most sought after, being ideal for ships' masts and structural beams in buildings. In the middle of the century, the urbanization of the US opened up a new market for dressed timber of all kinds. In the 20th century, further dramatic increases in the population of North America coincided with a new demand for newspapers, which required more forestry.

GIANT RAFTS
Intensive forestry brought with it a particular method of woodcutting and a new way to transport the lumber. With a superabundance of trees and a low-cost workforce, companies insisted that the trees should be hand-trimmed with axes in situ. The massive trunks were then assembled into enormous 'rafts'. Fitted with sails and oars and crewed by dozens of men, the rafts descended the Saint Lawrence and the Ouataouais as far as Quebec, where they were unloaded for transport.

FELLING

This took place in fall and winter as freezing weather made it easier to work with an axe, the only available tool until the end of the 19th century. Horses towed the trunks to the river, where they were piled on the ice.

VANISHING FORESTS IN QUEBEC

The 19th century increase in the population of the Saint Lawrence Valley depleted the forests of the region, but there was never total deforestation, as growers took care to maintain forests on their own land. Now trees are replanted in areas where farming is not profitable.

A LOGGERS' CAMP

Loggers lived in crude cabins made of round tree trunks. In the first half of the 19th century, a camp would comprise a dormitory, kitchen and dining room all in one. Bunk beds lined the walls around a central area used for cooking baked beans – the staple of the loggers' diet. The log cabins remained but conditions gradually improved – most notably after the loggers' strike of 1934 and the enforcement of rules concerning hygiene.

THE 'DRIVE'

Even small waterways with locks were used to float logs downstream which, until recent years, was the only means of transporting them. The 'drive' involved steering clusters of logs downriver to the sawmill or factory. In spring, when the logging season was over, loggers became 'drivers' and would guide the tree trunks through the water with a pole to keep them away from obstacles – blasting a way through them, if necessary.

E.B. EDDY'S MANUFACTURING & LUMBERING ESTABLISHMENTS HULL. P.Q. CANADA.

BIG BUSINESS

Forestry continues to play a major role in the economy of Quebec, and employs thousands of workers. Paper and related products, as well as wood, are among the province's most important exports. The industry's main problem is maintaining its place in the market without using up its valuable resources.

Furniture

For a long time Quebec furniture-makers were dependent upon foreign designs, but in recent years they have evolved their own aesthetic. Before then, local carpenters would use native pine to copy furniture made overseas, inspired by 17th-century French furniture made for noble families and by the great English cabinet-makers. A native school of furniture-making was established in the province which, following the European trend in the 1920s, rejected the historical approach to the craft. New ideas and designs became especially evident in pieces designed and produced in Montreal.

17TH-CENTURY FURNITURE
Now rare in Nouvelle-France, the finest examples can be found preserved in religious communities.

BUILT-IN FURNITURE
When building houses in the second half of the 18th century, workmen would sometimes build the furniture at the same time and fit it into the rooms, thus saving space. In spite of widespread demolition of old buildings, ornate doors from some of this furniture have been preserved and can be seen in museums in the province.

CARPENTERS' CREATIONS
In the absence of a domestic tradition of fine cabinet-making, most furniture was produced by carpenters until the early 19th century. Assembled from wooden panels with molding, they were chiefly inspired by and modeled on architectural features.

CHAIRS
The lack of clearly defined stylistic categories, combined with the imagination of skilled craftsmen, has resulted in a wide variety of chair designs.

GRANDFATHER CLOCK
Veneered and inlaid, the English-style grandfather clock became extremely popular in the 1820s, when they began to be made in the province by local cabinet-makers. In Montreal, Ira Twiss launched a model that was mass-produced by Michel Bellerose in Trois-Rivières.

VICTORIAN ERA
Furniture made in the second half of the 19th century took its inspiration from times past. Italian Renaissance designs were followed by French-style Second Empire, before tastes became even more eclectic and demand increased for luxurious pieces in the style of those being made by the flourishing workshops of Flanders and Germany.

MULTI-FUNCTIONAL DESIGNS
Houses tended to be small and interiors modest. The result was ingenious designs for pieces of furniture that had several uses, such as benches that became beds and tables that turned into chairs.

NEW DESIGN
Among the plethora of objects that have won Montreal its reputation for new design is this Baby Face chair (*below*), part of a series from the OMNI collection by Jean-Francois Jacques.

MONTREAL FURNITURE SCHOOL
The renowned École du Meuble de Montreal reacted against conventional furniture design in favor of modern ideas. When Jean-Marie Gauvreau designed this dressing table and stool in 1928, his main inspiration was the work of Henry van de Velde and the Art Deco movement.

● Transport on the Saint Lawrence

For centuries, dugouts and bark canoes were the only craft found on the Saint Lawrence River, but the arrival of European fishermen in the early 16th century, followed by Jacques Cartier and then the first settlers, was to change all that. The Saint Lawrence was the backbone of the country, and it was the first feature the new colonists saw. The river soon became crowded with maritime and local traffic of all kinds. Its banks and those of its tributaries were lined with towns and villages. With a vital part to play in trade and industry as well, boats and ships of all kinds have continued plying their way up and down the river since the 17th century.

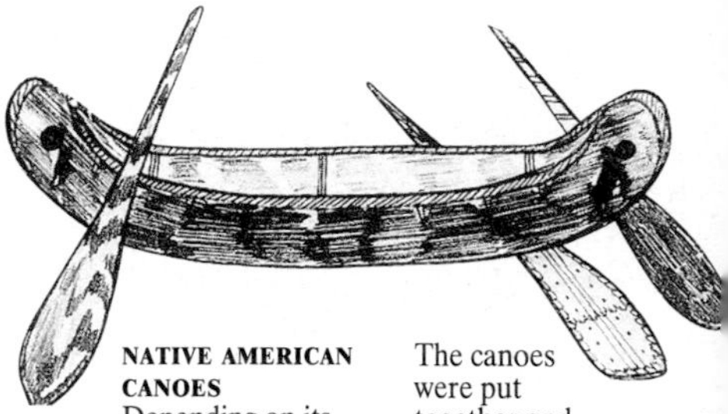

NATIVE AMERICAN CANOES
Depending on its size, the Algonquin canoe (*above*) could hold up to 14 people. It was designed for transporting and trading in furs ●*48*, and made from birch bark, lined with strips of cedar.

The canoes were put together and stitched using roots that had been peeled and split, and finally caulked with a mixture of spruce gum and animal fat, which sealed it from the water and the elements.

WELCOME ABOARD
In 1809 a prominent Montreal brewer named John Molson ● *52* started a steamboat service between Montreal and Quebec. The journey, which had taken up to three weeks in sailing vessels, now took less than two days from beginning to end.

BAR TO STARBOARD
In the 19th century, the government put buoys in the river and built lighthouses ▲ *302* to keep river traffic off the reefs in the Saint Lawrence. There were also river pilots ▲ *258*. For many centuries, ice closed the river in the winter months, but now ice-breakers allow year-round navigation for virtually every type of craft.

In the 1750s most vessels employed to carry colonists and their effects between Europe and Nouvelle-France were sailing ships

MASTS AND SAILS
of less than 150 tons. On average the voyage across the Atlantic took two months. By the 1880s, sailing ships bringing English settlers to Nouvelle-France weighed up to 2,000 tons. Some of these ships were manufactured in the shipyards of Quebec.

SHIPYARDS
In the years after 1660 a number of shipyards were established in the colony. Between 1739 and 1759 the royal dockyard in Quebec built a dozen men-of-war ships destined for the French Navy. By the 19th century, the region was dotted with shipyards building small coastal craft, and the British Royal Navy would boast 2,000 ships of the line built in Quebec.

● Maple sugar time

Maple sugar time coincides with the spring equinox. From mid-March onward, for a month and a half, sugar-makers are busy in the sugar shack, leaving the farm to look after itself. Although Native Americans prepared a sugar residue from maple water (sap), it was the arrival of the Europeans with metal utensils that kick-started the exploitation of the maple sugar industry. Sugar time is almost like carnival, and has all kinds of traditions. It also symbolizes the end of the long winter and the coming of spring.

THE HARVEST
Maple water was originally collected from maple trees using a tomahawk to make a cut and inserting a piece of wood to direct the sap into a crock on the ground ■ 36. In the 19th century, a juniper twig would be fixed in a groove on the tree, and a bucket suspended to catch the sap. The collector would transport the sap with a yoke across his shoulders and snowshoes on his feet, emptying the buckets into a barrel, which was mounted on a sleigh and then drawn back to the shack by a horse. Since 1960 factories have used a system of suction-operated plastic pipes.

MANUFACTURE
In former times the collected sap was boiled outdoors in a cauldron suspended over the fire. In the 19th century, the cooking took place in a tin pot, under a temporary shelter. Permanent shacks were first built in the mid-19th century. Once the sap becomes dark and thick and has come to the boil over the fire, the syrup is ready. To make maple candy, the maple syrup must be evaporated over a gentle heat. Finally, when drops of candy harden on exposure to air, the mixture can be vigorously creamed to make maple sugar ● 100 and then molded into loaves or small sweets.

TANOBE

HABITS AND CUSTOMS
Maple syrup production has long been associated with customs, beliefs, legends and sayings. For example, the cuts should not be made in the trees till the 'sugar birds' (a kind of bluetit) had come. And when a boy was first allowed to sleep in the shack and became involved in the supervision of the boiling, he was considered to be a man. Another saying holds that 'Easter brings the sugar, or brings it to an end'. Such traditions are now a fixed part of Quebec's cultural identity.

'Maple sugar, maple candy,
Maple syrup sure is dandy.'

Children's song from Quebec

SUGAR PARTY
When the day's work in the sugar shack is done, harvesting the sap and making the products that can be obtained from it, it's time to throw a party. Festive meals feature pea soup, beans, ham and eggs with maple syrup, broiled bacon, pancakes with more syrup, and taffy (a type of candy) hardened in the snow. Every sugar party has its own traditional folk dances.

BIG BUSINESS
In 1994 Quebec produced 5 million gallons of syrup (18 million litres), 90 percent of Canada's output and 70 percent of all the syrup in the world.

● Hunting

The first colonists quickly became keen hunters. Unlike the legal system they were used to back home in France, the seigneurial system gave all settlers the right to hunt. Methods varied according to the type of game they were tracking. Hunting provided food and was also vital for the development of the fur trade, which became the major source of income for many Quebecois. Today hunting is strictly controlled, and Quebec is one of the best-stocked regions for game in North America.

HUNTING WITH THE HORN
The Canadian moose is the largest member of the deer family in North America. It can stand up to 6 feet (1.8m) tall at the withers and weigh as much as 1,350lbs (600kg). It is usually hunted in the rutting season, when a small horn is blown to imitate the female's belling sounds. This technique was acquired from the Native Americans.

CONTROLS
As early as 1721 there was a law forbidding anyone to kill, sell or buy partridges between 15 March and 15 July 'on pain of a fifty pound fine'. But the first state-employed gamekeepers did not appear until the late 19th century. Today, the hunting of game, large or small, takes place in national parks and reserves in 'Zones d'Exploitation Contrôlée' (ZEC) with official permits, or on private land with the owner's permission.

DIFFERENT HUNTERS
The Native Americans whom the early French settlers met relied on hunting for their survival. The French colonists and, later, French Canadians, hunted game as much for food as for their furs. Hunting as a sport only began in the second half of the 19th century, when it was largely the preserve of British army officers.

BOW AND ARROW
Hunting game such as deer and bear with a bow and arrow has become increasingly popular over the last 20 years. The times of year when this type of hunting may be undertaken are strictly controlled, and generally begin before the rest of the hunting season.

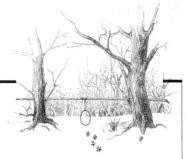

HUNTING SMALL GAME
Trapping hares in a snare has always been popular in Quebec. Snares are set throughout the fall, and the hares collected during fall and winter. Hares are used regularly in stews and pies, especially in wooded areas of the province.

WILDFOWLING
Between Montreal and Quebec, especially around Sorel and Lake St Peter ■ 22, wildfowl hunting from a floating hide is a favorite pastime. Making decoy birds out of wood has become an art form in itself.

● Fishing

The inhabitants of Quebec are fortunate to have a vast network of waterways consisting of hundreds of lakes and rivers, teeming with fish. Many different kinds of fish were important components of the early settlers' diet. Fishing as a sport has been popular in urban areas since the 18th century, although regulations governing the sport were not laid down until after 1800, when officers from the British army first took an interest. The number of parks and game reserves dedicated to fishing has mushroomed over the last 20 years.

PRIVATE CLUBS
In the 19th century, the growth of tourism and the expansion of the railroad system attracted many fishermen to the plains of the Laurentides and the Appalachians ■ 20. The first angling clubs were formed in 1883 and the government began to issue permits in order to conserve stocks. Membership of these clubs, originally reserved for the wealthy, has become more relaxed. New controls over the sport (ZEC) were introduced by the Quebec government in 1978.

FISHING IN WINTER
Many fishermen brave the cold in winter and travel to frozen lakes and rivers, where they make small holes about 3 feet (1m) apart. A baited line is placed in each one (*see below*) and the fish, attracted by the light of day, swim towards the surface, and are hooked.

TRADITIONAL METHODS
In the past, Inuits and Native Americans fished using a *nigog*, a type of harpoon. They would search for their prey in creeks or sometimes build a dam of rocks across a river to trap fish such as eels or salmon, which were then speared. Weirs – latticework devices that were set across streams – were also used. As fish passed through openings in the weir they could be easily captured.

TROUT

When the snow melts, brook trout, one of the most sought-after fish, can be found in almost every lake and river in southern Quebec, along with rainbow trout (*above*), gray trout (or weakfish) and brown trout, which is a well-known culinary specialty of the area.

QUANDARY

Choosing between artificial flies, metal spinners and live bait, such as earthworms, has long been a fisherman's problem. Their decision is based on many factors, such as the weather, water color, water depth, and the habits of the fish they're after. A bit of luck helps, too.

FISH IN THE NORTH

Each year, large numbers of fishermen are drawn to Abitibi
▲ *230* in the Mauricie
▲ *240* or to the north of Lac Saint-Jean
▲ *320* in search of the pike (*below*) or its cousin, the yellow pike. Both species like cold, deep water, and catching them requires a lot of patience and skill. Their flesh has a subtle, delicate flavor.

'SALMO SALAR': THE KING OF FISH

In late spring, the Atlantic salmon leaves the sea to spawn in the tributaries of the Saint Lawrence River. Until 150 years ago salmon regularly swam upstream to Montreal, where they were caught. However, population growth and industrialization have now driven the salmon back to the rivers around the Gulf of Saint Lawrence, where they are now caught with artificial flies (*above*). The balance of the rod, thickness of the line and the type of fly all help to encourage the fish to rise and investigate the lifelike little insect on the surface. Catching them is then a fairly easy process.

87

The first Canadians, whose culture came direct from 17th-century France, had next to no involvement in sport. It was not until the arrival of the British in 1760 that they discovered the pleasures of physical exercise as a leisure activity. Team sports started to become popular in the 1850s, with the introduction of baseball, football and especially ice hockey, which became a national passion. Played by children in almost every back street in Quebec, ice hockey (and, in the warmer months, ball hockey) has created many national superstars. Since the 1970s, an ecological conscience and a renewed interest in the outdoor life has been responsible for new open-air activities such as cross-country skiing, cycling and canoeing.

CHATEAU FRONTENAC

SKI·ING, SKI·JORING
HUSKY·DOG SLEDDING
SKATING, HOCKEY, CURLING
TOBOGGANING ···
BOB·SLEDDING & SNOWSHOEING

Winter Sports in Old QUEBEC

NATIVE AMERICAN GAMES
At first the chief means of transport in the province, canoeing has evolved into a competitive sport as well as a popular leisure activity. Similarly, snowshoes and toboggans, both traditional requirements for cold winters, have become recreational as much as functional. Lacrosse was adopted from the Native Americans by the British, and is now one of the most popular sports played in Quebec.

BRITISH IMPORTS

The British contribution to sport in Quebec has been remarkable in its quantity and diversity. No less than 20 new sports were introduced to the province in the 19th century, including curling (*below left*), boxing, cricket, rifle shooting, ice skating, swimming, golf and tennis.

RIOT AT THE FORUM

In March 1955, Maurice Richard (*right*) was on the point of becoming ice hockey's top scorer when he was suspended for the remainder of the season for deliberately injuring an opponent during a match in Boston. Richard was so popular that this disciplinary action sparked one of the worst riots in Quebec's history, at the Montreal Forum, home of Richard's team, the Montreal Canadiens.

ICE HOCKEY

Canada's national sport was first introduced in Montreal among British militia who were garrisoned there in the 1870s. Points are scored by hitting a hardened rubber 'puck' into a goal with a stick. Players wear ice skates on a rink that measures about 200 by 85 feet (60 by 25m). There are five players in each team apart from the goalkeepers, and a game consists of three 20-minute periods.

THE MONTREAL CANADIENS

Founded in 1909, this famous ice hockey team was originally entirely French-speaking. The team is one of four who founded the National Hockey League (NHL) in 1917, and has won the coveted Stanley Cup an unrivaled 25 times. Some of its stars, such as Maurice Richard, Guy Lafleur and Patrick Roy (*below*) have become legends.

SKIDOO

Armand Bombardier invented the snowmobile (skidoo) in 1922, a tracked vehicle with steerable skis in front, ideal for use in snow and on rough terrain ▲ *212*. Frequently used by farmers and rescue teams, since the 1960s it has also become a popular sport. Motor-racing star Gilles Villeneuve ▲ *221* began his career racing snowmobiles. Since 1988 Abitibi has organized long-distance rallies, with teams coming to compete from all over the world.

● Preserving tradition

A vital part of the heritage of the province, traditional knowledge and customs are flourishing in Quebec, passed down from one generation to another by those familiar with the traditional languages and way of life. For example, craftsmen, such as accordion-makers, boatbuilders or weavers, are intent on preserving the ancient traditions of their work. Musicians, too, such as fiddlers, continue to enliven everyday life with traditional airs and dances. Others have perfected the art of storytelling, recounting the old tales in a performance that can hold an audience spellbound. All of these people and thousands like them continue to preserve and keep alive the great traditions, linking the present with the past.

MUSICIANS AND DANCERS

Inverness in the Bois-Francs ▲ 247 has become an important center for traditional music and dance, involving the whole community and forging an invaluable link between English- and French-speaking cultures. Immigrants from many countries ensure a rich and vibrant array of different music and dance styles. The musicians play Irish jigs and reels, and the dance-steps are called by descendants of Scottish immigrants, whose English is liberally sprinkled with French, Scottish and Irish expressions. And everyone dances together, regardless of background.

STORYTELLERS
In former times, storytellers would move from one camp to another, telling their tales to loggers in the forests, who had little to entertain them when their day's work was done, especially in winter. A story might last for hours. The subjects were varied but often featured Ti-Jean, a legendary lumberjack and favorite hero of Canadian folklore. The tradition of telling unlikely but fascinating tales still thrives in Quebec: at Saint-Raphael near Saint-Michel-de-Bellechasse ▲ 288, fantastic storytellers keep their listeners enthralled all evening long, and pass their repertoire from father to son.

Montmagny ▲ 288 is world famous for making accordions of the highest quality.

ACCORDION MAKERS
The instrument has always been popular in this region of Quebec and the skill of the Messervier

family in particular has established the town's reputation. Their highly prized instruments can be found all over the world, and Montmagny now hosts the Carrefour Mondial de l'Accordéon, an important accordion festival.

BOATBUILDERS
Seafaring traditions are an integral part of the history of the Île d'Orléans ▲ 276. Until the 1950s people came from great distances to have a *chaloupe* built here. These are small sailing craft, between 9 and 36 feet in length (3 to 12m), with no deck. They are powered by sail or oars, and traditionally made from cedar and pine. When making these boats, the *chaloupiers* worked by eye alone, with no written plans. Such skills are passed down from generation to generation, and cannot be learned from any book.

ANIMAL SCULPTORS
This once-popular art form has undergone a revival in Quebec. There is a family at Saint-Ubalde de Portneuf ▲ 250 that has been carving animals for four generations. At least nine members of the Richard-Lavallée family have been or still are sculptors. *Right:* Aimé Desmeules at work in Saint-Paul-de-la-Croix on the lower Saint Lawrence.

● Songs and singers

In the 1970s, the inhabitants of Montreal often traveled to Mont Royal ▲ *182* to listen to their favorite artists singing about their love for Quebec and their longing for its independence.

Probably the most common form of cultural expression in the world, music has a special relevance to this French-speaking region in the heart of North America. At the end of the 1950s, old-fashioned ballads and folk songs gave way to a new style of singing that expressed a passion for the land of Quebec and the soul of the people who lived there. During the Quiet Revolution these songs had a political message and were vital to the search for national identity. Today, many singers from Quebec have won recognition and worldwide acclaim.

Left to right: Claude Léveillée, Yvon Deschamps, Jean-Pierre Ferland, Gilles Vigneault, Robert Charlebois.

LA BOLDUC: A SONG FOR EVERY OCCASION
In the 1930s, Mary Travers ▲ *307*, known as La Bolduc, enjoyed huge success as a chronicler of her times in sharp-witted words and music. Accompanied by 'mouth music' (harmonica), she sang about the people and their work, daily events and lifestyle, the news, politics and the landscape of her beloved Quebec.

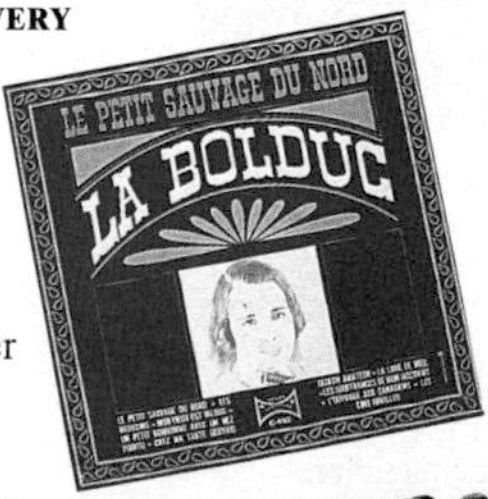

POETRY IN SONG
Artists such as Felix Leclerc (1914–88) ▲ *241*, Gilles Vigneault (b. 1928) ▲ *334*, Raymond Lévesque (b. 1928) and Claude Léveillée (b. 1932) celebrated the country they loved in haunting music and song. They also prepared the way for a whole new generation of singer-songwriters and vocalists, such as Georges Dor ▲ *330*, Pauline Julien (1928–98) ● *56*, Claude Gauthier and the Bozos, who have continued the vocal tradition all over Quebec, delighting sell-out audiences wherever they go.

ROCK BANDS (1960–80)
There was no way that rock 'n' roll would leave Quebec untouched. All over the province, groups of long-haired youngsters dreamed of matching the success of their idols in Britain and the US. Some made it right to the top – for example, bands like Beau Dommage (*left*), Finjan, Les Séguin, Harmonium, Corbeau and many more sang about love, peace and freedom, blaming society for the troubles they saw around them.

92

STARDOM (1980–90)

Bands broke up to pursue solo careers, and new names came to the fore, such as Luc de Larochellière, Jean Leloup and Marie-Denise Pelletier. Some singers went on to achieve worldwide fame, such as Celine Dion and the Acadian Roch Voisine.

SWITCHED OFF! (1990)

All over the musical world, the 1990s witnessed a return to acoustic music. Lyrics were given a new importance, and groups were smaller. Singer-songwriter Richard Desjardins (*above*) had been little known before this decade, but his fans multiplied over this period, bringing him fame and fortune.

CHARLEBOIS

SHOCKING WORDS AND SOOTHING SOUNDS

If 1968 was known for student unrest, it was also the year when Robert Charlebois (b. 1944) and Louise Forestier got together to put on their revue *L'Osstidcho*, an extraordinary fusion of Quebec street slang, Anglicisms and old French. It was a fantastic success, as well as an inspiration to other creative spirits, such as the radical Diane Dufresne (*right*). Renowned as an interpreter of the work of Luc Plamondon, who wrote the musical *Starmania*, Dufresne sings of rebellion, freedom, protest and madness. In a career spanning more than 25 years, she has achieved distinction as singer, scriptwriter, director and actress. Her 1994 rock album *Détournement Majeur*, featuring her own songs, was a worldwide success.

If such dramatists as Gratien Gélinas, Marcel Dubé and Michel Tremblay were the leading lights in the theatrical world in the second half of the 20th century, directors and designers have taken center stage now. Several brilliant playwrights have injected new life into drama, with thanks to the many fine actors who are continuing Quebec's great theatrical tradition. Thought-provoking new productions of the classics, as well as much innovative and experimental theater, are the hallmarks of drama in the province today. Choreographers in Montreal gave their art a radically new language in the 1980s and have won distinction, gaining the capital an enviable reputation for contemporary dance.

RENAISSANCE MAN
Actor, producer and director Robert Lepage (*above*) has been hailed as the Jean Cocteau of theater in Quebec. His original and dynamic approach to drama has influenced a new generation of actors and directors. Recently he was involved with the world-famous Cirque du Soleil, and is currently working on an opera based on George Orwell's *1984* with the conductor Lorin Maazel.

ENERGY
Spinning through the air in ways that seem to defy gravity, the work of the dance company La La La Human Steps, choreographed by Edouard Lock, is characterized by a fierce and brilliant energy.

CARBONE 14
This Montreal-based theater company, founded in 1980 by Gilles Maheu, explores sex, love, passion, God and death in *The Dormitory* (*above*), a show that brought Carbone 14 overnight success as well as undisputed notoriety.

The contemporary dance department at the University of Montreal has been exceptionally influential in turning out important choreographers onto the international scene.

HUMANISM

In 1983, Jean-Pierre Perreault produced a brilliant and witty show called *Joe*, a celebration of the working man in which 32 dancers dressed in hats and overcoats stamped, strutted, ran and leapt about the stage in choreography that seemed to draw inspiration from the work of L.S. Lowry.

MARGIE GILLIS

This internationally acclaimed dancer, in the Isadora Duncan and Martha Graham tradition, is also an athlete and actress. Her dramatic portrayals of raw emotion are universally recognizable.

REINVENTING THE CIRCUS

A world away from tamed animals cringing beneath the trainer's whip, the captivating Cirque du Soleil continues to delight audiences all over the world with its heady mix of magic, music and imagination.

KITCHEN SINK, MONTREAL-STYLE

Written in *Joual*, the patois of working-class Montreal, Michel Tremblay's 1968 play *Les Belles-Soeurs* dealt vividly and compassionately with the plight of downtrodden women in the provincial capital. Its effect was instant and electric: the play was hailed as 'the single most important event in the history of Quebec theater'. The English translation (*The Guid Sisters*) was also well received.

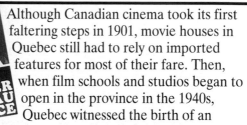

Although Canadian cinema took its first faltering steps in 1901, movie houses in Quebec still had to rely on imported features for most of their fare. Then, when film schools and studios began to open in the province in the 1940s, Quebec witnessed the birth of an indigenous local industry. After the advent of television in 1952, soap operas became everyone's favorite entertainment. In the 1960s both commercial and art cinema developed simultaneously, with several 'serious' movies attracting international attention. In the last 20 years feature films and documentaries have flourished, with many important young directors achieving recognition, who are keen to change the esthetic and cultural traditions of the movie industry.

Films from Quebec began to exert a powerful influence on the development of the industry in the early 1960s, notably with *Pour la Suite du Monde* (*above*) by

DOCUMENTARIES
Pierre Perrault and Michel Brault. In this movie, which tells of a group of local people trying to organize an old-fashioned beluga hunt, the directors take a searching look at the relationship between the different elements that make up the community, as well as their search for national identity.

STATE SUPPORT
Without state support, cinema in Quebec would struggle to exist. Both the Canadian and Quebec governments have been financing movie production for at least 50 years, and the National Film Board of Canada in Montreal has gained a worldwide reputation. As well as giving generous support, the Board also awards the industry certain fiscal privileges.

ANIMATION

Quebec has long been known for its animated films, made by such figures as Norman McLaren (*left: Blinkety Blank*) and Frédéric Back (*below: Homme qui plantait des arbres*). Co Hoedeman has also won many awards. Both art and cinema, animation uses many different techniques.

ENTERTAINMENT AND THE ART-HOUSE MOVIE

Movies made in Quebec since the 1940s have been predominantly French-speaking and created for two types of audience: art-house aficionados and those in search of entertainment. This split makes it difficult for the industry to define its personality within the plethora of foreign movies. Despite this problem, many directors and actors have succeeded, such as Denys Arcand (*below: Le Déclin de l'empire américain*), Claude Jutra, Gilles Carle and Micheline Lanctôt (*right: La Vraie Nature de Bernadette*), Geneviève Bujold and Carole Laure.

DER UNTERGANG DES AMERIKANISCHEN IMPERIUMS

CORPORATION IMAGE M-M und OFFICE NATIONAL DU FILM DU CANADA zeigen DER UNTERGANG DES AMERIKANISCHEN IMPERIUMS
Ein Film von DENYS ARCAND · Produziert von RENÉ MALO und ROGER FRAPPIER
mit DOMINIQUE MICHEL · DOROTHÉE BERRYMAN · LOUISE PORTAL · PIERRE CURZI
RÉMY GIRARD · YVES JACQUES · GENEVIÈVE RIOUX · DANIEL BRIÈRE und GABRIEL ARCAND
Kamera GUY DUFAUX · Schnitt MONIQUE FORTIER · Musik FRANÇOIS DOMPIERRE nach Motiven von HANDEL · Ausführende
Produzenten PIERRE GENDRON · Produzenten RENÉ MALO · ROGER FRAPPIER · Drehbuch und Regie DENYS ARCAND

tv
HEBDO

LOUIS se marie...

...le curé meurt!

EN PRIMEUR À LA TÉLÉ

JURASSIC PARK

SOAP OPERA

For the last 50 years, viewers have breathlessly watched the daily lives of their favorite soap characters. The popularity of these programs owes as much to escapism as to reality.

● Food: *cipaille*

Cipaille (also known as *ci-pâte*) is a meat and pastry stew similar to the old-fashioned 'sea-pie' from which it derives its name. Rich and nourishing, it is the perfect meal for a freezing winter's day. The Quebec diet enjoyed by the colonists was made up of meat, plenty of game, fish in certain regions, fatty bacon, potatoes and onions. Just like Lac Saint-Jean pie, the local specialty, and rabbit in white wine, *cipaille* is almost considered to be a national dish in Quebec, though the ingredients can change from one region to another. In Gaspésie, for example, it is made with fish.

INGREDIENTS
2lbs/900g pork fillet, 2lb/900g venison or beef, a 3lb/1.4kg chicken, a 3–4lb/1.4–1.8kg duck (wild if possible), 8 slices of streaky bacon, 2 pints/1,200ml of rich stock.

THAT'S NOT ALL!
4 onions, 2oz/50g parsley, 2oz/50g celery leaves, 1lb/450g potatoes, ¼ tsp savory (or thyme), ½ tsp marjoram, a pinch each of cinnamon and grated nutmeg, salt, pepper.

1. Chop the onions, parsley and celery leaves. Peel the potatoes and cut into cubes.

2. Cut the pork, venison, and boned, skinned chicken and duck into 1in/2.5cm cubes. In separate bowls blend each of the four meats with the raw onions, chopped celery leaves, chopped herbs, spices and salt and pepper to taste. Cover and chill overnight in the refrigerator, keeping the raw meat well away from other fresh foods.

COOKING
1. Line the base of a large ovenproof dish with bacon slices.

2. Add the pork mixture with a quarter of the cubed potatoes and pour over a quarter of the warm stock. Cover with ⅛ in/½ cm layer of pastry pricked with the point of a knife.

3. Repeat step 2 with the chicken and duck, and then venison, each separated by a layer of pastry.

4. Cover the whole pie with a thicker layer of pastry (½ in/1cm).

5. Put a lid on the dish and bake at 300°F/150°C for 2 hours and 30 minutes, basting occasionally with stock. Reduce the heat to 210°F/100°C and continue to cook for another 2 hours 30 minutes.

2½lb/1.2kg plain flour, 2 tsp salt, 2 tsp baking powder, 3 eggs, 12oz/360g lard, 13 fl oz/375ml boiling water.

1. Into a hole in the middle of the flour put salt and baking powder. Add the beaten eggs, lard cut into small pieces and knead well. Gradually add boiling water until you have a pastry that is slightly softer than shortcrust.

2. Cover with a clean cloth and chill in the refrigerator for at least 2 hours, until firm enough to be rolled out.

6. Serve hot, accompanied by pickled beetroot, dill pickles and pickled onions.

99

Quebec specialties

CHECK SHIRT
These come in two thicknesses: woolen for winter, and flannel for warmer weather.

GALOSHES
A pair of rubber galoshes is indispensable for keeping the feet warm and dry in rain and snow.

SPIRITS
Quebec has two liqueur specialties: Caribou, a mixture of alcohol and red wine; and Dubleuet, made from blueberries at Lac-Saint-Jean ▲ 321.

BEER
Quebec is justly proud of its beer, rejecting mass-produced flavorless products in favor of locally produced varieties made by craftsmen. There are many different types, such as Maudite, Fin du Monde, Saint-Ambroise and Boréale.

MAPLE PRODUCTS
Originally collected to make sugar, today maple sap yields a wide range of commercial products, such as the classic and ever-popular maple syrup (*below*), and Tire (*bottom and above*), a kind of candy hardened by pouring it onto snow. Some gourmet treats are reserved for sugar parties at harvest time ● 82, such as maple water (sap) and Réduit, a liquid that is half-way between water and syrup.

THE PRESS
Quebec has six mass-circulation daily papers: *Le Devoir*, *La Presse*, *Le Journal de Montreal*, *The Gazette*, *Le Journal de Quebec* and *Le Soleil*, as well as two popular weekly magazines: *Voir* and *The Mirror*.

ICE HOCKEY AND SKATING
As well as being the country's national sport ● 88, ice-hockey is big business. Hockey sticks and pucks are manufactured and sold by the thousands. Skating is enjoyed by almost everyone in the province. Just about every village has its own indoor as well as outdoor rink.

Quebec through the seasons

Two extremes, *102*

Coping with winter, *104*

Springtime, *106*

Summer at last, *107*

Fall: the first frosts, *108*

It has been said that in Quebec there are only two seasons: winter and July. That is not strictly true, although winter is definitely the most dominant of the four seasons, balanced by a short but splendid summer. These two extremes have been part of the national identity for centuries: the very first explorers noticed that Nouvelle-France only had two seasons, winter and summer. In 1603, Samuel Champlain ▲ *254* passed his first winter here, and its severity unsettled him; throughout the summer, nothing had led him to expect such a shocking contrast.

He later noted: 'Winter surprised us, coming much earlier than we had expected, and putting paid to many of our plans ... it is impossible to understand this country without having spent a winter here, since during the summer everything is so pleasant – the forests, the landscape, and the waters teeming with fish of every kind. But winter here lasts for six months of the year.' Half a century later, when the region was settled by colonists from France, Pierre Boucher ▲ 239, a Huron interpreter, soldier and finally seigneur of Boucherville, wrote a book intended to encourage people from his native land to come and settle in the province. He wrote: 'I shall say a word here about the seasons. One can really only count two of them, as the climate passes rapidly from great cold to great heat, and from great heat to great cold, and this is why we only speak of winter and summer.' Again in the 18th century, people remarked on this duality, which tended to gloss over the beauty of spring and fall. In the mid-20th century the geographer Raoul Blanchard explained their apparent absence by saying the winter 'eats away at spring and starts to bite again in late autumn'. Canadian artist, Horatio Walker, says: 'I live in the midst of difficulties, hemmed in by snow on the deserted Île d'Orléans, but cannot leave the wonder of Quebec in winter.'

CUTTING THE ICE
River ice was cut into blocks with enormous saws and stored for use in the hot months of summer.

103

● Quebec through the seasons
Coping with winter

The experience of more than 350 winters has led generations of Quebec residents to evolve their own culture rather than try to impose a European response to conditions here. The organization of everyday life and the development of appropriate technologies – even the creation of pastimes to while away the long months of winter – have all shaped the identity of present-day Quebec, where its inhabitants are regularly faced with the harsh reality of the climate. Learning to adjust has not been an easy process: the first colonists who settled in Nouvelle-France were often thrown into deep despair by the fearful conditions, and soon realized that their old way of life would be impossible in the hostile elements.

THE FIRST COLONISTS PREPARE FOR WINTER IN NOUVELLE-FRANCE
Early settlers built their houses along the same lines as they did back home in France, but they soon found that having a fireplace in the living-room meant a lot of heat was lost. In spite of the intense cold, the pioneers still wore European-style dress, so they suffered from chilblains and all kinds of aches and pains exacerbated by their poor diet, which largely consisted of salted meat. Before long, they learned to imitate the Native Americans, using sledges and snowshoes to travel and thus reduce the solitude that winter imposed. It soon became clear that if the colonists were to put down roots here, they would have to adapt quickly in order to survive.

LEARNING TO ADAPT
Thanks to a certain economic prosperity brought by the fur trade, the inhabitants were able to afford to take measures to reduce their hardship.

Windows once covered with paper were glazed and then double-glazed, the north walls of houses were built to be solid with no openings and the interior fireplace gave way to a stove. Meat was put out to freeze under the snow, while other farm produce was stored in cellars and outhouses. The most popular pastimes were tobogganing and sleigh-riding

● 88. The trick lay in learning to adapt the harsh cold to their advantage instead of sitting around complaining about it. Once they understood this principle, they were able to cope much more easily.

ADAPTING PROVED EASIER FOR SOME THAN OTHERS
In logging camps ● 76 in the newly colonized regions ■ 18, living conditions were similar to those the first settlers had endured. With the growing industrialization after 1850, many factory workers found themselves out of work in wintertime and they had to use what little money they had to buy food and wood for fuel. Adapting well to winter depended on choosing an appropriate way of life.

SURVIVING WINTER TODAY
Over the years the people of Quebec

have come to love winter, even cruising effortlessly through it. New technology has made life easier in such areas as house building, motoring, the building and clearing of highways, the design of sports equipment and clothing for work and leisure. Ski resorts, ice rinks, cross-country skiing trails, snowmobiles and snowshoes all make use of the freezing weather to enhance the quality of life for Quebec residents. But all the time, two crucial factors have to be borne in mind to avoid hardship and suffering: power supplies have to be maintained, and the highways kept open across the province. It is ultimately the same battle against cold and isolation that was fought daily by the early settlers.

● Quebec through the seasons
Springtime

It's not just winter that has its own defining characteristics; the beginning of spring is like a rite of passage in Quebec. Winter fades away as the warm weather arrives to send the melting snow on its way. While March often brings lashing storms and wild weather, it also heralds the return of migrant birds and the beginning of spring. This is sugar time in the province as well ● *82*, and the old traditions are just as popular now as they were centuries ago, adding sparkle to the last interminable weeks of winter, when the snow still lies on the ground. Historically, spring was also the time for all kinds of renewed activity, such as making soap out of scraps of animal fat left over from winter, spreading skeins of linen out on the snow to bleach in the sun and, in May, soaking bundles of wool in the nearest stream. And this is still the time when cattle are turned out into the fields after a long winter in the stable and work on the farm begins all over again.

Agriculture is one of the foremost industries in Quebec, and the countryside comes alive with activity as winter turns to spring in late March. As waterways everywhere are swollen with the melting snow, logs are floated down-river and formed into huge rafts ● *76* on their way from the forest to the sawmill or pulp factory. Just like their country cousins, city-dwellers take to the streets, enjoying the warmth and embarking on outdoor projects, such as giving their houses a lick of paint – but even with all this activity, there is still time for a weekend's camping or exploring the countryside on a bicycle. Larger cities also open sidewalk cafés reminiscent of those in European cities. In spring, snow geese congregate near Quebec City, a sight that never fails to impress the many visitors who travel to the area just to see these famous birds.

Summer traditionally begins on St John's Day (June 24), a few days after the summer solstice. Centuries ago, the first colonists spoke of an 'extremely great heat' and described the difficulties of dealing with mosquitoes and other biting insects unknown to European settlers. Native Americans taught them how to smear their bodies with grease to keep the insects at bay. They also taught them the secrets of growing corn, squash and tobacco, all of which still thrive in the summer months in Quebec. The cycle of crop growing and harvesting has continued unchanged for almost 300 years, with the addition of vegetables from the garden and wild fruits that vary the diet. In

the past, there might have been a ride out in the trap on Sundays, something that modern visitors to Quebec or Montreal can still do today, providing a taste of the pace of life in days gone by. The traditional get-togethers to shuck corn on the cob and enjoy a picnic with family and friends in the countryside are a harbinger of autumn in the province. And outside, in cafés on the sidewalks, there are tables and chairs for passers-by to enjoy the last rays of the summer sun.

Quebec through the seasons
Fall: the first frosts

As early as September, the warmth of the summer sun is tempered by the first chills of fall. Summer starts to fade away as the unmistakable signs of winter approach. This is known as 'the prettiest season of all, when the leaves on the trees are at their most beautiful,' as the botanist Marie-Victorin once said. He loved the golden fairyland of fall colors he saw in the forest: shades of ocher and vermilion contrasted with the verdant green of pine and spruce. For several years, there has been an annual 'Festival des Couleurs' in the Laurentides, which attracts nature lovers from far and wide. Indian summer ■ *21*, the last manifestation of the warm and sunny days, usually puts in an appearance in late October and is followed by cold rain and the first snows, which soon melt as hunters fire the last shots of the season. By St Catherine's Day (November 25), chill is setting in and winter knocks at the door. In times past, When society was predominantly rural, the end of the harvest signaled a period in which everything was gradually moved back to the homestead; food was preserved, and the wood stove was lit. By All Saints', when the animals were traditionally brought back to the stables, all the preparations for the long winter ahead had been completed and folk were already beginning to think about their Christmas dinner. Summer has always been the only season in which you can forget about winter: whether at the start or the finish, spring and fall are both eroded by the winter's chill.

Architecture

The classical style in
   Nouvelle-France, *110*
Canadian architecture
   in the 18th century, *112*
British classicism (1780–1825), *114*
Neoclassicism (1825–60), *116*
Historical styles of the
   19th century (1825–1914), *118*
19th-century church architecture, *120*
Religious heritage in the countryside, *122*
From tradition to modernism (1900–40), *124*
Architecture of the Quiet Revolution
   (1950–75), *126*
Postmodernism (1975 to present), *128*
The way ahead, *130*

The classical style in Nouvelle-France

For a hundred years, between 1660 and 1760, builders and master craftsmen continued to take French traditions and styles across the Atlantic with them to the New World, which was still a French province. The esthetic of the great châteaux was faithfully copied along the banks of the Saint Lawrence by men who wanted to build a mighty capital to rival the one back home – but it was not to be.

Roof timbers with double crossbeams

Mansard roof

The Sulpician Seminary in the 18th century

THE CLASSICAL CITY

Classical plans included fortified city walls for defense and also, as a sign of sophistication, to separate the city from the suburbs outside. In 1716, the engineer Chaussegros de Léry drew up a plan for the expansion of Quebec, which included fortifications with a west wall, keep, and upper and lower town all laid out with precise regularity; it was only completed in the early 19th century ▲ 262.

17TH-CENTURY GROINED VAULTING

The French classical style called for sophisticated stonework. The earliest vaulting in Nouvelle-France still shows the incredible skill required by architects and stonemasons to design and assemble such elegant features that could cope with the terrific force exerted on them.

18TH-CENTURY BARREL VAULTING

The art of vault-building declined when locally trained craftsmen replaced those who had traveled from France. To ensure stability, these less-skilled workers built vaults that were semicircular in section, exerted immense force on the walls, but could have no openings.

THE CLASSICAL STYLE

The Sulpician Seminary in Montreal ▲ 169 (*above*) was built in stages between 1685 and 1715 on palatial lines. Initially there were three buildings on two storeys surrounding a courtyard. The main building stood over three vaulted levels of kitchens, storerooms and cellars. The mansard roof was replaced, around 1735, by a brick-built level, which was topped by a pitched roof.

CLASSICAL BELL-TOWER

Consisting of a double drum topped with cupolas, this typical 17th-century bell-tower (*below left*) is from the old church of Sainte-Anne-de-Beaupré (c.1689). It was later moved to the commemorative community chapel ▲ *280*.

BAROQUE DECORATION

The canopy from the church at Neuville ▲ *250* is typical of the Louis XIV style, when this type of ornament, inspired by one Bernini designed for St Peter's in Rome, was popular in Parisian churches. Imported from France at the end of the 17th century to decorate the chapel of the episcopal palace of Mgr de Saint-Vallier, this was considered to be the most exquisite ornament in Nouvelle-France.

CLASSICAL TOWN HOUSE

Charles Aubert de la Chesnaye was a wealthy citizen of Quebec who had his town house enlarged when he was ennobled by the king. This type of dwelling, built around a central courtyard and consisting of a series of apartments, was exclusively reserved for those of noble blood.

THE CLASSICAL IDEAL

The Château Saint-Louis in Quebec ▲ *260* was built for Governor Frontenac by François de La Joué in 1692, and it was completed by Chaussegros de Léry in 1725. Its superb symmetry, tripartite façade, two storeys and high roof topped with points represented classical perfection 'à la Française' in Nouvelle-France. This château remained the residence of the colony's governor until 1834. Today a boardwalk runs beneath it.

DESIGN FOR LIVING, 18TH-CENTURY STYLE

The palace of Quebec's commanding officer ▲ *259* was rebuilt in 1715, with two wings hosting a series of rooms at the front and overlooking the garden. In the 18th century, drawing rooms, antechambers and bedrooms boasted built-in cupboards and wardrobes.

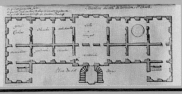

From the early 18th century onward, builders and architects were home-grown Canadians trained in Canada. Strict regulations to prevent fire made for simpler building styles, devoid of decoration. This austere style became modified over the years, and remained the typical French style of construction until well after the Conquest in 1760.

QUEBEC TOWN HOUSE
(*Right*) Built on top of vaulted cellars, this typical town house has chimneys placed against interior walls to conserve heat, and they stood well clear of the roof to minimize the risk of fire. On top is a sloping roof with a simple timber frame that could be removed in the event of fire.

MONTREAL TOWN HOUSE
(*Above*) The oldest houses in Montreal date from between 1780 and 1800, replacing earlier single-storey buildings.

A COTTAGE NEAR MONTREAL
(*Below*) In the late 17th century, this type of cottage would have had two rooms: a living-room and bedroom. A century later such dwellings had doubled in size, with four rooms on the ground floor.

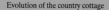

Evolution of the country cottage

A COTTAGE NEAR QUEBEC
(*Left*) Cottages were originally made of wood, but as the years went by, they were built of stone and became much larger. In the 18th century, a typical cottage still had just a living room and a bedroom.

CHURCH DESIGNS IN NOUVELLE-FRANCE

COUNTRY CHURCH
The chapel of the Petit-Cap Seminary (*above*) has a sober elegance typical of church design at this period.

Jesuit design

Augustinian design

TOWN AND COUNTRY
In 1743, the church of the Holy Family on the Île d'Orléans ▲ *277* (now demolished) was modeled on a church built by the Jesuits in Quebec in 1666. In this way society's conception of beauty in architecture spread out from its urban origins (*below right*).

Maillou design

AN 18TH-CENTURY PROTOTYPE
(*Below*) Following its destruction by fire in 1726, the palace of the commanding officer of Quebec ▲ *259* was rebuilt in accordance with new fire regulations. It was to serve as a model of dependable and secure construction, based on the new safety laws, while the design of its façade resembled a terrace of town houses.

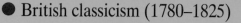

● British classicism (1780–1825)

Once they had settled into their new colony, the British
began to introduce the Palladian style of architecture
and their own systems of town planning. Family houses
were built in streets around the city center: market
squares gave way to streets lined with shops, which
connected the heart of the city to its suburbs, while
on the edges of the town were prosperous villas.

COUNTRY HOUSES
In 1781 Governor
Haldimand built
himself a house that
dominated the
Quebec landscape
from the
Montmorency Falls
▲ 276. The design
drew its inspiration
from the colonial

architecture of the
American South:
a huge porch with
columns supporting
an overhanging,
straight roof became
the ideal of an
elegant country
house, reminiscent
of classical Palladian
design (*left*).

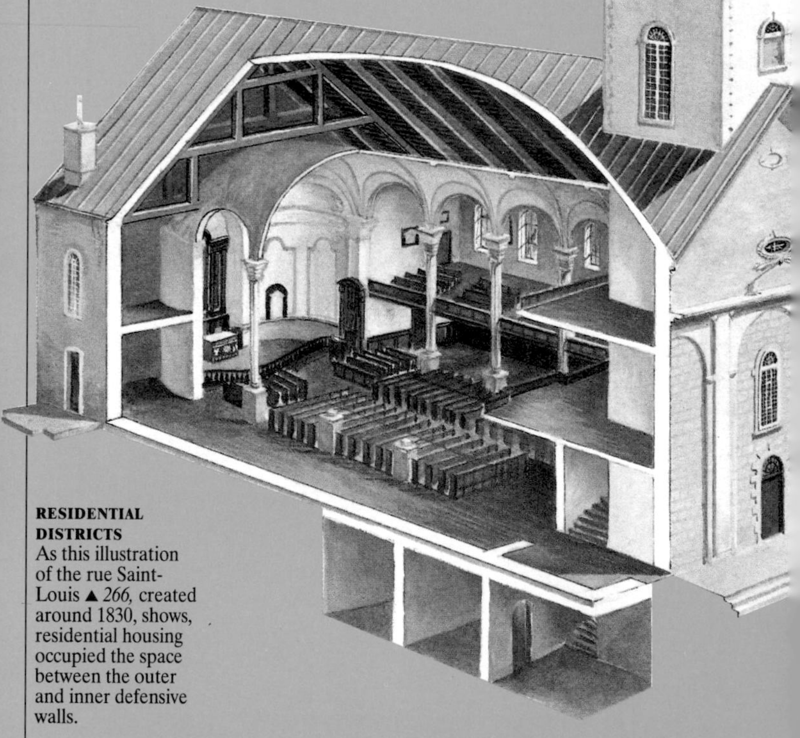

**RESIDENTIAL
DISTRICTS**
As this illustration
of the rue Saint-
Louis ▲ 266, created
around 1830, shows,
residential housing
occupied the space
between the outer
and inner defensive
walls.

COUNTRY PARISH
St Stefen in Chambly
(1820) ▲ *208* was one
of the first Anglican
churches in Lower
Canada.

**RELIGIOUS
ARCHITECTURE**
To assert dominance
in its latest colony,
the new rulers were
quick to establish the
presence of the
Anglican Church by
building Holy Trinity
Cathedral in Quebec
▲ *261*. Typically
English in style, it is
rectangular in layout,
with a high steeple,
three naves, first-
floor galleries, a
double row of
windows on
each side, and
closed wooden
pews as
principal
features.

THE CLASSICAL ENGLISH STYLE
Built in 1818 to a design by François Baillairgé, the old jailhouse at
Trois-Rivières ▲ *239* shows all the characteristics of the English
Palladian style, as built in Lower Canada: open façade with wing,
its central section set forward from the rest, three storeys, and
a pediment. The house was built from quarry stone with vertical
bands of rustication at the corners.

French-style town house

Classical British town house

**PALLADIAN STYLE: A
NEW WAY OF LIVING**
Town houses
retained their
outward appearance,
but were now
designed to house
single families. Living
space was set out
around a central hall,
giving onto rooms on
all floors. The wider
French town house
was replaced by
narrower, deeper
dwellings, which
complicated the
access to stables,
yards and
outbuildings to
the rear.

CITY CENTER
Around the Place d'Armes in Quebec ▲ *261*,
the British built new administrative buildings,
such as the Anglican cathedral and the law
courts. They also remodeled existing
buildings there, making the Château Saint-
Louis ▲ *260* look more English in style.

British and American architects introduced the neoclassical style, based on ancient classical models, to Lower Canada. Their designs showed a discipline and attention to detail that was applied to both the interior and exterior of their constructions, though it failed to win the colonists away from their traditional styles. As a result, a style peculiar to the province emerged – one that was essentially French, but that incorporated many features of the predominant style of the period.

MEMORIALS AND MONUMENTS
Largely because it involved going back to classical sources, neoclassicism proved ideal for commemorative monuments. The one erected to Nelson on the Place Jacques Cartier in Montreal (1809) ▲ *171*, celebrates the English admiral who lost his life at Trafalgar (*left*). The obelisk (*right*), whose shape is based on those found in ancient Egyptian temples, is a symbol of death: this is the Wolfe-Montcalm Memorial (1827), dedicated to two heroes who died in battle on the Plains of Abraham.

ARCHITECTURAL ORDERS
With the arrival of neoclassicism, architecture became an academic discipline, no longer simply the 'craft of building houses'. It was soon taught in colleges and universities, requiring a wide range of skills, as this model of different orders (c.1835) at the seminary of Nicolet ▲ *244* shows (*above*).

NEOCLASSICISM AND IMITATION
The Papineau house on the Rue Bonsecours ▲172 in Montreal shows the style that was prevalent when it was renovated in 1831. It was covered in carved wooden cladding and painted gray to take on the appearance of dressed stone blocks (*below*).

PAPER MODEL
The project above, for a retable in the Church of the Hôtel Dieu at Quebec (1829), was designed by Thomas Baillairgé and is typical of the neoclassical period: the design is entirely architectural, although there is no building as such.

NEO-GRECIAN RELIGIOUS ARCHITECTURE
The US evolved this style, which was inspired by ancient Greek models. The Plymouth Trinity Church at Sherbrooke (1848) ▲215 shows some of its distinctive features: doric columns with no base and pilasters, and an antique-style portico on the façade.

'LOWER CANADA'S FINEST ARCHITECT'
Thomas Baillairgé (1791–1859) earned this sobriquet, after designing most of the religious buildings in the province between 1825 and 1845.

A CIVIC STYLE
At the time it was built, Bonsecours Market (W. Footner, 1845) ▲172 was the largest neoclassical building in North America. Its doric portico and impressive dome dominate Old Montreal.

Historical styles of the 19th century (1825–1914)

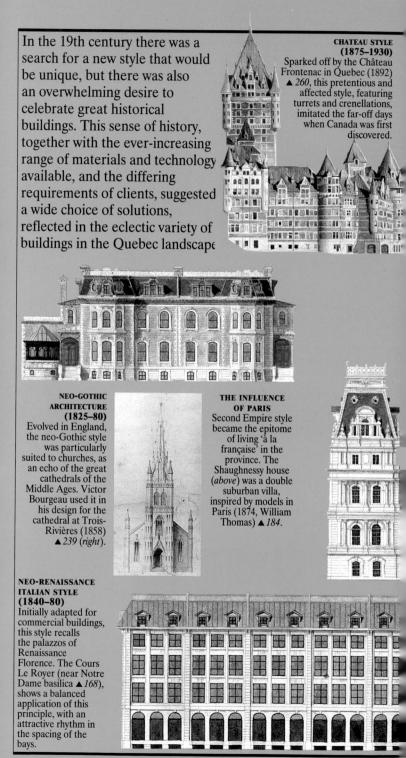

In the 19th century there was a search for a new style that would be unique, but there was also an overwhelming desire to celebrate great historical buildings. This sense of history, together with the ever-increasing range of materials and technology available, and the differing requirements of clients, suggested a wide choice of solutions, reflected in the eclectic variety of buildings in the Quebec landscape.

CHATEAU STYLE (1875–1930)
Sparked off by the Château Frontenac in Quebec (1892) ▲ *260*, this pretentious and affected style, featuring turrets and crenellations, imitated the far-off days when Canada was first discovered.

NEO-GOTHIC ARCHITECTURE (1825–80)
Evolved in England, the neo-Gothic style was particularly suited to churches, as an echo of the great cathedrals of the Middle Ages. Victor Bourgeau used it in his design for the cathedral at Trois-Rivières (1858) ▲ *239* (*right*).

THE INFLUENCE OF PARIS
Second Empire style became the epitome of living 'à la française' in the province. The Shaughnessy house (*above*) was a double suburban villa, inspired by models in Paris (1874, William Thomas) ▲ *184*.

NEO-RENAISSANCE ITALIAN STYLE (1840–80)
Initially adapted for commercial buildings, this style recalls the palazzos of Renaissance Florence. The Cours Le Royer (near Notre Dame basilica ▲ *168*), shows a balanced application of this principle, with an attractive rhythm in the spacing of the bays.

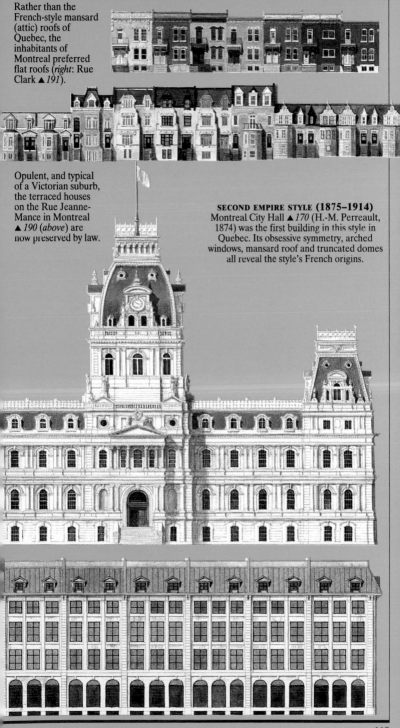

Rather than the French-style mansard (attic) roofs of Quebec, the inhabitants of Montreal preferred flat roofs (*right*: Rue Clark ▲ 191).

Opulent, and typical of a Victorian suburb, the terraced houses on the Rue Jeanne-Mance in Montreal ▲ 190 (*above*) are now preserved by law.

SECOND EMPIRE STYLE (1875–1914)
Montreal City Hall ▲ 170 (H.-M. Perreault, 1874) was the first building in this style in Quebec. Its obsessive symmetry, arched windows, mansard roof and truncated domes all reveal the style's French origins.

After the Conquest, the Church in Canada assumed
responsibility for the interests and the culture of the
Catholic French-speaking majority. As they took
charge of education, health and other social
concerns, the Church erected buildings
in towns and villages that remain
memorials to its degree of
involvement and its
omnipresence.

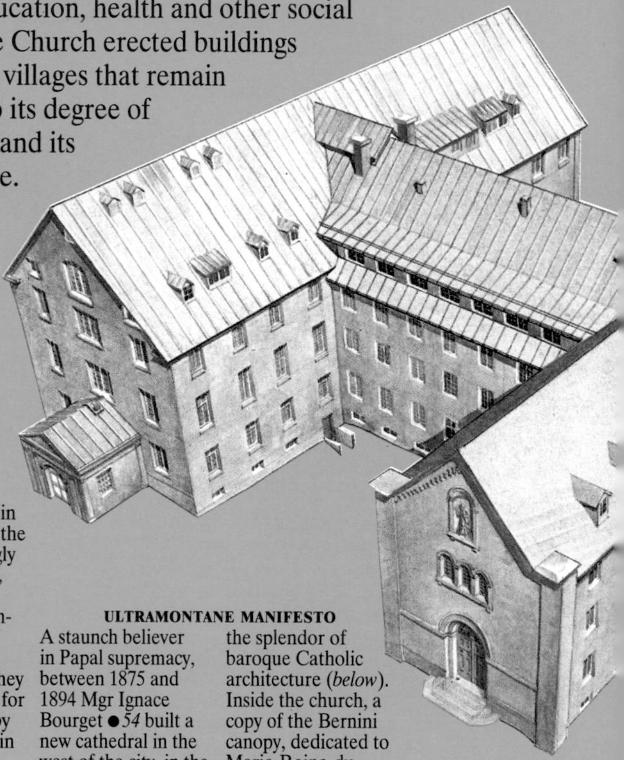

**NATIONALIST
MANIFESTO**
Opposed to the
secularization of
important
institutions, clergy in
Quebec promoted the
concept of a strongly
nationalist Church,
representing the
views of the French-
speaking majority
there. In 1881, the
architect J.F. Peachey
completed designs for
a church inspired by
the Trinité church in
Paris. Saint-Jean-
Baptiste (*below*) was
for years considered
the national
monument of
French-
Canadians
in the capital
▲ 270.

ULTRAMONTANE MANIFESTO
A staunch believer
in Papal supremacy,
between 1875 and
1894 Mgr Ignace
Bourget ● 54 built a
new cathedral in the
west of the city, in the
heart of the English-
speaking quarter.
The bishop chose a
scaled-down model of
St Peter's in Rome,
which was designed
by Victor Bourgeau,
as a potent symbol of
the splendor of
baroque Catholic
architecture (*below*).
Inside the church, a
copy of the Bernini
canopy, dedicated to
Marie-Reine-du-
Monde ▲ 175, served
as a reminder of the
unconditional
submission to the
ideology of the
Counter-
Reformation.

The Romano-Byzantine style in many ways exemplified the Church in Canada (and New England) by recalling its imperial origins. Monumental in scale, these churches were subject to a wide variety of designs, like Notre-Dame-du-Perpétuel-Secours in Holyoke (Massachusetts), by the architect Louis Caron, Junior.

BELL-TOWERS DOWN THE AGES
A fusion of French (pierced drum) and English (louvred screen) features, metal bell-towers are a hallmark of the regional landscape.

CITY CONVENT
Churches, hospices, convents and colleges are a feature of urban landscapes everywhere. The house of Bon-Pasteur ▲ 195 in Montreal (also known as 'Good Shepherd House') was built entirely of gray stone between 1846 and 1893, and is typical of the religious style; wings extend the main building, with a chapel at the center. This type of building was designed to be easily enlarged if the need arose. Today it has been converted into chic apartments, while the chapel has become a recital hall for chamber music.

CHURCH-BUILDERS
If he met with the approval of the clergy, a workman could become a contractor and even architect. This is how many church-building dynasties began, such as the Giroux, who brought the finest craftsmen to Saint-Casimir at Portneuf (*left*) ▲ 250 and executed orders from all over French-speaking Canada and New England.

121

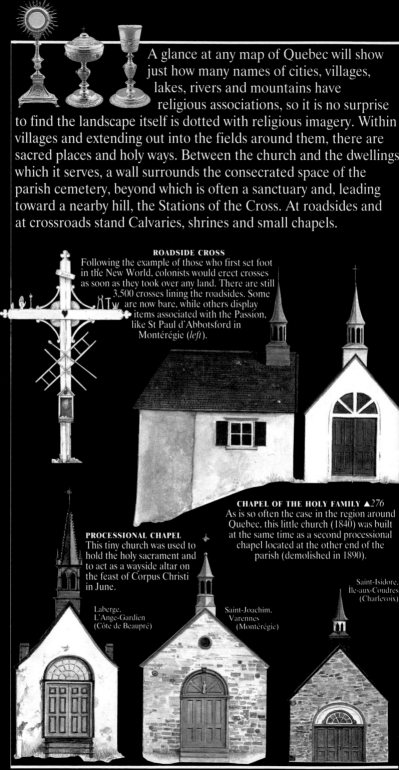

A glance at any map of Quebec will show just how many names of cities, villages, lakes, rivers and mountains have religious associations, so it is no surprise to find the landscape itself is dotted with religious imagery. Within villages and extending out into the fields around them, there are sacred places and holy ways. Between the church and the dwellings which it serves, a wall surrounds the consecrated space of the parish cemetery, beyond which is often a sanctuary and, leading toward a nearby hill, the Stations of the Cross. At roadsides and at crossroads stand Calvaries, shrines and small chapels.

ROADSIDE CROSS
Following the example of those who first set foot in the New World, colonists would erect crosses as soon as they took over any land. There are still 3,500 crosses lining the roadsides. Some are now bare, while others display items associated with the Passion, like St Paul d'Abbotsford in Montérégie (*left*).

CHAPEL OF THE HOLY FAMILY ▲*276*
As is so often the case in the region around Quebec, this little church (1840) was built at the same time as a second processional chapel located at the other end of the parish (demolished in 1890).

PROCESSIONAL CHAPEL
This tiny church was used to hold the holy sacrament and to act as a wayside altar on the feast of Corpus Christi in June.

Laberge,
L'Ange-Gardien
(Côte de Beaupré)

Saint-Joachim,
Varennes
(Montérégie)

Saint-Isidore,
Île-aux-Coudres
(Charlevoix)

Trois-Rivières-Ouest
(La Mauricie)

Saint-Germain
(Saint Lawrence Bay)

Yamaska-Est
(Montérégie)

CALVARY

This is the most elaborate kind of roadside cross. It shows the crucified Christ, sometimes with the two thieves, the Virgin and Mary Magdalene. Calvaries appeared in the province in the mid-18th century, when the Stations of the Cross found a new lease of life. There are still around 60 along the banks of the Saint Lawrence, almost all of which are made from carved wood.

PLACE OF PILGRIMAGE

Quebec has the three largest places of pilgrimage north of Mexico ▲186, 278, 249. In addition, there are about 80 rural places of pilgrimage, the great majority of which are very small. These include the hermitage of Saint-Antoine at Lac Bouchette (*left*, one of 23 paintings by Charles Huot).

THE VARENNES CALVARY

Made of iron, this is the largest Calvary in Quebec. It dates from 1829, with figures from 1850.

PARISH BUILDINGS

The typical structure of a village consists of church and adjacent cemetery, a large presbytery, village hall (formerly the center of community life) and sometimes a school where the teaching is by the clergy. L'Islet-sur-Mer (*above*) ▲ 289 is a classic example, with its church containing an art collection and a museum of church furniture.

123

● From tradition to modernism (1900–40)

At the beginning of the 20th century, the urban landscape was undergoing a period of drastic change. There were now buildings with steel frames, made of concrete, all with increased mechanization and an electricity supply. However, Canada was intent on preserving its national identity, and did not want styles known as 'international' to erode its own vernacular designs.

ART DECO
The University of Montreal ▲*186* (Ernest Cormier, 1926) introduced classical rationalism devised by French architects, such as Perret, Garnier and Roux-Spitz, in the first decades of the 20th century. Their influence was to have enormous impact on design and the decorative arts in North America, and introduced the concept of the skyscraper, the most potent of all capitalist symbols.

DOMESTIC COMFORT
English 16th- and 17th-century houses projected an image of elegance and comfort, and 'Mock-Tudor' style was immensely popular up to World War 2.

The half-timbered façade, tall chimneys, and gables on this house, built in Quebec by Harry Staveley, conceal a modern interior behind their cozy appearance.

EUROPEAN MODERNISM
In 1938 Baron Empain invited the Belgian architect A. Courtens to design buildings in Estérel, at Sainte-Marguérite-du-Lac-Masson ▲ *218*. The architect of this country house (*above*) introduced the international style to Quebec.

REGIONALISM
Firmly fixed in the collective subconscious, regional styles of design enliven the landscape of the province. The Manor of Saguenay (1939) in Jonquière ▲ *322* celebrates medieval Normandy, the home of explorer Jacques Cartier.

Architecture was soon being taught in art schools. Cultural institutions and big businesses liked what they saw: the Sun Life building ▲ *178* (1913–33) employed this rather self-conscious approach to add gravitas to its company's name.

DOM BELLOT AND MODERN GOTHIC
After winning much acclaim in France, the Benedictine monk and architect Paul Bellot (1876–1944) brought his radical style to Quebec. It made much use of polygonal concrete and polychrome brick parabolic arches (*right*), which pleased both the purse and the piety of the Church in Canada. The layout of the abbey at Saint-Benoît-du-Lac ▲ *213* (1939, *above*) solved the problem of fitting modern design into natural surroundings.

125

Architecture of the Quiet Revolution (1950–75)

In the 1950s, Quebec took the first steps toward creating a progressive society and freeing itself from the yoke of tradition. Like the rest of North America, the province had long been resistant to contemporary change but after the Quiet Revolution Quebecois discovered the attractions of functionalism combined with expressionism, in the hands of some brilliant and imaginative architects.

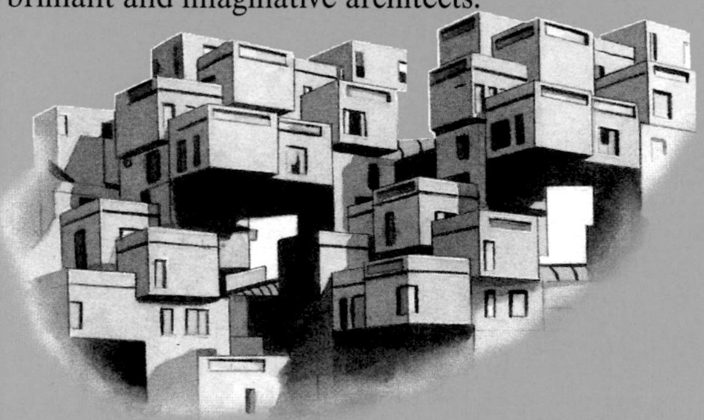

BOXES FOR LIVING
The promising young architect Moshe Safdie completed the above project while still a student, exploring the form and economy of stackable prefabricated concrete cubic modules designed for modern habitation. The completed assembly proved an attractive answer to the monotony of much existing design, but was, unfortunately, rather costly.

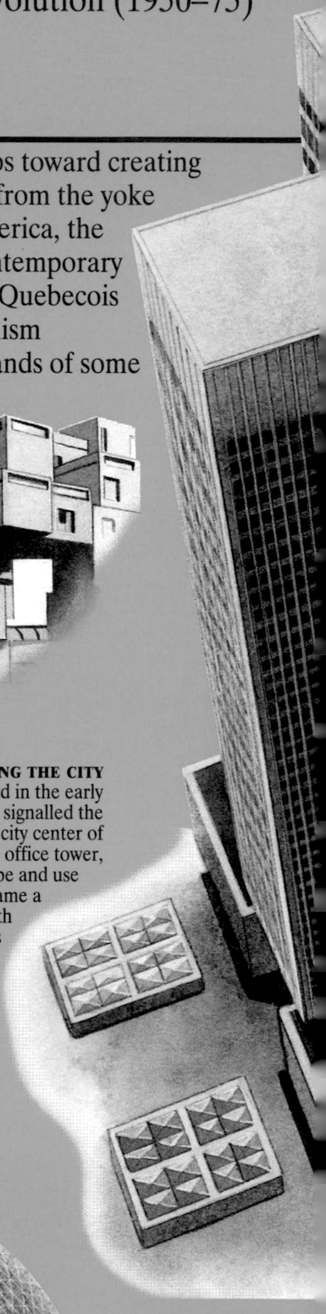

REINVENTING THE CITY
Place Ville-Marie, conceived in the early 1960s by the architect I.M. Pei, signalled the westward movement of the city center of Montreal ▲ *178*. With its tall office tower, innovative lines, cruciform shape and use of original materials, it soon became a symbol of the new North American city, with its contemporary skyline. With a shopping center in the basement, it also became an underground city, mirroring the skyscraper above.

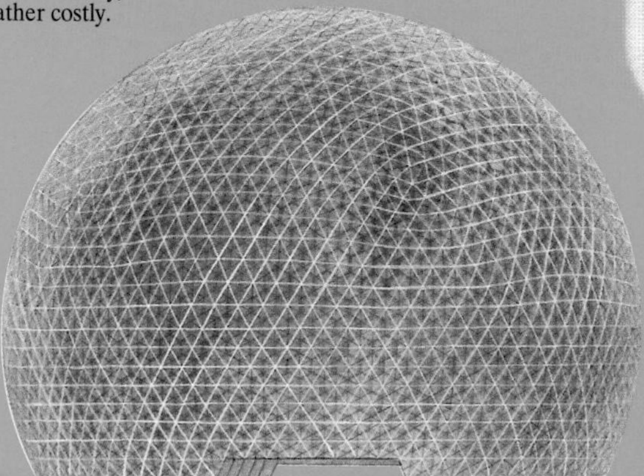

MONUMENTAL TECHNOLOGY
EXPO 67 was a virtual laboratory of technology. Buckminster Fuller's geodesic dome housing the United States Pavilion became one of Montreal's most famous buildings ▲ *198* (*left*).

SPIRIT OF FREEDOM
Freed from the traditional shackles which had distinguished its architecture before Vatican II, the Church began to explore the possibilities offered by the new technology. Notre-Dame-de-Fatima at Jonquière ▲ *322*, (P.M. Côté, 1963) dominates its surroundings with two large concrete semi-cones linked by glass panels.

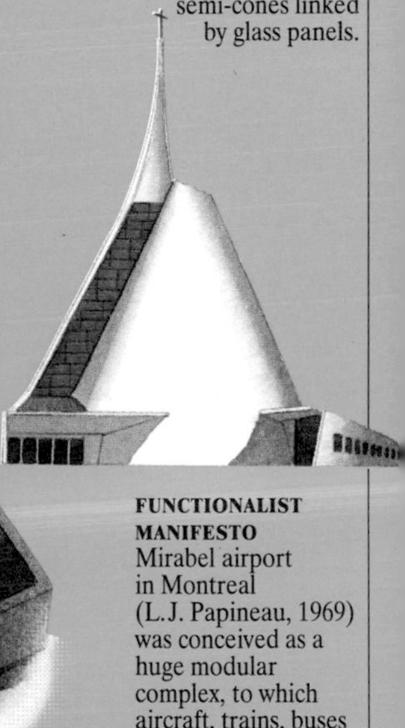

FUNCTIONALIST MANIFESTO
Mirabel airport in Montreal (L.J. Papineau, 1969) was conceived as a huge modular complex, to which aircraft, trains, buses and automobiles would carry passengers swiftly and efficiently. The severity and quality of the building, like a giant courtyard enveloped in a glass-curtain wall, brings to mind Mies van der Rohe's dictum that 'less is more'.

● Postmodernism (1975 to present)

Postmodern architecture was born when critics accused functionalism of being élitist and out of touch. Some architects sought a return to traditional values, considering the local context of their designs. This change of approach invested the landscape with a refreshing diversity, attracting people who had previously been architecturally unaware.

DESIGNER-LANDSCAPE
With fine parks and plazas, Montreal is blessed with original and innovative architectural features in both natural and urban surroundings. Sculptures by Melvin Charney in the Place Berri set off their environment

ORNAMENTAL SKYSCRAPER
Topped by a spectacular triangular cap, the 1000 de La Gauchetière ▲ 177 (LeMay & Associates, 1989) slices into the urban Montreal landscape. The variety of materials used in its construction (glass, marble, aluminum and granite) and its attractive geometric façades set this skyscraper apart from buildings of the preceding era.

NEW AGE JUNCTION
The 1000 de La Gauchetière (*above*: interior) stands at one of the principal transport junctions in the city, used every day by an estimated 40,000 people. Its main area with its imaginative décor frames shops, walkways, a winter garden and an ice rink.

SCULPTURE MUSEUM
Overlooking some archeological remains as well as the port, the sculpture museum at Pointe-à-Callière ▲ 173 (D. Hanganu, 1992) enhances the appeal of the exhibits within.

A NEW DISTRICT

Meticulous planning and imaginative design have been used in combination with traditional themes to create this new development at Sainte-Foy on the rue du Campanile (Gauthier, Guité, Roy; d'Anjou, Loisan, 1983). Gabled houses and a public market are set around an attractive clocktower.

EUROPEAN POSTMODERNISM

Peter Rose's design for the Canadian Centre for Architecture (1989) balances traditional classical forms with contemporary beauty of line.

URBAN LIVING

Economy, comfort and style have all been used to create the Georges-Vanier homes (R. de la Riva, 1993). Their interiors are modern and spacious, but the façades recall typical rows of Montreal houses: enough to tempt families back to live in the city center.

NEW TYPE OF SKYSCRAPER

Instead of conventional rectangles, architects Kohn Pedersen Fox reinvented the skyscraper at 1250 René-Lévesque Blvd W (1992) in Montreal. Finely calculated to scale the occupants to their environment, and the building to the city, the combinations of volume and texture are visually seductive and have transformed a basically functional building into a jewel in the urban landscape.

WINTER GARDEN

The building at 1250 René-Lévesque Blvd W plays its part in the everyday life of the city. Instead of dreary façades and dusty plazas, the public have a winter garden with a shelter that helps to prolong summer in Montreal.

● The way ahead

Uncertain circumstances and drastic government spending cuts have forced architects and developers to limit their plans. In future, projects will have to be cost-effective as well as socially relevant.

MOLSON CENTER

With seating for 21,500 people, Canada's new auditorium in Montreal (LeMay & Associates, Le Moyne, Lapointe, Magne) opened in 1996 with an ice-hockey festival ● 89. It combines a multi-functional building complex with the historic Windsor Rail Station, its vast façade dominating the square where it stands and giving the city a new backdrop to festival events.

THE FAUBOURG-QUEBEC PROJECT

A new district has grown up on a former stretch of industrial wasteland west of Old Montreal ▲ 168 which, when complete, will house 5,000 residents. The quarter has favored a French urban style with intimate clusters of houses rather than monotonous stretches. With its attractive streets and park extending along the river, the development ranks as one of the finest to emerge in the 21st century.

REDEVELOPING PARLIAMENT HILL

As the capital prepares to celebrate it's 400th birthday, history and landscape are being brought into play for this important project at the heart of the city. Right beside Old Quebec ▲ 270, where there were once unfinished highways, Dufferin-Monmorency and René-Lévesque Blvds (Gauthier, Guité, Roy Coord) set the historic city against a natural background. Around the Parliament Building and the latest skyscrapers there will be refreshing and sensitively conceived parks, avenues and gardens. This superbly realized project is designed to rekindle a sense of local identity and bring new life into the district.

Quebec as
seen by painters

Figures in a landscape, *132*
City life: then and now, *134*
Ethnic origins, *136*
Realist landscapes, *138*
Abstract landscapes, *140*

Figures in a landscape

'Through having to wrest their life from the land or the belly of the ocean, these people have come to look like their surroundings, gnarled and scaly like the earth's crust.'

Noël Audet

Like *The Village of Baie-Saint-Paul*, painted around 1910 by Clarence Gagnon ● *131* (1881–1942), *Percé* (1), painted between 1955 and 1960 by Lorne Bouchard (1913–78), is sometimes referred to as 'tourist art'. By emphasizing the vast expanses of snow and the harshness of the landscape, the Montreal-born artist has successfully painted what visitors to the region would see. But there are some interesting touches in Bouchard's painting, such as the old-fashioned boat and the open-air workshop. Bouchard continually searched for faster drying mediums for outdoor painting. *The Sawyers* (2), painted by Horatio Walker (1858–1938) in 1905, and *Country Station* (3), by Jean-Paul Lemieux (1904–90), appear more in contact with their subjects. Walker was influenced by the Barbizon school of landscape artists, and inspired in particular by the French artist Jean François Millet (1814–75) to capture on canvas the old crafts that were disappearing as industrialization advanced. He worked alone in his studio on the Île d'Orléans ▲ *276*: Clarence Gagnon was one of the few painters he allowed on 'his' island. Lemieux belonged to another generation, and lived to see the Quiet Revolution ● *56*. He set his face to the present rather than the past, and strove to find his individual voice and that of Quebec.

For many years director of the Art Association as well as President of the Royal Canadian Academy of Arts, William Brymner (1855–1925) painted his *Champ de Mars in Winter* **(1)** in 1892. Brymner exerted a strong influence on Quebec artists, such as Clarence Gagnon ● *133* (1881–1942), Edwin Holgate (1892–1977) and Robert Wakeham Pilot (1897–1967), his son-in-law. Pilot painted some fine Quebec landscapes, such as *Ice Rink, Dufferin Terrace* **(2)**. Completed around 1960, this painting is an excellent example of a naturalist-style cityscape. The artist preferred painting winter sports and horse-drawn carriages to the harsh realities of urban life. The magnificent view it shows of Dufferin Terrace on the Saint Lawrence is typical of Pilot's style. In 1928, in an interview with the Canadian critic Jean Chauvin, Pilot said that he considered himself 'a classical painter' because of his 'balance, sense of proportion and distaste for anything bizarre'. *Hyman's Tobacco Store* **(3)** is the subject of a lively picture by Adrien Hébert (1890–1967), painted in 1937. It shows a busy street dominated by a billboard advertising a brand of American cigarettes that was extremely popular before World War 2. Unlike his more pastoral contemporaries, such as Gagnon and Walker, Hébert celebrated the modern city, rejecting the country scenes they favored. He had great enthusiasm for urban architecture of all kinds, including the grain silos on the Montreal dockside ▲ *173*.

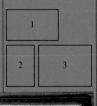

1	
2	3

Zacharie Vincent (1812–86), whose real name was Tchariolin, was of Huron descent and studied with the French-Canadian artist Antoine Plamondon (1804–95). Around 1845, he painted his *Zacharie Vincent and his Son Cyprien* **(1)**. His painting may well have been a response to a work created by his teacher, entitled *The Last of the Hurons*. The tribe was obviously still alive and well. Marc-Aurèle de Foy Suzor-Coté (1869–1937) ● *139* chose to paint one of the old settlers in his *Portrait of François Taillon* **(2)**. Suzor-Coté's subjects seemed to focus more on individuals, brought to life in works that could almost be called sculpted caricatures. Williem von Moll Berczy (1748–1813), born at Wallerstein in Saxony, arrived in Quebec in 1798, where he painted *The Woolsey Family* **(3)** in this 1809 conversation piece. English-speaking Quebec merchant John William Woolsey stands in the background. He had married a French-Canadian, Julie Lemoine-Despins, herself the daughter of a merchant in Montreal. Zacharie Vincent's wife, Marie Falardeau, was also French-Canadian, but there's no knowing whether Taillon had married a Native American or an English-speaker.

A.Sezer-Coté

In his painting entitled *Thaw, March Evening, Arthabaska* **(3)**, painted in 1913, Marc-Aurèle de Foy Suzor-Coté shows the strong influence of the Impressionist painter Claude Monet. He depicts a particular time of day and year, with melting snow in the twilight in his native region of the Bois-Francs ▲ *247*. Marc-Aurèle Fortin (1888–1970) was particularly fond of painting large trees, as this landscape with tall elms **(1)** shows. It was painted at Sainte-Rose, his birthplace, around 1926. Fortin is one of the key 20th-century painters in Quebec, and liked to portray nature as he found it in the outlying areas of big cities, like the Ahuntsic quarter in Montreal or his favorite Sainte-Rose. Celebrated for his vigorous and colorful landscapes, Arthur Lismer (1885–1969) was, with Alexander Young Jackson (1882–1974), one of the Group of Seven, who painted in Quebec, notably at Charlevoix ▲ *276*. The Group were modernist landscape painters who rejected archaic representational painting. His picture, entitled *Baie-Saint-Paul, Quebec* **(2)**, painted in 1931, recalls the snowy landscape by Clarence Gagnon on the title page of this section ● *131*.

| 1 | 2 |

| 3 |

● Abstract landscapes

'REFUS GLOBAL'
'Total Refusal' was an anti-establishment and anti-religious manifesto signed by a group of 16 artists, including Borduas and Riopelle in Montreal, in 1948. They rejected the academic approach to painting, favoring spontaneity and experimentation.

Paul-Emile Borduas (1905–60) and Jean-Paul Riopelle (1923–2002) were extremely progressive artists of the avant-garde who totally rejected conventional views of the outside world. In *Légers Vestiges d'automne* **(1)**, painted in 1956, Borduas expresses his own vision of winter in Quebec. In spite of its absurdist title, *Non, non, non, non ... non* **(2)**, painted in 1961, is an extraordinarily beautiful and dazzling confection of color and form, recalling the radiance of medieval stained glass combined with the rhythmic virtuosity of Jackson Pollock.

Quebec as
seen by writers

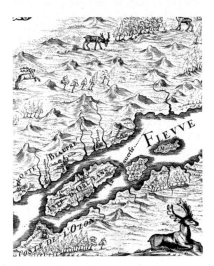

Nouvelle-France, *142*

Canadian natives, *144*

Famous words, *146*

Travelers, *148*

Nature, *153*

Modern fiction, *156*

Nouvelle-France

THE FIRST EXPLORER

Navigator Jacques Cartier (1491–1557) made three voyages to the North American continent. In 1534 he was appointed by Francis I to explore North America, in an attempt to find a passage through to the Pacific Ocean. On his first voyage he reached Newfoundland within 20 days, sighted the Îles-de-la-Madeleine and Prince Edward Island (which he thought was the mainland) and found the Saint Lawrence River. He made a second voyage in 1535 and explored the Saint Lawrence up to what is now Montreal. On his third voyage in 1541, Cartier was under the command of Jean-Francois de la Rocque de Roberval as they made an unsuccessful attempt to colonize the area. Upon Cartier's return to France in 1542, he settled in his hometown of St Malo. The following extract comes from his description of events in 1536, during his second voyage.

"We took with us three men of Hochelaga to bring us to the place. All along as we went we found the way as well beaten and frequented as can be, the fairest and best country that can possibly be seen, full of as goodly great oaks as are in any wood in France, under which the ground was all covered over with fair acorns. After we had gone about four or five miles, we met by the way one of the chiefest lords of the city, accompanied with many more, who, as soon as he saw us, beckoned and made signs upon us, that we must rest in that place where they had made a great fire and so we did … we went along, and about a mile and a half farther, we began to find goodly and large fields full of such corn as the country yieldeth … in the midst of those fields is the city of Hochelaga, placed near and, as it were, joined to a very great mountain, that is tilled round about, very fertile, on the top of which you may see very far. We named it Mount Royal."

JACQUES CARTIER, QUOTED IN
THE MARINER OF S. MALO;
A CHRONICLE OF
THE VOYAGES OF
JACQUES CARTIER,
BY STEPHEN LEACOCK,
'CHRONICLES OF CANADA', GLASGOW, BROOK & CO, TORONTO, 1915

GOVERNOR OF QUEBEC

Samuel de Champlain, (c.1570–1635) was a French explorer, founder of Quebec and first governor of Nouvelle-France. He travelled to North America several times between 1603 and 1608, and founded a settlement at Quebec in 1608, which became the center of the French fur trade. Champlain was first appointed governor of Quebec in 1612, and then again in 1625. He escaped the city after its capture by British privateers and when he returned in 1633, he was made governor for a third time and died there two years later.

"We set out the next day, continuing our course in the river as far as the entrance to the lake. There are many pretty islands here, low, and containing very fine woods and meadows, with abundance of fowl and such animals of the chase as stags, fallow-deer, fawns, roe-bucks, bears, and others, which go from the main land to these islands. We captured a large number of these animals. There are also many beavers, not only in this river, but also in numerous other little ones that flow into it. These regions, although they are pleasant, are not inhabited by any savages, on account of their wars; but they withdraw as far as possible from rivers into the

'History is everywhere, around us, beneath us; from the depths of yonder valleys, from the top of that mountain, history rises up and presents itself to our notice, exclaiming: "Behold me!"'

P. J.O. Chaveau

interior, in order not to be suddenly surprised. The next day we entered the lake, which is of great extent, say eighty or a hundred leagues long, where I saw four fine islands, ten, twelve, and fifteen leagues long, which were formerly inhabited by the savages, like the River of the Iroquois ... there are also many rivers falling into the lake, bordered by many fine trees of the same kinds as those we have in France, with many vines finer than any I have seen in any other place; also many chestnut-trees on the border of this lake, which I had not seen before. There is also a great abundance of fish, of many varieties: among others, one called by the savages of the country Chaoufarou, which varies in length, the largest being, as the people told me, eight or ten feet long. I saw some five feet long, which were as large as my thigh; the head being as big as my two fists, with a snout two feet and a half long, and a double row of very sharp and dangerous teeth ... Continuing our course over this lake on the western side, I noticed, while observing the country, some very high mountains on the eastern side, on top of which there was snow. I made inquiry of the savages whether these localities were inhabited, when they told me that the Iroquois dwelt there, and that there were beautiful valleys in these places, with plains productive in grain, such as I had eaten in this country, together with many kinds of fruit without limit. They said also that the lake extended near mountains, some twenty-five leagues distant from us, as I judge. I saw, on the south, other mountains, no less high than the first, but without any snow."

SAMUEL DE CHAMPLAIN, *VOYAGES OF SAMUEL DE CHAMPLAIN,*
ED. EDMUND F. SLAFTER, PRINCE SOCIETY,
BOSTON, 1878

FIRST SIGHT

George Ramsey, 9th Earl of Dalhousie (1770–1838) succeeded to his father's Earldom in 1788 while serving in the army. In 1809 he was created Lieutenant Governor of Quebec, in which role his most memorable achievement was the founding of Dalhousie University in 1818.

"The steeples of Quebec ... covered with tin look like massive silver; grand and singularly striking at first sight."

GEORGE RAMSEY, 9TH EARL OF DALHOUSIE,
JOURNAL, JULY 1, 1819

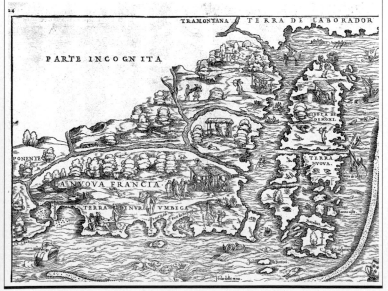

Canadian natives

UNDERSTANDING NATIVE AMERICAN CULTURE

Duncan Campbell Scott (1862–1947) was born in Ottawa, the son of a Methodist minister. He was educated at various schools in Ontario and Quebec where his father was posted. Scott wanted to go to university and become a doctor, but neither he nor his family could afford it so, at 17, he joined the Department of Indian Affairs where he rose to become the Deputy Superintendent. In 1883, at the age of 21, Scott met the poet Archibald Lampman ● 155 who inspired him to begin writing poetry. Scott's official position made him well aware of his compatriots' lack of knowledge of native culture, and his condemnation of their greed when dealing with natives is forceful. The poem 'At Gull Lake' suggests that there can be no marriage, no compromise between the white and Native American nations except those that end in tragedy, and explains Scott's belief that the First Nations were doomed to extinction.

"Then burst the storm —
The Indians' screams and the howls of the dogs
Lost in the crash of hail
That smashed the sedges and reeds,
Stripped the poplars of leaves,
Tore and blazed onwards,
Wasting itself with riot and tumult —
Supreme in the beauty of terror.
The setting sun struck the retreating cloud
With a rainbow, not an arc but a column
Built with the glory of seven metals;
Beyond in the purple deeps of the vortex
Fell the quivering vines of the lightning.
The wind withdrew the veil from the shrine of the moon.
She rose changing her dusky shade for the glow
Of the prairie lily, till free of all blemish of colour
She came to her zenith without a cloud or a star,
A lovely perfection, snow-pure in the heaven of midnight.
After the beauty of terror the beauty of peace.
But Keejigo came no more to the camps of her people;
Only the midnight moon knew where she felt her way,

Only the leaves of autumn, the snows of winter
Knew where she lay."

DUNCAN CAMPBELL SCOTT, FROM 'AT GULL LAKE, AUGUST, 1810',
PUB. IN *THE GREEN CLOISTER*, MCCLELLAND, TORONTO, 1935

MONTAGNAIS

An Antane Kapesh, born in 1926 near Fort Chimo (Kuujjuaq), was the first Montagnais writer to make a name in white society. Kapesh was forced to live under white rule as she grew up and her memories reflect her struggle to express and maintain a collective Montagnais identity. She writes in her native language.

"What will you leave me, Grandfather?
All of my territory with everything you find on it
All kinds of animals, fish, trees, all the rivers,
that is the heritage I leave you.
Down through the generations
that is what you will need for survival.
Don't ever forget what I am going to tell you.
During your lifetime do as I do – respect all the animals,
don't ever make them suffer before you kill them,
don't ever waste anything by killing more than you need,
and don't ever try to keep an animal in captivity
because the
animals are necessary for the survival of future
generations."

AN ANTANE KAPESH,
'A DYING INNU MAN TO HIS GRANDSON',
FROM *QU'AS-TU FAIT DE MON PAYS?*, PUB. ÉDITIONS
IMPOSSIBLE, QUEBEC, 1979

NATIVE LOVE STORY

Leonard Cohen, who was born in 1934 in Montreal, is a poet and novelist as well as an internationally famous singer-songwriter. His novel Beautiful Losers, *published in 1966, tells of a love triangle, where the lovers are united by their obsessions and fascination with a mythic 17th-century Mohawk saint, Tekakwitha. The book has become a Canadian classic.*

"Catherine Tekakwitha, who are you? Are you (1656–1680)? Is that enough? Are you the Iroquois Virgin? Are you the Lily of the Shores of the Mohawk River? Can I love you in my own way? I am an old scholar, better-looking now than when I was young. That's what sitting on your ass does to your face. I've come after you, Catherine Tekakwitha. I want to know what goes on under that rosy blanket. Do I have any rights? I fell in love with a religious picture of you. You were standing among birch trees, my favorite trees. God knows how far up your moccasins were laced. There was a river behind you, no doubt the Mohawk River. Two birds in the left foreground would be delighted if you tickled their white throats or even if you used them as an example of something or other in a parable. Do I have any right to come after you with my dusty mind full of the junk of maybe five thousand books? I hardly even get out to the country very often. Could you teach me about leaves? Do you know anything about narcotic mushrooms?"

LEONARD COHEN, *BEAUTIFUL LOSERS*,
NEW CANADIAN LIBRARY,
TORONTO, 1966

Famous words

A WANDERING CANADIAN

Antoine Gerin LaJoie (1824–79) was born in Yamachiche, Lower Canada. He was one of the organizers of the Institut Canadien, of which he was several times president, and he edited the magazine La Minerva *in Montreal for several years. He wrote one of the best-known Canadian folk songs, 'A Wandering Canadian', as a lament for the Canadians driven into exile after the 1837–8 Patriot Rebellion ● 40.*

'A wandering Canadian
Banished from his home
Traveled in tears
Through foreign lands.

One day, sad and thoughtful,
Seated beside the waters,
He addressed these words
To the fugitive current:

"If you see my country,
my unhappy country,
Go, say to my friends
That I remember them.

Oh days so full of charms
You have disappeared.
And my country, alas,
I'll never see it again.

No, but while dying
O! my dear Canada,
My languishing gaze
Will turn to you.'"

ANTOINE GERIN-LAJOIE,
'UN CANADIEN ERRANT'
[A WANDERING CANADIAN],
1842

THE MOUNTAIN

A.M. Klein (1909–72) was born in Ratno, Ukraine, into a Russian Orthodox Jewish family who emigrated the following year to Montreal. His post-war poems are considered his best. They portray Quebec culture from a unique perspective that is distinctly his own, and personify Montreal as static, secure, alive and individual.

"Who knows it only by the famous cross which bleeds
into the fifty miles of night its light
knows a night-scene;
and who upon a postcard knows its shape–
the buffalo straggled of the laurentian herd,–
holds in his hand a postcard.

In layers of mountains the history of mankind,
and in Mount Royal
which daily in a streetcar I surround my youth, my
childhood –
the pissabed dandelion, the coolie acorn,
green prickly husk of chestnut beneath mat of grass –
O all the amber afternoons
are still to be found.

There is a meadow, near the pebbly brook,
where buttercups, like once on the under of
my chin
upon my heart still throw their rounds of
yellow.

And Cartier's monument, based with
nude figures
still stands where playing bookey
Lefty and I tested our gravel aim
(with occupation flinging away our
guilt)
against the bronze tits of Justice.

And all my Aprils there are
marked and spotted
upon the adder's tongue, darting
in light,
upon the easy threes of trilliums,
dark green, green, and white,
threaded with earth, and rooted
beside the bloodroots near the
leaning fence-corms and
corollas of childhood,
a teacher's presents.

And chokecherry summer
clowning black on my
teeth!"

A.M. KLEIN,
EXTRACT FROM
'THE MOUNTAIN',
A.M. KLEIN: COMPLETE POEMS,
ED. ZAILIG POLLOCK,
UNIVERSITY OF TORONTO PRESS,
TORONTO, 1990

● Quebec as seen by writers

Travelers

A YANKEE IN CANADA

Henry David Thoreau (1817–62) was born in Concord, Massachusetts. From 1841 to 1843, he lived in the house of Ralph Waldo Emerson and was introduced to the philosophy known as transcendentalism. In 1845, Thoreau moved to a hut on Walden Pond, just outside of Concord. There, he spent most of his time observing nature and meditating. Most of Thoreau's writing were published after his death. They include Excursions *(1863),* The Maine Woods *(1864),* Cape Cod *(1865), and* A Yankee in Canada*(1866). In the late 1840s and the 1850s, Thoreau made a number of excursions – to Maine in 1853 and 1857; to Cape Cod in 1849, 1850, 1855, and 1857; and to Quebec in 1850.*

"The view from Cape Diamond has been compared by European travellers with the most remarkable views of a similar kind in Europe, such as those from Edinburgh Castle, Gibraltar, Cintra, and others, and preferred by many. A main peculiarity in this, compared with other views which I have beheld, is that it is from the ramparts of a fortified city, and not from a solitary and majestic river cape alone that this view is obtained ... I still remember the harbour far beneath me, sparkling like silver in the sun – the answering headlands of Point Levis on the south-east – the frowning Cape Tourmente abruptly bounding the seaward view in the north-east – the villages of Lorette and Charlesbourg on the north – and farther west, the distant Val Cartier, sparkling with white cottages, hardly removed by distance through the clear air – not to mention a few blue mountains along the horizon in that direction. You look out from the ramparts of the citadel beyond the frontiers of civilization. Yonder small group of hills, according to the guide-book, forms the portals of the wilds which are trodden only by the feet of the Indian hunters as far as Hudson's Bay."

EXCURSIONS AND POEMS:
THE WRITINGS OF HENRY DAVID THOREAU,
HOUGHTON MIFFLIN, BOSTON, 1906

A TALE OF A CITY

English novelist Charles Dickens (1812–70), fierce critic of the evils of Victorian society, with its injustice and hypocrisy, spent much time travelling and campaigning during the 1840s. In this account, he describes a trip to Niagara, Toronto, Kingston, Montreal and Quebec that he made in May, 1842.

"We left Kingston for Montreal ... and proceeded in a steamboat down the S. Lawrence river. The beauty of this noble stream at almost any point, but especially in the commencement of this journey when it winds its way among the thousand Islands, can hardly be imagined. The number and constant successions of these islands, all green and richly wooded; their fluctuating sizes, some so large that for half an hour together one among them will appear as the opposite bank of the river, and some so small that they are mere dimples on its broad bosom; their infinite variety of shapes; and the numberless combinations of beautiful forms which the trees growing on them present: all form a picture fraught with uncommon interest and pleasure ...   The impression made upon the visitor by this Gibraltar of America, its giddy heights, its citadel suspended, as it were, in the air; its picturesque steep streets and frowning gateways; and the splendid views which burst upon the eye at every turn, is at once unique and lasting. It is a place not to be forgotten or mixed up in the mind with other places, or altered for a moment in the crowd of scenes a traveller can recall. Apart from the realities of this most picturesque city, there are associations clustering about it which would make a desert rich in interest. The dangerous precipice along whose rocky front Wolfe and his brave companions climbed to glory; the Plains of Abraham, where he received his mortal wound; the fortress so chivalrously defended by Montcalm; and his soldier's grave, dug for him when yet alive, by the bursting of a shell, are not the least among them, or among the gallant incidents of history ... The city is rich in public institutions and in Catholic churches and charities, but it is mainly in the prospect from the site of the Old Government House and from the Citadel, that its surpassing beauty lies. The exquisite expanse of country, rich in field and forest, mountain-heights and water, which lies stretched out before the view, with miles of Canadian villages, glancing in long white streaks, like veins along the landscape; the motley crowd of gables, roofs and chimney tops in the old hilly town immediately at hand; the beautiful St Lawrence sparkling and flashing in the sunlight; and the tiny ships below the rock from which you gaze, whose distant rigging looks like spiders' webs against the light, while casks and barrels on their decks dwindle into toys, and busy mariners become so many puppets; all this framed by a sunken window in the fortress and looked at from the shadowed room within, forms one of the brightest and most enchanting pictures that the eye can rest upon."

CHARLES DICKENS,
AMERICAN NOTES FOR GENERAL CIRCULATION,
CHAPMAN AND HALL, LONDON, 1842

THE FALLS OF MONTMORENCY

Anthony Trollope (1815–82) was born in London to a bankrupt barrister father and a mother who supported the family with her earnings as a writer. Trollope worked as a senior civil servant in the post office, but his claim to fame was as a novelist. He published more than 40 novels and many short stories. In writing a book entitled North America, *Trollope was very conscious of his mother's work,* The Domestic Manners of the Americans, *which had been published in 1832. He wrote: 'I had entertained for many years an ambition to follow her footsteps there, and to write another book.'*

"Quebec is a very picturesque town; from its natural advantages almost as much so as any town I know. Edinburgh, perhaps, and Innspruck may beat it ... the best part of the town is built high upon the rock – the rock which forms the celebrated plains of Abram; and the view from thence down to the mountains which shut in the St Lawrence is magnificent. The best point of view is, I think, from the esplanade, which is distant some five minutes' walk from the hotels. When that has been seen by the light of the setting sun, and seen again, if possible, by moonlight, the most considerable lion of Quebec may be regarded as 'done', and may be ticked off from the list ... Strangers naturally visit Quebec in summer or autumn, seeing that a Canada winter is a season with which a man cannot trifle; but I imagine that the mid-winter is the best time for seeing the Falls of Montmorency. The water in its fall is dashed into spray, and that spray becomes frozen, till a cone of ice is formed immediately under the cataract, which gradually rises till the temporary glacier reaches nearly half way to the level of the higher river. Up this men climb – and ladies also, I am told – and then descend, with pleasant rapidity, on sledges of wood, sometimes not without an innocent tumble in the descent. As we were at Quebec in September, we did not experience the delights of this pastime. As I was too early for the ice cone under the Montmorency Falls, so also was I too late to visit the Saguenay River, which runs into the St Lawrence some hundred miles below Quebec. I presume that the scenery of the Saguenay is the finest in Canada."

ANTHONY TROLLOPE, *NORTH AMERICA*,
HARPER & BROTHERS, NEW YORK, 1862

AMERICAN HUMOR

Ar`temus Ward is the pseudonym of Charles Farrar Browne (1834–67), an American humorist who was born in Waterford, Maine. As a reporter on the Cleveland Plain Dealer, *he began in 1858 a series called 'Artemus Ward's Letters' that made him famous on both sides of the Atlantic. The letters were supposedly written by a carnival manager who commented on current events in a New England dialect that was augmented by bad grammar and misspelled words. In 1859, Browne joined the staff of the New York humorous weekly* Vanity Fair *and later turned successfully to lecturing. He traveled to Canada in 1864 and 1865.*

"Quebeck was surveyed and laid out by a gentleman who had been afflicted with the delirium tremens from childhood, and hence his ideas of things was a little irreg'ler. The streets don't lead anywhere in partic'ler, but everywhere in gin'ral. The cit is bilt on a variety of perpendicler hills each hill bein a trifle wuss nor t'other one. Quebeck is full of stone walls and arches, and citadels and things. It is said no foe could ever get into Quebeck, and I guess they couldn't. And I don't see what they's want to get in there for."

CHARLES F. BROWNE,
'ARTEMUS WARD IN CANADA', 1865

'Quebec
ranks by herself among
those Mother-cities of whom
none can say, "This reminds me".'

RUDYARD KIPLING,
LETTERS TO THE FAMILY, 1907

PORTRAITS OF PLACES

Henry James (1843–1916) wrote 20 novels, 112 short stories, 12 plays and a number of works of literary criticism. He was born in New York and he traveled back and forth between Europe and America throughout his youth. He studied with tutors in Geneva, London, Paris, Bologna and Bonn, and briefly attended law school before making literature his main focus. In the 1880s James wrote many travel pieces, which were collected in Portraits of Places *(1883),* Tales of Three Cities *(1884), and* A Little Tour of France *(1885).*

"His first impression will certainly have been that not America, but Europe, should have the credit of Quebec … As we rattled towards our goal in the faint raw dawn, and … I began to consult the misty window-panes and descried through the moving glass little but crude, monotonous wood, suggestive of nothing that I have ever heard of in song or story, I felt that the land would have much to do to give itself a romantic air. And, in fact, the feat is achieved with almost magical suddenness. The old world rises in the midst of the new in the manner of a change of scene on the stage. The S Lawrence shines at your left, large as a harbor-mouth, gray with smoke and masts, and edged on its hither verge by a bustling water-side faubourg which looks French or English, or anything not local that you please; and beyond it, over against you, with its rocky promontory, sits the ancient town, belted with its hoary wall and crowned with its granite citadel. Now that I have been here a while I find myself wondering how the city would strike one if the imagination had not been bribed beforehand. The place, after all, is of the soil on which it stands; yet it appeals to you so cunningly with its little stock of transatlantic wares that you overlook its flaws and lapses, and swallow it whole."

HENRY JAMES, 'QUEBEC, 1871',
IN *PORTRAITS OF PLACES*, 1883

"Quebec is the most interesting thing by much that I have seen on this Continent, and I think I would sooner be a poor priest in Quebec than a rich hog-merchant in Chicago."

MATTHEW ARNOLD, *LETTER TO WALTER ARNOLD*,
28 FEBRUARY 1884

HOCHELAGA

Eliot Warburton (1810–52) was an Irish-born lawyer, but made his living as a travel writer. His brother George (1816–57), an army officer, was stationed at Montreal from 1844 to 1847, and wrote of his travels in Quebec. His book Hochelaga *was to become staple reading for a generation of travelers to Canada. George's work was edited by Eliot, who added his own flowery touches to the prose.*

● Quebec as seen by writers

"Take mountain and plain, sinuous river, and broad, tranquil waters, stately ship and tiny boat, gentle hill and shady valley, bold headland and rich, fruitful fields, frowning battlement and cheerful villa, glittering dome and rural spire, flowery garden and sombre forest – group them all into the choicest picture of ideal beauty your fancy can create; arch it over with a cloudless sky, light it up with a radiant sun, and lest the sheen should be too dazzling, hang a veil of lighted haze over all, to soften the lines and perfect the repose,– you will then have seen Quebec on this September morning."

GEORGE D. WARBURTON, *HOCHELAGA; OR, ENGLAND IN THE NEW WORLD*,
ED. ELIOT WARBURTON,
WILEY & PUTNAM, NEW YORK, 1846

QUAINT QUEBEC

Henry Ward Beecher (1813–87) was a Congregational clergyman, born in Litchfield, Connecticut. He was the brother of writer Harriet Beecher Stowe. Henry was ordained in 1837 and held only three pastorates during his 50-year ministry. He was an active abolitionist but decried the use of violence to win freedom for the slaves. He travelled extensively and he and his sister had an intimate knowledge of Canada as they often helped slaves to escape across the border.

"A Curious old Quebec! – of all the cities on the continent of America, the quaintest ... It is a populated cliff. It is a mighty rock, scarped and graded, and made to hold houses and castles which, by a proper natural law, ought to slide off from its back, like an ungirded load from a camel's back. But they stick. At the foot of the rocks, the space of several streets in width has been stolen from the river ... Away we went, climbing the steep streets at a canter with little horses hardly bigger than flies, with an aptitude for climbing perpendicular walls. It was strange to enter a walled city through low and gloomy gates, on this continent of America. Here was a small bit of mediaeval Europe perched upon a rock, and dried for keeping, in this north-east corner of America, a curiosity that has not its equal, in its kind, on this side of the ocean ... We rode about as if we were in a picture-book, taming over a new leaf at each street! ... The place should always be kept old. Let people go somewhere else for modern improvements.
It is a shame, when Quebec placed herself far out of the way, up in the very neighbourhood of Hudson's Bay, that it should be hunted and harassed with new-fangled notions, and that all the charming inconveniences and irregularities of narrow and tortuous streets,

> 'A boundless vision grows upon us: an untamed continent, vast wastes of forest verdure, mountains silent in primeval sleep; river, lake, and glimmering pool; wilderness oceans mingling with the sky.'
>
> Francis Parkman

that so delight a traveller's eyes, should be altered to suit the fantastic notions of modern people ... Our stay in Quebec was too short by far. But it was long enough to make it certain that we shall come back again. A summer in Canada would form one of the most delightful holidays that we can imagine. We mean to prove our sincerity by our conduct."

HENRY WARD BEECHER, *EYES AND EARS*,
COLLECTED FROM THE *NEW YORK LEDGER*,
WITH A FEW PIECES FROM *THE INDEPENDENT*,
BOSTON, 1862

HAWKINS'S PICTURE OF QUEBEC

"The scenic beauty of Quebec has been the theme of general eulogy. The majestic appearance of Cape Diamond and the fortifications, the cupolas and minarets, like those of an eastern city, blazing and sparkling in the sun, the loveliness of the panorama, the noble basin, like a sheet of purest silver, in which might ride with safety a hundred sail of the line, the graceful meandering of the river St Charles, the numerous village spires on either side of the St Lawrence, the fertile fields dotted with innumerable cottages, the abode of a rich and moral peasantry – the distant falls of Montmorency – the park like scenery of Point Levis – the beauteous Isle of Orlean – and more distant still, the frowning Cape Tourmente, and the lofty range of purple mountains of the most picturesque form, which, without exaggeration, is scarcely to be surpassed in any part of the world."

ALFRED HOPKINS,
HAWKINS'S PICTURE OF QUEBEC,
PRINTED FOR THE AUTHOR BY NEILSON & COWAN, 1834

NOBLE QUEBEC

English poet Rupert Brooke (1887–1915) was a gifted writer whose early death in World War I contributed to his idealized image in the interwar period. Brooke traveled in Europe, North America and the South Seas for the Westminster Gazette, *sending back narratives and poems for publication.*

"Is there any city in the world that stands so nobly as Quebec? ... Quebec is as refreshing and definite after the other cities of this continent, as an immortal among a crowd of stockbrokers ... You are in a foreign land, for the people have an lein tongue, short staure, the quick, decided, cinematographic quality of the movement, and the inexplicable cheerfulness, which makes a foreigner."

RUPERT BROOKE, *LETTERS FROM AMERICA*, 1913,
SIDGWICK & JACKSON, LONDON, 1916

Nature

IN THE WILDERNESS

Frances Brooke (1724–89) was an English author who wrote The History of Emily Montague *(1769), said to be the first Canadian novel – and even the first in North American literature. Brooke lived in Canada from 1763 to 1768, while her husband was chaplain in the British garrison at Quebec. She set her novel primarily in the city. The plot is a traditional love story told in letters written among four friends in England and Quebec. The work is best known for its convincing account of life and the amusements to be had in a rugged British garrison town. It also includes interesting portrayals of the French-Canadian working class, then known as 'habitants', and the Native Americans. First published in 1769,* The History of Emily Montague *brings the 18th-century novel to the new world.*

"It is sufficient employment ... to contrive how to preserve an existence. Not only does the cold bring … on a sort of stupefaction, but it also suspends the very powers of the understanding. Genius will never mount high where the faculties of mind are benumbed for half the year."

FRANCES BROOKE,
THE HISTORY OF EMILY MONTAGUE, 1769

WINTER

Charles Mair (1838–1927) was the first Canadian poet of the nature school. He might in many senses be called the first Canadian poet, as his first volume was published in 1868, one year after Confederation. Dreamland *was a small volume of 150 pages, written when Mair was 30. The 33 poems constitute the first attempt to deal with Canadian nature, in the manner of Keats and the other classic poets.*

"When gadding snow makes hill-sides white,
And icicles form more and more;
When niggard Frost stands all the night,
And taps at snoring Gaffer's door;
When watch-dogs bay the vagrant wind,
And shiv'ring kine herd close to shed;
When kitchens chill, and maids unkind,
Send rustic suitors home to bed–
Then do I say the winter cold,
It seems to me, is much to bold.

When winking sparks run up the stalk,
And faggots blaze within the grate,
And, by the ingle-cheek, I talk
With shadows from the relm of fate;
When authors old, yet ever young,
Look down upon me from the walls,
And songs by spirit-lips are sung
To pleasant tunes and madrigals –
Then do I say the winter cold
Brings back to me the joys of old.

When morn is bleak, and sunshine cool,
And trav'llers beards with rime are gray;

When frost-nipt urchins weep in school,
And sleighs creak o'er the drifted way;
When smoke goes quick from chimney-top,
And mist flies through the open hatch;
When snow-flecks to the window hop,
And childrens' tongues cling to the latch,–
Then do I sigh for summer wind,
And wish the winter less unkind.

When merry bells a-jingling go,
And prancing horses beat the ground;
When youthful hearts are all aglow,
And youthful gladness rings around;
When gallants praise, and maidens blush
To hear their charms so loudly told,
Whilst echoing vale and echoing bush
Halloo their laughter, fold on fold,–
Then do I think the winter meet,
For gallants free and maidens sweet."

CHARLES MAIR,
EXTRACT FROM 'WINTER',
DREAMLAND, CITIZEN PUBLISHING,
OTTAWA 1868

AUTUMN MAPLES

Archibald Lampman (1861–99) was an important Canadian poet of the Confederation group, whose most characteristic work sensitively records the feelings evoked by scenes and incidents of the outdoors. He was a romantic, melancholy, passionate poet who died tragically young. Throughout this poetic life, Duncan Campbell Scott ● 144 was his admirer, friend, fellow poet, and, in the end, his editor.

"The thoughts of all the maples who shall name,
When the sad landscape turns to cold and gray?
Yet some for very ruth and sheer dismay,
Hearing the northwind pipe the winter's name,
Have fired the hills with beaconing clouds of flame;
And some with softer woe that day by day,
So sweet and brief, should go the westward way,
Have yearned upon the sunset with such shame
That all their cheeks have turned to tremulous rose;
Others for wrath have turned to rusty red,
And some that knew not either grief or dread,
Ere the old year should find its iron close,
Have gathered down the sun's last smiles acold,
Deep, deep, into their luminous hearts of gold."

THE POEMS OF ARCHIBALD LAMPMAN,
ED. AND WITH AN INTRODUCTION BY DUNCAN CAMPBELL SCOTT, 1900

LAKESHORE

Francis Reginald Scott (1899–1975) was born in Quebec City. He was educated at Bishop's College, Quebec, and at Oxford University, where he held a Rhodes scholarship. Scott was elected to the Royal Society of Canada in 1947, awarded the Lorne Pierce Medal for distinguished service to Canadian literature in 1962, and received a Molson Prize for outstanding achievements in the arts, the humanities, and the social sciences in 1967. In landscape poems such as 'Lakeshore', he established a northern evolutionary view of Canadian nature that later influenced such poets as Al Purdy and Margaret Atwood.

"The lake is sharp along the shore
Trimming the bevelled edge of land
To level curves; the fretted sands
Go slanting down through liquid air
Till stones below shift here and there
Floating upon their broken sky
All netted by the prism wave
And rippled where the currents are.

I stare through windows at this cave
Where fish, like planes, slow-motioned, fly.
Poised in a still of gravity
The narrow minnow, flicking fin,
hangs in a paler, ochre sun,
His doorways open everywhere.

And I am a tall frond that waves
Its head below its rooted feet
Seeking the light that draws it down
To forest floors beyond its reach
Vivid with gloom and eerie dreams.
The water's deepest colonnades
Contract the blood, and to this home
That stirs the dark amphibian
With me the naked swimmers come
Drawn to their prehistoric womb.

They too are liquid as they fall
Like tumbled water loosed above
Until they lie, diagonal,
Within the cool and sheltered grove
Stroked by the fingertips of love.

Silent, our sport is drowned in fact
Too virginal for speech or sound
And each is personal and laned
Along his private aqueduct."

F.R. SCOTT, EXTRACT FROM
'LAKESHORE', *EVENTS AND SIGNALS*,
RYERSON PRESS,
TORONTO, 1954.

Gabrielle Roy

Modern fiction

THE TIN FLUTE

Canadian author Gabrielle Roy (1909–83) was born in poverty in Manitoba, and raised on her mother's stories of Quebec. Her landmark novel, set in the working-class world of Saint-Henri, Quebec, was Bonheur d'occasion *(later translated as* The Tin Flute*), published in 1945. Gabrielle Roy, though passionate about Montreal and Quebec, was a latecomer to the province and never felt comfortable with the label of Quebecois, French-Canadian or even Canadian writer. Her reputation suffered in Quebec towards the end of her life because of her refusal to become politically engaged on the side of the separatists.*

"The street was absolutely silent. There is nothing more peaceful than St Ambroise Street on a winter night. From time to time a figure slips by, as if drawn to the feeble glimmer of a store front. A door opens, a square of light appears on the snow covered street, and a voice rings out in the distance. The passerby is swallowed up, the door bangs shut, and only the spirit of the night reigns in the deserted street between the pale glow of lighted windows on one side and the dark walls bordering the canal on the other. At one time the suburb had ended here; the last houses of Saint-Henri looked out on open fields, a limpid, bucolic air clinging to their eaves and tiny gardens. Of the good old days nothing is left now on St Ambroise Street but two or three great trees that still thrust their roots down under the cement sidewalk. Mills, grain elevators, warehouses have sprung up in solid blocks in front of the wooden houses, robbing them of the breezes from the country, stifling them slowly. The houses are still there with their wrought-iron balconies and quiet façades. Sometimes music penetrates the closed shutters, breaking the silence like a voice from another era. They are lost islands to which the winds bear messages from all the continents, for the night is never too cold to carry over alien scents from the warehouses: smells of ground corn, cereals, rancid oil, molasses, peanuts, wheat dust and resinous pine. Jean had chosen this remote, little-known street because the rent was low, and because the deep rumble of the quarter, the whistle blowing at the end of day, and the throbbing silence of the night spurred him on to work."

GABRIELLE ROY,
BONHEUR D'OCCASION,
TRANS. HANNAH JOSEPHSON
AS *THE TIN FLUTE,*
MCCLELLAND & STEWART,
TORONTO, 1947

Quebec itineraries

Montreal, *164*

Montérégie, *204*

Estrie, *210*

The Laurentides–Lanaudière, *216*

From Montreal to Hull, *222*

Ottawa and Hull, *226*

Abitibi–Témiscamingue, *230*

Around James Bay, *234*

Trois-Rivières, *238*

Saint Maurice Valley, *240*

Around Les Bois-Francs, *244*

Chemin du Roy, *248*

Quebec City, *252*

Chaudière–Beauce River, *274*

Côte-de-Beaupré and Charlevoix, *276*

South Shore and Lower Saint Lawrence, *288*

Gaspésie, *298*

Îles-de-la-Madeleine, *310*

Lac-Saguenay-Saint-Jean, *317*

North Shore, *328*

Lower North Shore, *334*

Nunavik, *335*

▲ Slide in front of the Château Frontenac in Quebec ▼ Rue Viger in Montre

▼ Rue Sainte-Catherine in Montreal

▲ 'My country is not a country, it is winter' (Gilles Vigneault)   ▼ The Chic Choc Mountains

▲ The Laurentides   ▼ Saguenay Park

▼ Fall colors

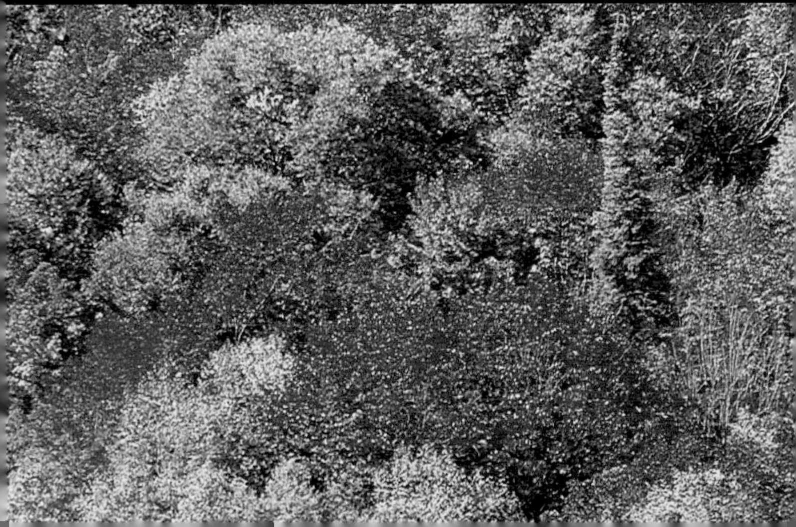

▲ A pumpkin farmer

▼ The logging industry

▼ A silica mine

Montreal

History of Montreal, *164*
Old Montreal, *168*
City center, *174*
The underground city, *176*

Mont Royal, *182*
Golden Square Mile, *184*
Outremont and Côte-des-Neiges, *186*
'The Main', *188*
Mont-Royal Plateau, *190*
'Latin Quarter', *194*
Maisonneuve, *196*
Bridges and islands, *198*
Along the Lachine Canal, *200*
Montérégie, *204*
The Rebellions of 1837–8, *206*
Estrie, *210*
The Laurentides, *216*
Lanaudière, *219*
Between Montreal and Hull, *222*

Montreal, a huge, cosmopolitan sprawl, with 3 million inhabitants, is the largest city in Quebec. It is not only the biggest French-speaking city outside France, it is also a hub of ethnic and cultural diversity, the meeting point of the civilizations that have forged Quebecois culture and an interface between the Francophone and Anglophone worlds. Its streets, buildings and monuments bear witness to the successive influences they have experienced.

From Hochelaga to Ville-Marie

FORTIFICATIONS
Montreal was once surrounded by a stone wall, built between 1717 and 1744, and demolished between 1801 and 1817 to allow the town's growth. Fragments can still be seen on the Champ-de-Mars ▲ 171.

In 1535, when Jacques Cartier first visited Hochelaga, this farming village on the outskirts of Mont Royal, on Montreal Island, had been occupied by the Iroquois for centuries ● 44 and boasted a population of around 1,500. Hochelaga and its inhabitants disappeared from the map, however, in the 16th century, until the Frenchman Paul Chomedey de Maisonneuve founded Montreal in 1642 with an expedition of 40 men. This first

settlement was a missionary colony financed by a group of devout Frenchmen (hence its name of Ville-Marie). Despite its difficult beginnings, marked by skirmishes with the Iroquois, a small town grew up on the riverbank.

The fur capital

Missionary ideals soon gave way to the lure of the fur trade. Montreal's location at the confluence of the Saint Lawrence and Ottawa rivers made it a useful port for the Native-American convoys bringing pelts from the west. In 1660, merchants began to organize expeditions and set up trading posts. As a result, the town found itself heading a huge empire spreading over the central and western part of the continent. The population was slow to expand, however, and by 1760 it was only around 4,000. At this point, Montreal resembled a small French town, with perimeter walls, merchants' and craftsmen's houses, convents, and a church and general hospital, but the population had begun to extend beyond the walls.

The British trading city

After the Conquest, a new wave of merchants (mostly Scots) took control of the fur trade, but for several decades Montreal maintained the appearance of a small French town. In the early 19th century, however, this situation changed quickly, as population influx into the territory transformed Montreal into the urban center of a vast rural hinterland. Its merchants became intermediaries for the growing trade between Great Britain and its Canadian colonies, and they invested in navigation and the first railroads to create a transport network that extended deep into the countryside and made the city a vital link in the continent's trading routes. Its population mushroomed after the arrival of thousands of immigrants from England, Scotland and, above all, Ireland. By 1831, Montreal had 27,000 inhabitants and, for the first time, the British formed the majority. The British influence

SYMBOLS UNITED
In 1809, a column (*below*) that rendered homage to Admiral Horatio Nelson ▲ *171* was built in a square that was named after Jacques Cartier in 1847 ▲ *170*.

left its imprint on the architecture, which followed the canons of the Victorian era. The English-speaking middle classes dominated the economy and endowed the city with its first university, McGill ▲ *179*, as well as various other cultural institutions. English became the language of public life and business; the marginalized French-speaking population could only make their presence felt through their Catholic institutions. The religious revival of the 1840s ● *54* engendered a proliferation of churches and convents that changed the face of the urban landscape. Over time, the two communities came to be divided geographically, with the French speakers concentrated in the eastern part of the city and the Anglophones predominantly living in the west.

The driving force of Canada

In the mid-19th century, industrialization turned Montreal into Canada's most important manufacturing center. The need for manpower was initially satisfied by an exodus from Quebec's rural areas and then by immigration from Europe,

THE PORT
The port has played a key role in both the history of Montreal and the relationship between Canada and Europe. The first permanent quays were installed in 1830 and warehouses were soon built close by. Right up to the 1960s, the port was closed in winter because of ice floes. The resumption of navigation in springtime was a major event, and crowds flocked to welcome the first ship of the season, whose captain was presented with a walking stick topped by a golden knob. Today, the port remains open all year round, due to advanced methods of breaking the ice.

Montreal History

**INDUSTRY IN THE
19TH CENTURY**
The focus was on
spinning, garment-
making, tobacco,
metal and steel
products, railroad
materials and
foodstuffs. The
footwear industry
was also very
important – and
remains so today.

**THE
BANK OF
MONTREAL**
This was founded in
1817, making it the
oldest in Canada.
It was long a symbol
of the economic
power of the city's
English-speaking
businessmen ● 52; its
present head office
on the Place d'Armes
dates back to 1848
▲ 169.

MONT ROYAL
Its slopes are the
setting for middle-
class mansions, two
huge cemeteries, a
lake, the University
of Montreal and a
park, created 1873–81
to preserve the area's
natural heritage and
make space for
leisure activities.

which reached its peak in the early 20th century. The population of the metropolitan area of Montreal soared from 57,000 in 1851 to 250,000 in 1891, and topped the half-million mark on the eve of World War 1. The suburban boroughs of Saint-Henri, Maisonneuve, Rosemont, Côte-des-Neiges and Ahuntsic emerged as the city grew. Each one presented social, ethnic and architectural peculiarities that made it a distinctive microcosm. Around 1866, the French-speakers regained their ascendancy, and their high-fliers carved out increasingly large niches in politics and business. They founded Montreal's first Francophone university, the Laval University of Montreal ▲ 195 (later the University of Montreal), placing the city in the vanguard of French-Canadian culture. English, however, remained the dominant language for financial affairs, and Montreal's large English-speaking middle class wielded enormous influence throughout Canada. Its banks, railroads and manufacturing and trading companies penetrated the entire country and increased the city's prosperity still further. At the turn of the century, immigration brought in new groups, particularly Jews from Eastern Europe and Italians, but also other Europeans and Chinese. These new arrivals tended to cluster together in separate neighborhoods, endowing Montreal with a hitherto unknown cosmopolitan air ● 52 and an increasingly diverse cultural mix. The city's expansion led to development schemes, vestiges of which are still visible today. The construction of countless warehouses and office buildings energized Old Montreal, while enormous factories dominated the landscape of the suburbs. The middle class subsequently left Old Montreal and built magnificent houses on the flanks of Mont Royal, in an area that would later be known as the Golden Square Mile ▲ 184. In 1874, the local authorities turned the peak of this mountain into a public park. In the working-class neighborhoods, the small gabled houses inherited from the French gave way to apartment blocks, including the distinctive triplexes ▲ 193, to meet the housing needs of the expanding labor force.

> 'All around me, there are cars, unknown pedestrians ... concrete, steel in movement. It roars, rumbles, crashes and soars to the sky in grayish petals.'
>
> Roger Fournier

A great North American city

1914 saw the start of a transitional phase marked by the two world wars and the devastating effects of the Depression in the 1930s. The population of the metropolitan area reached one million in 1931 and two million in 1961. The British influence lost ground to that of the US. American architectural models won favor, and the first skyscrapers appeared in the city center ● *126*. Urban technology, cars, the mass media and consumerism all joined forces to make Montreal a major North American city.

The modern city

From 1960 onwards, these transformations intensified and modified the image of Montreal. A new city center was developed, along with an underground city ● *126*, ▲ *176*. It is served by the subway (1966) and by a network of freeways that encouraged the growth of new suburbs dependent on cars. The decline of the manufacturing industries undermined the economy, which has since focused on service industries. This resulted in Montreal relinquishing its place as Canada's foremost city to Toronto, but it has consolidated its status as Quebec's financial and cultural capital. Since the Quiet Revolution ● *56*, French has taken on an increasingly high profile. Almost all major Francophone corporations have their head offices in Montreal, and the foremost French-language television channels are concentrated there, emphasizing its role as the standard-bearer of Quebecois culture. What's more, signposts in English, once predominant, have disappeared from the streets. The long-established communities with European roots have been joined by immigrants from all over the world; together, they make up a quarter of the city's population. Montreal has become more cosmopolitan and acquired international renown by organizing the World Fair in 1967 and the Olympic Games in 1976. Its four universities also extend its field of influence, as does the city's involvement in international Francophone organizations.

ONE ISLAND, ONE CITY
After several years of debate, the various municipalities on Montreal Island gave way to a single city divided into districts.

Montréal 1976

CALDER'S STABILE
The work on the left, by the American sculptor Alexander Calder (1898–1976) was constructed for the World Fair, which was held in 1967 on the islands of Sainte Hélène and Notre Dame ▲ *198*.

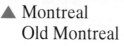

The migration of the business sector to the current city center after 1945 allowed Old Montreal to retain its unique character and its special place in the heart of the locals. Its narrow, winding streets are the heritage of the French regime and the Sulpician administration ● *50*, which drew up the plans for it in 1672. The architecture, mostly dating from the 19th century, is remarkable: even the warehouses, such as those on rues Sainte-Hélène, Notre-Dame, Saint-Pierre, Le Moyne and Le Royer ● *118*, are adorned with magnificent sculpted façades. Declared a historic district by the Quebecois government in 1964, Old Montreal revolves around the Places d'Armes, d'Youville and Jacques-Cartier. It is crossed by rues Saint-Paul and Notre-Dame, while its frontiers with the rest of the city are traced by rues McGill and Saint-Antoine and Victoria Square (formerly a hay market), which were developed after the demolition of the old city walls and the renovation project (1804–21). Old Montreal can be reached via Victoria Square, the Place d'Armes or the Champ-de-Mars, as well as via the bicycle paths running along Rue Berri and the Lachine Canal ▲ *200*.

THE ORGAN OF NOTRE DAME
The large organ in the basilica boasts 5,722 pipes. Installed in 1891, it was the 26th made by the famous Casavant workshop ▲ *209*, and the first to be equipped with four keyboards. It was electrified in 1924 and restored in 1991.

Notre Dame Basilica ★

The history and architecture of this parish church have made it a distinctive religious symbol. When the original 17th-century church on Rue Notre-Dame became too small to welcome the faithful of the city's only parish, it was replaced by the present building (completed in 1829, although its towers were added in 1843). By opting for a grandiose basilica – the biggest religious building in North America at the time –

> 'Every day, the face is renewed, the body is more beautiful than before. More beautiful, I say. I love this city, I love this woman.'
>
> Jean-Guy Pilon

the Sulpicians sought to rival the bishop's palace and, above all, the Protestant churches. They hired architect James O'Donnell, a Protestant, Irish New Yorker, who adopted the neo-Gothic style, exceptional in a Catholic church. From 1874 to 1880, the self-taught architect Victor Bourgeau created the interior design out of wood that was sculpted, gilded and painted in bright colors; his high altar can still be seen today, in front of an old window. Philippe Hébert sculpted the figures of Jeremiah and Ezekiel on the pulpit.

'WEDDING CHAPEL'. The Sacré Coeur Chapel (built 1881–91) behind the basilica, was popularly known as the 'wedding chapel'. Profusely decorated with paintings and wood trim, it was damaged by a fire in 1978 and rebuilt in 1980 along modern lines (although some of the original wood trim has been restored).

PLACE D'ARMES
The focal point of this square hemmed in by skyscrapers is the statue commemorating Maisonneuve ▲ 164, created by Philippe Hébert in 1895.

Old Saint Suplice Seminary

Still occupied by the Sulpicians today, the old seminary, put up between 1682 and 1685, then enlarged on several occasions, is the oldest building in Montreal's historic quarter ● 110. In 1848, the Sulpicians resolved to rebuild according to plans drawn up by John Ostell, but they abandoned the project after the completion of the east wing. They then chose Rue Sherbrooke as the site for their Great Seminary, which was finished in 1857. To the rear, the grounds of the old seminary include a 17th-century private garden, complete with a vegetable patch.

THE SULPICIANS IN MONTREAL
The order of Saint Suplice, founded in Paris in 1641, has played a major role in the social, cultural and economic development of Montreal, from the time its first priests arrived in 1657, right up to the present.

Place d'Armes ★

The square took on its present configuration after the demolition of the first Notre Dame Church, in 1830, and its bell tower, in 1843. Before that, it had been bounded by the north face of the church and served as a cemetery until 1799, when it became a military parade ground. A bust of King George III of England was unveiled in the square in 1773, but it was subsequently thrown down a well (it's now on show in the McCord Museum ▲ 180). The surrounding buildings include, on the east side, Montreal's oldest skyscraper (1888), erected by the New York architects Babcock, Willard & Cook for New York Life Insurance, and its Art-Deco neighbor, the Aldred Building (*right*), designed by the local firm of Barrott & Blackader in 1929.

Aldred Building. Place d'Armes. Montreal. Que., at night

Edifice Aldred, Place d'Armes, Montreal, Qué.

169

Rue Saint-Jacques

Rue Saint-Jacques is Canada's time-honored financial powerhouse. Its buildings, embellished with sculptures, evoke the Scottish trading cities that were the birthplaces of many of Montreal's 19th-century architects. Several buildings can be visited during working hours, such as no. 53, the former BANQUE DU PEUPLE (1873), which was once the only French-speaking institution on the street, and no. 380, the ROYAL BANK (1928), whose roof once sported the beacons now set on the Place Ville-Marie ▲ *178*. On the corner of Victoria Square, the WORLD TRADE CENTER has its own inner alleyway, on the site of a street that formerly bounded the fortified city wall.

MONTREAL'S 'WALL STREET'
Rue Saint-Jacques and Place d'Armes became Canada's financial center as the increasing activity and prosperity of the port attracted first banks and then insurance companies from Britain, Canada and the US.

BANK OF MONTREAL
The sober façade with aluminum capitals (replacing the original ones, damaged by pollution) belies the lush interior design: green syenite pillars, black marble pedestals, gilded bronze capitals, brass grilles and chandeliers and a marble cenotaph.

Bank of Montreal

Founded in 1817, the Bank of Montreal was the first bank to open in the whole of Canada. The building seen today was erected in 1848 by John Wells, drawing on the forms of Palladian villas and the Pantheon in Rome. The pediment sculpted by Sir John Steele bears the bank's coat-of-arms and depicts Canada's trade growth. In 1905, the New York architects McKim, Mead & White enlarged the building, replacing the dome that had been removed in 1859 and creating a large banking hall, a good example of Beaux-Arts architecture ● *125* inspired by Roman basilisks. The bank also has an unusual exhibition of money boxes.

OLD COURT HOUSE
The Old Law Courts, dominated by a tinned copper dome that once housed a library for the use of lawyers, judges and other legal professionals, was the headquarters of the organizing committee for the 1976 Montreal Olympic Games. The interior decor – replete with stucco, wood trim and trompe l'œil effects – has been restored.

Court houses

The presence of three law courts on Rue Notre-Dame illustrates the extent to which the legal profession put down roots in Old Montreal. The oldest stands at no. 155, built in 1856 by architects Ostell & Perrault. It was adorned with a dome and a cast-iron interior staircase in 1894 and complemented by an annex (no. 100) with a tunnel link in 1925. The second court house, known as the Cormier Building, after its principal architect, Ernest Cormier ▲ *185*, is now home to the MUSIC CONSERVATORY, which regularly organizes concerts by both students and teachers. Its doors open on to a foyer lit by a large glass roof and Art Deco chandeliers, the work of Edgar Brandt's Parisian workshop. The present court house dates from 1971.

Place Jacques-Cartier

Place Jacques-Cartier emerged in 1804 after property developers bought the ruins and gardens of the fire-ravaged Vaudreuil Castle. They then gave the site to Montreal's local authorities to set up a new market, to complement the one on today's Place Royale. The square continued to be used for this purpose until the 1960s.

NELSON'S COLUMN ● *116*. This monument, erected in 1809 by public subscription, was the first to celebrate the victory of Admiral Horatio Nelson (1758–1805) in the Battle of Trafalgar (1805), and predates its counterpart in London. The original statue was unable to resist pollution or vandalism and was replaced by a glass-fiber replica. A tourist office now occupies the building that was once the Silver Dollar Saloon.

City Hall

The borough of Montreal was born in 1833, with Jacques Viger as its first elected mayor. The municipal council initially met under the tanks of the local water company, then in the Bonsecours market, before moving into the City Hall in 1878. The building was devastated by a fire in 1922 but was rebuilt four years later within the original walls and with an additional story ● *117*. Place Vauquelin provides access to the CHAMP-DE-MARS, a space cleared for military parades after the dismantling of the fortifications; the latter were restored in 1992 to leave visible their foundations and outline.

Château Ramezay

This castle – originally built in 1706 by Claude de Ramezay, the Governor of Montreal (1703–24) – has frequently been rebuilt and modified. It has served as a base for the West Indies Company, the Faculty of Medicine and the Court House – and it was the headquarters of American General Montgomery, who arrived in 1775 to rally Canadian support for the American colonies rebelling against British rule. It has been used by Montreal's Society of Archeology and Numismatics as a history museum since 1895.

'CONCORDIA SALUS'
Montreal's device and emblem were created in 1833 by Jacques Viger in a climate of ethnic tension. The beaver was the symbol of the French Canadians (it was later replaced by the fleur-de-lis). The rose represents the English; the thistle, the Scots and the clover, the Irish.

PLACE JACQUES-CARTIER
This old market square is dominated by the City Hall. It was from its balcony that General de Gaulle proclaimed on July 24 1967: 'Long live Montreal! Long live Quebec! Long live free Quebec!' This was the slogan used by the independence movement against the federal government.

NOTRE DAME DE BONSECOURS
Situated on the thoroughfare of Rue de Bonsecours, the chapel bears witness to the prominent position of churches in the Ville-Marie: the Notre Dame Basilica was also originally set in a strategic position on Rue Notre-Dame.

Bonsecours

CHAPEL OF NOTRE DAME DE BONSECOURS. This building, which was consecrated in 1773, replaced an earlier wooden chapel (1657) that burnt down in 1754. In subsequent years, Notre Dame de Bonsecours has undergone numerous modifications. Its popular title of the 'sailors' chapel' is evidence of its close relationship with the port, further underlined by the commemorative models of boats hanging in the nave and the large copper statue of the Virgin Mary looking out over the river.

MAISON DU CALVET. This rare example of an 18th-century urban residence is situated just opposite the chapel, near the Papineau House ● *117*. Pierre du Calvet, a French Huguenot who settled in Montreal in 1766, was imprisoned by the British due to his sympathies for American revolutionaries.

BONSECOURS MARKET ● *117*. This building, designed by William Footner, is one of the enduring symbols of Old Montreal. When the market opened in 1847 it boasted refrigeration chambers, the City Hall, a prison and a concert hall, but it later became a hub of the financial district. Its Doric columns are cast iron and its dome, which has twice been damaged by fire, was restored in 1978. It was converted into offices in 1964, but since 1992 it has been made available for public use.

OLD PORT. Although the French settlers put quays and jetties on the river bank, it was not until the 19th century that the port was fully developed and turned into the pillar of Montreal's prosperity. New quays were built along Rue de la Commune, soon followed by piers that incorporated the islet of Normand. A long dyke with stockades was also installed to protect the city from the drifts that accumulate when the

> 'Ropes are hung everywhere, going upward and crossways, taut for the acrobats, loose for the rope dancers, already knotted for the scoundrels. An authentic virgin forest.'

Jean-Jules Richard

winter ice begins to thaw. Twenty years ago, new docks were established in the eastern part of the island, and the original port now has only the harbor station and the last of the great silos, a testimony to Montreal's importance in the wheat trade that also served Le Corbusier as a model of functionality and purity of form in his book *Toward a New Architecture*. The relocation of the port left a huge space at the city's disposal. The site of the Old Port now buzzes with activity year round, thanks to its ice rink, exhibition spaces and performances, as well as its promenades, pond and panoramic views of the city.

PLACE D'YOUVILLE. This square was created in 1832, when the Petite Rivière was filled in to make way for the Sainte-Anne Market. The Parliament of United Canada met in this market until 1849, when British Orangemen set light to it.

The Old Port neighborhood.

The HISTORY CENTER, set in the former headquarters of the fire service (1903), offers a portrait of Montreal's neighborhoods and population. Further south lies a wing of the old hospital founded by the Charon brothers in 1694, then run by the Gray Nuns. This order was created in 1755 by Marguerite d'Youville. When the nuns moved to the new convent in Rue Guy in 1871, they knocked down the chapel and the eastern wing of the hospital, to prolong Rue Saint-Pierre and build warehouses. On the western side, close to Récollets suburb, the square opens on to Rue McGill ▲ *179* and the headquarters of the Grand-Tronc, a railroad company (founded 1852) responsible for the 1859 construction of the Victoria Bridge ▲ *199*.

POINTE À CALLIÈRE. On the eastern side, Place d'Youville gives on to the Pointe à Callière, the site of the ARCHEOLOGY MUSEUM. Built in a postmodern style ● *128*, the museum opened in 1992 to mark the 350th anniversary of the founding of Ville-Marie. The museum comprises three distinct sections: a modern nucleus (designed by Dan Hanganu in the shell of the Royal Insurance Building, but gutted by a fire in 1953) fitted out with a multimedia display, an exhibition area and a panoramic restaurant; the archeological crypt, under the old Place Royale, which preserves the remains of the fortifications; and the old customs house, built by John Ostell (1838).

THE GRAY NUNS
In 1671, Marguerite Bourgeoys founded the Congregation of Notre Dame ▲ *185*. In 1755, Marguerite d'Youville went on to found the Sisters of Charity, known as the 'Gray Nuns' because of the color of their habits – and, rumor had it, because they sold the natives alcohol that turned them *gris* (gray, but also meaning drunk). Sisters of Charity proved exceptional administrators and spread all across North America.

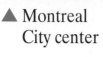

It is more appropriate to speak of Montreal not as a city center but as several concentrations around squares running along an east-west axis that take in rues Sainte-Catherine, Sherbrooke and René-Lévesque, at the foot of Mont Royal. The very idea of a city center is inextricably linked with the relationship between the two French and English linguistic communities. This is illustrated by the efforts to create a city center in the eastern Francophone sector, around the Berri-UQAM subway station, in response to the business center to the west, traditionally associated with the Anglophone community. Today, the city center revolves around Dorchester Square and Rue Sainte-Catherine and, apart from the lively Latin Quarter, it extends, from east to west, from the Place des Arts and the Desjardins complex to the boundaries of Westmont, and, from south to north, from the Sulpicians' territory, encompassing the Great Seminary (1857), Montreal College (1871) and the towers of the Mountain Fort (c.1696), to Rue de la Gauchetière.

THE ICE CASTLE
Dorchester Square was the setting for Montreal's winter carnival, first held in 1883. An ice castle was built in the southern part of the square and its capture, after snow-shoers overcame the staunch resistance of the firemen who defended it from their attacks, was celebrated by the firework display that marked the end of the carnival.

Dorchester Square

Dorchester Square, formerly Dominion Square, has become a place for relaxing. It stands on the site of the old Saint Anthony's cemetery, a resting place for Catholics created amidst orchards in the 18th century. This became overcrowded in the Victorian era and was considered insalubrious, so it was closed and replaced by today's cemetery of Notre Dame des Neiges ▲ *183*, which opened its gates on Mont Royal in 1855. Saint Anthony's cemetery was then neglected for years, when its mortal remains, including those of the victims of a cholera epidemic in 1832, were relocated. This exhumation caused a great stir and eventually led to the creation of the square in 1872, intersected by Boulevard René-Lévesque. It went on to

CONTRASTING VIEWS
The cathedral and the old YMCA dominated Dorchester Square at the end of the 19th century. Writer Mark Twain (1835–1910) said that it was impossible to throw a stone there without breaking a church window. The photo on the right shows the importance that trees have in today's square, which is now lined with skyscrapers.

play a major role in Montreal's official ceremonies in the 19th and 20th centuries. This is illustrated by several monuments, such as a memorial to the heroes of the Boer War (1899–1902), the work of George W. Hill and the Maxwell architectural firm; a tribute to the first Prime Minister of Canada, Sir John A. MacDonald (1895); and one dedicated to Sir Wilfred Laurier, made by Émile Brunet (1953). There is also a cenotaph, put up in 1924, and canons used in the Crimean War.

The Cathedral and Saint George's Church

Dorchester Square is surrounded by imposing buildings that bring together the worlds of religion and finance. Several churches, mostly Protestant, used to surround first the cemetery and then the square, but today the sole survivors are the Catholic Cathedral of Marie Reine du Monde ● 120 and the Anglican Saint George's Church.

MARIE REINE DU MONDE. On the façade, the copper-plated wooden statues represent the parishes that financed the cathedral's construction. The bas relief adorning the recumbent statue of Monseigneur Bourget, sculpted by Philippe Hébert (1903), evokes its subject's major achievements, the construction of the cathedral and the exploits of the Papal Zouaves. The interior displays paintings celebrating the history of Catholicism in Montreal.

SAINT GEORGE'S CHURCH. This was built in 1870 on the site of an old Jewish cemetery. Its modest exterior contrasts with the remarkable interior, embellished by its roof structure, oak trim and stained glass. The tower was added in 1894 and endowed with its chiming clock five years later.

St. James Cathedral and Bourget Monument, Montreal.

CATHOLICS MAKING THEIR PRESENCE FELT
After the great fire of 1852 destroyed his cathedral in the Latin Quarter, Mgr Ignace Bourget, the Bishop of Montreal from 1840 to 1876, decided to build a new half-size replica of Saint Peter's in Rome. Its location was chosen to ensure a Catholic presence in the city center, amidst the array of Protestant bell towers. The building work lasted from 1870 to 1894.

▲ The underground city

Montreal boasts an enormous underground complex that dates from the ambitious project to build Place Ville-Marie (1954–62), when the architects drew up a structure with an underground surface area equal to that of the tower block above it. They also divided the space imaginatively so that offices, stores and restaurants were all mixed together. This original concept has evolved over the years to create a separate pedestrian area that has breathed new life into the city center.

INTEGRATION WITH THE SURFACE
The subway can be reached by no fewer than 154 access points. They avoid entrances opening directly on to the street in favor of large halls in the neighboring buildings because of the harsh winter conditions.

The subway's logo (a vertical cross inside a circle) indicates the passageways leading to the stations. The design of each station has been entrusted to a separate architectural firm, in order to encourage visual and cultural diversity.

URBAN INFRASTRUCTURE
The underground city is structured around a network of 18 miles (29km) of subterranean pedestrian passageways that serve almost 2,000 stores (about half those in the city center), ten subway stations, two railroad stations and more than 10,000 parking spaces. This maze of corridors is also connected to seven hotels, the main cultural venues and congress halls and 80 percent of the offices.

AN EXTENSION OF THE PUBLIC DOMAIN
Although municipal authorities were solely responsible for creating the subway system, much of the underground city owes its existence to private capital; most of the passageways are the result of private business schemes rather than one plan. As a consequence, the huge network has been expanded at different times over the years, making it difficult to achieve unity.

Since 1966, the scale and originality of Montreal's underground network have been internationally recognized: one American architectural magazine described Montreal as 'the first North American city to cross the threshold of the 21st century'.

AN ARCHITECTURAL WONDER

The Cathedral Promenades under Christ Church Cathedral (1988) form a shopping mall that is totally buried underground. To achieve this feat, engineers raised the entire building and placed it on pillars (*right*). The stone spire was replaced by one made of aluminum.

FIRST STEPS

Underground Montréal grew up around Place Ville-Marie (*above*) ● 126. Developers made use of excavations dating from 1918 (the result of boring a railroad tunnel under Mont Royal) to install an underground shopping mall, two floors of parking spaces and a marshaling yard. These facilities were linked to the adjacent buildings through underground passageways.

THE SECTORS

The underground city is divided into three main areas: Place Ville-Marie; the stretch from the Place des Arts ▲➞*181* and the Palais des Congrès; and the department stores and apartment buildings of Rue Sainte-Catherine and Boulevard de Maisonneuve.

THE DEPARTMENT STORES

Faced with stiff competition from suburban shopping malls, department stores in the city center have invested in the construction of passageways linking them directly to the subway and the main buildings nearby.

Left: a cross-section of La Gauchetière

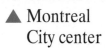

The Concourse–Windsor Station–Montreal

To arrive in a Fine Station is to complete a Fine Trip

WINDSOR STATION
In 1889, the Canadian Pacific Railway opened Windsor Station, thereby accelerating the transformation that was underway in the center of Montreal. Drawn up by the New Yorker Bruce Price – also responsible for the Château Frontenac in Quebec ▲ 260 – and enlarged several times in the same neo-Roman style, the station raised the social standing of the railroad and marked its entrance into the heart of Montreal, as it had previously been confined to the foot of the hill. Saved from the wrecker's ball in 1971 and restored in the 1980s, the station is now part of the Molson Center, a new sports arena that is home to the ice-hockey club Les Canadiens de Montréal.

Windsor Hotel

The construction of the Windsor Hotel in 1878 by G.H. Worthington at the junction of rues Peel and Dorchester (now René-Lévesque) changed the atmosphere of Dorchester Square by adding a metropolitan touch. After a fire in 1953, the original building was demolished and replaced by a tower block occupied by the Canadian Imperial Bank of Commerce (1962), with a work by Henry Moore on display in the lobby, while the annex that was added in 1923 has now become office space.

Sun Life

In 1914, the Sun Life Assurance company left Old Montreal to set up shop in Dorchester Square, in a formidable building ● *125* made with 50,000 tons of gray granite quarried in Quebec's Eastern Townships. It was constructed in various stages: the initial south-facing colonnade was enlarged first in 1925 and then in 1931, without any loss of architectural unity. When it was finally completed, it was not only a symbol of Montreal's economic power but also the biggest building in the British Empire. During World War 2, its vaults guarded the gold reserves of several European countries, including Great Britain. Another outstanding office block stands to the north of the square: the DOMINION SQUARE BUILDING, put up in 1928 by the architectural firm Ross & MacDonald, is worth a detour for the bronze wall lamps and trompe l'œil paintings in its lobby. Its first floor now houses the city's Infotouristique Center.

Place Ville-Marie

Place Ville-Marie ● *126*, the symbol of modern Montreal and nucleus of the underground city ▲ *176*, was built in 1962 on the trench of the railroad tunnel dug between 1912 and 1918 by the Canadian Northern Railway to create access to the city. The square was designed by I.M. Pei, who was also responsible for the Louvre Pyramid in Paris. Its cross shape allowed him to create the biggest expanse of office floor space under a single roof anywhere in the world. At night, the powerful revolving spotlights set on the Royal Bank Tower make this skyscraper a distinctive beacon of the city center.

Avenue McGill-College

A street was first laid on this site in 1840, when McGill
University subdivided the property that had been bequeathed
by James McGill. From the vantage point of Place Ville-
Marie, it provides an impressive view of the university,
Royal Victoria Hospital (1893) and the cross on Mont Royal.
It has been subjected to many alterations over the years,
including those of town-planner Jacques Gréber (1935).
In 1988, after heated debates, the street was widened to
create the current avenue.

McGill campus

The Royal Institution for the Advancement of Knowledge
(now known as McGill University) was founded in 1821,
making it the oldest of Montreal's four universities. It owes its
existence to the legacy of James McGill and originally
occupied Burnside, McGill's former home, before moving to
McGill College (now the Pavilion of Arts), which was

**THE 'ENLIGHTENED
THRONG'**
A sculpture by
Raymond Masson
called *Enlightened
Throng* (*above*) was
installed in 1986 on
Avenue McGill-
College, at the foot of
the BNP building.
'I barely notice today
the lawns of the
McGill Campus, with
the old elms under
which we used to
wait, or the old
beeches, at whose
feet lovers thought
they were hidden in
summertime but were
being spied on ...'
Jean Basile,
La Jument des Mongols

purpose-built in 1839 by John Ostell. It acquired international
standing under rector William Dawson (1855–93).
THE CAMPUS. The main campus, financed by Montreal's
leading Anglophone families, comprises a series of stone
buildings adorned with coats of arms. A monument to James
McGill stands in front of the central pavilion. One interesting
building is the REDPATH MUSEUM, known for its natural history
collections and for its architecture. Constructed as a home for
the university's geological collection, it was one of the first
Canadian buildings specifically designed as a museum.

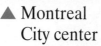

McCord Museum

Opposite the university, the McCord Canadian History Museum, set in the old Student's Union, possesses a wide-ranging collection that embraces the country's indigenous communities and their traditions. The museum, which was enlarged in 1992, is home to the Notman Archives, which include more than 450,000 old photos, mostly taken by William Notman, a local photographer of Scottish origin.

This photograph of a building gutted by fire is part of the Notman collection.

Phillips Square

This square, dominated by a statue of Edward VII by Philippe Hébert (1914), was created in the 1840s, when Thomas Phillips divided up the old Frobisher estate in imitation of London's residential squares. In the 1880s, when the Rue Sainte-Catherine grew into the city's main shopping street, the square became an emporium attracting big spenders from far and wide.

STORES. What is now LA BAIE was once Henry Morgan's Colonial House and the property of the Hudson Bay Company. It was built in 1889, when Morgan moved his store from Victoria Square. The BIRKS jewelry store (1894), built by Edward Maxwell in 1894 but subsequently enlarged, occupies the western side of the square. The eastern side once housed the gallery of the Montreal Art Association, which later moved to Rue Sherbrooke to become the Beaux-Arts Museum ▲ *184*. To the south, the CANADIAN CEMENT building is made entirely of ... cement.

TWO CHURCHES. Two churches on either side of the square show the evolution of the city center. The Anglican CHRIST CHURCH CATHEDRAL opened in 1869; surprisingly, it is now complemented by the Cathedral Promenades ▲ *177*, a

'LE 9E' RESTAURANT Toronto's Eaton Company, once famous for its mail-order service, opened a branch on Rue Sainte-Catherine in 1927. Four years later, this store was endowed with a magnificent Art Deco restaurant inspired by the dining room of the steamship *Ile-de-France*, designed by Jacques Carlu, also responsible for the Palais de Chaillot in Paris. The paintings are the work of Natacha Carlu.

shopping mall installed under the building to raise funds. Similarly, it was decided to build a row of stores in front of the SAINT JAMES UNITED METHODIST CHURCH (1888), to the east, to cover the building's maintenance costs. Now set in the heart of the fur trading neighborhood, the church has conserved its remarkable interior.

In the early 20th century, Victoria Square was surrounded by numerous bell towers; these can still be glimpsed today between the skyscrapers.

Saint Patrick's Basilica

Montreal's Irish community established itself in the 19th century and is now an integral part of the city's social fabric ▲ *200*; Saint Patrick's Day (March 17) is celebrated by a huge street procession running down Rue Sainte-Catherine. The Basilica was built between 1843 and 1847 on a plot facing Victoria Square that was a gift from the Sulpicians. Its superb interior has much to admire. To the south, a garden leads to the Rue de La Gauchetière and the old Irish neighborhood, now Chinatown ▲ *188*. The buildings around the basilica also bear fascinating vestiges of the industrial prosperity of the early years of the last century. This area was mainly occupied by printing houses, hence its nickname of Paper Hill.

IMPERIAL MOVIE THEATER
The 'super palaces' appeared around 1915 when the movie industry set about attracting a more affluent clientele with enormous, sumptuously decorated theaters. The Imperial opened in 1916 with 2,400 seats. Recently restored, it is the flagship of Montreal's cinema architecture.

North–South Axis

This axis is the result of attempts to consolidate the eastern, Francophone city center by means of a series of property developments on land formerly belonging to religious orders. The DESJARDINS COMPLEX (1977) and its inner square are the focal point. Another prominent landmark is the Place des Arts, with its CONTEMPORARY ART MUSEUM. Founded in 1964, this is the only museum in Canada exclusively devoted to contemporary art: the collection traces the main trends in Quebecois art since the 1950s. To the north stand the old technical college and the CHURCH OF SAINT JOHN THE EVANGELIST (1879).

Mont Royal has three peaks. One is occupied by Westmount, a residential neighborhood mainly inhabited by Anglophones; the second, by the University of Montreal and two cemeteries; and the third by a 250-acre (100ha) park, the pride and joy of the locals. It was created between 1873 and 1881 by Frederick Law Olmstead (1822–1903), the landscape gardener who designed

Central Park in New York. 'The Mountain', a welcome leisure area in the very heart of Montreal, offers unbeatable views of the city, the Saint Lawrence River and the South Shore.

DOWN WITH TRAMS
The park was designed to control the expansion of the city and to preserve the site's natural environment. Access to the mountain soon proved a contentious issue. In 1896, local women opposed the construction of a tramline on the grounds that the noise and traffic would prevent them from 'enjoying nature'.

THE MONT ROYAL CHALET
This chalet, built in 1932, serves as a youth center. Inside, models of giant squirrels hold up the ceiling and mounted paintings depict scenes from the history of both Montreal and Canada. Outside, it is fronted by an immense square and a baroque balustrade (*above*) that overlooks the city center.

THE BEST VIEWS IN MONTREAL

Mont Royal has three belvederes that provide excellent views of various parts of the city. In addition to those of the chalet and Westmount ▲ *185*, the Camillien-Houde belvedere looks out over the Mont-Royal plateau ▲ *190*.

THE CEMETERIES

In 1854, after a cholera epidemic, the local authorities decided to transfer the city's cemeteries to the mountain as a safety measure ▲ *174*. The Catholic cemetery abounds in elements intended to emphasize the religious nature of the site. Many well-known figures from the arts and the business world are buried here. The Protestant cemetery, shared by the Anglican, Methodist, Presbyterian and Baptist churches, is modeled on an English garden.

GETTING THERE

Mont Royal can be reached in several ways: on foot, along paths leading from the Avenue des Pins and the Avenue du Parc; by the number 11 bus (from Mont-Royal subway station) or by car, via the Camillien-Houde road.

ACTIVITIES

Since the end of the 19th century, Mont Royal Park, with its 60,000 trees, numerous plant species and countless squirrels, has supplied the citizens of Montreal with a haven of peace and quiet. It is criss-crossed with footpaths that make it possible to explore the woods, either on foot or on skis. One path ends at the foot of a large metal cross (which is lit up at night) dating from 1924. It replaces and pays tribute to the first wooden cross, which was erected by Maisonneuve, the founder of Montreal, in 1643 ▲ *164*. The park is also much appreciated for its Beaver Lake, an expanse of water introduced in 1958 to replace marshland; in wintertime, it becomes a delightful skating rink. For the last few summers, Sunday strollers have found themselves entertained by the drumming enthusiasts who regularly assemble at the foot of the mountain.

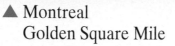

'So, costumed images passed by in front of me, haunting your architectural archives: the trapper at the trading posts where furs were portaged; the lord in his manor lit by chandeliers; the Scot wandering through his enormous, pillared bank ... All those presents emanating from your past.'
A. M. Klein, 'Montreal'

In the early 19th century, Montreal's middle classes started leaving the old city ▲*164* to settle on the southern slopes of Mont Royal, in an area now bounded by the Avenue des Pins, the Boulevard René-Lévesque and rues Bleury and Côte-des-Neiges. The large estates on the mountain gave way to smaller plots on which financial and industrial magnates built sumptuous mansions: by the turn of the century, it was estimated that the inhabitants of this neighborhood possessed 70 percent of Canada's wealth – hence the name 'Golden Square Mile'. After World War 1, the stress of the city center led these rich families to move further afield, particularly to Westmount, a borough set on one of the three peaks of Mont Royal ▲*182*. Although the Golden Square Mile has witnessed demolitions and the construction of apartment blocks, it still boasts some splendid houses, particularly to the north of Rue Sherbrooke. Lower down, the SHAUGHNESSY HOUSE (now part of the CANADIAN CENTER FOR ARCHITECTURE ● *129*, Rue Baile) and the prestigious MOUNT STEPHEN CLUB (Rue Drummond) are also relics from this glorious past.

Rue Sherbrooke

MUSÉE DES BEAUX-ARTS ★. The Montreal Society of Artists, founded in 1847 and renamed the Montreal Art Association in 1860, was nurtured by the private collections and donations of the neighborhood's wealthy population. In 1879, it opened a museum on Phillips Square ▲*180*. Since 1912, the institution has occupied an impressive building (no. 1380) made of Vermont marble and designed in the Beaux-Arts style ● *125*.The museum displays an excellent selection of paintings by Canadian and European artists, sculptures (*left*: a bronze by Robert Tait McKenzie), engravings, drawings and decorative art.
MAISON FORGET. Louis-Joseph Forget (1853–1911) was, along with his nephew Rodolphe ▲ *284*, one of the few French-speakers who managed to penetrate Montreal's business circles in the 19th century. In 1893, he built himself a villa (no. 1195) inspired by Second Empire architecture. This was purchased in 1927 by a club for veteran officers of World War 1; it remained in its hands for 45 years, before being taken over by the philanthropic Macdonald-Stewart Foundation in 1962.
ROSS HOUSE. This house, situated at no. 3644 on Rue Pell, was designed by the architect Bruce Price ▲ *260*. It was commissioned in 1892 by James Ross, an engineer for the Canadian Pacific, and then enlarged in 1905 by the Maxwell brothers, who were responsible for the construction of several houses in the area. In the early years of the 20th century, Ross House was a nerve center of Montreal's high society.

A YOUNG DANDY When James Ross died in 1913, his son John Kenneth inherited the family residence. John already owned two houses in the neighborhood, as well as horses and properties in the country. His extravagant lifestyle soon led to financial difficulties, however, and in the build-up to the Depression of the 1930s he was obliged to sell his paintings (including works by Rembrandt, Rubens and Millet) and to part company with his houses in the town and country.

Avenue des Pins

ARDVANA. This house (no. 1110), built in 1894 by the Maxwell brothers for the banker Henry Meredith, stands out because of its brick walls; this material was usually confined to working-class areas or industrial buildings.

MAISON CORMIER. In 1931, Ernest Cormier ● *124*, a famous engineer and architect, created a house (no. 1418) with a waterfall for his personal use and went on to live in it until 1975. It was in this masterpiece of Quebecois Art Deco that Pierre-Elliot Trudeau (1919–2000), the former Canadian Prime Minister, spent the last years of his life.

Westmount

The borough of Westmount, founded in 1874, dominates the city center from the western side of Mont Royal. A random stroll through its streets will reveal striking stone and brick residences built for the rich English-speakers who settled here in the early years of the 20th century. It is also possible to find rural houses dating from the 18th and 19th centuries (particularly in the streets around Rue Côte-Saint-Antoine).

VILLA MARIA. This imposing house is set back from the old borough of Westmount, in the territory of Montreal. A drive lined with maple trees opens on to magnificent mid-19th-century convent buildings (a girls' school and a barn). These belong to the Sisters of the Notre Dame Congregation, Montreal's oldest religious community. The main building was put up in 1803 by James Monk, a senior administrator for the British colony. The Villa Maria is one of Montreal's most beautiful monuments.

RAVENSCRAG
In 1863, Sir Hugh Allan, a Scottish shipbuilder and financier, commissioned a small castle in an Italianate style (1024, Avenue des Pins) that allowed him to enjoy the view of his ships docked in the port from its towers. This symbol of the architecture on the Golden Square Mile was bequeathed to the Royal Victoria Hospital in 1944 (*above*).

VOCATION AND EDUCATION
In 1657, Marguerite Bourgeoys, the founder of the Congregation of Notre Dame, opened the first school in Montreal, showing no qualms about setting up her classroom in a stable. Her community went on to play an important role in the education of young girls.

Below: a house in Westmount

'And if one breathes easily on the slopes of Mont Royal, if the noise of the city is a mere murmur, if civilization remains within easy reach, then, as I think Flaubert would have said, a high price must be paid for the privilege of this space and altitude.'
Jacques Godbout, *Liberty*

Today, the northern slopes of Mont Royal are divided between the Montreal neighborhood of Côte-des-Neiges and the old borough of Outremont ('over the mountain'). Although little is known about the period preceding the arrival of the French, we do know that the colonization process was instigated in 1694 with the royal cession of land on the Côte-Sainte-Catherine to some noble families and was then consolidated in 1698, when the Sulpicians commissioned Gedeón of Catalonia to survey the future Côte-Notre-Dame-des-Neiges. This area was crossed by several streams and soon grew into a village specializing in leather tanning. In the 19th century, Outremont, on the more sheltered and fertile side of the mountain, was used by French Canadian and Scottish market gardeners to grow the Montreal melon; this fruit was much appreciated by the hotels of New England but ceased to be grown for decades, until very recently. In the 19th century, trips to Outremont by horse and carriage or tram were extremely popular not only with the locals but also with travelers stopping over in inns or snowshoers' lodges, and with members of the golf and hunting clubs. The borough, with its plateau and views extending to the Lower Laurentides, attracted gentlemen farmers and, later on, hospitals and universities, which erected some notable buildings. French-speaking Outremont, lush and wealthy, and cosmopolitan Côte-des-Neiges, steeped in history, have both been home to several eminent personalities.

Saint Joseph's Oratory

THE HISTORY OF A BASILICA. Every year, millions of visitors and pilgrims flock to Saint Joseph's Oratory, which is inextricably linked with Notre Dame College, just across the way. In 1869, the priests of the Holy Cross improvised a school in an inn before moving to a newly completed stone building in 1881. This has since been enlarged several times. The oratory was founded by Brother André, a miracle-worker beatified in 1982, who was the college porter. In 1904, he put up the small wooden chapel that now stands behind the basilica. The oratory's crypt was built in 1916, but the major construction work was undertaken between 1924 and 1955, including the concrete dome, designed by Dom Bellot; other major architects involved were Viau, Venne, Parent and Cormier. The result was one of the world's biggest churches, with an impressive belvedere. The Way of the Cross was added in 1962.

The Oratory inspires such devotion that some pilgrims climb its steps on their knees. It celebrates the feast of Saint Joseph (March 19) and the beatification (May 23) and birthday (August 9) of Brother André.

University of Montreal

One recurring concern of Montreal's French-speakers was the establishment of a university to replace its branch of the Université Laval de Quebec; it was not until 1920 that they were granted this right. Today, the University of Montreal ● *124* is one of the most important in the Francophone world.

Côte-Sainte-Catherine

This old trail and toll road is characterized by its interesting topography, history and architecture.

PRESTIGIOUS HOUSES. The building at no. 543, erected in 1817 by the Bagg brothers, served as a warehouse for the Hudson Bay Company before becoming the seat of the municipal council. On the corner of Rue MacDougall, the MAISON DE L'OUTRE-MONT, which gave its name to the borough, was built in 1838 by Louis-Tancrède Bouthilier. In 1887, the Clerics of Saint-Viateur bought a farm in the area, only to subdivide it in the early 20th century and create Outremont and Saint-Viateur parks.

SAINT VIATEUR'S CHURCH. This church at the junction of rues Bloomfield and Laurier was opened in 1913. Its interior was decorated in 1921 by Guido Nincheri ▲ *196*.

RIALTO AND OUTREMONT THEATERS
The Rialto (1923) and the Outremont (1928, *above*) have been listed as historic monuments to prevent them being converted into shopping malls. In their early years, these neighborhood 'palaces' presented countless movies and vaudeville shows. In both cases, the interior decoration was the work of Emmanuel Briffa, a Montreal resident of Maltese origin responsible for fitting out more than 200 theaters all over Canada.

153, MAPLEWOOD
This private house was built in 1935 for Sévère Godin, the secretary to Sir Herbert Holt, the former chairman of the Royal Bank of Canada.

Traditionally, Boulevard Saint-Laurent, otherwise known as 'The Main', marks the boundary between the Anglophone west and Francophone east of Montreal, as well as being the backbone of the 'immigrants' corridor'. Over the last century, successive waves of newcomers have forged a multicultural environment.

PORTUGUESE QUARTER
The Portuguese residents of Montreal arrived relatively recently (1960–75). They have settled to the east of Boulevard Saint-Laurent, where they have spruced up and enlivened a neighborhood that was falling into decay.

HAÏTIENS
ASIATIQUES

MÉTROPOLITAIN

PARC JARRY
PETITE ITALIE

RUE JEAN-TALON

RUE DANTE

QUARTIERS
JUIF
GREC

AV. SAINT-VIATEUR

RUE BERNARD

RUE LAURIER

LE VILLAGE

AV. DU MONT-ROYAL

QUARTIER PORTUGAIS

SMOKED MEAT

RUE PRINCE-ARTHUR

RESTOS "IAI"   RUE SHERBROOKE

BRIC A BRAC

BD. RENÉ-LÉVESQUE

RUE SAINTE-CATHERINE

"REDLIGHT"

RUE DE
LA GAUCHETIÈRE

QUARTIER CHINOIS

RUE DE LA
COMMUNE

VIEUX MONTREAL

GREEK QUARTER
The Greek community, clustered around The Main, is now one of the largest in Montreal. Its kebab joints are deservedly famous, and well worth a try.

A HIVE OF ACTIVITY
Boulevard Saint-Laurent is one of the city's liveliest thoroughfares. Its small stores make up a veritable League of Nations. Its buzzing atmosphere after dark makes it a focal point for nighttime revelry.

CHINATOWN
Originally established in the late 19th century on Rue de La Gauchetière, Chinatown has now spread to The Main itself. Its numerous restaurants and grocery stores serve as a meeting place for a community that is widely scattered all over the city.

RED LIGHT DISTRICT

Montreal's answer to the Pigalle is subdued these days but, before the 1980s, Michel Tremblay declared: 'We were on The Main ... we hadn't gone to the Coconut Inn to mess around being fancy or subtle! We had come to drink and have a good time.'

LITTLE ITALY

Italians, mainly from the Molise region, started settling in northern Montreal in the early 20th century. They have since dispersed, but their cafés, restaurants and grocery stores on Rue Dante or around the Jean-Talon Market are a reminder of their continuing influence on the city.

CULINARY CONTRIBUTIONS

Ashkenazi Jews have enriched Montreal's cuisine with smoked meat (in particular, the smoked beef sandwich made with rye bread) and bagels (small, slightly sweetened ring-shaped bread rolls).

JEWISH QUARTER

Ashkenazi Jews from Eastern Europe have constituted one of Montreal's principal cultural communities for over a century. There are abundant signs of their presence on The Main, which was the center of their collective life for many years.

189

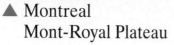

'The Plateau' is a huge natural terrace to the east of Mont Royal that looks out over the city center. Originally made up of several autonomous villages that merged into Montreal in the early 20th century, it has now been absorbed into the city's grid system. The Plateau has attracted a varied population through its intense cultural life, ethnic diversity ▲ 188 and small-town atmosphere, which almost makes it possible to forget the hectic rhythm of the nearby city center.

Mile End

RUE DROLET
This part of the Plateau has preserved

houses dating back to the start of Montreal's initial property boom; the group on the north side of Rue Roy (1873) is painted in vivid colors.

AROUND LAHAIE PARK
The area to the edge of Lahaie Park and the Church of Saint-Enfant-Jésus-du-Mile-End (*below*) constitute the institutional center of Saint-Louis-du-Mile-End, which separated from Coteau-Saint-Louis in 1878. The mansion houses, banks, convents and former city hall, built in 1905 by Joseph-Émile Vanier, bear witness to the rapid expansion that once transformed this old village into the third largest city in Quebec.

Coteau-Saint-Louis, the first village on the Plateau, was founded in 1846, near the quarries that provided the gray limestone used for Montreal's public buildings and middle-class houses. The route down first Rue Berri, then Rue Gilford, near Boulevard Saint-Joseph, follows the traces of the quarries that wound through the fields and lured the first settlers.
CHURCH OF SAINT MICHAEL THE ARCHANGEL.
This building with neo-Byzantine touches – the bell tower is in the form of a minaret – was erected in 1915 by the French-Canadian architect Aristide Beaugrand-Champagne for the Irish Catholics. The dazzling frescos on the dome were painted by Guido Nincheri ▲ 187, a prolific Florentine interior decorator. The church is now used by the Polish community.
A COMPOSITE POPULATION. The successive waves of immigrants from different cultures is reflected in the variety of Mile End's places of worship, particularly on Rue Saint-Urbain. Further south of the Church of Saint Michael the Archangel lies the Greek CHURCH OF SAINT MARKELA, on the site of the old Tifereth Israel Synagogue, installed in 1947 in a house originally built in 1905. Further down, the MONTREAL BUDDHIST CHURCH stands next to a MIKVAH, used for ritual ablutions by orthodox Hassidic Jews from central Europe, who are concentrated around rues Esplanade, Jeanne-Mance and Hutchison, to the north of Rue Fairmount.

Saint-Jean-Baptiste and Saint-Louis

The area to the south of today's Avenue Mont-Royal once comprised enormous farms owned by Montreal's leading families (the Courvilles, Guys, Cherriers, Vigers and Papineaus), but in the mid-19th century property developers bought them up and divided them into plots that attracted workers and craftsmen.
A WORKING-CLASS TOWN. The population of Saint-Jean-Baptiste mushroomed as a result of the manufacturing industries set up on Boulevard Saint-Laurent and the arrival of the tram. Its center, now a listed heritage site, is dominated by the CHURCH OF SAINT-JEAN-BAPTISTE. This symbol of French Canadians' religious faith and Catholic power was built in 1915 by the architect Casimir Saint-Jean in an Italian neo-baroque style. It is now also

used for concerts (of both religious and secular music); its large organ, made by the Casavant company ▲ *205*, is one of the most powerful in Montreal.

THE PORTUGUESE COMMUNITY. The Portuguese, who mainly arrived from the Azores in the 1960s, were at the forefront of the revitalization of the Saint-Jean-Baptiste, which was threatened by the city's relentless expansion. Their houses can easily be recognized by the devotional tiles set close to the doors and the vines climbing up the colorful façades. Rue Rachel leads to the new CHURCH OF SANTA CRUZ (on the corner of Rue Saint-Urbain), which is the hub of community life.

THE JEWISH COMMUNITY. Jews settled in the Saint-Louis neighborhood in the interwar years. Although the small Beth Schloime Synagogue (*below right*), on the corner of

IN THE BACK STREETS
A stroll down the small Rue Grolt reveals children playing in the street and lush Mediterranean-style front gardens where nostalgic immigrants nurture vines and fig trees in defiance of the northern climate.

rues Clark and Bagg, is still active, the sweat shops and the days when Yiddish was the principal language on The Main are long gone. The neighborhood still bears traces of the great influx of Jews from central Europe in the late 19th and early 20th centuries. The Jewish community has given Montreal many celebrities, trade union leaders, writers and poets, such as Leonard Cohen ● *53* ▲ *145*. Kosher butcher's stores with delicious smoked meat and aromatic bagel shops mark the trail toward Avenue Parc, where fish restaurants with a Greek flavor start to take over.

The heart of the Plateau

To the east of Rue Saint-Denis, the elegant Victorian houses give way to some of the most prized treasures of Montreal's popular heritage.

'MONDAY IS WASHDAY'
Miyuke Tanobe, an artist of Japanese descent, chronicles working-class life.

IN LAFONTAINE PARK Lafontaine Park is an oasis of greenery in the Mont-Royal Plateau. The locals use it to unwind all year long and, in winter, one of the two lakes is transformed into a skating rink. The park's paths and trees abound in squirrels that are as docile as they are greedy!

MONASTERY AND CHURCH OF NOTRE-DAME-DU-TRÈS-SAINT-SACRAMENT. In the late 19th century, the architectural team of Resther and Son built the monastery of the Pères-du-Très-Saint-Sacrament and the Saint Basile boarding school – now a cultural center – whose pinnacles tower above the flat roofs of the houses on the Plateau. The church, classified as a historic monument, is embedded in the imposing monastery complex. Its high nave, with a polychromatic design by Toussaint-Xénophon Renaud, and its two rows of side galleries – extremely rare in Montreal's Catholic churches – were restored after a fire in 1982.

AROUND LAFONTAINE PARK. The nucleus of the Plateau – stretching to the west, north and east of Lafontaine Park – is a showcase for most of Montreal's styles of residential architecture: small wooden buildings on Rue Pontiac, pioneers of urban development, nestle alongside two-story homes on rues Saint-André and Boyer. At the junction of the latter with Rue Marie-Anne, the residences sport turrets. There are also the famous 'triplexes' typical of Montreal. On both sides of Avenue Mont-Royal, the streets dotted with churches and monumental parish schools display façades with outdoor staircases. These are covered in snow or ice in winter. However, in summer their steps become ringside seats for the spectacle of neighborhood life that the writer Michel Tremblay depicted in his famous *Chronicles of the Mont Royal Plateau*. RUES RACHEL and DU PARC-LAFONTAINE are ideal for a stroll, as are RUES SAINT-HUBERT, CHRISTOPHE-COLOMB, DE LANAUDIÈRE, GARNIER AND FABRE. Although the Plateau has become a prosperous neighbourhood, many of its houses and flats have no yards or gardens; the park affords locals a chance to experience nature. Most of the park's neighbouring streets are residential, but on the south, Notre-Dame Hospital and the main municipal library create an institutional boundary along Sherbrooke Street.

'When Marcel disappeared for whole days … that meant that he had literally been abducted to Lafontaine Park to be tossed around in a ridiculous fashion on a plank of wood tied to two ropes.'
Michel Tremblay

'These outdoor staircases are a geographical nonsense; they would be fine in Genoa, Algiers or Granada, but they seem reckless in a country where the ice makes them extremely slippery and dangerous.'

Raymond Tanghe

THE MONTREAL TRIPLEX

The new working-class areas that grew up between 1900 and 1930 witnessed the appearance of the triplex (three-story apartment building), which has become the most common type of dwelling in Montreal. Although the triplex retained some features of previous architectural styles, it introduced a systematic use of back alleys and plots of identical dimensions. It is made up of three to five L-shaped apartments, each with six to eight rooms that form a line stretching to the back alley. The striking, large balconies and rear verandahs almost look like proscenium theater stages. At the front, the façade is set back from the street to allow room for a small front garden. The outdoor staircases – whether straight, S-shaped or spiral – allow for more space inside and give each family a separate entrance to their home, thereby reproducing the autonomy of a rural house in an urban setting. The façades, adorned with a false pediment and often decorated with finials, are sometimes marked with the building's completion date. Their balconies are supported, in later designs, by wooden pillars and enclosed by wrought-iron balustrades. Recently environmentalists have encouraged triplex owners to create gardens on their roofs to save fuel and insulate.

193

This neighborhood grew up as a result of the natural division that occurred between the French- and English-speaking populations around 1850, when the moneyed élite began leaving Old Montreal ▲ *168* for the quieter suburbs. In the late 19th and early 20th centuries, the Francophone bourgeoisie took over a neighborhood in the city center but, when Outremont began to be developed between 1900 and 1920, this area was inhabited mainly by traders and working-class families. It was already a lively place but it experienced a new injection of vitality with the establishment of the University of Quebec in 1969 and the opening of innumerable cafés: this dynamism has earned it the nickname of 'Latin Quarter'.

MONTREAL INTERNATIONAL JAZZ FESTIVAL
For the last 15 years, the annual Montreal Jazz Festival ▲ *352*, and particularly the bustling streets of the Latin Quarter, have played host to one of Canada's

biggest musical events. Artists of an extremely high caliber, such as Ray Charles, B. B. King, Miles Davis, Cab Calloway, Charlie Haden and local hero Oscar Peterson ▲ *200* have performed to ever larger audiences. It now assembles over 2,000 musicians from all over the world and up to one and a half million music fans.

Carré Viger

HOTEL VIGER. This former Canadian Pacific Railroad terminus, put up by Bruce Price in 1897, follows the architectural style of the other hotels built by this railroad company, such as the Château Frontenac in Quebec ▲ *260*. The hotel closed in 1935 but the government took it over in 1946 and converted it into accommodation for World War 2 veterans and their families. It is now occupied by local authority offices and still bears the name of Jacques Viger (1787–1858), a former militia officer, civil servant, politician, author and collector who has been permanently linked with the history of Montreal since his appointment as the city's first elected mayor in 1832.

Rue Sainte-Catherine

MAISON ARCHAMBAULT. This building on the corner of Rue Berri, erected in 1928, reflects the dynamic nature of the entire neighborhood by playing host to a store called the Maison Archambault, a symbol of the entrepreneurial spirit of Montreal's Francophones. Founded in 1896, it originally specialized in musical instruments and

sheet music but has since branched out to sell a variety of records and books.

PLACE ÉMILIE-GAMELIN OR SQUARE DU 350E. This park, opened in 1992 to mark the 350th anniversary of the founding of the city, is distinguished by its modern layout. It lies opposite the Chapel of Notre Dame de Lourdes, built in the Byzantine style by Napoléon Bourassa, the grandson of Louis-Joseph Papineau ▲ *224*.

Rue Saint-Denis

UNIVERSITÉ DU QUÉBEC À MONTRÉAL (UQAM). This university emerged as a result of the protests of 1968 and has established itself as a pacesetter in Quebec's cultural life. Its

modern buildings occupy the site of the Church of Saint-Jacques and have incorporated both its neo-Gothic spire, dating from 1830, and its transept, built 60 years later. Opposite the bell tower of Saint-Jacques stands the former École Polytechnique (1903), which is constructed with limestone in the Beaux-Arts style ● *125*; this relic from the Laval University of Montreal is now used by the UQAM.

SAINT-SUPLICE LIBRARY. This monument at no. 1700 was built in the Beaux-Arts style by Eugène Payette, who won an architectural competition in 1912. The interior boasts several stained-glass windows (*left*) and is organized around a series of mezzanines. The library contains numerous rare books available for consultation and it sometimes puts on thematic exhibitions.

Rue Sherbrooke

MONT-SAINT-LOUIS. This former college, situated at no. 244, to the west of Rue Saint-Denis, was built between 1887 and 1909 in the Second-Empire style ● *118*. It offered courses in business, technology and science. It was left empty for years but has now been converted into luxury apartments. Further west, at no. 104, lies the Bon-Pasteur Monastery ● *121*, built from 1846 to 1888 for the Bon-Pasteur Sisters.

Carré Saint-Louis ★

Enclosed by the Rue Saint-Denis to the east and the Rue Laval to the west, this square is an oasis of peace. Its large trees and fountains provide a refreshing respite from Montreal's summer heat; in winter, the colored roofs of the surrounding middle-class houses are obscured by snow.

ÉMILE NELLIGAN (1879–1941)
The Romantic poet Émile Nelligan is closely associated with Rue Laval and the Saint-Louis neighborhood and has become a symbol of the Bohemian scene at the turn of the 20th century. Irish on his father's side and Canadian on his mother's, he embodied the image of the young *poète maudit*. At the age of 20 he was admitted to a psychiatric hospital, where he died 42 years later. In the preface to Nelligan's collected work (1904), Eugène Seers, alias Louis Dantin, wrote: 'Émile Nelligan is dead. It barely matters that our friend's eyes have not been extinguished … Neurosis, that unrelenting divinity that bestows death along with genius, has consumed and taken away everything … It has crushed him mercilessly, as it did Maupassant and Baudelaire, … as it will crush sooner or later all those dreamers …'

CARRÉ, PLACE, SQUARE …
Carré Saint-Louis (Quebecois use *carré* as well as the French/English terms *place* and square) leads to the Rue Prince-Arthur. Restaurants, stores and musicians combine to make it a lively street in the Latin Quarter.

Maisonneuve sprung up to the east of Montreal at the end of the 19th century, when a group of French Canadian industrialists and landowners decided to create a rival to Montreal. In effect, it did become Quebec's second largest industrial city, but overambitious construction projects brought it to the brink of ruin and it was annexed by Montreal in 1918. Nowadays, its main tourist attraction is the sports complex built for the 1976 Olympics, but its architectural richness and community life should not be overlooked.

THE BOTANICAL GARDENS
Montreal's Botanical Gardens were founded in 1931 by Brother Marie-Victorin ▲ 247. Its 180-acre (73ha) expanse and 30,000 species and varieties of plants are only surpassed by Kew Gardens in London. It comprises ten greenhouses and some 30 outdoor gardens. The Chinese garden, with its kiosks and pavilions, reproduces an aquatic setting based on the classical gardens of the Ming Dynasty. An insectarium with almost 130,000 insects from all over the world rounds off the spectacle; butterfly lovers are particularly catered for, as most of the specimens found in Quebec are on display.

Château Dufresne

This building, once owned by the brothers Oscar and Marius Dufresne, dominates the former city of Maisonneuve. In 1900, their father Thomas took advantage of the local authorities' generosity to open up a shoe factory; very soon after, Marius Dufresne, an architect and municipal engineer, was commissioned

to undertake a huge development program for the new city. Between 1915 and 1918 he also built this 44-room hotel that reflected the social aspirations of Maisonneuve's ruling élite. The originality of the Château Dufresne lies in its interiors (*above*: the smoking room) and its murals painted by the Florentine artist Guido Nincheri ▲ 187. It was turned into a school in 1948 but was then abandoned in 1961. Just before the 1976 Olympics, businessman and patron of the arts David M. Stewart took on the task of restoring it and putting back much of the original furniture. The building is now used for temporary exhibitions.

Olympic Complex ★

PANORAMIC TOWER
A funicular train runs to the top of the Olympic Stadium's mast. It towers 575 feet (175m) above the city and offers stunning views of Montreal Island and the plain.

OLYMPIC STADIUM. This stadium, which took 15 years to build, aroused great controversy when it was conceived by the French architect Roger Taillibert, because of the immense size and cost, but it has proved to be a landmark in modern architecture. The huge upside-down saucer was supported by 34 consoles with cantilevers that stretch for up to 200 feet (60m) and support almost all the other elements, including the terraces with a seating capacity of 60,000.
Today, the stadium is used for a variety of shows including rock concerts, baseball games, motocross competitions and trade fairs.

BIODOME. The huge concrete shell of the Olympic velodrome – a major technical achievement in itself – was the site chosen by the Montreal authorities in 1992 for a museum of the environment called the Biodome. It recreates four ecosystems from the Americas (tropical rain forest, forest drained by the Saint Lawrence, the maritime Saint Lawrence area and the Arctic); thousands of plants and animals live and reproduce here under meticulously controlled atmospheric conditions. The Biodome is also a center for scientific research.

Maisonneuve neighborhood

The major development schemes drawn up by Maisonneuve's city planners went on to inspire the American City Beautiful and British Garden City movements. Four public buildings have survived from those heady days: the city hall, the market, the public baths and the fire station. Maisonneuve is also an excellent and well-preserved showcase for the charm and originality of working-class residential architecture.

CITY HALL. Built by the architect Cajetan Dufort in the Beaux-Arts style ● *125* and opened in 1912, the city hall has an impressive façade broken up by Corinthian columns. It now serves as a community arts center.

CHURCH OF THE TRÈS-SAINT-NOM-DE-JÉSUS. Built between 1903 and 1906 by the architect Charles-Aimé Reeves, this was the first church in Maisonneuve. Its lavish interior décor was the work of Toussaint-Xénophon Renaud. Its organ is one of the finest produced by the Maison Casavant ▲ *205*.

THE MARKET. The Maisonneuve market, completed in 1914, stands at the end of Boulevard Morgan; designed in the Beaux-Arts style, it was the most monumental of all the public buildings that emerged from the development program, selling agricultural produce then livestock.

BOULEVARD MORGAN. Marius Dufresne built the PUBLIC BATHS, along with a gymnasium, on this thoroughfare in 1915. Its Beaux-Arts style was inspired by New York's Grand Central Station. Further along, to the south of Boulevard Ville-Marie, the FIRE STATION, also the work of Dufresne, was directly inspired by the Unity Temple erected by Frank Lloyd Wright (1867–1959) in Chicago. Now disused, it awaits an initiative that can justify its restoration.

ON THE MARKET SQUARE
The Maisonneuve market, recently fitted out with a new pavilion, seems to have recovered its former vitality. The center of the square contains one of the masterpieces of the sculptor Alfred Laliberté, *The Woman Farmer*, with four bronze figures representing the market's activities.

'Hochelaga-Maisonneuve is a village within a city. On summer evenings, when I go down the Valois coast, people seem to be talking to each other from one side of the street to the other with such intimacy that I see the two palisades of duplex houses like walls of a single corridor and I feel as if I'm in a big House, surrounded by a Family.'
Robert-Guy Scully

SPORTS CITY
The Olympic Stadium, with a surface area of 640,000 sq feet (59,307 sq m), hosts concerts, operas and trade fairs. Since the 1976 Olympics, it has also held some of Quebec's most important sporting events. Montreal's baseball team, the Expos, play here regularly.

197

Montreal Island, one of a cluster of islands, has a total of 22 road and rail bridges. Before the first wooden bridges were put up across the Back River, to the north, the crossing had to be made in a ferry boat or, in winter, on ice bridges that could bear the weight of trains. Although the oldest and most spectacular structures are located along the stretch to the south where the river widens, several more all the way around the island are well worth a visit.

THE 1967 EXPO
This international event came to Montreal due to the efforts of Mayor Jean Drapeau (*right*), who went on to organize the 1976 Olympics. The World Fair (Expo) was installed on the 'Land of Men', Saint Hélène Island and Notre Dame Island, created from the fusion of other islets. The survivors of the Expo's futuristic architecture include the geodesic dome ● *126*,

United States Pavilion (converted into a Water Museum in 1995) and the French Pavilion (*left*), designed by architect Jean Faugeron, and now the Montreal Casino.

AROUND MONTREAL
To the west, the Bridge of Sainte-Anne-de-Bellevue links up with Perrot Island, while to the east, a tunnel-bridge leads to the Boucherville Islands. To the north, the Papineau Bridge straddles the Back River from the site of the village of Sault-au-Récollet, near the island's oldest church (1752). Boulevard Gouin and Visitation Island Park stretch along the edge of the reservoir.

JACQUES-CARTIER BRIDGE
Although the port administration drew up plans for a two-storey bridge from Montreal to Longueuil in 1874, the current 2½-mile (4km) bridge was only begun in 1925 and finished in 1930. Its construction required four million rivets and over 10,000 gallons (40,000 l) of paint. The former Le Havre Bridge was rechristened in 1934 to celebrate the 400th anniversary of Jacques Cartier's first voyage.

VICTORIA BRIDGE
The Victoria Bridge,
(1854–9, *above*),
built by Robert
Stephenson for the
Grand Trunk Railway
Company, was
opened with great
pomp and ceremony
by the Prince of
Wales in 1860. It
crossed the Saint
Lawrence for the first
time, linking
Montreal with the
ports of New
England, which were
not paralyzed by ice
during the winter. In
1898, the original
single-track tube was
replaced by the
present structure,
with two railroad
tracks and two roads,
one of which was
once a tramway that
linked the suburbs to
Old Montreal train
station (on the corner
of rues McGill and
Youville).

ÎLE SAINTE-HÉLÈNE
Named by Champlain ▲ *254* in 1611, in honor
of his wife, the Île Sainte-Hélène (*above*) was
sold to the British Crown in 1818 by Baron de
Longueuil. The Duke of Wellington went on
to build a fort here to guarantee the defense
of the continent. In 1874, the city of Montreal
created a park, before taking possession of
the island in 1908 and later using it as a
prisoner-of-war camp. The fort now contains
the David W. Stewart Museum.

CHAMPLAIN BRIDGE
This bridge (*below*),
opened in 1962,
provides a link to the
Île des Socurs and
allowed it to be
urbanized. The great
architect Ludwig
Mies van der Rohe
contributed to the
development plans
and drew up some
buildings, including
the gas station.

▲ Montreal
Along the Lachine Canal

'What high spirits these kids from Saint-Henri had! ... Exotic produce from the land – molasses from Barbados, bananas from Jamaica, rum from the Antilles – all passed under their eyes en route to warehouses steeped in the aromas of the Tropics.'

Gabrielle Roy

Since the 17th century, Montreal's local authorities had dreamed of enabling boats to cross the south-west of Montreal Island and avoid the dangerous rapids on the Saint Lawrence. This finally became a reality in 1821, when 500 laborers, mostly Irish, dug the 7-mile-long (11km) canal and built the seven locks on the way to the village of Lachine, a major fur-trading post. The continuous increase in traffic gave rise to several enlargements of the canal until the opening of the sea link in 1959, dug in the bed of the Saint Lawrence itself. The original canal, of crucial importance to Montreal's industrial heritage, was finally closed in 1970 and is now a park, complete with a bicycle path, that connects the port of Montreal with Lachine.

Saint-Henri

The opening of the canal turned Saint-Henri-des-Tanneries, originally a small tanning village founded in the 17th century, into one of the most important industrial centers in Canada. This French-speaking working-class neighborhood boasts a rich popular heritage.

WORKERS' HOUSES. Like its neighbors, the HOUSE OF CARPENTER JOHN CLERMONT (1870), wedged between the railroad track and Rue Saint-Augustin, displays vestiges of the old village of Saint-Augustin, which joined up with Saint-Henri-des-Tanneries to form the town of Saint-Henri. In Rue Saint-Ambroise, which runs alongside the canal and its industrial sites, the HOUSES OF LOUIS RICHARD (1890) illustrate this period of growth, when laborers crammed into precarious wooden houses. Rows of working-class triplexes ▲ 193 can be seen around the George Étienne Cartier Park, created after Saint-Henri was annexed by Montreal in 1905.

ATWATER MARKET. Built in 1933 as part of a public works program to alleviate the devastating effects of the Great Depression, the Art Deco Atwater Market has received a new injection of life after a recent restoration; its food produce attracts shoppers from all over Montreal.

PETITE-BOURGOGNE. This neighborhood has been deeply marked by an urban development project in the late 1960s that destroyed most of its 19th-century atmosphere. The survivors include the CHURCH OF SAINTE CUNÉGONDE (1906), designed in the Beaux-Arts style ● 125 by Jean-Omer Marchand, and the stone cottages with sloping roofs on RUE COURSOL.

OSCAR PETERSON
In the late 19th century, the Petite Bourgogne became home for a Black-American community, mainly employed as porters in Montreal's railroad stations. This was the birthplace of Oscar Peterson, one of the great names of jazz; he served his musical apprenticeship in now forgotten local cabarets.

Pointe Saint-Charles

MAISON SAINT-GABRIEL.
This building is one of the oldest in Montreal. The old farm was purchased in 1668 by the Notre Dame Congregation, founded by the teacher Marguerite

Bourgeoys, to house the 'King's Daughters' ● 51.
A remarkable example of Nouvelle-France architecture,
the house contains a well-stocked museum that evokes
everyday life in the original colony. The two Catholic
churches (of Saint-Gabriel and Saint-Charles), side by side
on RUE CENTRE, are evidence of the cohabitation of French
Canadians and Irish in this working-class neighborhood
since the mid-19th century.

THE CANAL
This waterway, later
accompanied by a rail
link, gave rise to what
was, until World
War 1, the largest
industrial center in
Canada.

Lachine

In 1667, the
Sulpicians conceded
this territory to
Robert Cavalier de
La Salle, an
adventurer and
explorer who went
on to discover
Louisiana and
dreamed of finding
a passage to China
– hence the derisive
name of 'La Chine
[China]' given to
his domain.
TOWN MUSEUM.
Lachine,
strategically placed
for the exchange of
merchandise, owes
its existence to the
fur trade. In the
town's golden era, the house of Jacques LeBer and
Charles LeMoyne – built between 1669 and 1685 – served
as both a trading post and residence. It is now a museum of
the town's history.
FUR TRADE INTERPRETATION CENTER. When Lachine
became an important commercial center, the Hudson Bay
Company set up its headquarters and warehouse there in
1826. The latter now houses this museum devoted to the
fur trade.
OPEN-AIR MUSEUM. Lachine went into decline after
the closure of the canal, its lifeblood for over 500
years, but it has experienced a renaissance thanks
to a new appreciation of its heritage and its location
beside Lake Saint-Louis. The open-air museum on
the huge jetty of René-Lévesque Park and the banks
of the lake displays 36 monumental sculptures by
contemporary artists.

THE RAPIDS
The power of the
Lachine rapids is
most apparent when
the river's water level
drops in summer:
thrill-seekers can go
down them in a boat,
safe from all danger
except a drenching.
Numerous water
birds take refuge
here. In the early
17th century, the
explorer Samuel de
Champlain found a
heron colony on one
of the islands at the
head of the rapids. It
is still there today,
and its home is now
known as Heron
Island.

A tanner in his
workshop

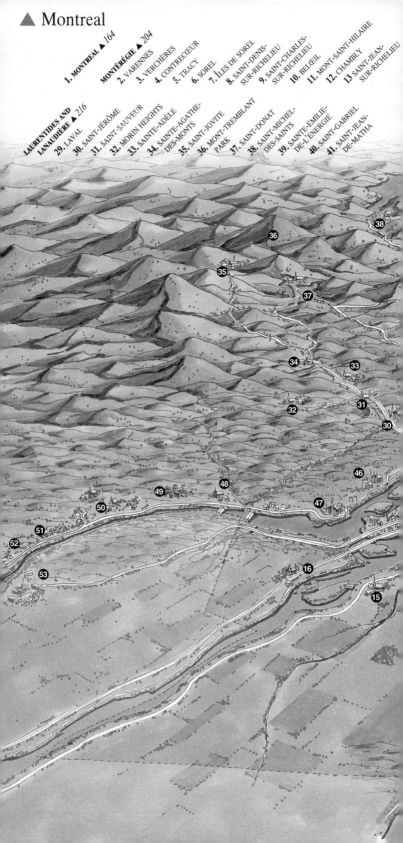

▲ Montreal

1. MONTREAL ▲ 164

MONTÉRÉGIE ▲ 204
2. VARENNES
3. VERCHÈRES
4. CONTRECŒUR
5. TRACY
6. SOREL
7. ÎLES DE SOREL
8. SAINT-DENIS-SUR-RICHELIEU
9. SAINT-CHARLES-SUR-RICHELIEU
10. BELŒIL
11. MONT-SAINT-HILAIRE
12. CHAMBLY
13. SAINT-JEAN-SUR-RICHELIEU

LAURENTIDES AND LANAUDIÈRE ▲ 216
29. LAVAL
30. SAINT-JÉRÔME
31. SAINT-SAUVEUR
32. MORIN HEIGHTS
33. SAINTE-ADÈLE
34. SAINTE-AGATHE-DES-MONTS
35. SAINT-JOVITE
36. MONT-TREMBLANT PARK
37. SAINT-DONAT
38. SAINT-MICHEL-DES-SAINTS
39. SAINTE-ÉMILIE-DE-L'ÉNERGIE
40. SAINT-GABRIEL
41. SAINT-JEAN-DE-MATHA

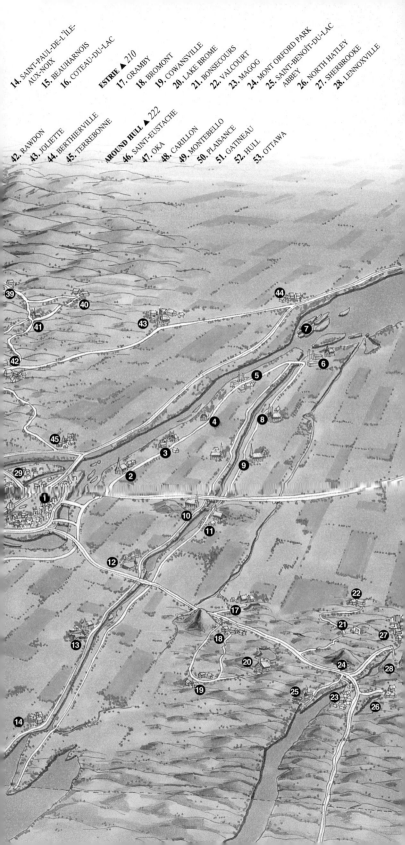

14. SAINT-PAUL-DE-L'ÎLE-
    AUX-NOIX
15. BEAUHARNOIS
16. COTEAU-DU-LAC
ESTRIE ▲ 210
17. GRAMBY
18. BROMONT
19. COWANSVILLE
20. LAKE BROME
21. BONSECOURS
22. VALCOURT
23. MAGOG
24. MONT ORFORD PARK
25. SAINT-BENOÎT-DU-LAC
    ABBEY
26. NORTH HATLEY
27. SHERBROOKE
28. LENNOXVILLE

42. RAWDON
43. JOLIETTE
44. BERTHIERVILLE
45. TERREBONNE
AROUND HULL ▲ 222
46. SAINT-EUSTACHE
47. OKA
48. CARILLON
49. MONTEBELLO
50. PLAISANCE
51. GATINEAU
52. HULL
53. OTTAWA

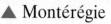

⏱	2 days
🚗	185 mi/295 km

THE MONTÉRÉGIENNES
Contrary to popular belief, these hills are not extinct volcanoes. They were formed in the Cretaceous period as a result of a rapid solidification of magma that extended up to 2 miles (3km) below ground level. A series of glacial cycles eroded the surrounding lowlands, leaving the hills exposed to view. One of these is Mont Royal ▲ *182*, which gave Montreal its name. The hills on the Montérégie plain are Monts Saint-Bruno, Saint-Grégoire and Saint-Hilaire, Rougemont, Yamaska and Rigaud.

Montérégie is an immense plain crossed by the tranquil River Richelieu and marked by the presence of six of the isolated hills known as the Montérégiennes. Today, nothing could seem more peaceful, but this plain has been the stage for several violent confrontations over the course of the centuries ▲ *206*. It has long been an agricultural region but it has also attracted industry, including advanced aeronautical and aerospace technology.

Sorel

Montérégie is bounded by a panoramic road running alongside the Saint Lawrence River from Longueuil to Sorel,

passing through Varennes and Verchères. Sorel was founded in 1642 and acquired a fort in 1665; this survived for many years, but there are no traces left today. The town was once famous for its shipyards, but these are now closed. The CHURCH OF SAINTE-ANNE-DE-SOREL contains eleven paintings by Marc-Aurèle de Foy Suzor-Côté (1869–1937), depicting the lives of Saint Anne and the Virgin Mary.

A YOUNG HEROINE
In 1692, Madeleine de Verchères, aged 14, defended a fort against the Iroquois for eight days, with the help of only two men. A bronze statue was put up in her memory in 1927 in the village of Verchères.

SOREL ISLANDS. The Île aux Fantômes, Île de Grace and Île du Moine are just some of the many enchanting islets accessible by boat. All of the houses there are built on pillars to protect them from flooding during the springtime rise in the water level. These islands and the channel separating them from the bank of the Sorel are the setting for the novel *The Unexpected Arrival* by Germaine Guèvremont (1893–1968). Pé Island has a WRITING MUSEUM that traces the history of Quebecois literature and presents exhibitions about its authors.

The Lower Richelieu

Successively named the Iroquois, Saint-Louis and Chambly, the Richelieu River originates in Lake Champlain, on the American border, and runs into the Saint Lawrence. The three forts situated on its banks vouch for its strategic importance as a navigational and trading route. Its waters have been the haunt of canoes, steamers and barges but are now only used by pleasure boats.

SAINT-DENIS. Its location on the Richelieu encouraged this town to develop numerous craft industries in the early 19th century, such as pottery ▲ 208 and hatmaking, with a special emphasis on beaver-skin top hats. Some old buildings have survived as witnesses to this former prosperity. In 1837, Saint-Denis was the site of the Patriots' only victory over British troops in the Rebellions ▲ 206. The MAISON NATIONALE DES PATRIOTES records the impact of these events on local history.

BELŒIL ★. From Saint-Denis, the trail of the Patriots leads to Saint-Charles, where a ferryboat crosses to Saint-Marc, on the other side of the river. From there, the road leads to Belœil, which provides a panoramic view of Saint-Hilaire, with its mountain and church.

Mont-Saint-Hilaire

The birthplace of Ozias Leduc (1864–1955) and Paul-Émile Borduas (1905–60) ● 140, Mont-Saint-Hilaire is considered a crucible of Quebecois painting.

ROUVILLE-CAMPBELL MANOR. This estate belonged to the Hertel de Rouville family for nearly 150 years before it was bought in 1843 by Thomas Edmund Campbell, who built a mock-Tudor manor house. The Barcelona-born painter-sculptor Jordi Bonet (1932–79), who emigrated to Quebec in 1954, restored the house in 1969 as his studio. It is now a luxury hotel.

SAINT HILAIRE CHURCH. This church, built in 1837, boasts one of the oldest organs manufactured by the Casavant brothers. The interior décor is the work of Ozias Leduc; as well as stenciling on vaults and walls, he painted 15 canvases portraying the sacraments, the Evangelists, the Nativity, the Ascension, the Assumption and Saint Hilary of Poitiers.

MAISON CASAVANT
Joseph Casavant (1807–74) was a renowned blacksmith when he tried his hand at making organs in 1837. In 1879, his sons Claver and Samuel founded Casavant Frères in Saint-Hyacinthe. The firm has become famous for the quality of its instruments and for its innovations, such as the electric organ. It remains a pioneer in the field today. Its crowning glory is the organ in Montreal's Notre Dame Basilica ▲ 168.

OZIAS LEDUC (1864–1955)
The intimacy of the region and the contours of Mont-Saint-Hilaire, seemingly squeezed between the Richelieu and the mountain, certainly had an effect on this painter. He was fascinated by expansive landscapes, whether serene or stormy, but also produced religious frescos: he decorated 31 churches and chapels in Quebec, the rest of Canada and New England.

▲ The Rebellions of 1837–8

In 1837 and 1838, the Richelieu Valley was the stage for significant military confrontations. The causes and aspirations of the rebellion are diverse and complex. In Lower Canada, the issues of allegiance to Great Britain and the colony's future gave rise to disagreements between the 'Canadian' (French-speaking) majority and the British minority. The elected legislative Assembly clashed with the Councils appointed by the Governor of the colony. Tensions were exacerbated by the inequitable distribution of wealth and problems associated with property ownership. The episode of the Rebellions should also be seen in a broader context, marked by the independence of the American colonies, nationalism in Europe and the triumph of Liberalism.

RURAL SOCIABILITY
In the villages, the cohabitation of a diversified population encouraged social interaction as well as the emergence of political protest. *Right*: the village of Saint-Denis-sur-Richelieu.

SEVERE REPRISALS
Hundreds of rebels were imprisoned; some were locked up in Montreal's Pied-du-Courant prison. Twelve Patriots were hanged and 58 deported to Australia.

PUBLIC ASSEMBLIES
In the face of the Crown's persistent refusal to grant their demands ● *40*, the reformers convened a series of public assemblies in 1837. The most important of these took place on October 23 in Saint-Charles. The participants openly defied the authorities by displaying the tricolor flag and wearing red hats. The following day, a manifesto inspired by the American Declaration of Independence was published.

THE PATRIOTIC PRESS
The freedom acquired by the press under the British regime made it possible to disseminate the demands for reform. *L'Echo du Pays* set about promoting economic education and the concept of democracy.

L'ECHO DU PAYS.
INDUSTRIE, PROSPERITE ET UNION.

ST. CHARLES VILLAGE DEBARTZCH.

| VOL. I. | JEUDI, 6 JUIN 1833. | NO. 15. |

The newspaper published in Saint-Charles.

ARMED CONFLICTS
Tension mounted in the summer of 1837 as a confrontation brewed. In early November, orders were given to arrest Patriot leaders. The conflict blew up: after a setback at Saint-Denis (November 23), the Army triumphed at Saint-Charles (November 25) and regained control of the region. It could then turn its attention to the rebels to the north of Montreal, particularly those of Saint-Eustache ▲ *222*.

A SECOND ATTEMPT IN 1838
After this setback to their movement, several Patriots took refuge in the US, where they started to organize another uprising. The secret society of the Frères Chasseurs (Hunting Brothers) was formed in late 1838. This new movement was characterized by a more radical repudiation of the monarchy, the clergy and the landowners. It was soon suppressed, however; 800 rebels were taken prisoner, and 108 of these faced a court martial.

SAINT-HILAIRE MOUNTAIN ★. The most imposing of all the Montérégiennes dominates the plain and offers stunning views of the region. Lake Hertel, born from the melting of glaciers, nestles on its sugar-loaf peak. The massif is inhabited by 45 species of mammals, including the roe deer, and 180 species of birds, such as the blue jay. In 1978 this mountain was declared a UNESCO Biosphere Reserve, and the MONT SAINT-HILAIRE NATURE CONSERVATION CENTER was set up as a resource for naturalists and all those who enjoy open-air activities.

APPLE GROWING
In 1620, Louis Hébert ▲ 269 planted the first apple trees in Nouvelle-France. Three hundred years later, the Sulpicians provided the Montreal area with its first apple orchard. Today, 90 percent of Quebec's apple production comes from Montérégie, and both Mont-Saint-Hilaire and Rougemont are famous for their orchards. In the former case, apples are the mainstay of its economy; it even boasts a museum dedicated to them!

Chambly

The main attractions of Chambly are its fort, pond, canal and rapids. The French built the Saint-Louis Fort in 1665 as protection against attacks by the Iroquois; it was subsequently rechristened the Chambly Fort in honor of Jacques Chambly, who was granted the land in 1672. The British occupied it after the Conquest of 1760 ● *39* and used it to fight against the Americans in the British-American War of 1812. The fort was restored in 1982 and now serves as a museum chronicling the town's history. A canal with nine locks was opened in 1843 to facilitate navigation.

SAINT STEPHEN'S CHURCH ● *115.* In the 19th century, Chambly received an influx of British and American Loyalists, and in 1820 Saint Stephen's Church was built for their benefit. Although its exterior resembles that of Catholic churches, its interior is distinguished by a sobriety typical of Protestant churches.

POTTERY
This industry, which thrives on the local glacial clay, emerged in Saint-Denis ▲ *205* in the early 19th century and has, since 1840, spread across the valley, particularly in Saint-Jean. The Stone Chinaware Company lent its collections to international exhibitions in Anvers (1885) and London (1886). Other companies have continued the tradition by specializing in earthenware tiles.

Saint-Jean-sur-Richelieu

VIEUX-SAINT-JEAN. This town has been a lively commercial center since the 17th century. Originally a staging post for fur traders, then for loggers, Saint-Jean was endowed with a shipyard around 1750. The construction, in 1836, of Canada's first railroad, linking Laprairie with Saint-Jean, gave a further boost to its activity. Four years later, the town had become a prime mover in local pottery: the HAUT-RICHELIEU REGIONAL MUSEUM tells the story of the region's pottery industry. There is also a military history museum, which dates back to 1666.

L'ACADIE. This village, close to Saint-Jean, was founded in 1768 by Acadians returning from 13 years of exile in the US. The historic village known as ONCE UPON A TIME THERE WAS A SMALL COLONY recounts their adventures ▲ *308*.

Saint-Paul-de-l'Île-aux-Noix

FORT LENNOX. The Île aux Noix has played an important role in Canada's military history. In 1759, the French started building a fort on the island but were unable to complete it before the Conquest the following year ● *39*. During the American War of Independence (1775–83), it was captured by Americans trying to invade Canada. In 1812, in the British-American War, the fort was taken over by the British, and in 1837 it was one of the places used to imprison the Patriots ▲ *206*, before it was deserted in 1870. Its museum provides a glimpse of military life in days gone by, while the park that has been created on the island is a good place to relax.

THE LACOLLE BLOCKHOUSE. Built in 1782, this building is the oldest of its kind in Quebec. It now houses a museum devoted to events that have marked the history of the Richelieu Valley.

South-west Montérégie

MELOCHEVILLE. Pointe-du-Buisson was inhabited by the Iroquois for centuries and objects reflecting their everyday life, such as arrows and harpoons, have been unearthed here. The ARCHEOLOGICAL PARK allows visitors to observe digs and explore the footpaths.

BEAUHARNOIS HYDROELECTRIC POWER STATION. This power station, built between 1929 and 1961, is one of the biggest in the world. It is situated on the Saint Lawrence and takes advantage of the powerful flow of its waters. A museum presents a permanent exhibition illustrating the electrification of the Montreal region ● *68*.

COTEAU-DU-LAC. This was the site of the first canal with locks in the Americas, built by the British in 1779. Upper Canada then used it to receive imports, and fortifications were added in 1812 to ensure its protection. The foundations are visible today, along with a reconstruction of a blockhouse, on the COTEAU-DU-LAC HISTORICAL SITE, which also presents thematic exhibitions.

▲ Estrie

⏱ 3 days

🚌 125 mi/300km

CANTONS DE L'EST OR ESTRIE?
In 1858, the writer Antoine Gérin-Lajoie coined the phrase *Cantons de l'Est* to give the region a French alternative to the Eastern Townships. Nearly a century later (1946), Monseigneur O'Brady came up with a new term – Estrie – and this went on to be recognized by the government. Now, through one of the quirks of Quebecois toponymy ● *62*, Estrie is approached by the freeway of the Cantons de l'Est.

GRANBY ZOO
The small town of Granby boasts one of Canada's most important zoos, with more than 1,000 animals from 200 different species (several of them in danger of extinction). Apart from its African mammals and exotic birds, the zoo has a large reptile house in which tortoises, iguanas and snakes are encouraged to move freely.

The region to the southeast of Montreal, between Montérégie ▲ *204* and the Appalachians, was first populated in the late 18th century, after the American Revolution (1775–82), as colonists left the US to settle in nearby Canada. Their allegiance to the British Crown earned them the epithet of Loyalists. They settled first in Ontario and then in Quebec, on land divided into 'townships'. They broke with the tradition of the *rangs* (narrow, rectangular fields) by creating plots that were almost square in shape ■ *19*. As Quebec lies to the east of Ontario, the territory occupied by these Loyalists became known as the Eastern Townships. Around 1850, logging and railroad construction attracted many French Canadians in search of work, giving the area a linguistic duality that is still in evidence today.

Granby

This town owes its name to John Manners (1721–70), the Marquess of Granby (in the English Midlands) and commander of the British forces in Canada. In 1776, he was granted vast tracts of land in this area by King George III. A relatively young town (1859), Granby is proud of its collection of European fountains. The most spectacular – in the middle of Lake Bolvin, not far from the town center – is fitted out with no fewer than seven jets of water. A stroll down rues Elgin, Dufferin and Mountain reveal magnificent Victorian residences, such as the BROWNIES CASTLE on Rue Elgin. This home was built by the English-speaking writer and native of Granby, Palmer Cox (1840–1924), who became famous for his fairy tales inspired by Scottish folklore.

Bromont

This new town (1964), equipped with a major industrial park, has prospered by taking advantage of its superb natural position. It stands near a mountain endowed with a ski resort, an aquatic park and bicycle trails. Bromont has also earned fame as an equestrian center: every June, it plays host to an important competition, the Bromont International, that features riders from both Europe and North America.

L'ACADIE. This village, close to Saint-Jean, was founded in 1768 by Acadians returning from 13 years of exile in the US. The historic village known as ONCE UPON A TIME THERE WAS A SMALL COLONY recounts their adventures ▲ 308.

Saint-Paul-de-l'Île-aux-Noix

FORT LENNOX. The Île aux Noix has played an important role in Canada's military history. In 1759, the French started building a fort on the island but were unable to complete it before the Conquest the following year ● 39. During the American War of Independence (1775–83), it was captured by Americans trying to invade Canada. In 1812, in the British-American War, the fort was taken over by the British, and in 1837 it was one of the places used to imprison the Patriots ▲ 206, before it was deserted in 1870. Its museum provides a glimpse of military life in days gone by, while the park that has been created on the island is a good place to relax.

THE LACOLLE BLOCKHOUSE. Built in 1782, this building is the oldest of its kind in Quebec. It now houses a museum devoted to events that have marked the history of the Richelieu Valley.

South-west Montérégie

MELOCHEVILLE. Pointe-du-Buisson was inhabited by the Iroquois for centuries and objects reflecting their everyday life, such as arrows and harpoons, have been unearthed here. The ARCHEOLOGICAL PARK allows visitors to observe digs and explore the footpaths.

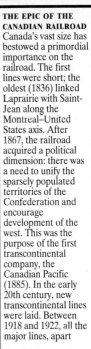

BEAUHARNOIS HYDROELECTRIC POWER STATION. This power station built between 1929 and 1961, is one of the biggest in the world. It is situated on the Saint Lawrence and takes advantage of the powerful flow of its waters. A museum presents a permanent exhibition illustrating the electrification of the Montreal region ● 68.

COTEAU-DU-LAC. This was the site of the first canal with locks in the Americas, built by the British in 1779. Upper Canada then used it to receive imports, and fortifications were added in 1812 to ensure its protection. The foundations are visible today, along with a reconstruction of a blockhouse, on the COTEAU-DU-LAC HISTORICAL SITE, which also presents thematic exhibitions.

THE EPIC OF THE CANADIAN RAILROAD
Canada's vast size has bestowed a primordial importance on the railroad. The first lines were short; the oldest (1836) linked Laprairie with Saint-Jean along the Montreal–United States axis. After 1867, the railroad acquired a political dimension: there was a need to unify the sparsely populated territories of the Confederation and encourage development of the west. This was the purpose of the first transcontinental company, the Canadian Pacific (1885). In the early 20th century, new transcontinental lines were laid. Between 1918 and 1922, all the major lines, apart from that of Canadian Pacific, were nationalized to form the Canadian National. The CANADIAN RAILROAD MUSEUM in Saint-Constant (to the south of Montreal) celebrates these endeavors.

🕐 3 days

🚌 125 mi/300km

CANTONS DE L'EST OR ESTRIE?
In 1858, the writer Antoine Gérin-Lajoie coined the phrase *Cantons de l'Est* to give the region a French alternative to the Eastern Townships. Nearly a century later (1946), Monseigneur O'Brady came up with a new term – Estrie – and this went on to be recognized by the government. Now, through one of the quirks of Quebecois toponymy ● 62, Estrie is approached by the freeway of the Cantons de l'Est.

GRANBY ZOO
The small town of Granby boasts one of Canada's most important zoos, with more than 1,000 animals from 200 different species (several of them in danger of extinction). Apart from its African mammals and exotic birds, the zoo has a large reptile house in which tortoises, iguanas and snakes are encouraged to move freely.

The region to the southeas
Montérégie ▲ 204 and th
populated in the late 18th cer
Revolution (1775–82), as colo
nearby Canada. Their allegian
earned them the epithet of L
Ontario and then in Quebec,
'townships'. They broke with t
(narrow, rectangular fields) b
almost square in shape ■ 19.
of Ontario, the territory occup
known as the Eastern Townshi
railroad construction attracted
search of work, giving the area
in evidence today.

Granby

This town owes its name to Joh
Marquess of Granby (in the En
commander of the British force
granted vast tracts of land in thi
relatively young town (1859), G
of European fountains. The mo
of Lake Bolvin, not far from the
with no fewer than seven jets of
Elgin, Dufferin and Mountain r
residences, such as the BROWNIE
home was built by the English-sp
Granby, Palmer Cox (1840–1924
fairy tales inspired by Scottish fo

Bromont

This new town (1964), equipped
has prospered by taking advantag
position. It stands near a mountai
an aquatic park and bicycle trails.
fame as an equestrian center: eve
important competition, the Brom
features riders from both Europe

L'ACADIE. This village, close to Saint-Jean, was founded in 1768 by Acadians returning from 13 years of exile in the US. The historic village known as ONCE UPON A TIME THERE WAS A SMALL COLONY recounts their adventures ▲ 308.

Saint-Paul-de-l'Île-aux-Noix

FORT LENNOX. The Île aux Noix has played an important role in Canada's military history. In 1759, the French started building a fort on the island but were unable to complete it before the Conquest the following year ● 39. During the American War of Independence (1775–83), it was captured by Americans trying to invade Canada. In 1812, in the British-American War, the fort was taken over by the British, and in 1837 it was one of the places used to imprison the Patriots ▲ 206, before it was deserted in 1870. Its museum provides a glimpse of military life in days gone by, while the park that has been created on the island is a good place to relax.

THE LACOLLE BLOCKHOUSE. Built in 1782, this building is the oldest of its kind in Quebec. It now houses a museum devoted to events that have marked the history of the Richelieu Valley.

South-west Montérégie

MELOCHEVILLE. Pointe-du-Buisson was inhabited by the Iroquois for centuries and objects reflecting their everyday life, such as arrows and harpoons, have been unearthed here. The ARCHEOLOGICAL PARK allows visitors to observe digs and explore the footpaths.

BEAUHARNOIS HYDROELECTRIC POWER STATION. This power station, built between 1929 and 1961, is one of the biggest in the world. It is situated on the Saint Lawrence and takes advantage of the powerful flow of its waters. A museum presents a permanent exhibition illustrating the electrification of the Montreal region ● 68.

COTEAU-DU-LAC. This was the site of the first canal with locks in the Americas, built by the British in 1779. Upper Canada then used it to receive imports, and fortifications were added in 1812 to ensure its protection. The foundations are visible today, along with a reconstruction of a blockhouse, on the COTEAU-DU-LAC HISTORICAL SITE, which also presents thematic exhibitions.

THE EPIC OF THE CANADIAN RAILROAD
Canada's vast size has bestowed a primordial importance on the railroad. The first lines were short; the oldest (1836) linked Laprairie with Saint-Jean along the Montreal–United States axis. After 1867, the railroad acquired a political dimension: there was a need to unify the sparsely populated territories of the Confederation and encourage development of the west. This was the purpose of the first transcontinental company, the Canadian Pacific (1885). In the early 20th century, new transcontinental lines were laid. Between 1918 and 1922, all the major lines, apart from that of Canadian Pacific, were nationalized to form the Canadian National. The CANADIAN RAILROAD MUSEUM in Saint-Constant (to the south of Montreal) celebrates these endeavors.

BEL ŒIL

| 🕐 | 3 days |
| 🚗 | 125 mi/300km |

CANTONS DE L'EST OR ESTRIE?
In 1858, the writer Antoine Gérin-Lajoie coined the phrase *Cantons de l'Est* to give the region a French alternative to the Eastern Townships. Nearly a century later (1946), Monseigneur O'Brady came up with a new term – Estrie – and this went on to be recognized by the government. Now, through one of the quirks of Quebecois toponymy ● *62*, Estrie is approached by the freeway of the Cantons de l'Est.

GRANBY ZOO
The small town of Granby boasts one of Canada's most important zoos, with more than 1,000 animals from 200 different species (several of them in danger of extinction). Apart from its African mammals and exotic birds, the zoo has a large reptile house in which tortoises, iguanas and snakes are encouraged to move freely.

The region to the southeast of Montreal, between Montérégie ▲ *204* and the Appalachians, was first populated in the late 18th century, after the American Revolution (1775–82), as colonists left the US to settle in nearby Canada. Their allegiance to the British Crown earned them the epithet of Loyalists. They settled first in Ontario and then in Quebec, on land divided into 'townships'. They broke with the tradition of the *rangs* (narrow, rectangular fields) by creating plots that were almost square in shape ■ *19*. As Quebec lies to the east of Ontario, the territory occupied by these Loyalists became known as the Eastern Townships. Around 1850, logging and railroad construction attracted many French Canadians in search of work, giving the area a linguistic duality that is still in evidence today.

Granby

This town owes its name to John Manners (1721–70), the Marquess of Granby (in the English Midlands) and commander of the British forces in Canada. In 1776, he was granted vast tracts of land in this area by King George III. A relatively young town (1859), Granby is proud of its collection of European fountains. The most spectacular – in the middle of Lake Bolvin, not far from the town center – is fitted out with no fewer than seven jets of water. A stroll down rues Elgin, Dufferin and Mountain reveal magnificent Victorian residences, such as the BROWNIES CASTLE on Rue Elgin. This home was built by the English-speaking writer and native of Granby, Palmer Cox (1840–1924), who became famous for his fairy tales inspired by Scottish folklore.

Bromont

This new town (1964), equipped with a major industrial park, has prospered by taking advantage of its superb natural position. It stands near a mountain endowed with a ski resort, an aquatic park and bicycle trails. Bromont has also earned fame as an equestrian center: every June, it plays host to an important competition, the Bromont International, that features riders from both Europe and North America.

Cowansville

This small textile town on the banks of the right branch of the River Yamaska is steeped in Loyalist tradition. It is distinguished by its splendid brick-and-wood Victorian houses. The Rue Principale contains a former branch of the Eastern Townships Bank, now converted into a community center. The town also possesses a small neo-Gothic Anglican church (1854).

From Lake Brome to Magog

LAC-BROME. This town is a collection of seven hamlets scattered around the lake; their names bear witness to the British influence on the region (Knowlton, Foster, Bondville, and so forth). Most of Estrie's English-speakers are concentrated between Lake Brome and Lake Massawippi, situated further south, by the American border. The architecture in

Lac-Brome is characterized by a range of Victorian and neo-Gothic houses, as well as buildings following the American vernacular model ● *118*. The small village of KNOWLTON boasts not only stores, art galleries and fine inns but also the BROME COUNTY HISTORICAL MUSEUM, set in buildings dating back to the 19th century.

BONSECOURS. In 1989, a mining company bought a deposit of high-quality quartz crystals close to the village of Bonsecours. It is one of the few places in the world where such crystals are found in sufficient abundance to make their extraction feasible. The mine is operated by the Mines Cristal Kebec Company. It offers guided tours that explain the site's

BROME COUNTY HISTORICAL MUSEUM
This museum is run by a regional history society created over a century ago (1897). One of the buildings houses a military museum, opened in 1921 by the Canadian Prime Minister, Sir Robert Borden. The collection includes a Fokker D VII (*left*) that dates back to World War 1. The museum also contains recreations of a 19th-century law court and general store.

THE WINE TRAIL
In 1979, the Estrie region went into the wine and cider trade, particularly in Dunham, to the south of Granby. Despite its severe winters, Quebec produces around 220,000 bottles of wine every year, over half of which comes from Estrie.

211

geology and history, the extraction techniques and the technological and industrial applications of quartz.

VALCOURT. This town proclaims itself as the world capital of snow-biking. It was here that Joseph-Armand Bombardier (1907–64) designed and built his first 'skidoos'. He obtained a manufacturing permit in 1937 and went on to build an enormous industrial complex. Today, Bombardier is a multinational company that produces not only snow bikes but also airplanes, trains (both engines and cars) and a variety of mechanical parts. A museum presents displays about the company's founder, his first workshop and the history of snow-biking.

BOMBARDIER'S FIRST TRIAL
In 1922, at the age of 15, Joseph-Armand Bombardier made his first motor vehicle (*above*) to allow him to travel in the snow. This prototype was propelled by a helix and a four-cylinder motor engine taken from an old Model T Ford that his father had given him as a present. When the latter saw the result, he ordered his son to destroy the contraption as he considered it highly dangerous.

Magog-Orford

The Magog-Orford ski resort is rightly considered the hub of Estrie's tourist industry. It benefits from its unbeatable location, tucked between Mont Orford and Lake Memphremagog.

MAGOG. This town has developed on the basis of its textile and tourist industries. It is set on the banks of Lake Memphremagog (a Native-American word meaning 'large expanse of water'), which stretches majestically for 26 miles (42km), right into the American state of Vermont. Legend has it that it is inhabited by Memphre, a close cousin of the Loch Ness monster and just as elusive. The lake provides the setting for several summertime activities and boat trips are organized to reveal its natural splendors and explain its history and folklore. Magog also provides the finishing line for the INTERNATIONAL SWIMMING MARATHON across the lake, which attracts swimmers from various countries with a tradition of long-distance swimming. This race is the focal point for a number of cultural and sporting events, which culminate in a painting symposium in August. When winter comes, Magog is popular with skiers from Montreal and the US who flock to the slopes and trails of this region.

LAKE MEMPHREMAGOG
The lake, surrounded by mountains and spectacular scenery, is one of the region's major tourist attractions.

MONT ORFORD PARK. This provincial park, dominated by Mont Orford (2,875 feet/876m), is one of the area's most alluring spots for tourists. It plays host to several sporting activities, including skiing (both downhill and cross-country), hiking and mountain biking.

The park also contains ORFORD ARTS CENTER, an institution founded in 1951 that every year invites young musicians to revel in the beautiful setting and take master classes from the renowned performers that participate in the ORFORD FESTIVAL. This festival puts on some 30 classical music concerts. In mid-September, Mont Orford becomes the stage for yet another festival, appropriately titled The Explosion of Colors. Taking advantage of the breathtaking backdrop provided by the foliage at this time of year, a series of activities are organized (including a symposium of the visual arts and exhibitions of regional produce).

SAINT-BENOÎT-DU-LAC ABBEY ★. Lake Memphremagog is surrounded by stunning landscapes and second homes that range from humble chalets to sumptuous villas. Saint-Benoît-du-Lac Abbey ● *125* rises up like a beacon on the lake's west bank. In 1913, the Benedictine monks of Saint Wandrille Abbey left their native Normandy to settle on this site and prepare the ground for the construction of a monastery. The abbey was finally built between 1939 and 1958 in accordance with plans drawn up by a French monk, Dom Paul Bellot (1876–1944), who was also responsible for the dome of Saint Joseph's Oratory in Montreal ▲ *186* and Solesme Abbey in Sarthes, near Paris. More recently, guest quarters and a magnificent bell tower have been added. Mass is said every day to the accompaniment of Gregorian chants. The monks grow fruit and make cheese, and their produce is on sale in situ. This monastic complex exudes harmony and serenity.

Before being named
Governor-in-Chief of
British North
America (1816),
Sir John Coape
Sherbrooke had had a
distinguished career
in the British army.
During the war
between the US and
Great Britain
(1812–14), the troops
under his command
captured Castine
(Maine), enabling the
British to control a

large part of this
State throughout
most of the conflict.

NORTH HATLEY ★.
The village of North
Hatley is an ideal
spot for a relaxing
break. It is situated at
the northern tip of
Lake Massawippi,
amidst lush natural
scenery. In the second
half of the 19th
century, the site
attracted rich summer
visitors who built
themselves magnificent
houses. These days, the
village offers tourists
several self-catering
cottages and small art
shops. It also organizes an annual international competition
of native art; the prizewinners' work is exhibited in October
and November.

Sherbrooke

THE BIRTH OF A TOWN. A fur trading post ● *48* was
established at the confluence of the Saint Lawrence and
Magog rivers under French rule, on a spot now known as
Grandes Fourches ('Great Forks'). Around 1795, Gilbert
Hyatt, an exiled American whose assets had been seized by
his government, took advantage of the current of the
Saint-François River to set up a mill in the settlement,
which at that time hosted only three families. The hamlet
acquired the name of Hyatt's Mill, in homage to Gilbert
and his brothers, who were granted several plots of land
by the government. Other Loyalist families followed Hyatt
to his retreat and the little village soon boasted about ten
sawmills and a population of traders, craftsmen and farmers.
Around 1817, the villagers decided to rechristen their
village in honor of Sir John Coape Sherbrooke,
the Governor-in-Chief of the British colonies in
North America. In the second half of the 20th
century, Sherbrooke began to attract French-
speakers and became industrialized. Since then,
it has consistently grown in importance and is now
endowed with a university, modern hospitals,
thriving businesses and a host of summer music
festivals ◆ *351*. Sherbrooke is now recognized as
the regional capital and often called the 'Queen of the
Eastern Townships', but its expansion has not prevented it
from preserving several precious souvenirs of its past. Its
Vieux-Nord (Old North) neighborhood has retained many
houses from the 19th century, in styles ranging from
American vernacular and Second Empire to Queen Anne
and neo-Gothic ● *118*.
SHERBROOKE SEMINARY MUSEUM. This museum, in a
redbrick building dating from 1898, is divided into two distinct
galleries. The main gallery is devoted to the natural sciences
(with stuffed animals, plants and minerals); the other displays
furniture, Native-American objects and works of art,

**CRAFTIER
THAN THE DEVIL**
The Estrie region is
dotted with round
farmhouses. Peasants
built them in this
shape because,
according to an old
superstition, it
afforded them
protection against
the Devil, who was
supposedly in the
habit of hiding in
corners!

including several
engravings by Rodolphe
Duguay (1891–1973)
and watercolors by
William Henry Bartlett
(1809–54).

**PLYMOUTH-TRINITY
UNITED CHURCH.**
This church, set on
a promontory close
to the river, reflects
the influence of the
colonial architecture
of New England.
Neoclassical in style,
it was built in 1855 for
the benefit of the Congregationalists in the region.
It is adorned with stained-glass windows celebrating the
memory of local figures who played an important role
in the development
of the community.

ART MUSEUM.
This
museum,
which
occupies a
building
formerly
used as the
law faculty of
Sherbrooke
University, offers an
interesting collection of Quebecois art,
including paintings by Marc-Aurèle de Foy
Suzor-Coté ● *139* and Robert Whale (1805–87).
Native art is well represented, with particularly
outstanding paintings by Arthur Villeneuve
▲ *323*.

LENNOXVILLE. This small town with Loyalist
origins a few miles to the south of Sherbrooke is
the site of a long-established Anglophone
institution: Bishop University (*above*). It
occupies an imposing building erected in 1843,
following the model of a college at Oxford
University in Great Britain. Similarly, the
plans for SAINT MARK'S CHAPEL – which was
incorporated into the university in 1853 – were
drawn up in England. Its Gothic structure is
embellished with wooden statues and stained-
glass windows. Parts of the campus and chapel
were destroyed by a fire in 1891, but
restoration work has allowed the buildings to
recover their original appearance. The
UPLANDS MUSEUM is set in a beautiful
Palladian mansion ● *118,* built in 1862.
It regularly hosts thematic exhibitions
focusing on the history of the region.
It also contains an art gallery that
promotes artists from Estrie.

A COLLEGE CHAPEL
The history of Saint
Mark's Chapel is
closely linked to that
of Bishop University.
The whole complex is
based on the
Anglican church
colleges. In keeping
with the collegial
tradition, the chapel's
pews (1891) do not
face the altar but are
arranged opposite
each other, in tiers,
on either side of a
central aisle. Another
striking feature is the
set of eight kneeling
angels with folded
wings.

▲ Laurentides and Lanaudière

The exact boundaries of the Laurentides are a matter for debate. According to history books, a territory of this name first emerged to the northwest of the islands of Montreal and Laval; geographers insist, however, that the name designates the mountainous massif that extends across all the Quebecois part of the Canadian Bouclier. This area, bounded to the south by the Mille-Îles and Ottawa rivers and to the north by the Lièvre Valley, is divided into two distinct sections: the Lower Laurentides ▲ *222* and the Laurentides themselves, 'an immense maze of hills and valleys' (according to Raoul Blanchard, 1947), covered with forests. Today, the region is famous for its natural scenery and resorts.

THE COLONIZATION OF THE HIGHLANDS: A UTOPIA?
In the late 19th century, missionary colonizers, in their efforts to attract families to the Laurentides, enthusiastically depicted the area as 'the true California for our young Canadians'. Nevertheless, even now barely three percent of the land is cultivated or devoted to pasture.

The first settlers

Several thousand years ago, nomadic populations of hunter-gatherers were already roaming the Laurentides. Over the course of the centuries, they developed certain skills, as can be seen from the pottery and wall paintings discovered on the territory of the Petite-Nation Algonquins. In the early 17th century, Samuel de Champlain ▲ *254* came into contact with the Weskarinis, whose hunting territory straddled the Laurentides and the Ottawa area. This ethnic group was annihilated after repeated attacks by the Iroquois between 1650 and 1653. The Lower Laurentides began to be occupied in the mid-19th century by seigneuries established by the overflow of colonists from the Saint Lawrence Valley. In 1870, a colonization movement set on conquering 'the North' emerged, coupled with an energetic campaign to prevent the emigration of French Canadians to the Protestant, Anglophone US. This was led by the famous Father Labelle (statue, *left*), who, from 1888 to 1890, combined his priestly duties with a post as junior minister for colonization.

Saint-Jérôme

The village of Saint-Jérôme, now considered the cradle of the Laurentides, was born in 1834 with the official creation of the parish of Saint-Jérôme-de-la-Rivière-du-Nord. It was here that the movement to colonize the lands of 'the North' began to take shape in 1870, headed by the young parish priest, Antoine Labelle. Twelve years later, the establishment of the Rolland paper company on the banks of the River Nord took the region into the industrial era. The town expanded quickly and earned its place as the capital of the Laurentides on the administrative, political and religious levels.

AROUND THE CATHEDRAL. The center of Saint-Jérôme is endowed with an imposing church with neo-Byzantine touches ● *121*. It opened in 1900 and was declared a cathedral in 1951. It looks out on a bronze statue by Alfred Laliberté (1878–1953), erected in honor of Father Labelle, the 'King of the North'. Also prominent is the former law court, a three-storey Beaux-Arts building ● *125* erected between 1922 and 1924. Since 1978, it has housed the VIEUX-PALAIS EXHIBITION CENTER, which has played an important role in promoting local culture. It specializes in contemporary art shows.

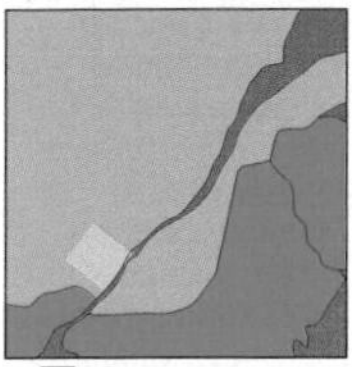

The Highlands

For many years, the term 'Highlands' was used to describe the vast territories in western Canada where trappers ● *48* went in quest of furs. Under the influence of Claude-Henri Grignon, the author of *Tales of the Highlands*, a soap opera that was highly popular in the 1960s and 1970s, its name has gradually come to mean the

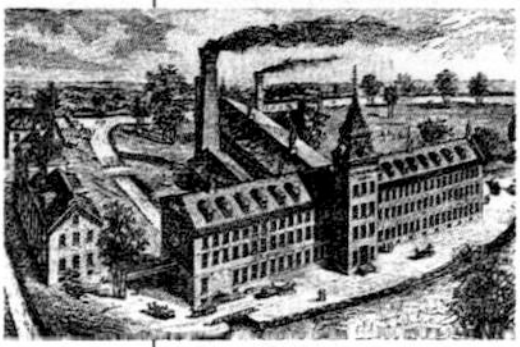

A THRIVING BUSINESS
In 1882, Jean-Baptiste Rolland (1815–88) answered the call of Father Labelle and set up a paper mill in Saint-Jérôme. The borough gave him a $10,000 subsidy and exemption from taxes for 25 years. After some initial difficulties, the firm started to prosper and went on to forge an international reputation.

A MAN AND HIS SIN
Jean-Pierre Masson (*above*) played a miserly mayor in *Tales of the Highlands*.

Laurentides, the setting for the series. After the failure of the colonization movement, the Highlands have taken on a new lease of life as a tourist attraction.

WINTER SPORTS. Way back in 1930, the little village of SHAWBRIDGE boasted the first mechanical ski-tow in the whole of North America. Subsequently, a number of downhill-skiing resorts sprang up, making it possible to develop an efficient infrastructure. The region is now well equipped with hotels, summer theaters, art galleries, specialist stores and renowned restaurants.

TOURIST RESORTS. SAINT SAUVEUR contains an interesting SKIING MUSEUM, while SAINT-ADÈLE is chiefly known for the 'Village of the Seraphim', a reconstruction

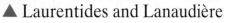

WINTER CHALETS
The Saint-Jovite region welcomed its first tourists between 1890 and 1920. Members of the French-Canadian lower middle classes came here to build round wooden 'camps', chalets that are very different from today's models.

of buildings typical of the colonization period. SAINTE-AGATHE-DES-MONTS is also popular with visitors, partly for its setting by the Lac des Sables, a lake bordered by a string of opulent houses that bear witness to the area's appeal to rich Montreal families in the early 20th century. The Highlands have many more delightful small villages to offer, including SAINT-FAUSTIN, SAINTE-MARGUERITE ● *124*, VAL-DAVID and MORIN HEIGHTS.

Mont-Tremblant Region

SAINT-JOVITE. This region was particularly close to the heart of Father Labelle. The village of Saint-Jovite (1875), once the nerve center of the logging industry, has gradually turned into a tourist resort, while preserving its traditional character. It is overshadowed by Mont Tremblant (3,068 feet/935m), slightly to the north.
MONT-TREMBLANT PARK ★. In 1894 this former forestry reserve became the first park created by the Quebec government. Originally called the park of the 'Montagne Tremblante' ('trembling mountain'), it is extremely popular with nature lovers, due to its abundant lakes and rivers. It is possible to practice a variety of sports, depending on the time of the year: skiing, snowshoeing, snow-biking, canoeing, sailing, cycling, and others.

RAFTING
From April to October, specialist companies organize trips in inflatable dinghies down the River Rouge.

The Rouge Valley

The development of this area was sparked by agriculture and logging. Today, however, the local economy revolves around a handful of small businesses, a few public institutions and nature tourism, particularly hunting and fishing. The local place names ● *62* indicate the Catholic clergy's role in the colonization of the region as well as the Native-American presence, with villages such as La Conception, L'Annonciation, L'Ascension, Sainte-Véronique and La Macaza (the name of a Native American who established a settlement on this site) and Lakes Saguay (from *sagwa*, meaning 'to run into' in Algonquin) and Nominingue. The name of the Lanaudière region has its roots in history. It perpetuates the memory of Charlotte de Lanaudière, who was the daughter of the Lavaltrie

seigneur and the wife of the businessman Barthélemy Joliette, the descendant of a famous explorer ▲ 258 and founder of the regional capital (Joliette). Lanaudière is often referred to as the 'Green Region', meant in both the literal and the metaphorical sense. Every possible shade of green seems to be on display here in the natural surroundings, but it is also a young region, developed only relatively recently, that serves as a microcosm of Quebec itself, with all its varied landscapes, activities, lifestyles and aspirations. Lanaudière is divided into three main areas, running north to south: the Heights, the Piedmont and the Plain.

The Heights

Nature remains largely unspoilt in this part of Lanaudière, which has drawn on its lakes, rivers and wide, open spaces to develop recreational activities and attract tourists. After the ski resort of Saint-Côme, the road descends unexpectedly to Sainte-Émélie-de-l'Énergie, a village nestling in the hollow of a valley. (The 'energy' in question is that of the first settlers, who arrived in 1854.) Heading back north, the road winds along the banks of the River Noire in a steep-sided valley gouged out by glaciers, before returning to higher ground.

SAINT-ZÉNON. This hamlet, created in 1866 by Théophile-Stanislas Provost, proclaims itself as the highest in all Quebec (2,300 feet/700m). This former lumber station is set among lush hills with stunning views of the surroundings, particularly the Vallée des Nymphes (Valley of the Nymphs). The area is unbeatable for its views and is also extremely popular with trout fishermen ● 86.

THE PARC DES SEPT-CHUTES. This nature park is endowed with exceptional scenery; its abundance of wildlife and spectacular views of lakes and dense forest make it ideal hiking country, although you should make sure you have good maps and proper equipment. The rocks here are among the oldest in the world.

THE MATAWINIAN DREAM
In the early 1860s, a young priest from this region, Théophile-Stanislas Provost, became concerned about the exodus of Quebecois seeking work in American factories and proposed the colonization of the land to the north of Montreal. He saw this territory as a 'Promised Land' and its colonization as divinely ordained. Father Provost was the first leader and advocate of northern development, slightly predating the more famous Father Labelle ▲ 216.

SAINT-DONAT
The village of Saint-Donat, in the southern part of Mont-Tremblant Park, is tucked beside Lake Archambault amidst spectacular wooded mountains.

▲ Laurentides and Lanaudière

SAINT-MICHEL-DES-SAINTS. This village owes its creation (1863) to another priest, Father Brassard, under the inspiration of Father Provost. It lies close to LAKE TAUREAU, a huge artificial reservoir (nearly 440 miles/700km in circumference) that serves to regulate the flow of water from the Saint-Maurice River ▲ 240. Further north, the village of Manawan is inhabited by Atikameks, a hospitable Native-American community. It is possible to explore this bracing region of lakes and forests by canoe, by snow bike or in a sled drawn by dogs.

Piedmont

The hills and villages of Piedmont offer a stimulating mix of nature and culture. This part of Lanaudière is particularly abundant in maple trees, which turn scarlet and gold when the fall arrives.

BETWEEN SAINT-GABRIEL-DE-BRANDON AND RAWDON. The village of SAINT-GABRIEL-DE-BRANDON, set on the edge of Lake Maskinonge, was once the most popular tourist destination between Montreal and Trois-Rivières. Today, the excitement of those heady days has long evaporated, but the village has managed to preserve much of its charm. SAINT-JEAN-DE-MATHA is considered one of the crowning glories of Canadian cross-country skiing, because of the facilities on the Coupée Mountain and its 50 miles (85km) of ski trails. The village also contains a museum devoted to the strongman Louis Cyr. In this area, numerous gaps in the slopes sweeping down to the plain allow water to rush through, creating stunning sites, such as the MONTE-À-PEINE (*opposite, bottom right*), the DALLES GORGES and the DORWIN FALLS.

ECOLES DE RANG
For many years, these rural schools (*below*) enabled children from isolated regions to

attend primary school without having to leave their parish or travel long distances.

RAWDON. This settlement grew up in the 1810s when Irish immigrants put down roots here. They were followed by Scots, Acadians and Eastern Europeans, making it one of the most cosmopolitan towns in all Quebec. Rawdon has opened a museum that recounts the history of its various communities, while the CANADIANA VILLAGE presents a reconstruction of a 19th-century village, with over 50 buildings transported from different parts of Canada. Its treasures include an *école de rang* (country school) dating from 1835 (*left*), a general store (1888), an inn (1843) and other rural houses.

The Plain

Below: Lake Taureau

This area by the banks of the Saint Lawrence was one of the first to be colonized by the French and its fertile plains allowed agriculture to thrive. The landscape between Joliette and Lanoraie, particularly around Saint-Thomas, is characterized by its tobacco fields set out in checkerboard formation.

JOLIETTE. The capital of Lanaudière is endowed with superb houses dating from the late 19th century, as well as a museum renowned for its collection of sacred art. The town's motto, 'Joliette, land of music', reflects both its traditions and its International Festival of Lanaudière.

THE ARROW SASH
The manufacturing of arrow sashes ● 75 originated in the early 19th century in the area around L'Assomption, to the south of Joliette, and French-Canadian trappers ● 48 turned them into a highly fashionable accessory that set them apart from their Scottish rivals.

BERTHIERVILLE. This town, set on the land of the Autray estate (1672), looks out on the Berthier Islets, as remarkable in their way as the Bayous of Louisiana. Their extraordinary natural heritage constitutes a veritable aquatic paradise, with a maze of waterways looked down on by thousands of birds. Berthierville is also the hometown of Gilles Villeneuve, one of the first Quebecois to excel in the world of motor-racing. A museum celebrates the memory of this former member of the Ferrari team, who was killed in 1982 during a qualifying heat for the Belgian Grand Prix. Cuthbert Chapel, named after General Wolfe's aide-de-camp ▲ 252, was the first Protestant church in Quebec (1786), but for over 20 years it has been used as a cultural center.

THE *CHASSE-GALERIE*
Lumberjacks used to celebrate the New Year in a flying canoe, having first made a pact with the Devil. This legend, passed down orally and popularized by Honoré Beaugrand, a Lanoraie writer, exemplifies the wanderlust of the Quebecois.

TERREBONNE. This town on the north bank of the Mille-Îles River attracted settlers in the early 18th century because of its location and its fertile soil (its name means literally 'good land'). The 'old' quarter is packed with beautiful stone and wood buildings, such as the Masson Manor (1850). The Île des Moulins ● 66 similarly offers a collection of impressive 19th-century industrial buildings.

The Ottawa River, which has its source in the Great Lakes of Ontario, is named after a Native-American tribe. It was the main route for the fur trade, and also went on to play a key role in the logging industry. The Ottawa Valley was not colonized until the 19th century;

☑ 2 days

🚗 155 mi/250km

A GIANT WITH A HEART OF GOLD
Joseph Favre, or Jos Montferrand, was born in Montreal in 1802. After distinguishing himself as an amateur boxer in the city's taverns, he set off for the Ottawa River in 1823, to try his hand at tree felling ● 76. His subsequent career as a lumberjack, timber driver and raftsman soon made him a legendary character in Quebec, because of his kindness, charisma, agility and immense strength.

the first settlers were English, Irish and Scottish, as reflected in the abundance of British place names: Buckingham, Templeton, Wakefield, Ripon, Masham, Aldfield, Hull, and many more. Accordingly, Ottawa was divided along the lines of the British townships system, apart from the Petite-Nation seigneury, which was bestowed on Monseigneur de Laval in 1674 and later bought by the Papineau family.

THE BLAINVILLE SEIGNEURY
The second half of the 18th century witnessed a population boom on the north bank of the Mille-Îles River ▲216. Sainte-Thérèse, which was home to the seigneur of Blainville, stood out as the intellectual, religious and cultural center of the Lower Laurentides for 150 years, largely through the influence of its Catholic high school.

Saint-Eustache

After years of winning acclaim for its farm produce, this village was rapidly urbanized in the second half of the 20th century and now forms one of Montreal's residential suburbs.

SAINT-EUSTACHE CHURCH. The Palladian façade ● 114 still bears traces of the cannonballs fired by the British army during the battle against the Patriots of the North ▲ 206 on December 14, 1837.

GLOBENSKY MANOR. This house was built in 1862 by the family of the same name after it inherited the Saint-Eustache seigneury. Maximilien Globensky and his sister Hortense had taken sides against the Patriots ▲ 206 in 1837. Later on, Louis-Joseph Papineau became a close friend of the young Marie-Louise Globensky. The manor house now serves as the town hall and cultural center.

> 'Let us be carried away to the banks of the fiery Ottawa,
> in the strangleholds of its rugged rocks,
> its heavy waves twisting in frenzied torrents.'

Louis Fréchette

LÉGARÉ MILL. This mill, built in 1762, is of exceptional historic interest because it has never gone out of operation. It is still possible to buy its sacks of wheat and buckwheat flour.

Oka

Oka means 'golden fish' in Algonquin. The village fell under the Deux-Montagnes seigneury, given to the Sulpicians by the King of France in 1717 to set up a mission there. In around 1740, the priests built a CALVARY ● *122*, made up of seven chapels with walls decorated with copies of French paintings. Only three of these chapels are standing today, in what is now the Oka municipal park. In 1945, some of Oka's territory was restored to the Native Americans, who had occupied it since the 18th century. The Iroquois have rechristened the village Kanesatake ('below the coast').

THE CISTERCIAN ABBEY. Oka's first Trappist monks arrived in 1881 and they completed their first monastery in 1890. They are still there today, and continue to produce the Oka cheese that follows the recipe of French Port-Salut and has become famous throughout North America. The monks also opened an agriculture school in 1908, but this closed in 1962.

SAINTE-SCHOLASTIQUE. Not far to the north of Oka, this village takes in the land and seigneurial Sulpician manor house of Belle-Rivière, along with a small Protestant church built by former Catholics who had apostatized their faith after Montreal's diocesan authorities refused to grant a religious burial to the Patriots of 1837.

CARILLON. It was in Carillon, formerly known as Long-Sault, that Adam Dollard des Ormeaux died in 1660 at the hands of the Iroquois. Like Grenville, further to the west, Carillon is flanked by dangerous rapids on the River Ottawa, so it was decided, in 1834, to build canals to link Ottawa with Montreal. An old barracks building now serves as the unmissable ARGENTEUIL MUSEUM, replete with military mementos, furniture, period costumes, Native-American art and vintage photographs.

DOLLARD DES ORMEAUX (1635–60) In 1660, Nouvelle-France was at war with the British, who had joined forces with the Iroquois. The soldier Adam Dollard des Ormeaux and his men prepared to ambush the Long-Sault Iroquois with the help of the Hurons and the Algonquins. Their plan failed, they were taken by surprise, and subjected to a siege of several days, during which an accidental explosion killed several men. The nine survivors were captured by the Iroquois, who tortured them before killing and eating them. Legend says that Dollard was sacrificed to prevent a more substantial attack against Montreal, securing his status as national hero.

One of the pavilions of
Château Montebello

LOUIS-JOSEPH PAPINEAU (1786–1871)

This Montreal-born lawyer and politician was elected to the Legislative Assembly in 1809 as a representative of the Canadian Party (Patriots). His moderate views became more radical in the 1830s; his attacks against the unelected Legislative Council became more strident and he advocated Lower Canada's independence. In 1837, the population rose up after Britain refused to give in to his demands. Papineau became a fugitive and went into exile in the US and then France. Granted an amnesty in 1845, he returned and settled in Montebello, where he died in 1871, having made another brief foray into politics in 1854.

Montebello

The Petite-Nation seigneury was granted by the French regime in the 17th century, before the arrival of the British, and it is the only place in the region with a French feel. It was bought by the Papineau family in 1801.

LOUIS-JOSEPH-PAPINEAU MANOR. This severe-looking house on Cape Bonsecours was built by the leader of the 1837–8 Rebellions ▲ 206 on his return from exile in the fall of 1845. Its tower contains the great Patriot's library. Less than half a mile away, a small funeral chapel made of rough stones shelters the mortal remains of members of the Papineau family. The estate now belongs to the Canadian Pacific railroad company, which put up the CHÂTEAU MONTEBELLO, a large hotel built with logs between 1930 and 1933, in the midst of the Great Depression. It was used by the Seigneury Club, a private sports club whose members came from the Canadian English and American middle classes.

THE RESCUE OF LADY ABERDEEN

In the spring of 1896, the carriage of the wife of Lord Aberdeen, the Governor General of Canada, fell into the icy waters of the River Ottawa. The men of Pointe-Gatineau went to her rescue and managed to save her. As a token of her gratitude, she gave the parish of Saint-François-de-Sales an engraved clock (which can still be seen today).

Around Hull

PLAISANCE. The construction of watermills ● 66 and the ready access to waterfalls brought prosperity to this village in the 19th century. The site of the North National Mills has been excavated to reveal the secrets of the village's industrial past; the findings are on display in the CENTRE D'INTERPRÉTATION DU PATRIMONIE (Heritage Museum) in the old presbytery. The Plaisance Nature Reserve offers trails for cyclists and hikers to investigate the fauna of the swamplands. In late April and early May, wild geese gather here before setting off on their long journey northward.

GATINEAU. This town, on the confluence of the Ottawa and Gatineau rivers, was founded by Canadian International Paper, which established a pulp mill here in 1926. The 'modern-style' architecture of the houses built near the mill to house the firm's administrative staff illustrates the American influence characteristic of domestic architecture in Ottawa's border areas. The view from the CHURCH OF SAINT-FRANÇOIS-DE-SALES by the Quai des Artistes takes in the federal capital, Ottawa, on the opposite side of the river. Its neo-Gothic style ▲ 118 is enhanced by stained-glass windows dating from 1902 and gold-leaf wood trim in the interior (1886).

Ottawa and Hull

Ottawa, *227*
Hull, *228*
The Vérendrye Wildlife Reserve, *230*
Abitibi, *230*
Témiscamingue, *231*
The caribou or *tuktu*, *232*
Highway 109, *234*
Radisson, *234*

Often called 'the National Capital Region', the two cities of Hull and Ottawa share a common destiny, despite the Quebec-Ontario border that divides them in the symbolic form of the Ottawa River. Altogether, the Hull-Ottawa region has a population of around one million, making it the fourth largest urban spread in Canada.

History

The first permanent settlements around the Chaudières Falls date from the early 19th century. Both Hull, created in 1800 by American Loyalists led by Philemon Wright, and Bytown (Ottawa), founded in 1827 by Lieutenant-Colonel By, became important centers for the lumber industry. Once the first log raft had been dispatched to Quebec in 1807, the area followed the rhythm of the lumber camps: every winter men were hired to cut down the big red and white Ottawa pines. This is the land of the raftsmen ● *76*, fired up by 'shiners' – legendary brawls between French-Canadian and Irish timber drivers renowned for their brutality. When Bytown became the capital of the new United Canada in 1858 (in accordance with the wishes of Queen Victoria), it took on a new appearance when the Parliament buildings were put up on the promontory of Barrack Hill.

1. RIDEAU CANAL
2. CANADIAN PARLIAMENT
3. NOTRE DAME CATHEDRAL-BASILICA
4. NATIONAL GALLERY OF CANADA
5. CANADIAN MUSEUM OF CIVILIZATIONS

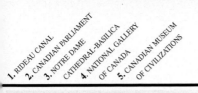

'This almost Arctic village of lumberjacks transformed by royal decree into a political arena,' in the words of Professor Goldwin Smith from Toronto, has become a peaceful, picturesque city.

Ottawa

The capital of Canada is dotted with parks and numerous museums. The Parliament and the civil service activity mark the pace of the city, as well as the activity of the area around the Rideau Canal.

RIDEAU CANAL ★. This canal, built in 1826 for military use, crosses Ottawa and links Lake Ontario with the Ottawa River via 125 miles (200km) of waterways that are now reserved for the use of pleasure boats. In winter, a stretch of around 4 miles (7km) is made available to ice-skaters.

PARLIAMENT HILL ★. The three buildings of neo-Gothic inspiration that comprise the CANADIAN PARLIAMENT sit on a cliff towering almost 165 feet (50m) above the Ottawa River. The original buildings, made of local sandstone, were finished in 1876 but burned down in 1916. Only the library, a polygonal architectural treasure, resisted the fire. The present buildings (1917) are more austere.

DOWNTOWN. The old working-class neighborhood by the right bank of the Rideau Canal still has the character of a lively shopping area from a hundred years ago. The stalls of BYWARD MARKET display flowers, fruit and vegetables, just as they have done since 1840. THE NOTRE DAME CATHEDRAL-BASILICA (1846) is adorned with mahogany wood trim.

AN ENTHUSIASTIC VISITOR
The British novelist Anthony Trollope (1815–82) visited the Ottawa Parliament in 1862, when it was yet to be completed. He was sufficiently impressed, however, to declare: 'I have no hesitation ... in giving my warmest commendation to [the architects] as regards beauty of outline and truthful nobility of detail ... I know of no modern Gothic purer of its kind, or less sullied with fictitious ornamentation.'

PARLIAMENT CLOCK TOWER
The chiming clock, based on 17th-century Dutch models, is one of the oldest in North America.

227

Below: the Rideau
Canal in summer

BAL DE NEIGE ON THE RIDEAU CANAL
This annual festival takes place in a fairytale setting of ice sculptures, snow and hoar frost, with a host of activities to distract from the biting cold. A local delicacy is also on offer: beaver's tail, an extremely sweet pastry, somewhere between a pancake and a waffle, dusted with brown sugar and cinnamon.

RUE SUSSEX. The historic quarter stretches along the Sussex Promenade from the Parliament to RIDEAU HALL, the residence of the Governor General of Canada. To the east of the street lies an urban landscape barely touched since the 19th century; to the west, there is a stunning panoramic view of the Ottawa River and Hull. To the north, the promenade comes to an end at the NATIONAL GALLERY OF CANADA, a spacious glass building designed by the Montreal architect Moshe Safdie, which opened in 1988. It contains an unrivalled collection of Canadian art, including works by the Group of Seven ● *139*, and Emily Carr, as well as a display of Inuit art ▲ *342*. The promenade also passes the charming RIDEAU FALLS and the official residence of the Canadian Prime Minister.

MUSEUMS. Ottawa's status as a capital city has made it a depository for a number of museum collections. Dinosaurs and animal specimens are on show in the CANADIAN MUSEUM OF NATURE, while the NATIONAL MUSEUM OF SCIENCE AND TECHNOLOGY boasts the largest refractive telescope in the whole country.

Hull

For years, Hull was a working-class suburb of Ottawa and it has preserved some striking relics of its industrial past. On the riverside, the Eddy pulp mill (1890) ● *77* and the small gabled houses, with narrow façades hiding long, thin apartments,

evoke the working-class neighborhood of yesteryear. In the 19th century, another smaller river, the Ruisseau de la Brasserie, was once flanked by craftsmen's workshops, but now only the THÉÂTRE DE L'ÎLE has survived as a relic of those times. The city center, however, has been totally transformed by the state-of-the-art MAISON DU CITOYEN and the skyscrapers on PLACE DU CENTRE; only the little cafés on Place Aubry and the main street recall days gone by.

OTTAWA'S GREEN BELT
The Rideau Canal and the Ottawa River are both bounded by an array of gardens. The Promenade Rockcliffe crosses the park of the same name and provides splendid views of the river. The Promenades Reine-Élisabeth and Colonel-By along the Rideau Canal border on parks that burst into color during the tulip season: Queen Juliana of Holland, who took refuge in Canada during World War 2, donated thousands of bulbs every year.

CANADIAN MUSEUM OF CIVILIZATIONS ★.
Douglas Cardinal, a Native-American architect from
Alberta, wanted the museum's exterior to recall the coasts
of the American continent, eroded over thousands of years
by wind, water and glaciers. The main gallery, devoted to the
six First Nations of the Canadian West, presents totem poles
and artworks characteristic of these peoples, while the
history room tells Canada's epic story.

PIONEERS' ROUTE. A footpath running alongside
the Ottawa River from Hull to Aylmer was
once used by portagers to avoid waterfalls
that were impassable by canoe. It crosses
Hull's Brébeuf Park, where a monument
commemorates the era of great
explorers, like Des Groseillers,
Radisson and La Vérendrye.
The SYMMES HOTEL, at the western
end of the path, once provided
accommodation for travelers going up
the Ottawa River. This neoclassical
building ● *116* with Regency touches
dates from 1831. The Hull–Aylmer
road passes the luxurious RIVERVIEW
HOUSE, built in 1865 by Edward
Skead, a prosperous lumber
merchant. This English-style manor
house now serves as the Hull Music
Conservatory. Aylmer contains period
houses that perfectly illustrate the British
influence on local architecture.

Native
American bag
displayed in
the Canadian
Museum of
Civilizations.

GATINEAU VALLEY. Beyond the River Ottawa, the
panoramic road tracking the River Gatineau leads to
Gatineau Park then, 100 miles (160km) further north,
to the La Vérendrye Wildlife Reserve ▲ *230*. This valley was
populated in parallel with the advance of the timber industry
● *76*. Even now, logs can still be seen floating past the banks
of little villages like WAKEFIELD, founded in 1830.

GATINEAU PARK
In 1938, the Canadian
government, under
the administration of
the Prime Minister
William Lyon
Mackenzie King
(1874–1950), set
about acquiring land
here to guarantee the
protection of forests.
Since then, Gatineau
Park has expanded
and now covers
135 sq mi. (356 sq
km) devoted to
environmental
conservation and
research. It also hosts
the former summer
residence of
Mackenzie King,
whose barn has been
turned into a tea
room. The park is
open to visitors
throughout the year,
but the symphony of
colors on view in fall
from the Champlain
Belvedere is
particularly
breathtaking.

229

▲ Abitibi-Témiscamingue

AbitibI-Témiscamingue is an isolated region to the northwest of Quebec that has a wealth of natural resources in immense, sparsely populated open spaces. Its eventful history has been marked by agricultural colonization, the lumber industry and a gold rush, but nature has always been the determining factor.

La Vérendrye Wildlife Reserve

The road from Grand-Remous to Val-d'Or spans 185 miles (300km) of forests and lakes. It is here that the Ottawa River springs up from countless small sources of water. The wildlife reserve, inhabited by species like the black bear, the beaver and the great northern diver, is crisscrossed by hiking trails and offers several sporting activities.

⏱ 4 days

🚌 265 mi/425km

'I can hear the smelting works in full flow; for those of you who do not know, this is where the rock is burned, along with countless youngsters. [...] Do you hear the rumour, the company law? "You must die if you want to live, my friend".
      Richard Desjardins
      ...And I slept in my car

A FROZEN DEATH
In 1912, the prospector Stanley Siscoe discovered a mine that now bears his name, but he is better known for the circumstances of his death. In March 1935, he was flying back from Montreal when a fierce storm obliged his pilot to make an emergency landing on a lake. After waiting for help for two days,

Siscoe, hungry and frozen to the marrow, decided to walk southward. He was found dead from exposure, with banknotes scattered around him.

Abitibi

This region is characterized by its rocky soil and an abundance of black spruce trees. The discovery of mineral deposits around the Cadillac Fault in the 1920s sparked off a gold rush; in 25 years, about 50 mines were opened up and millions of tons of gold, copper and silver were processed in the area, attracting prospectors, miners and businessmen. Several boom towns sprung up as a result.

VAL-D'OR. The forest, like the mines, has made an enormous contribution to the development of this town, founded in 1935. The BOURLAMAQUE MINING VILLAGE, which officially became a neighborhood of Val-d'Or in 1965, was created in 1934, when a company built some round log cabins for the families of their employees. Sixty or so of these are still inhabited and one has been turned into a museum that elucidates the town's history.

AMOS. After Val-d'Or, Highway 111, which leads to James Bay ▲ *234*, passes through Amos. This town, divided by the Harricana River, is the oldest in Abitibi: the settling of 'Abitibi of the railroad' began here in 1912 and, subsequently, several farming villages like Senneterre and Barraute grew up alongside the railroad track linking this isolated region to the rest of Quebec.

The CATHEDRAL OF SAINTE-THÉRÈSE-D'AVILA, built in 1922, is distinguished by its Romano-Byzantine design, circular shape, stained-glass windows and mosaics. Nearby, the Algonquin village of Pikogan (1954) boasts a Native-American chapel in the form of a teepee.

MALARTIC. This town is extremely popular with hunters and fishermen. The main street is flanked by houses with fake, Western-style façades topped with gables, reflecting its past as a mining town. The REGIONAL MUSEUM OF MINES, created by miners themselves, focuses on the history of this industry and the nature of the local minerals. A reconstruction of a mine enables visitors to experience life below the earth's surface.

ROUYN-NORANDA. This town was the starting point for the 1926 gold rush. A stroll around Lake Osisko reveals Naranda's architectural heritage, comprising houses for the mining companies' management and other, more modest ones for their employees. The bleakness of the rocky landscape belies the fact that it holds within its depths so many labyrinthine galleries of gold and copper mines. The site of the MAISON DUMULON comprises a house and general store dating from 1924 that now serve as a museum of the town's history.

Témiscamingue

After Rouyn-Noranda the road leads to the magnificent Lake Témiscamingue. This area is predominantly rural and its landscape is reminiscent of southern Quebec, with its lush, rolling hills.

ANGLIERS. This tourist resort on the banks of the Lake des Quinze contains a museum that celebrates the logging industry ● 76. Its prize exhibit is the tug *T. E. Draper*, built in 1929, which visitors are welcome to board; they can also explore a reconstruction of a lumber yard from the 1940s.

VILLE-MARIE. A fur trading post was first established on the shores of Lake Témiscamingue in 1606. It was fortified in 1785 and remained operative into the 19th century. Its remains can be seen in FORT TÉMISCAMINGUE PARK. THE MAISON DU COLON, dating from 1881, was the town's first private house. It served as temporary lodging for numerous families of colonists but has now been converted into a museum of the history of Témiscamingue.

TÉMISCAMING. Témiscaming, built on the mountainside in 1917, is the region's only industrial town. There is a strong British influence here, due to its proximity to Ontario.

Statue paying tribute to Abitibi's miners, in Val-d'Or.

ABITIBI-TÉMISCAMINGUE INTERNATIONAL FILM FESTIVAL

Created in 1982 on the initiative of three local movie buffs, the festival takes place in late October in Rouyn-Naranda. Every year it presents almost 80 movies from around 20 different countries, a quarter of them premières, with famous guests invariably on hand. Despite the region's isolation (Montreal is 435 miles/700km away), the festival has doubled the size of its original program and tripled its attendance since it first opened.

▲ The caribou or *tuktu*

The caribou plays a key role for the region's nomadic peoples. Both Inuits and Native Americans depended entirely on it for their survival and their annual travels corresponded with the migration of caribou herds. This cervid is omnipresent in the imaginative world of these northern peoples, lying at the heart of their myths, stories, songs and hunting epics. It has inspired artists from prehistory to the present and has been depicted with veneration on sculpted stone or wood, in paintings, on film and in the spoken word.

THE CARIBOU
The caribou population in Nunavik is divided into two distinct groups. The 300,000-strong Aux-Feuilles-River group live in the Ungava Peninsula; the George-River group, which numbers around 600,000 heads, occupies the land slightly further south. The caribou's perpetual migrations are determined by its feeding requirements. In winter, it moves to the southwest, in the direction of James Bay ▲ *234*, where it finds vast expanses of lichen under the snow. In summer, it prefers the shrubs of the Arctic tundra, particularly those in the scorched forests. The young are born in May and June, when the females go on their own to the peat bogs further north.

Female caribou

HUMAN USES OF THE CARIBOU
In the desert-like immensity of the Great North, the caribou has traditionally been a priceless resource for human inhabitants. Its meat, bone marrow, fat and the plants in its stomach make up a reasonably balanced diet. Its supple, insulating skin is ideal for making blankets and clothes. Finally, its bones and antlers are turned into tools: its tendons serve as needles and its rawhide as *babiches* – cords used, among other things, to tie up snowshoes.

Adult caribou

'The land was here before men.
The very first men came from the land.
From the land, everything came from the land, even the caribou.'

Chant of the Tundra, Inuit poem

INDIGENOUS FASHION
Native American and Inuit craftsmen invented tailoring techniques and winter clothes that have had a great impact on contemporary manufacturers. They used caribou skin to make coats, *kamik* (winter shoes), moccasins and gloves, all richly decorated and ideally suited to the Nordic lifestyle ▲ *338*. Without them, humans would have been unable to survive the hardships of this glacial desert.

PRAYERS TO THE GREAT CARIBOU SPIRIT
When a shaman ▲ *340* sings, the vibrations of his voice and the sound waves emanating from the caribou skin stretched across the frame of his drum are prayers that enable him to communicate with the spirit world. He speaks to Papakashtishkw, the great caribou spirit, the master of caribous, who will tell him where to hunt on his territory.

CARIBOU MAN: THE LEGEND
'The greatest Innu hunter of all time killed so many caribous that he endangered the survival of the herd. One day, he had a dream in which he married a female caribou. The next day, while in the tundra, he found a splendid female at the head of some of the remaining caribou. Just as in his dream, she offered to follow him. The man accepted and became Caribou Man. It is he who now controls the herd and teaches caribous only to let themselves be killed by hunters who deserve this prize. Many people say they've seen the Caribou Man and his female running in the tundra.'

Montagnais legend

EMBLEM
The caribou is the predominant figure on the elaborate coats-of-arms of the indigenous nations, and it is also featured on the Canadian 25-cent coin.

Highway 109

It is undoubtedly more practical to travel to Radisson by plane from Montreal or Val-d'Or, but it is also possible to take the long, 540-mile (866km) road from Val d'Or ▲ 230. After Amos, inhabited areas disappear, giving way to the vast forests of the Radisson region. The northern town of MATAGAMI was created as a result of the local mining and logging industries. On leaving Matagami, it is essential to report at the checkpoint at kilometer 6, where travelers are given all the information they require. The road leading to Radisson crosses Cri territory, covered by boreal forest ■ 32, the domain of the black spruce, the beaver ▲ 242, the gray jay and ... insects with fearsome bites. Rivers with rushing brown water break up the monotonous landscape. Despite the extreme temperatures (–40°F/–40°C at night and no more than –4°F/–20°C by day) the winter cold is bearable if the appropriate clothes are worn. Although the landscape varies little, it is more impressive in winter, as the road is bounded by a dark green drape festooned with snow that may be frosty, powdery or fleecy, depending on the vagaries of the wind. The spruce forest is all-embracing and the silence is absolute and total.

Radisson

In winter, it is possible to see caribous ▲ 232 on the outskirts of Radisson, while grouse come to peck at the willow buds in the ditches. From Radisson, travelers can visit the Cri village of CHISASIBI, on the shore of James Bay, and the Robert-Bourassa power station ● 70, one of the gigantic hydroelectric facilities that form La Grande complex, named after the river that drives it. The power station, built between 1972 and 1985, extends 450 feet (137m) below ground level and has a power output of 7,500 megawatts. The dam is 530 feet (162m) high and nearly two miles (3km) long; the reservoir contains 15 billion gallons/60 million cu litres of water (with a reserve of 5 billion gallons/19.4 million cu litres) controlled by 30 locks. Along with the other two dams on James Bay, it supplies Montreal and its suburbs, as well as regions on the way, such as Abitibi and the Laurentides.

Trois-Rivières

Vieux-Trois-Rivières, 238

Saint-Maurice Valley, 240

Shawinigan, 240

La Mauricie National Park, 241

Saint-Jean-des-Piles, 241

La Tuque, 241

The beaver, 242

Around Les Bois-Francs, 244

The South Shore of the Saint
Lawrence, 244

The banks of the Saint-François
River, 245

Around Victoriaville, 246

Lake Saint-Pierre, 248

Between Trois-Rivières and
Quebec City, 249

1. TROIS-RIVIÈRES ▲ *238*
SAINT-MAURICE VALLEY ▲ *240*
2. SHAWINIGAN
3. GRAND-MÈRE
4. LA MAURICIE NATIONAL PARK
5. SAINT-JEAN-DES-PILES
6. LA TUQUE
AROUND BOIS-FRANCS ▲ *244*
7. SAINT-GRÉGOIRE
8. NICOLET
9. BAIE-DU-FEBVRE
10. ODANAK
11. DRUMMONDVILLE
12. ULVERTON
13. RICHMOND
14. SHERBROOKE
15. KINGSEY FALLS

16. WARWICK
17. VICTORIAVILLE
18. PLESSISVILLE
19. INVERNESS
20. THETFORD MINES
21. FRONTENAC PARK
22. MASKINONGÉ
23. LOUISEVILLE
24. YAMACHICHE
25. POINTE-DU-LAC
26. CAP-DE-LA-MADELEINE
27. BATISCAN
28. SAINTE-ANNE-DE-LA-PÉRADE
29. DESCHAMBAULT
30. DONNACONA
31. NEUVILLE
32. PONT-ROUGE

CHEMIN DU ROY ▲ 248

THE BARK CANOE
Light and easy to maneuver, the canoe is perfectly adapted to the turbulent rivers of Quebec. The roots of spruce trees were used to sew large strips of birch bark to a cedar-wood frame; plant resins were then applied to the joins to make them watertight. In the 18th century, large canoes known as *rabaskas*, 30 to 35 feet (10 to 12m) in length, were manufactured in Trois-Rivières and Nicolet to facilitate the transportation of furs and other merchandise.

History

Midway between Quebec ▲ 252 and Montreal ▲ 164, Trois-Rivières forms part of the second-oldest population center in the Saint Lawrence Valley, dating back to 1634, when the Sire of Laviolette set up a trading post where trappers and merchants could replenish their stocks. The choice of site was fortuitous: Trois-Rivières lies at the confluence of the Saint Lawrence (at the tip of Lake Saint-Pierre) and the Saint-Maurice ▲ 240. This strategic position is further enhanced by the proximity of the Bécancour, Nicolet and Saint-François rivers on the South Shore. All in all, the town is endowed with a wealth of what Native Americans call 'roads that walk' that served as routes for trade and traffic. Trois-Rivières lived off the fur trade but its population barely increased for almost a century and numbered about 600 at the time of the Conquest in 1760. It then took on a new lease of life, thanks to the population boom, the influx of Acadian immigrants and the emergence of markets for wheat and lumber. By the early 19th century, another natural resource was proving to be the town's driving force: the abundant supply of water was exploited to produce squared wood, sawing wood and paper pulp. In the 20th century, this renewable energy was turned into electricity.

Vieux-Trois-Rivières

The original village of Trois-Rivières, set on a terrace overlooking the river, replaced the first wooden fort in 1634. Its grid system, dating from 1649 and still intact today, comprises two parallel thoroughfares, rues Notre-Dame and Saint-Pierre, crossed by other streets at regular intervals. The settlement, enclosed by a staked palisade, included the parish church (demolished in 1908), Tonnancour Manor (1797), which served as a presbytery from 1820 to 1903, and a Récollet monastery and chapel. The latter, built of wood in the late 17th century, was replaced by stone buildings in the mid-18th century. The Ursuline convent, dating from 1697,

'FOUR-FOOT PITOUNES'
Wooden billets play a key role in the popular imagination in Quebec. They were formerly known as 'four-foot *pitounes*', on account of their regulatory size.

underwent several transformations between then and 1897. The Governor's residence and some 30 stone cottages were added in the 19th century. The dock that once ran along the Saint Lawrence and Rue Notre-Dame to the west of the enclosure was razed by two devastating fires, one in 1856, the other in 1908. The historic quarter of Vieux-Trois-Rivières, a protected heritage site since 1964, is well-endowed with art galleries, museums, a park, a terrace and fine views of the river.

URSULINE MUSEUM. At the heart of today's convent, this building dating from 1697 houses magnificent collections of embroidery, silverwork, sculpture and furniture produced between the 17th and 19th centuries.

BOUCHER DE NIVERVILLE MANOR. Although some of the roof trussing and walls were put up in 1668, the manor house did not achieve its definitive form until 1730. The stonework walls in the main hall are topped by a triangular roof clad with cedar shingles. A furniture exhibition displays tables, trunks and closets from the 18th and 19th centuries, as well as objects, including a saucepan made in the Saint-Maurice Forges ▲ *240*.

TROIS-RIVIÈRES PRISON. At the northern limits of the old settlement stands a beautiful, if suitably severe, Palladian building ● *115*: this is the town prison (1816), drawn up by the famous Quebecois architect, François Baillairgé (1759–1830) ▲ *255*. The old prison was recently incorporated into the QUEBEC MUSEUM OF FOLK CULTURE, which is completed by a new building that was constructed in the northwest corner of the site.

CATHEDRAL OF THE ASSUMPTION ● *118*. This neo-Gothic cathedral, built in 1858, was fitted with stained-glass windows made by Guido Nincheri between 1923 and 1934; these soften the somewhat austere interior.

DOCKSIDE PARK. Tiered terraces provide the setting for PULP AND PAPERS EXHIBITION CENTER, which contains products resulting from the transformation of ligneous fibers, along with models and videos on the industrial processes that have turned the town into the world's paper capital ● *72*.

PIERRE BOUCHER (1622–1717)
Boucher arrived in Nouvelle-France at the age of 13 and went on to become an interpreter and soldier. As Governor of Trois-Rivières, he approached Louis XIV in 1661 to convince him to develop the colony. His *True and Natural History of the Customs and Productions of the Lands of New France*, published in 1664, remains one of the best chronicles of the period. He was ennobled under the name of Boucher de Boucherville.

MAURICE DUPLESSIS (1890–1959)
This native of Trois-Rivières was Prime Minister of Quebec from 1936 to 1939 and was leader of the Union Nationale party from 1944 to 1959. His government was characterized by its exaltation of traditional rural life. Despite some useful measures, such as the establishment of a minimum wage, his leadership was considered a failure and provided impetus for the Quiet Revolution that followed ● *56*.

239

▲ The Saint-Maurice Valley

This foundry was
active from 1730 to
1883 and for a
hundred years it was
unrivalled in Canada.
It employed almost
500 workers, who
produced wrought
iron, cooking pans,
tools and kitchen
utensils.

The Saint-Maurice River has its source to the west of
Lake Saint-Jean ▲ *318* and runs for 350 miles (563km).
Although several hydroelectric dams have tamed its flow
since the early 20th century, this river with dark, powerful
waters is only calm in appearance and still dashes against
the dangerous rocks with alarming force. Before it became
a waterway that served to ferry logs and furs, the Saint-
Maurice had for thousands of years been the source of a
highly prized mineral – marsh iron.

Saint-Maurice Forges ★

In the late 17th century, the deposits of
iron oxide, limonite and ochers between
Yamachiche ▲ *248* and Champlain had
been discovered but not yet exploited.
The colony, however, increasingly needed
iron because cooking pots, axes, kitchen
utensils and nails were all being imported
from France at great expense. Canada's
very first iron works, the Saint-Maurice
Forges, were established in 1730 on the
right bank of the river, to the north of
Trois-Rivières. The SAINT-MAURICE NATIONAL
HISTORIC SITE offers an unforgettable tour of the remains
of the site (which closed down in 1883), revealing its
techniques and products while also evoking various aspects
of life in the forges.

'From one star to the
other, they have to
unloose billets
embedded in the ice,
run on moving logs or
cling to branches or
rocks on the shore
when the ice breaks
up and the water
wants to sweep away
everything in front of
it like an enraged
beast.'
Félix-Antoine Savard
*Menaud,
Master Driver*

Shawinigan

ENERGY CITY MUSEUM. A great deal of electricity is
required to produce aluminum, and American companies
began to take interest in the hydroelectric potential of the
Saint-Maurice River ● *68* around the turn of the 19th
century. The Shawinigan waterfalls offered suitable declivity
and power and, from 1899 to 1940, the biggest industrial
complex of the age grew up, with three hydroelectric power
stations, an aluminum factory, a pulp mill and twenty other
industrial plants spread around the town. Shawinigan was
planned by engineers concerned with new practicalities like
domestic hygiene and the creation of public parks. The
museum provides a fascinating trip through the 20th century,
with unmissable ports of call at the industrial site and the
Shawinigan-2 power station.

COMMON MERGANSER
The common merganser,
a type of duck that feeds
mainly on fish, often
overwinters in rivers where
the fast-flowing current
prevents ice from forming.

CHURCH OF NOTRE-DAME-DE-LA-PRÉSENTATION.
Impressive frescos by Ozias Leduc (1864–1955) ▲ *205*
illustrate the lives of the region's working classes. They trace
the recent history of its industries and depict activities
connected with the forest.

GRAND-MÈRE. The name refers to a rock whose shape is
like an old woman's head. The Algonquins called it *kokomis*
('your grandmother'). The installation of an electric power
station on the rock's original site made it necessary to move
it to a park in the town in 1948.

La Mauricie National Park ★

This vast territory – uninhabited, dotted with lakes and
covered with a dense spread of numerous varieties of trees –
is famous for its spectacular views. Hiking trails and didactic
nature-related activities lead visitors from one discovery to
another. Thrill seekers should not miss the camping and
canoeing excursions on offer: after paddling all day, the
night casts an all-embracing spell as the adventurers sit
around a campfire on the edge of a lake, the silence only
broken by the hooting of an eagle owl and the reply of
a merganser.

**THE FOUNDRY
WORKERS**
In this painting that
decorates the
Shawinigan church,
Ozias Leduc
illustrates Man's
redemption through
work.

Saint-Jean-des-Piles

The VISITORS' CENTER in the La Mauricie Park just outside
Saint-Jean-des-Piles explains the role of glaciations in forming
the territory's geological phenomena and the nature of the
forest cover, as well as illustrating the ecosystems of this
freshwater environment (150 lakes) and its array of wildlife.
A riverboat trip leads to Grandes-Piles, the setting for the
LUMBERJACK VILLAGE. Here, a lumber camp ● *76* from a
hundred years ago has been reconstructed, with its axe-
sharpening room, lookout tower and some 20 other buildings,
including a canteen where visitors can sample the typical
lumberjack diet: beans with lard, stew, pies and pancakes with
walnut syrup.

La Tuque

A rock in the form of a *tuque* (woollen hat) ● *74* is
the source of this town's name. A wide range of
sporting activities are on offer in this part of
upper Mauricie, while the PARK DES CHUTES
DE LA PETITE RIVIÈRE BOSTONNAIS contains
delightful hiking trails close to a 100-feet
(30m) waterfall.

**FÉLIX LECLERC
(1914–88)**
La Tuque was the
birthplace of Félix
Leclerc, a singer-
songwriter who was
also a novelist,
dramatist and poet.
His most famous
songs include *Bozo*,
Le Tour de l'île, *Le
P'tit Bonheur*,
*L'Hymne au
printemps* and *Moi,
mes souliers*. His work
paid tribute to
his homeland,
its people and
the richness
of its popular
culture.

▲ The beaver

Under French rule, the driving force of the economy was the trading of furs, particularly that of the beaver. Attempts to control the exportation of beaver pelts to Europe stirred up rivalries between the French, the British and various Native-American tribes. The beaver is not just a commercial asset, however; it also fascinates observers with its ceaseless labor. It builds dykes to stabilize the water level and, as the pools created through its efforts expand, wildlife is enriched and constantly renewed.

FIRST CONTACTS
In the 17th century, Europeans were already expressing great interest in the beaver's supposed medicinal properties. The Jesuit Louis Nicolas, for example, reported: 'The testicles of the Beaver, which Medicine calls castoreum [...] are excellent for several sicknesses, and women suffering from morning sickness feel very well when they are burned close to their nose ...'

An 18th-century depiction of a beaver burrow

A HIGHLY COVETED ITEM
Beavers were particularly cherished by trappers ● *48* in the 17th and 18th centuries because of the great demand for beaver pelts in Europe. Since Native Americans did not use money in their dealings, these beautiful pelts served as a yardstick by which the value of other objects could be calculated.

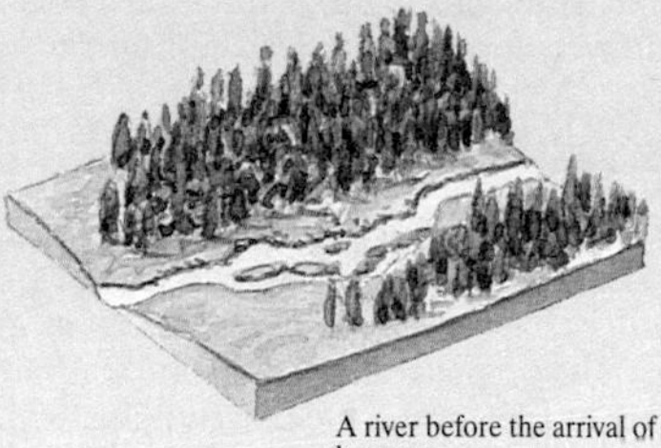

A river before the arrival of beavers

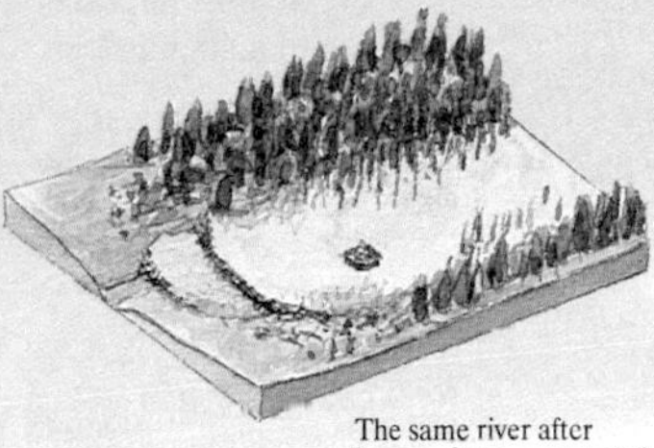

The same river after beavers have constructed their dam

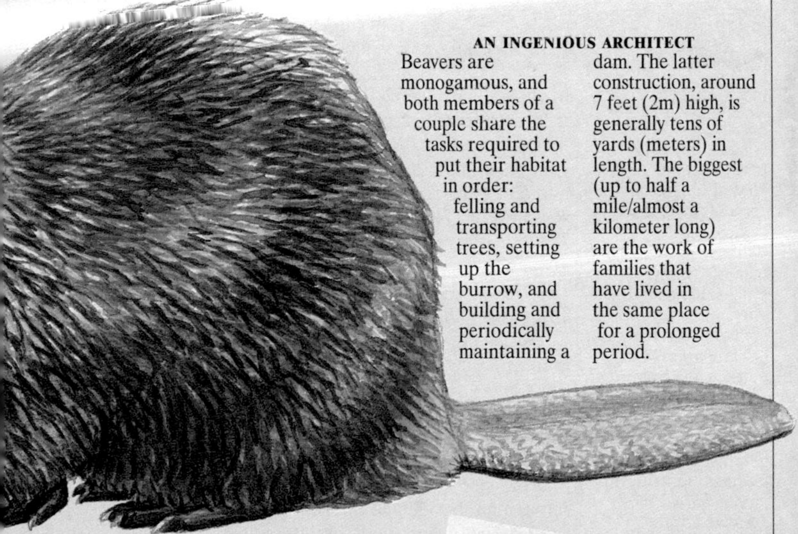

AN INGENIOUS ARCHITECT

Beavers are monogamous, and both members of a couple share the tasks required to put their habitat in order: felling and transporting trees, setting up the burrow, and building and periodically maintaining a dam. The latter construction, around 7 feet (2m) high, is generally tens of yards (meters) in length. The biggest (up to half a mile/almost a kilometer long) are the work of families that have lived in the same place for a prolonged period.

THE BEAVER'S BURROW

Beaver families build conical burrows upriver from the dams they construct to control the water level. The visible part of the burrow is less important than the underground part. It comprises a mass of logs and branches joined together with mud. Contrary to what was long believed, the burrow has just one chamber, with a floor situated above water level. The underwater entrance to the access tunnel is dug through the foundations. There is also a chimney to supply the burrow with ventilation.

ABATTEZ-LE PAR

VOTRE TRAVAIL

THE NATIONAL SYMBOL

The metaphor of the busy beaver is a recurring theme. Like the British bulldog, the Canadian beaver has established itself as a national symbol. It was even used in military propaganda to support the war effort. Today, this rodent can be found engraved on five-cent coins, framed by two maple leaves.

▲ Around Les Bois-Francs

🕐 2 days

🚗 170 mi/275km

NICOLET SEMINARY
Nicolet Seminary, one-time home of the Quebec Police Institute, is the work of

Jérôme Demers and Thomas Baillairgé ▲ 255. The building dates from 1827, making it one of the oldest of the classical schools after those of Quebec and Montreal, although it did not receive its first students until four years later. By building this school in a rural area, Mgr Plessis, the bishop of Quebec, hoped to counteract the dearth of religious vocations in the cities. Educational reforms in the early 1960s ● 56 led to the school's closure. In 1973, part of the façade and the walls of one wing were destroyed by fire; these have only recently been restored.

The immense plain on the South Shore of the Saint Lawrence River, opposite Trois-Rivières, extends right down to the Appalachians. Les Bois-Francs owes its name ('noble woods') to its forest with a mixture of broad-leaved trees like maple, wild cherry and elm – all abundant here. The area was slow to be populated, largely due to the threat of Native-American aggression in the 17th century. In the second half of the 18th century, first Acadians ▲ 308 and then British colonizers settled on the territory. The development of logging, farming and manufacturing industries gave rise to a string of small but lively towns in the 19th century.

The South Shore of the Saint Lawrence

SAINT-GRÉGOIRE. The first village you reach on the South Shore, after crossing the Laviolette Bridge from Trois-Rivières, was built by the Acadians in 1802. The original SAINT-GRÉGOIRE CHURCH, put up in 1806, was a modest building with rough-cast walls and a planked false vault hiding the ceiling. Five years later Brother Louis Demers, the priest in a local parish from 1764 to 1767 and the last Récollet from the monastery in Montreal, enriched it with some treasures from his community – a tabernacle made by Charles Chaboulié (1703) and an altarpiece sculpted in 1713 by Jean-Jacques Bloem, also known as Leblond. Urbain Brien, also known as Desrochers, was commissioned to create a décor worthy of this gift and came up with the tomb for the high altar, the entablature, the wainscoting and the side altars. Although the nave, main façade and interior have undergone several modifications since then, the choir remains unchanged.

NICOLET. This small town is not only a religious and administrative center but it has also grown into an important economic and cultural pacesetter for the region. The NICOLET SEMINARY (1826), a neoclassical palace, demonstrates the skill and originality of the architects of the period ● 116. THE MUSEUM OF RELIGIONS contains artworks, documents and archives, as well as mounting exhibitions designed to find common ground between spiritual beliefs from all cultures.

BAIE-DU-FEBVRE. This village is at the heart of the ecosystem of Lake Saint-Pierre ■ 22. The vast flood plain around it serves as a refuge for a wide diversity of aquatic animals. In April and October, Canada geese and barnacle geese are just some of the species that stop off here. A nature center allows visitors to observe them in their natural habitat.

The banks of the Saint-François River

ODANAK. The Abenaki once occupied a huge territory, stretching from the Saint-François River to the maritime provinces. Forming an alliance with the French, they took refuge on the South Shore of the Saint Lawrence, particularly in this little village. Ritual objects and costumes on show in the Abenaki Museum reflect their traditions and a guided tour of the village gives visitors some insight into their culture.

DRUMMONDVILLE. This town, founded in 1815, took its name from the then Governor of Lower Canada, Lord Drummond. A private company, British American Land, was responsible for distributing land and allocated plots to demobilized soldiers after the Anglo-American conflict ▲ *262*. Sawmills activated by the currents of the Saint-François River ● *66* cut up the tall pine trees felled by the colonists. In the early 19th century, the construction of hydroelectric dams ● *68* and the ready availability of local labor encouraged several companies to establish factories here. One of these sawmills is now in operation in the VILLAGE QUÉBECOIS D'ANTAN, a faithful reconstruction of a French Canadian community from 1810 to 1910, with its craftsmen, farm and traditional activities. In Voltiguers Park, named after a regiment of volunteers formed in 1812 (*below*), TRENT MANOR comprises a fine example of architecture in the Eastern Township style ▲ *210*, as it has retained the original walls, roof and interior decoration. Erected between 1837 and 1848 by George Norris Trent, a retired British naval officer, this building houses a center devoted to wines and cheeses. Every July, a major international folklore festival, the Mondial des Cultures, draws dancers and singers from all over the world to Drummondville.

A FAMILY OF ARCHITECTS
Louis Caron, born on November 25, 1848, founded a dynasty of architects that was extremely active in the Nicolet and Victoriaville areas. He designed 19 churches, as well as several impressive homes, such as the Poisson House (*below*) and Sir Wilfrid Laurier's residence.

ULVERTON MILL. This building, about 12 miles (20km) southeast of Drummondville, was built around 1849. The mill was used to card, spin and weave the wool produced by local stockbreeders and has now been restored to recreate the operation of a textile factory in the second half of the 19th century. Its attic was designed to make maximum use of the space, with the windows arranged to allow light to flood in.

Around Victoriaville

The road leading to Victoriaville is lined with small villages, such as RICHMOND and WARWICK, which have preserved excellent examples of 19th-century rural architecture, including some opulent residences.

ALFRED LALIBERTÉ (1878–1953)
This native of Les Bois-Francs was one of the most prolific sculptors of his day. He left a total of 925 sculptures ▲ *197*, many of which depict customs and professions of yesteryear. He also produced several busts (such as that of Wilfrid Laurier, *below*) and monuments.

KINGSEY FALLS. In the 1800s, the first colonists built a flour mill, sawmill and finally a paper mill on the banks of the River Ulverton, near the waterfalls. Today, the town is the headquarters of Cascades Inc., a company that specializes in recycling paper. A 22-acre (9ha) horticultural park, divided into thematic gardens, pays homage to Brother Marie-Victorin, a famous botanist from the vicinity. The gardens reflect the diversity and richness of Quebec's natural environment ■*20*.

VICTORIAVILLE. This town owes its name to Queen Victoria, who was on the British throne at the time of its creation (1861). Victoriaville has long been the region's financial powerhouse and, as such, it has a magnificent collection of Victorian private houses (*above*). The town now forms a borough with neighboring Arthabaska that serves as the gateway to Les Bois-Francs. (The best way to get your bearings is to climb Mont Sant-Michel as soon as you reach the historic quarter of Arthabaska.) In 1929, the LAURIER MUSEUM ★ was opened in the splendid home of the former Prime Minister of Canada, Sir Wilfrid Laurier (1841–1919). Built in 1876 by Louis Caron, this house is typical of an extravagantly decorated Italian-style villa, designed to display its owner's social standing. Laurier was born in Saint-Lin (Laurentides) but in 1869 he moved to Arthabaska, where he practised as a lawyer. He was elected to the Quebecois parliament two years later, before winning a seat in Ottawa in 1874. Highly acclaimed for his oratorical skills,

this liberal politician became the first French speaker to assume the post of Canadian Prime Minister in 1896 and he remained in power until 1911. The museum contains Laurier's original décor and furniture, as well as his art collection, notable for its pictures by the painter-sculptor Marc-Aurèle De Foy Suzor-Côté (1869–1937) ● *137* and sculptures by Alfred Laliberté (1878–1953) and Philippe Hébert (1850–1917). The PARMINOU THEATER allows the public access to its scenery workshops and wardrobe department.

PLESSISVILLE. This town, surrounded by maple trees, can claim to be the world capital of the sweet, typically North American products derived from these trees. In April, 'sugar time' ● *82* provides the excuse for a Maple Festival and there are parties in all the 'sugar shacks'.

INVERNESS ★. This village which, as the name suggests, was founded by Scottish immigrants (in 1845), is home to a BRONZE MUSEUM. This has fomented a revival of a lost art – that of the bell makers who used to cast their work in the sand at the foot of churches.

THETFORD MINES. The mining of asbestos fiber, which began in the late 19th century, has given rise to a highly distinctive industrial landscape: working-class towns, open-air quarries and slag heaps waiting to be recycled. The MINERALOGICAL AND MINING MUSEUM in Thetford Mines presents an exhibition describing the development of mining procedures and explaining the dangers and properties of asbestos.

FRONTENAC PARK. This park is distinctive because it contains microcosms of all the main natural landscapes in Quebec. The northeast section comprises a huge tundra – the most southerly of its kind – surrounded by boreal forest dominated by black spruce ■ *33*. Only in the northern Laurentides ▲ *216* are these two major biotypes found together. Most of the park is covered with deciduous forest, broken up by numerous lakes echoing to the strange but endearing call of the common loon.

croceum

canadense

BROTHER MARIE-VICTORIN
Conrad Kirouac (1885–1944) took the name of Marie-Victorin when he entered the religious order of the Frères des Écoles. He was a botany professor at the University of Montréal ▲ *187*, founded the Botanic Institute in 1922 and participated in the creation of the Montreal Botanical Gardens ▲ *196* in 1931. His work earned him an international reputation.

ASBESTOS STRIKE
Workers in the town of Asbestos (near Thetford Mines) went on strike in 1949. Their main demands were higher wages and a solution to the problem of asbestos dust. The strike was severely repressed, thereby unleashing a massive wave of solidarity all over Quebec.

AN ARTISTIC FAMILY
The Louiseville notary Joseph-Alphonse Ferron fathered three famous artists: Jacques (1921–1985) and Madeleine (b. 1922), both writers, and Marcelle (1924–2001), a painter who also worked with stained glass. They all forged original careers characterized not only by a love of arts and letters but also, above all, by their free thinking.

The road running along the left bank of the Saint Lawrence (Chemin du Roy) follows the route of the first carriage connection between Quebec and Montreal, which opened in 1737. This strategic link was created under orders from the colonial authorities, in the name of the king. A regular stagecoach service was established in the late 19th century. At this time the journey from Quebec to Montreal took three days.

Lake Saint-Pierre

Berthier gives on to the flood plain of the north bank of Lake Saint-Pierre ■ *22*, one of the places where the Saint Lawrence widens. The lake measures 46 by 10 miles (75 by 16km) but is only 10 ft (3m) deep. Its western entrance is dotted with about 100 little islands. Its abundance of fish (such as muskellunge and great pike) and plant life attracts numerous bird species, including the wood duck, teal and barnacle goose.

MASKINONGÉ. Although the fertile lowlands of the Saint-Pierre appealed to colonists, they soon realized that it was prudent to settle far from the banks to avoid the risk of flooding. So, the original parish of Maskinongé, founded in 1785, stood on a hill – the modern village lies further west. The old presbytery-turned-private house, at no. 167 on the Chemin du Pied-de-la-Côte, is the last vestige of the initial hamlet. Further along this road lie the Maison Doucet (no. 184), completed in 1794, and a group of three general stores (no. 192), built in 1827, 1870 and 1916.

LUXURY FOR THE PRIEST OF YAMACHICHE
The early-19th-century presbytery is complemented by a stonework 'refrigerator'. At the end of winter, its basement was filled with blocks of ice taken from a lake or a river ● *103*. Any cracks in the walls were stopped up with snow. A trap door set in the floor regulated the amount of cold air required to preserve food in the warmer weather.

LOUISEVILLE. There are beautiful houses grouped around the church square, including that of Doctor Léandre Hamelin, on the corner of rues Notre-Dame and Saint-Laurent (*above right*). This brick building dating from 1898 was inspired by the Queen Anne style; its ornamentation is original and its wooden décor highly elaborate. The profusion of decorative elements conforms to the esthetics of the Arts and Crafts movement, which rejected the standardization and simplification of manufactured architectural design.

YAMACHICHE. In the 19th century, Yamachiche was famous throughout the region for the artistry of its carpenters, brickmakers and masons. The craftsmen of the enterprising Héroux family have left evidence of their skills on the main street, where several façades feature accomplished brickwork that serves as counterpoint to their elegant wooden finishing.

POINTE-DU-LAC. Built shortly after 1775, the Tonnancour seigneurial mill (now an art gallery) has preserved some of its original machinery. Guided tours and hiking trails make this an enjoyable stopover.

Between Trois-Rivières and Quebec City

CAP-DE-LA-MADELEINE. This site has been occupied since 1649, when the Jesuits created a mission here. The simple church, surrounded by a shady park near the river, was built in 1717. The sanctuary of NOTRE-DAME-DU-CAP (1950), distinguished by its stained-glass windows and Casavant organ ▲ *205*, plays host to the province's third most important pilgrimage ▲ *186, 278*. The large gatherings of devotees of Our Lady of the Rosary date back to 1883, when a procession set out from Trois-Rivières.

BATISCAN. A visit to the old presbytery, completed in 1816, reveals fine furniture, décor and wainscoting. This imposing stone building used to form part of the village, until constant flooding drove its inhabitants to settle at a higher altitude.

SAINTE-ANNE-DE-LA-PÉRADE. This village bears the name of the river running through it, as well as that of the descendants of Thomas de Lanouguère, who obtained the original concession in 1672. His son, Pierre-Thomas Tarieu de La Pérade, married Madeleine de Verchères ▲ *204* in 1706. The remains of the manor where they lived until 1747 are still visible.

WINTERTIME
FISHING ● *86*
Around mid-December, the excitement of the wait for cold weather reaches bursting point, and the ice on the river is regularly inspected. Once the signal is given, tractors, trucks, drills and chain saws go to work on the ice. In just a few days, hundreds of colorful cabins spring up on the river. They have trap doors in the floor that are opened on to a hole in the ice before occupants light the stove and cast the lines. Until mid-February, tens of thousands of fish such as loaches are frozen outside the cabins. A typical dinner menu might be *gibelotte* (fish, potatoes, onions, lard, salt and pepper); pancakes with eggs and small fish, and caviar as white as snow. This tradition has made Sainte-Anne-de-la-Pérade the capital of winter fishing.

The cold, rushing waters of the Sainte-Anne River were once replete with salmon, but these disappeared in the mid-19th century due to the effects of the logging industry ● 76. Loach, however, still leave the sea to work their way upriver.

FROM GRONDINES TO CAP-SANTÉ. Most of this area was cleared between 1660 and 1680. Several villages, particularly Portneuf ● 121, still boast churches, mills and houses dating from the period of French rule. DESCHAMBAULT, formerly known as Cap-Lauzon, has a church built between 1834 and 1837, an old presbytery put up in 1815 (*left*) and a convent dating from 1860. The church in Cap-Santé (1754), surrounded by a presbytery (1849), sacristy and cemetery, overlooks the river from a narrow plateau.

DONNACONA. The Jacques-Cartier River, 'one of the most enchanting in the world' (according to British officer Frederick Tolfrey in 1845), rises in the Laurentian plateau behind Quebec; it cuts its way through the rocky substrate of the low terraces between Donnacona and Pont-Rouge before opening on to the Saint Lawrence. It was an abundant source of salmon for centuries before industry chased them away around 1915. Ecological groups reintroduced young salmon into the river in 1980; the results were promising until 1990, when work began on a hydroelectric power plant in Donnacona, severely limiting their numbers again.

PONT-ROUGE. Further into the hinterland, a toll post built in 1804 reminds the modern traveler that the Chemin du Roy straddled a spectacular gorge with the Jacques-Cartier River running below. This building, with its stunning views, can be reached by the bridge or by steps.

NEUVILLE. Here, stone houses run at various heights along a narrow terrace. The CHURCH OF SAINT-FRANÇOIS-DE-SALES, which has been enlarged and refurbished several times, has a splendid baldaquin with six cabled columns, given to the parish by the Bishop of Quebec in 1717 in exchange for wheat for the city's paupers. Originally commissioned in 1695 to decorate the chapel in the Bishop's Palace in Quebec City, it is a remarkable example of Quebecois ornamental sculpture ● 111. The sanctuary is completed by the high altar designed by François Baillairgé (1802) ▲ 255, the décor in the choir, conceived by local artists (1826), and some 20 paintings by Antoine Plamondon (1804–95), who was born in Neuville.

Quebec City

Quebec City, *252*

The Museum of Civilization, *256*

Within the walls of the Upper Town, *260*

The fortifications, *262*

The suburbs, *270*

Beauce and the River Chaudière, *274*

Côte-de-Beaupré and Charlevoix, *276*

Devotions to Saint Anne, *278*

Cap Tourmente, *282*

The South Shore and Lower Saint
Lawrence, *288*

▲ Quebec

1. PLACE ROYALE
2. MUSEUM OF CIVILISATION
3. CHURCH OF NOTRE-DAME-DES-VICTOIRES
4. FUNICULAR
5. CHÂTEAU FRONTENAC
6. DUFFERIN TERRACE
7. PLACE D'ARMES
8. HOLY TRINITY
9. CITY HALL
10. ST ANDREW'S CHURCH
11. CLARENDON HOTEL
12. PRICE BUILDING
13. NOTRE-DAME
14. BASILICA-CATHEDRAL
15. OLD SEMINARY
16. CAVALIER DU MOULIN PARK

TWO SOLITUDES, A MONUMENT
The city's oldest commemorative monument stands in the Park des Gouverneurs, near the Château Frontenac ▲ 260. The obelisk (1827–8) is dedicated to James Wolfe and the Marquis de Montcalm, killed in the battle on the Plains of Abraham. It bears this inscription: '*Mortem virtus communem. Famam historia. Monumentum posteritas dedit.*' (Their courage has brought them the same destiny; history the same reputation; posterity the same monument.)

Quebec City, the cradle of French civilization in the Americas, has an inexhaustible charm. This city, 'perched on a rock like an eagle's nest' (Xavier Marmier, 1808–92), is situated at the confluence of the Saint-Charles and Saint Lawrence Rivers. Its citadel on top of Cap Diamant makes the Quebecois capital the only fortified city in North America ▲ 262. Here, 'everything has a timeworn smell, everything speaks to the imagination', observed the historian James MacPherson LeMoine (1825–1912). The city had a similar enchantment for the American writer Henry David Thoreau ● 148, who visited it in 1850. He was stunned by its alleyways and fortifications: 'It was as much a reminiscence of the Middle Ages as Scott's novels.'

A privileged position

In the Algonquin language, *Kebec* means 'the place where the river narrows'. This location attracted the attention of Jacques Cartier in 1535–6 and later Samuel de Champlain, who set up a fur trading post here in 1608 ● 48. The French adventure in the Americas really started in Quebec City, and in the 17th and 18th centuries it established itself as the capital of Nouvelle-France, complete with its Governor General's residence, Intendant's Palace, fortifications and monasteries. It was the starting point for explorers, missionaries and trappers ● 48. In 1759, when France and England had been at war for three years, the future of the colony was decided here. The Marquis de Montcalm and his men resisted the attacks of the English troops all summer. Brigadier General James Wolfe, fearful of the winter, launched one

16. SAINT-LOUIS GATE
17. CHALMERS-WESLEY CHURCH
18. SANCTUARY OF NOTRE-DAME-DU-SACRÉ-COEUR
19. CERCLE DE LA GARNISON
20. HÔTEL-DIEU
21. URSULINE MONASTERY
22. LOUIS-SAINT-LAURENT BUILDING
23. MONTMORENCY PARK
24. KENT GATE
25. SAINT-JEAN GATE
26. CARRÉ D'YOUVILLE
27. HOUSE OF PARLIAMENT
28. CITADEL

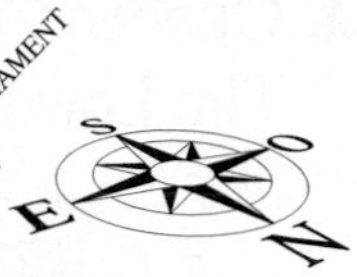

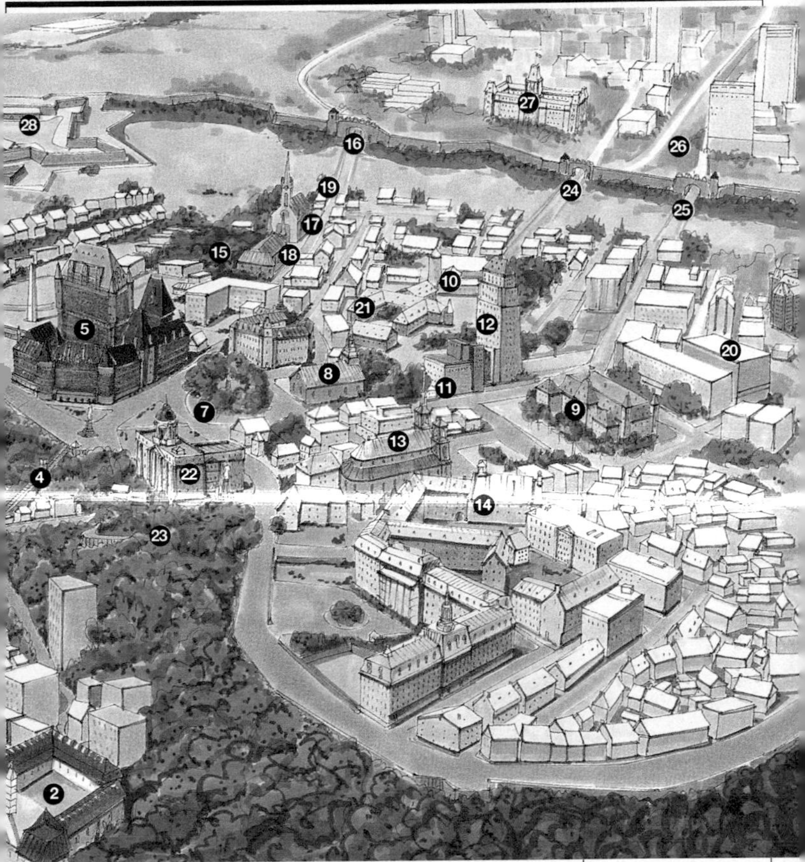

final assault: on the night of September 12–13, his soldiers captured a path leading to the top of the cliffs to the west of the city. By first light, the English army had occupied the Plains of Abraham, obliging Montcalm to engage in a pitched battle that turned out to be his swansong. The city fell into the hands of the English three days later. Under British rule, Quebec City was established as a major shipbuilding center and exporter of timber to England, as well as being the capital of footwear and corsetry until the Depression of the 1930s. Although the city's architecture and place names are resolutely French, they nevertheless reveal the considerable influence of English, Scottish and Irish immigrants in the 18th and 19th centuries. Nowadays, Quebec's economy rests on the two pillars of public administration and tourism.

THE END OF AN ERA
In September 1759, Wolfe and his 8,000 men succeeded in taking possession of the city and defeating Montcalm's army of 2,200 regular soldiers and 1,500 sailors.

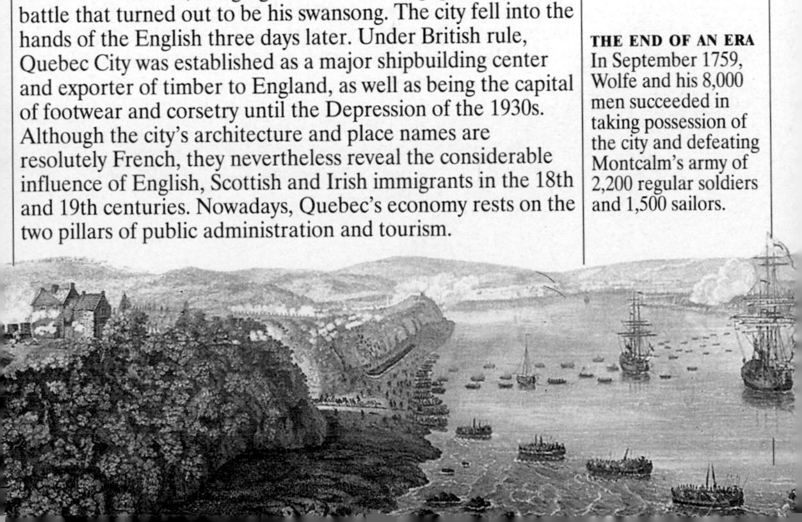

'L'ABITATION DE QUEBECQ'
Samuel de Champlain (c.1567–1635, *right*), arrived in Quebec City on July 3, 1608. He noted: 'I used some of our workers to cut them [the trees] down and make our house'. Quebec City was born.

ANSE-DES-MÈRES
The Continental System (1806–8) imposed on the English by Napoleon gave a boost to the Canadian lumber industry. The coves near Quebec City were ideal for gathering together logs before shipping them to England. By the time Maurice Cullen painted the picture *below* (1904), the port had been transferred to new docks to the east and west of the city.

I n 1608, Champlain built a settlement on the narrow strip of land between the river and the promontory. In the mid 17th century, the authorities and religious communities established themselves on the top of the cape while the businessmen and merchants occupied the lower ground by the river. In the 19th century, this area was enlarged by extending the land into the river. When Quebec City's importance as a port began to dwindle, around 1860, many financial and trading firms were obliged to move from the Place Royale to other neighborhoods.

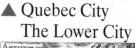

Around the Place Royale

A BUSINESS CENTER. It was in this square that the French colony took shape. In the early 17th century, the leading merchants set up shop around Champlain's original settlement. After the Conquest, the Place Royale reaffirmed its status as a business center and was the stage for a large public market in the first half of the 19th century. The old merchants' houses have now been restored to showcase the architectural styles prevailing under the French regime ● *110* and in the 19th century.

MAISON FORNEL. In 1723, the father of Louis Fornel, one of Quebec City's most important businessmen, gave him a house on the Place Royale which had been built in 1658.

The Maison Fornel was the site of intense commercial activity, as

its owner was heavily involved in cod fishing and seal hunting on the Labrador coast. After his death in 1745, his widow took over the business and expanded it to include a trading post in Tadoussac ▲ *328*. The house was destroyed by a fire in 1960 but was rebuilt two years later from a scale model dating from 1810. The building work brought to light a 17th-century well and magnificent vaulted cellars (1735) that extend underneath the Place Royale.

MAISON HAZEUR. This house on Rue Notre-Dame contains a museum that traces the 400-year-old history of the square using reconstructions, a multimedia show and a workshop where visitors can dress up in the costumes that merchants would have worn in 1800.

MAISON CHEVALIER ● *112*. This complex of houses from different periods stands close to the Place Royale. Jean-Baptiste Chevalier (c.1715–63), originally from Moulins in France, arrived in Quebec City in 1740. Twelve years later, Chevalier, by now a rich merchant and shipbuilder, bought a plot of land and some 'walls in ruins'. He hired the services of Pierre Renaud, also known as Canard, to oversee the construction of a large stone house resting on two enormous vaulted cellars. Although the Maison Chevalier was one of the few houses to remain unscathed by the English bombardment in 1759, it later succumbed to a fire. In 1807, it was bought by a major property developer, George Pozer, who converted it into the London Coffee House. In 1956, the Quebecois government took over the house, along with the neighboring buildings, to carry out restoration work. The complex is now administered by the MUSEUM OF CIVILIZATION ▲ *256*, which uses it to present 18th- and 19th-century interiors.

Church of Notre-Dame-des-Victoires

The construction of this church, on the very same spot as Champlain's original settlement, began in 1687 under the supervision of the architect Claude Baillif (c.1635–98). Like most of the buildings in the area, it was destroyed in 1759 during the siege of Quebec City. It was rebuilt three years later by the architect Jean Baillairgé (1726–1805) and has been restored several times since then. The church's name and frescos in the choir celebrate the victory of French troops over Admiral William Phipps in 1690 ▲ *262* and the wrecking of Admiral Hovenden Walker's fleet in the Saint Lawrence estuary in 1711. This shipwreck was interpreted by the citizens of Quebec as a second victory caused by divine intervention. The splendid high altar of painted and gilt wood contains a relic of Saint Lawrence, in whose honor Jacques Cartier christened the city's river ▲ *294*. The side chapel is dedicated to Saint Genevieve, the patron saint of Paris, and the French capital's tradition of distributing *petits pains* (bread rolls) on January 3 is followed here. (They were originally intended to alleviate food shortages.)

THE BAILLAIRGÉ FAMILY
In 1741, the architect Jean Baillairgé (1726–1805) emigrated to Nouvelle-France, where he founded a dynasty of architects, sculptors and painters. His son François (1759–1830) studied in France and his grandson (1791–1859) found fame in 19th-century Quebec City. Charles Baillairgé (1826–1906), a renowned architect, mathematician and engineer, belonged to the fourth generation.

THE *BRÉZÉ*
A model of the *Brézé* hangs from the vault of the Church of Notre-Dame-des-Victoires. It was this ship that bore the Marquis de Tracy and the Carignan-Salières regiment in 1665 to defend the colony against attacks by the Iroquois. Once peace had been re-established, many of the officers and soldiers settled in Quebec City.

▲ The Museum of Civilization

The Museum of Civilization opened to the public in 1988 as a place for discovery, reflection and surprises. Its thematic displays, embracing numerous exhibitions and activities, enable it to tackle both major topical issues and aspects of everyday life. It throws new light on human experience, on civilizations both at home and abroad, while remaining deeply rooted in Quebecois reality. Open, dynamic and accessible, geared toward participation and interaction, the Museum of Civilization has fast become a setting in which visitors can meet, exchange ideas and explore – in short, a new public space.

THEMATIC EXHIBITIONS

The wide diversity of the themes presented allows the museum to cater for an equally wide range of interests. The museum's exhibitions, both permanent and temporary, offer new ways of looking at the world and reflect mankind's dynamism and capacity for adaptation in both the past and the present. The subjects treated mainly revolve around the human adventure (the body, the elements, society, language and thought). They are approached from a multidisciplinary angle, combining performance, images, soundscapes and interactive elements. A visit involves complete immersion, with constant stimulation of the emotions, senses, intuition and intelligence.

ETHNOLOGICAL TREASURES

The museum's collection started to be assembled in the 1920s and now comprises over 60,000 pieces covering fields as varied as fashion, the professions, domestic life, furniture, glass, pottery, games and popular art. The collection traces the evolution of Quebecois society, without forgetting the crucial contributions of the Native Americans and the Inuits.

ARCHITECTURE

The Museum of Civilization has integrated perfectly into the layout of Old Quebec City by combining resolutely modern forms with a respect for the typical architectural character of the oldest French city in the Americas. The complex has absorbed two old buildings, the Maison Estèbe (1752) and the Bank of Quebec (1865). The skylights, bell tower and choice of materials (stone, copper and glass) also help to establish a blend of old and new. The roofs with their terraces and staircases allow summer visitors to stroll from one street to the next and enjoy views of the river.

ACTIVITIES

Every theme explored in an exhibition is also developed by complementary educational and cultural activities. In this way, visitors can investigate various aspects of a subject, honing in on areas or issues that particularly concern them. Guided tours, specialist workshops, symposiums, practical demonstrations, thematic weeks, theater, cinema and music are all put to use to create a pluralistic approach.

LOUIS JOLLIET
Born in Quebec in 1645, Louis Jolliet became famous for 'discovering' the Mississippi in 1673, along with the Jesuit Jacques Marquette. He also explored the coasts of Labrador.

Petit Champlain

Quebec once had two rues Champlain, one large and one small. The latter changed its name in the 19th century to become Little Champlain Street before being rechristened, around 1874, as 'Petit-Champlain'. (Ironically, this translation implies that it is Champlain who is little, not the street!) It is lined with shops run by artists and craftspeople. Small, picturesque staircases run up between the houses to the Boulevard Champlain and its café terraces. Petit-Champlain is also the embarkation point of the FUNICULAR (*right*), which provides a link with the Upper Town while avoiding a climb up the Casse-Cou steps or a detour around the coastal mountain.

The entrance to the funicular is in the MAISON LOUIS-JOLLIET, one of the oldest houses in the area, built only a few months after a terrible fire (1682) ravaged the Lower City. It is named after its original owner, the explorer Louis Jolliet (1645–1700). An old Beaux-Arts ● *125* fire station, completed in 1912, stands on Rue Dalhousie. This is now the headquarters of the theater company Ex Machina, whose artistic director is the internationally famous theatrical all-rounder Robert Lepage ● *94*.

CASSE-COU STEPS
The Casse-Cou ('break-neck') steps supposedly acquired their name in the 19th century, when they were treacherous underfoot.

QUEBEC CARNIVAL
Every February, Quebec has a winter carnival. Crossing the Saint Lawrence in a canoe is one of the most popular activities. During the 11 days of festivities, 'caribou' ● *100*, a mixture of red wine and alcohol, is consumed in copious quantities.

The Old Port

The port of Quebec City represented the gateway to the New World for thousands of European immigrants. However, it began to be eclipsed by Montreal ▲ *172* in the second half of the 19th century and gradually faded in importance as its facilities became obsolete. The current site of the Old Port was comprehensively refurbished in the 1980s to create a marina and a huge open-air amphitheater, known as the AGORA. It also contains a monument (1922) honoring the 'King's first pilot', Abraham-Martin, and recalling the countless dangers involved in navigation on the Saint Lawrence River ● *80*. Since the 19th century, insurance companies have obliged all boat-owners to use the services of a river pilot when negotiating the river.

BASSIN LOUISE A jetty was built between 1880 and 1883 on the estuary of the Saint-Charles River in order to protect schooners from the tides. This led to the creation of the Bassin Louise, a sheltered expanse of water which was named after the daughter of Queen Victoria and wife of the Marquess of Lorne, the Governor General of Canada (1878–83). These days, the Old Port's marina shelters hundreds of pleasure boats.

> 'On the streets of Quebec City,
> Come rain or shine,
> I like to go with my nose to the wind,
> Dreaming, my heart full of joy.'

Charles Trenet

A museum illustrates the role played by the port of Quebec City in the lumber and shipbuilding industries, as well as in receiving immigrants. Slightly set back from the docks, Rue Saint-Paul – once inhabited by grain merchants and spice wholesalers – has now been taken over by antique shops and art galleries.

NAVIGATING THE RIVER
Quebec City's once thriving port suffered a sharp decline in the 20th century due to increasing competition from Montreal as an industrial center, and the opening of a shipping route that allowed even ocean liners to reach the Great Lakes.

Îlot des Palais

Under French rule, the Intendant was the powerful right arm of the Governor, with responsibility for administrating the local economy, police and judicial system. In the 17th century, this senior civil servant was allocated a palace on the banks of the Saint-Charles River. The Intendant's original residence was an old brewery that had been put up by Talon and then bought by Louis XIV in 1686. It was the meeting place for the ruling Council, later the Supreme Court, but on January 6, 1713 it was destroyed by fire. Two years later, however, a second residence was built not far from the first site. The construction of this palace marked a turning point in the history of Canadian architecture ● *111*. It survived the bombardments of 1759 but in 1775 it was attacked by troops seeking to root out the Americans who had taken refuge there during the siege of Quebec City. Nearly a century later (1870), a new brewery was built on this spot. Nowadays, the site of the first palace serves as an archeological museum, whilst the vaults of the second are the setting for the exhibition 'Quebec, City of Archeology'. The GARE DU PALAIS, a complex designed in the Château style ● *118*, was opened in 1916; its entrance hall is topped with a glass roof depicting the Western hemisphere.

THE INTENDANT
Under French rule, the Governor was the direct representative of the King. All discussions on administrative issues were held in the Intendant's Palace (*below*), and civil servants were charged with making the resulting decisions known throughout the colony.

The upper city is enclosed by fortified walls ▲ 262. The Prescott, Saint-Louis, Kent and Saint-Jean gates open onto an impressive architectural complex that was home to Ursulines, Augustines and priests from the seminary in the 17th century. These days, there is still a nucleus of stone garrison buildings, interspersed with parks and squares. Between the Rue de la Fabrique and the walls lies the Latin Quarter, whose narrow streets have changed little since the 19th century.

LOUIS DE BUADE, COMTE DE FRONTENAC Frontenac, born around 1620 in Saint-Germain-en-Laye (France), was Governor of Nouvelle-France from 1672 to 1682, and again from 1689 to 1698. During both periods, he ruled the colony with a firm hand; he also became famous for his superb oratory and scathing rejoinders ▲ 262.

Details (stained glass and decorations) from the Château Frontenac.

Château Frontenac

The majestic outlines of this hotel, named after Louis de Buade, the Comte de Frontenac, have become one of the city's most well-known landmarks. The building stands on the promontory of Cap Diamant, near the spot chosen in 1620 by Samuel de Champlain to build the Saint-Louis fort. It was enlarged in 1629 and then again in 1692, when it became, at the request of Frontenac, the official residence of the Governor. It was later destroyed in the Conquest, and its subsequent replacement was burnt down in 1834. The Château Frontenac, designed by the American architect Bruce Price, opened in 1893. It is a prominent example of the Château style, and its identity was reinforced by extensions added in 1897 and 1899, as well as the imposing 18-floor central tower, which was completed in 1924. The Canadian Pacific Railroad Company ▲ 209 succeeded in acquiring the majority of the shares in the complex very early on (1897) and became the sole owner of the hotel. This awe-inspiring building was both the company's trademark and a national emblem, emphasizing the links between the birth of the Canadian Confederation (1867) and the need to unify the country by means of a railroad network.

DUFFERIN TERRACE ★. Dufferin Terrace, added in 1879, offers an impressive view of the river and the surrounding area. This long promenade in front of the Château Frontenac stretches down to Cap Diamant under the gaze of a statue paying homage to Champlain ▲ 254 and opens onto

the Promenade des Gouverneurs, overlooked by the Citadel ▲ 262. As the poet Alain Grandbois remarked in 1950: 'From this immense promontory, one discovered, and one still discovers, one of the most beautiful landscapes on the Planet Earth.'

Around the Place d'Armes

This former military parade ground has taken on a new life as a square enlivened by musicians and performers. In the center, the monument to Faith (1916) honors the first Récollets. The nearby FORT MUSEUM puts on a son-et-lumière show reconstructing the major events of the city's civil and military history. The QUEBEC WAX MUSEUM, with its replicas of famous figures like Columbus, Montcalm, George Washington and René Lévesque, occupies the former Maison Vallée (1732), on Rue Sainte-Anne, once occupied by Pierre-Joseph-Olivier, the Prime Minister of Quebec from 1867 to 1873.

Holy Trinity

The Episcopalian Cathedral of the Holy Trinity stands on the former site of the Récollets' living quarters and chapel, which were destroyed by a fire in 1796. Its quaintly English replacement was erected between 1799 and 1804 following plans drawn up by Captain William Hall and Major William Robe, who were inspired by St-Martin-in-the-Fields in London. Time seems to have stood still inside this cathedral. Its walls are bedecked with dozens of plaques celebrating 19th-century English families. The liturgical objects and the wood used for the pews (oak from the woods of Windsor Castle) were donated by George III (King of England 1738–1820). The gallery by the north wall contains a pew adorned with British coats of arms that is reserved for the Governor General or members of the Royal Family. The episcopal throne is made from the wood of an old elm under which, according to legend, Champlain smoked a peace pipe with Native Americans.

INTERNATIONAL HOSTS
In 1943 and 1944, the Allied leaders met in the Château Frontenac, to discuss, among other subjects, the final details of the Normandy landings. Winston Churchill and Franklin D. Roosevelt (*above*) were among those present. A year later, the Food and Agriculture Organization (FAO) of the United Nations was created here. The building also caught the fancy of Alfred Hitchcock, who used it for some scenes in his 1951 movie *I Confess*.

THE RÉCOLLETS
The first priests sent to Nouvelle-France belonged to the order of Récollets, known for their humble lifestyle. Their contribution to the development of the colony has been overshadowed by the achievements of more influential orders. They worked as parish priests, schoolteachers, army chaplains and missionaries.

The fortifications built on the promontory looming over the Saint Lawrence River run for over 3 miles (5km) around the upper city. The siege of Quebec City conducted by the English fleet under Admiral Phipps in 1690 led to the construction of some early fortifications, but it was nearly 50 years later when the engineer Chaussegros de Léry set about building the enclosure. Nevertheless, it was only in the 19th century that the site took on its definitive form with the completion of a star-shaped citadel, inspired by the work of the 17th-century French military engineer Marshal Vauban. Today, Quebec City can boast that it is the only fortified city in North America.

THE ENCLOSURE
In 1745, the British seized Louisbourg, a town now situated in Nova Scotia. This struck fear into the denizens of Quebec City and triggered the construction of a new enclosure, following plans drawn up by Gaspard-Joseph Chaussegros de Léry (*above*). This provided the city with protection, for a time, during the long siege of 1759 ▲ 252.

REMAINS OF A FIRST LINE OF DEFENSE (1690–1713)

In 1690, Admiral Phipps laid siege to Quebec City. Frontenac and his men put up such stout resistance that they forced the English to retreat. Several defensive structures, such as the redoubts on the cape, Cavalier-du-Moulin ▲ 266 and the Royal Battery (in the Lower City) were built in the following years.

'The only answer I have for your General will come from the mouth of my cannons and with gunshots.'

Frontenac (1690)

OUTMODED FORTIFICATIONS

The departure of the British garrison in 1871 rendered the fortifications obsolete. The population called for their demolition, arguing that they hindered the development of the city. They were only saved by a personal intervention from the Governor General of Canada, Lord Dufferin.

THE CAP DIAMANT CITADEL (1819–31)

Faced with the threat of an American invasion, the colonial administration decided to build the Quebec Citadel. Designed by the British engineer Elias Walker Durnford, it is in the form of an irregular pentagon, with two sides facing the river, two opposite the Upper Town and one pointing westward. The whole garrison could take refuge within it in the event of a siege or an uprising. The main entrance is the Dalhousie Gate (*above*).

Left: the Saint-Louis Gate (1878)

THE GREAT BATTERY (EARLY 19TH CENTURY)

The Napoleonic Wars made it advisable to build new fortifications to defend Quebec. The Great Battery (*above*), with its heavy smooth-bore artillery, constituted the main defense against possible attacks from the opposite bank of the Saint Lawrence.

PROTECTED SITE

In 1985, UNESCO classified Old Quebec City as a world heritage site, making the provincial capital the first North American city to receive such an honor.

263

A SPECIAL MAGIC
For decades, Quebec
has cast a spell over
visiting painters,
photographers,
novelists and poets.
Back in the 19th
century, it was

referred to as the
'Gibraltar of
America', and it has
also been compared
to both Naples and
Edinburgh.

A DYNASTY OF
PHOTOGRAPHERS
Between 1889 and
1977, the house at
the junction of rues
Saint-Jean,
Garneau and
Couillard was home
to a great lineage of
photographers, the
Livernois. This family
has left numerous
records of the city's
past (*right*).

Around the City Hall

The City Hall, which opened in 1896, stands on a site once
occupied by a school and church run by the Jesuits, until
they were outlawed after the Conquest of 1760. A large stone
in front of the building is the only remaining relic of this
earlier function.

ST ANDREW'S PRESBYTERIAN CHURCH.
In 1759, the British army numbered many Scotsmen
among its ranks and, when the hostilities ended,
some of them decided to settle in Quebec.
St Andrew's Presbyterian church, the oldest of
its kind in Canada, was built in 1810 on the corner
of rues Cook and Sainte-Anne. It is topped with
a striking Palladian clock tower.

CLARENDON HOTEL ★. This superb building on
Rue Sainte-Anne (no. 57), is the city's oldest hotel (1875).
It was originally designed by Charles Baillairgé ▲ 255 in
1858 as a printing press. The main
entrance is Art Deco in style.

PRICE BUILDING. Built in 1913,
the city's first-ever skyscraper
boasts 17 stories. It was
commissioned by Price
Brothers, a major logging
company which was based
in the Saguenay region
▲ 322. Influenced by the
Art Deco movement, it
resembles a pyramid,
becoming progressively more
narrow as it rises upward.
In common with many public
buildings in Quebec City, its roof
is clad with copper.

> 'To an American, these walls are the sign of the primacy
> of Quebec: one lifts one's hat to salute them.'
>
> Henry James

Notre Dame Basilica-Cathedral

The Notre Dame Basilica, with its
neoclassical façade, is one of the oldest
churches in the Americas. In 1629, after
the capture of Quebec City by the Kirke
brothers, Samuel de Champlain was
forced to abandon the city, but not before
vowing that he would build a church if
the colony ever came back into French
possession. Accordingly, when he
returned in 1633, Champlain organized
the construction of a chapel. It was
rebuilt after the fire of 1640 but then
destroyed in the siege of 1759. The
project to create a cathedral subsequently
fell to the Baillairgé family ▲ 255: first
Jean, followed by his son François, his
grandson Thomas and the latter's cousin,
Charles. In 1922, the interior was
seriously damaged by a fire. Restoration
work was carried out on the basis of plans
and drawings from the 18th century. The
décor, with its mixture of wood, plaster
and gilt, is a combination of several
styles. In the choir, the baldaquin by
sculptor André Vermare crowns the high
altar above a painting of the Immaculate
Conception. The stained-glass windows,
heavy columns and Casavant organ
▲ 205, with its 5,239 pipes, give the
basilica-cathedral a timeless air.

QUEBEC BASILICA
The cathedral was
promoted to the rank
of a minor basilica in
1874 and became
Canada's primatial
church in 1956. More
than 900 people,
including Frontenac
and three other
Governors of
Nouvelle-France, are
buried in the crypt.
The funerals of many
eminent Quebecois
(including Champlain
and René Lévesque)
have been held here.

The Old Seminary ★

The whitewashed walls of the old buildings of the Quebec
seminary stand in the shadow of Notre Dame. Canada's
first educational institution was founded in 1663 by
Mgr de Laval to provide training for priests. When the
Jesuits were obliged to leave after the Conquest, the school
opened its doors to all young people with a thirst for
knowledge. The Old Seminary is the sum of various successive
architectural interventions. The inner courtyard is surrounded
by wings named the 'Procure' (1678–81), 'Congrégation'
(1823) and 'Parloirs' (1823) that together form a complex
typical of 16th- and 17th-century French monastic
architecture. Since 1773, the Latin device on the sundial on
the wall of the Procure wing has warned that 'the days flee
like shadows'. Another feature is an oratory built in 1780 and
decorated with olive branches sculpted in 1785 by Pierre
Émond in honor of the Bishop of Quebec, Mgr Jean-Olivier
Briand (1715–94). It is possible to visit the exterior chapel
(completed in 1900), with its walls adorned with reliquaries.
Mgr Briand's chapel is also open to the public. The fine
collection amassed by the seminary's priests is spread over
the five stories of the MUSEUM OF FRENCH AMERICA.
The archives in the library contain several documents dating
from the period of French rule, as well as Canadian and
European incunabula.

**THE FIRST BISHOP OF
NOUVELLE-FRANCE**
François de Laval
(*below*) became the
first bishop of
Nouvelle-France in
1674. His diocese
extended right down
to Louisiana. It was
due to him that the
Seminary (1663) and
the Small Seminary
(1668) were created
for the city.

Rue Saint-Louis

THE OLD LAW COURTS. Rue Saint-Louis, the former hub of Quebec's legal profession, was once lined with the houses of judges and lawyers. Law courts were built here between 1799 and 1804, only to be razed by fire on February 2, 1873. Work began on new courts near the Place d'Armes in 1883, under the supervision of the architect Eugène-Étienne Taché (1836–1912), who was also responsible for the Parliament building ▲ *270*. The result, which opened in 1887, was inspired by 16th-century French architecture. The interior decoration (particularly the wood trim) recalls the French Renaissance, while other elements (such as the judges' benches) reflect the 'Fortress style' that was in vogue during this period. The law courts were transferred elsewhere in 1979 and the building on Rue Saint-Louis became the headquarters for the Ministry of Finance.

AROUND SAINT-LOUIS GATE. Rue Saint-Louis is endowed with some of Quebec City's most renowned restaurants, as

VUE DE LA HAUTE VILLE A QUEBECK.

well as several splendid houses. The FRENCH CONSULATE occupies the former home of the Duke of Kent (Queen Victoria's father), who lived in it when he was stationed in the Quebec City garrison from 1792 to 1794. The walls of the MAISON PÉAN, at no. 59, could tell tales of more than a few *liaisons dangereuses*, as its former owner, the beautiful Madame de Péan, born Angélique de Méloizes, was renowned for several love affairs, including one with the last Intendant of Nouvelle-France, François Bigot (1703–78). Close by, there is a tree which tends to attract attention from passersby because there is a cannonball entangled in its roots. It fell there during the Conquest but only became visible when the tree started to grow.

AUX ANCIENS CANADIENS
The small red-roofed Maison Jacquet on the corner of rues Saint-Louis and des Jardins was built in 1675–6 making it, reputedly, the oldest in Quebec. The restaurant *Aux Anciens Canadiens* is named after the famous novel by Philippe Aubert de Gaspé ▲ *289*, who lived here from 1815 to 1824.

THE CAVALIER-DU-MOULIN PARK
The far end of the Rue Mont-Carmel hides one of Old Quebec City's best kept secrets, the Cavalier-du-Moulin Park (*below*). A windmill was built here in 1663 and fortifications were added 30 years later ▲ *262*. It is backed by the bell towers of the Chalmers-Wesley Church and the Sanctuary of Notre-Dame-du-Sacré-Cœur.

'It is, for you and for us, the region of châteaux, old historic buildings, the purest language, the most lofty traditions ...'

Hervé Bazin

Chalmers-Wesley Church

This church on Rue Sainte-Ursule was built in 1852–3 and, with its slender steeple, constitutes a fine example of neo-Gothic architecture. It had barely been completed when it became the setting for a riot, after the preaching of the apostate Alessandro Gavazzi sent Irish Catholics into a fury. Another neo-Gothic church stands just opposite: the SANCTUARY OF NOTRE-DAME-DU-SACRÉ-COEUR, built in 1909–10 by the architect François-Xavier Berlinguet (1830–1916), is a replica of a chapel in Issoudun, France. Its superb windows and walls covered with commemorative plaques are particularly noteworthy.
CERCLE DE LA GARNISON. Tucked away on the coast leading to the citadel, the Cercle de la Garnison, founded in 1879, is the oldest military club in Canada. It first admitted civilians in 1895 – but it didn't start admitting women until 1977.

Quebec City prison

The façade of this building at the top of Rue Saint-Stanislas once sported an inscription that read: 'May this prison avenge the good on the wicked!' Quebec City's common prison was built between 1809 and 1814, following plans drawn up by François Baillairgé ▲ 255 to adapt to the winds of change blowing through Western penitential systems. Detention began to acquire a different function; it was no longer intent on isolating criminals in order to punish them but sought to create conditions that favored their rehabilitation into society. Baillairgé came up with a Palladian building comprising four cell blocks, each with three floors and a central, communal area. Prisoners were distributed according to age, sex and the severity of their sentence. Around 1860, a new prison was opened on the Plains of Abraham and the building was taken over in 1867 by Morrin College, which was affiliated to the McGill University in Montreal ▲ 179, but this closed down in 1902 due to a lack of students.

Today, the second story houses the library of the Quebec Literary and Historical Society, the oldest academic association in Quebec, which was founded in 1824.

IRISH RAGE
In 1853, Alessandro Gavazzi (1808–89) traveled to North America to raise funds for his struggle against the absolutism of pontifical authority. His tour started in the US, where his anti-Papist message was warmly received by Protestants. On June 9, 1953, he gave a sermon in the Chalmers-Wesley Church that compared the activities of the Papacy, and of Catholic priests in general, to the methods of the Inquisition. He was lucky to come out in one piece.

PROTEST
The construction of Quebec's prison gave rise to a heated debate between French- and English-speaking politicians, with the latter refusing to countenance subsidies financed by additional taxes on imported goods (such as tea and wine).

Hôtel-Dieu

The young French colony acquired its first hospital in 1637. Quebec City's Hôtel-Dieu was created under the auspices of the Duchess d'Aiguillon, Cardinal Richelieu's niece. The colonial authorities turned to the nuns of the Hôtel-Dieu in Dieppe to run the institution. The first three Augustines landed in Quebec City on August 1, 1639. The Hôtel-Dieu followed the practice of its French models by taking in sick people who were too poor to care for themselves, as well as abandoned children. The nuns also made efforts to convert the Native Americans to Catholicism. Nowadays, the hospital is administered by laymen, but the Augustines still live in their original convent. The hospital's chapel, added in 1800, is adorned with an altarpiece and sculptures conceived by Thomas Baillairgé ▲ 255. It also contains several paintings rescued from Parisian churches during the French Revolution by Abbot Philippe-Jean-Louis Desjardins and subsequently sent to Quebec City in 1817.

AUGUSTINES MUSEUM. This museum, adjacent to the hospital, displays a fascinating collection of surgical instruments and pharmaceutical utensils dating from the 17th century. The separate CATHERINE-DE-SAINT-AUGUSTIN CENTER honors the memory of this nun, who was beatified in 1989, with a reliquary sculpted in 1917 by Jean-Noël Levasseur (1690–1770).

Bon-Pasteur Museum

This museum is set in a neo-Gothic house built in 1887 that originally served as a maternity hospital. It now celebrates the work of the Servantes du Coeur Immaculé de Marie, better known as the Soeurs du Bon-Pasteur ('Sisters of the Good Shepherd'). This community, founded in 1850 by Marie

> 'Inside the walls of Quebec City, every house and every street has its own character, its own form, color and design.'
>
> Pierre Morency

Fitzbach, came to the rescue of needy women, taking charge of abandoned children and setting up missions all over the world.

The Old Ursuline Convent

More than three and half centuries after its creation, the order of the Ursulines still dedicates itself to the education of young girls. The oldest wings of its convent were built between 1685 and 1715. The chapel was rebuilt in 1902 but has preserved many elements of its 18th-century interior decoration. The impressive altarpieces and altars were all made by Pierre-Noël Levasseur. The Ursulines Museum and the Marie-de-l'Incarnation Center, with their array of objects connected with the order's activities, are open to the public. Also on show is the skull of the Marquis de Montcalm, who was buried in the Ursuline chapel in 1759.

Around Montmorency Park

THE POST OFFICE. The Louis-Saint-Laurent building, with its façade embellished by Beaux-Arts decorations ● *125*, was specifically designed in 1873 to be Quebec's post office. Its history is reflected by several philatelic displays. It stands opposite one of Quebec's most imposing monuments, dedicated to François de Laval, the first bishop of Nouvelle-France ▲ *265*. This statue by the sculptor Louis-Philippe Hébert (1850–1917) was unveiled in 1908 to mark the bicentenary of Laval's death. Providing a backdrop to it there is a superb park that also bears witness to the bishop's contribution to the city.

MONTMORENCY PARK. This park, crowning the coastal mountain, was once occupied by Quebec's first episcopal palace. It was in the chapel of this palace, built between 1691 and 1696 by Mgr de Saint-Vallier, that the members of the first House of Assembly of Lower Canada met in 1792. A series of parliamentary buildings were built here before the construction, in the late 19th century, of the House of Parliament ▲ *270*. The park is now home to a monument to Louis Hébert, which originally stood by the City Hall. Hébert (1575–1627), an apothecary by trade, settled in Quebec in 1617 and went on to be the first farmer and first seigneur of Nouvelle-France. His property covered the entire expanse of the present-day Montmorency Park.

Outside the fortifications

CARRÉ D'YOUVILLE. This square's location right by the Saint-Jean Gate has made it an important meeting place. It played host to a market from 1876 to 1930, but this was knocked down in 1932 to make way for PALAIS MONTCALM, a prestigious theater. The lawns running along the ramparts near the Saint-Louis Gate are used for a host of activities: in February, they are the site of the Carnival ice palace; in July they are occupied by the main stage for the International Summer Festival, and in August by the marquees of the Crafts Fair ◆ *350*.

Faubourg-Saint-Jean

FAUBOURG SAINT-JEAN. This neighborhood was once inhabited by craftsmen specializing in construction work. Its long streets lined with duplex houses with flat or sloping roofs are spread over two steep hills. The EPICERIE J. A. MOISAN graces the Rue Saint-Jean, the suburb's main shopping street. This grocer's store dating from 1871 has retained its old-fashioned atmosphere and is so well-stocked that it is almost like a museum of delicatessens. The neighborhood also boasts the neo-Gothic CHURCH OF SAINT-JEAN-BAPTISTE ● *120*, built between 1882 and 1884 with a façade recalling that of the Church de la Sainte Trinité in Paris. It is as impressive as any cathedral, and undoubtedly one of the most beautiful places of worship in the entire city, as well as being the masterpiece of the architect Joseph-Ferdinand Peachy (1830–1903).

THE CAPITOLE
The curved façade of the Capitole Theater has stood alongside the Saint-Jean Gate since 1903. The American architect Walter S. Painter came to terms with the narrowness of the plot to create an attractive Beaux-Arts building ● *125*.

PARLIAMENT HILL. The House of Parliament, an imposing building that draws on French classicism in its design, was built between 1877 and 1886, following the plans of the architect Eugène-Étienne Taché (1836–1912). The members of the National Assembly sit in its blue chamber, along the lines of the British Parliament, with members of the opposition sitting opposite the representatives of the party in power. The face of Parliament Hill has changed its appearance in the last half century, with the construction of new buildings between 1965 and 1974 to provide office space for civil servants and, more recently, a refurbishment of the House of Parliament ● *130*.

PARLIAMENT
Eugène-Étienne Taché based his plans for the House of Parliament on the wings and pavilions of the Louvre in Paris.

THE MUSEUM OF QUEBEC. This museum, which opened in 1933, is set on the edge of the Champs-de-Bataille Park, the battlefield where French troops were defeated by General Wolfe and his men. In front of the museum, a column topped with a helmet and sword indicates the spot where Wolfe died ▲ 252. The museum's collection comprises over 22,000 artworks (including paintings, sculptures, drawings and silverwork), mostly created within Quebec itself. The central pavilion, illuminated by a skylight, links the Gérard-Morisset pavilion to the Baillairgé pavilion, a former prison built between 1861 and 1871.

Outlying areas

The neighborhoods of Montcalm and Saint-Sacrement extend over a huge plateau overlooking the Saint Lawrence and the Saint-Charles valley. In the 19th century, this area was divided into large estates, but these were broken up and replaced by middle-class housing. Meanwhile, working-class families settled in the Lower City, which expanded to spill beyond the river bank and embrace the neighborhoods of Saint-Roch, Saint-Sauveur and Limoilou.

Saint Michael Defeating the Dragon (1705), preserved in the Museum of Quebec.

THE OLD JESUIT HOUSE. This building in the quiet district of Sillery stands on the site of an old Jesuit mission, built in 1637 to convert the Algonquins and the Montagnais, and lure them away from their nomadic life in the process. It comprised a house, a chapel and a fortified wall with four turrets. The whole complex was destroyed by a fire in 1657. The Old Jesuit House, built in the early 18th century, now presents exhibitions on popular traditions and Native American culture.

WENDAKE. The Hurons (Wendat), chased off their territory (Ontario) by tribal wars, fled to L'Ancienne-Lorette in 1673 and settled on land belonging to a Jesuit mission. In 1697, the Native Americans moved to new ground nearby and established the village of WENDAKE, which contains several houses and museums that reflect their ancestral lifestyle. The village also produces snowshoes, moccasins, winter boots and canoes.

A CITY STRUCK BY DISASTERS
Over the course of its history, Quebec City has been ravaged by several fires and bombardments (particularly that of the siege of 1759 ▲ 252). In 1845, Faubourg-Saint-Jean was devastated by flames (*center*).

THE HURONS
In the 17th century, the merry-go-round of alliances led the Hurons (*below*) to fight alongside the French.

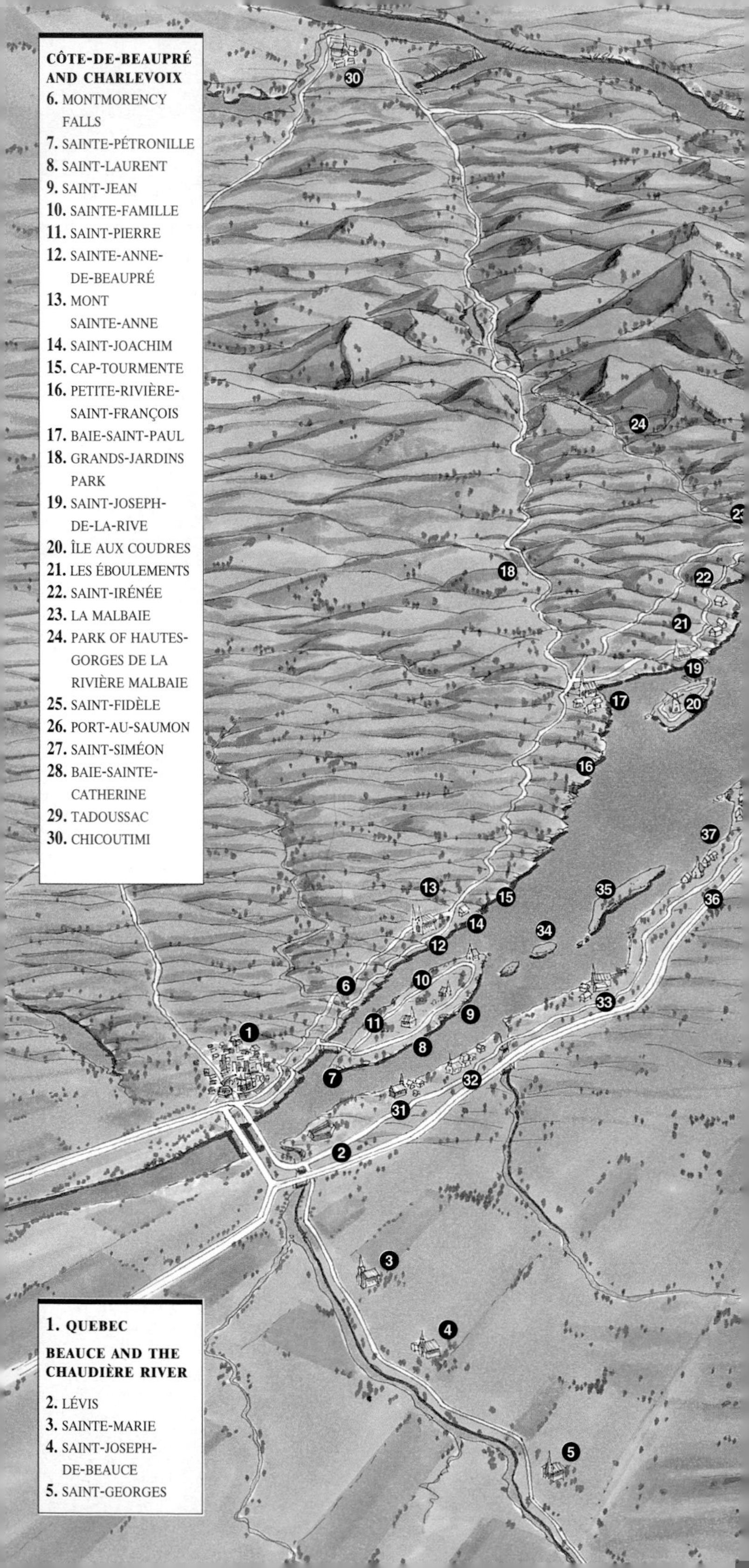

CÔTE-DE-BEAUPRÉ AND CHARLEVOIX

6. MONTMORENCY FALLS
7. SAINTE-PÉTRONILLE
8. SAINT-LAURENT
9. SAINT-JEAN
10. SAINTE-FAMILLE
11. SAINT-PIERRE
12. SAINTE-ANNE-DE-BEAUPRÉ
13. MONT SAINTE-ANNE
14. SAINT-JOACHIM
15. CAP-TOURMENTE
16. PETITE-RIVIÈRE-SAINT-FRANÇOIS
17. BAIE-SAINT-PAUL
18. GRANDS-JARDINS PARK
19. SAINT-JOSEPH-DE-LA-RIVE
20. ÎLE AUX COUDRES
21. LES ÉBOULEMENTS
22. SAINT-IRÉNÉE
23. LA MALBAIE
24. PARK OF HAUTES-GORGES DE LA RIVIÈRE MALBAIE
25. SAINT-FIDÈLE
26. PORT-AU-SAUMON
27. SAINT-SIMÉON
28. BAIE-SAINTE-CATHERINE
29. TADOUSSAC
30. CHICOUTIMI

1. QUEBEC

BEAUCE AND THE CHAUDIÈRE RIVER

2. LÉVIS
3. SAINTE-MARIE
4. SAINT-JOSEPH-DE-BEAUCE
5. SAINT-GEORGES

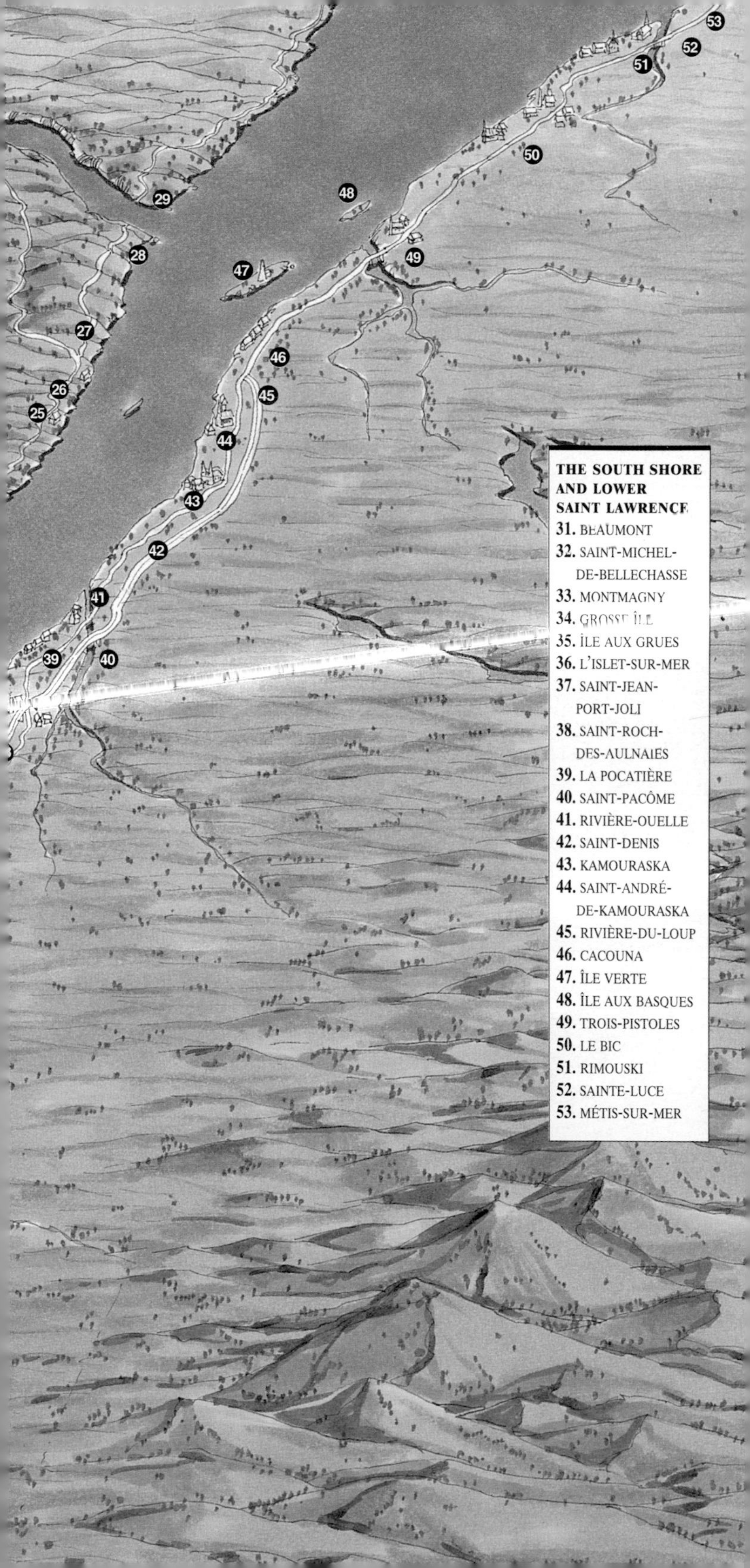

THE SOUTH SHORE AND LOWER SAINT LAWRENCE

31. BEAUMONT

32. SAINT-MICHEL-
DE-BELLECHASSE

33. MONTMAGNY

34. GROSSE ÎLE

35. ÎLE AUX GRUES

36. L'ISLET-SUR-MER

37. SAINT-JEAN-
PORT-JOLI

38. SAINT-ROCH-
DES-AULNAIES

39. LA POCATIÈRE

40. SAINT-PACÔME

41. RIVIÈRE-OUELLE

42. SAINT-DENIS

43. KAMOURASKA

44. SAINT-ANDRÉ-
DE-KAMOURASKA

45. RIVIÈRE-DU-LOUP

46. CACOUNA

47. ÎLE VERTE

48. ÎLE AUX BASQUES

49. TROIS-PISTOLES

50. LE BIC

51. RIMOUSKI

52. SAINTE-LUCE

53. MÉTIS-SUR-MER

◪	1 day
🚌	60 mi/100km

The Beauce region extends over an enormous plain drained by the Chaudière River, which originates in Lake Mégantic, near the US border. Even though it becomes mountainous toward the south, it is characterized by its fertile land (just like its French namesake). The local economy was once totally dominated by agriculture but has now diversified to take in logging and manufacturing industries. Beauce is famous for its maple groves, its folklore and the enterprising spirit of its inhabitants.

Sainte-Marie

ICE BRIDGE
Over the course of centuries, the crossing between the two banks of the Saint Lawrence has been achieved in several different ways (by canoe, horse-drawn ferry and steamboat). The arrival of winter often saw the formation of an 'ice bridge'. A roadmaster marked out the route with wooden poles and regularly monitored the state of the ice.

A DYNASTY. The town of Sainte-Marie (*left*) is spread along both banks of the Chaudière River. It once formed part of the seigneury granted in 1736 to Thomas-Jacques Taschereau, the first in a long line of influential figures. His son Jean-Thomas (1778–1832) was one of the cofounders of the newspaper *Le Quotidien* (1806), renowned for the patriotism of its editorial line. In 1820, he fathered the first cardinal of Canadian origin, Elzéar-Alexandre Taschereau. This family would later come to include a prime minister, Louis-Alexandre Taschereau (1867–1952), who governed the province from 1920 to 1936. The MAISON TASCHEREAU, the imposing, neoclassical family residence, can still be seen today.

Lévis

A STRATEGIC POSITION. This town, located just across the river from Quebec, owes its name to the Chevalier François-Gaston de Lévis (1719–87), the Marquis de Montcalm's second-in-command ▲ *252*. FORT NO. 1 (built in the style of Vauban ▲ *262*), was built in 1865 to protect Quebec City against a possible American attack, and the MARTINIÈRE FORT (1907) bears witness to the importance of the site and its elevated positions surveying the expanse of the river.

MAISON DESJARDINS. This neo-Gothic cottage (1882), built with stacked beams and clad with shingles, stands on a foundation of embossed freestones. The founder of the popular Desjardins savings bank (*right*), which now controls an immense network, lived here for almost 40 years. These days, the building plays host to exhibitions on the history of the organization, which has over 1,200 branches and more than four million account holders.

Canada 8
Postage
Postes

Alphonse Desjardins
1854·1920

Saint-Joseph-de-Beauce

A RICH INSTITUTIONAL PAST. The village of Saint-Joseph-de-Beauce contains five buildings, constructed between 1865 and 1947, that are devoted to worship and education. Together, they comprise the Saint-Joseph institutional complex, classified as a heritage site. The CHURCH (1867), facing the Chaudière River, has a narrow, neoclassical façade with a projecting tower crowned with a narrow belfry. The PRESBYTERY (1892), with its terraced, ridge-tile roof and redbrick facing, is an impressive house with two identical façades, one overlooking the river and the other facing onto the main street. The old ORPHANAGE (1908) is a more modest continuation of the CONVENT, a Second Empire building topped with a high, ornate roof in the form of a pyramidal tower (1889). The convent is now the setting for the MARIUS-BARBEAU MUSEUM, which presents exhibitions about the region's history, culture and traditions. The complex is completed by the LAMBERT SCHOOL (1911, enlarged in 1947), with stark decor that reflects early 20th-century trends. The town is dominated, however, by the old LAW COURTS (1857–66), a neoclassical vestige of Saint-Joseph's former status as Beauce's judicial center.

Saint-Georges

The opening of the Kennebec road between Quebec City and Boston in 1830 fomented the economic expansion of Saint-Georges. The parish church (1902), laid out like a basilica, towers over the west bank of the Chaudière. It is crowned with three steeples, one of which reaches a height of 245 feet (75m), giving it the appearance of a cathedral. The colorful interior, set off by an abundance of gilt, only increases the impression of sumptuousness. Outside the church's entrance, a replica of horseback figures designed by the sculptor Louis Jobin (1845–1928) depicts Saint George slaying the dragon. The original (1912) of this wooden sculpture clad with gold-plated copper – the first equestrian statue by a Quebecois – is on show in the municipal library.

JOS. LOUIS

MayWest

A VISIONARY
Born in Lévis in 1854, Alphonse Desjardins was first a soldier, then a journalist and civil servant in the House of Commons in Ottawa. Aware of the havoc wreaked by usurious loans on workers with modest incomes, he set up his first savings bank in the kitchen of his house in 1901. By the time of his death in 1920, his business had over 200 branches to its name, spread over Quebec, Ontario and New England.

VACHON CAKES
The former family residence of J. A. Vachon in Sainte-Marie is now home to a museum chronicling the early days of the Vachon Patisserie, famous for its 'little cakes' (*below*), which were sold in Quebec and beyond.

▲ Côte-de-Beaupré and Charlevoix

⏱ 3 days
🚌 160 mi/260km

The Côte-de-Beaupré and the Charlevoix region – named in honor of the Jesuit François-Xavier Charlevoix (1682–1761), the first historian of Nouvelle-France – were some of the first parts of Quebec to be populated. Until the 19th century, their main activities were inshore navigation, shipbuilding and fishing, but for many years they were isolated by an absence of roads and the interruption of river traffic in winter. These days, the logging industry is the driving force of the economy in the Charlevoix region, which is particularly spectacular, with its steep river banks, rugged landscape and large parks ▲ 286.

Montmorency Falls

These 270-ft-high (83m) falls – narrower than the Niagara Falls but 100 ft (30m) higher – and the river that feeds them both owe their name to Champlain. He christened them after Charles, the Duke of Montmorency, the viceroy of Nouvelle-France from 1620 to 1625. During the siege of Quebec City in 1759, General Wolfe ▲ 252 dispatched a party of soldiers to set up a camp not far away. The site is now endowed with a cableway, footbridges and hiking trails that offer stunning panoramic views. Another attraction is a house built in 1850 for the colony's Governor General in 1781 to replace the Haldimand Manor ● 114. This house provided accommodation for the Duke of Kent, Queen Victoria's father, before being turned into first a hospital then an hotel.

Île d'Orléans

In 1635, Jacques Cartier discovered an island that he called the 'Isle of Bacchus' on account of the wild vines that grew there. A year later, it was renamed after the Duke of Orléans, the second son of François I. This thin strip of land, dotted with coves and headlands, is 20 miles (32km) long. In 1648, some colonists settled on the tips of the island, but raids by Iroquois drove them away in 1656. The survivors decided to put down roots

THE WHITE LADY
In 1759, during the siege of Quebec ▲ 252, a young woman from Beauport found out that her fiancé, a

soldier, had been killed in battle. In desperation she threw herself into the Montmorency Falls (*above*). Legend has it that the ghost of the White Lady can be seen in the spray of the falls when there is a full moon.

'The island is like Chartres
it is high and clean
with naves
with arched corridors
and cliffs.
In February
the snow is pink
like woman's flesh
and in July
the river is warm
on the sand bars.'
Félix Leclerc,
The Tour of the Island

'For a traveler from the old world, Canada East may appear a new country [...] But to me [...] It appeared as old as Normandy itself.'

Henry D. Thoreau

nearer the coast, in Sainte-Famille. At the instigation of Mgr de Laval ▲ 265, the villages of Saint-Laurent and Saint-Jean were developed between 1665 and 1675. The Île d'Orléans then passed into the hands of various seigneurs and new parishes were created.

SAINTE-PÉTRONILLE ★. From the end of the 19th century, several middle-class families moved from Quebec City to Sainte-Pétronille (below), a parish to the far south of the island. As a result, the village and its surroundings were soon studded with opulent villas. The painter Horatio Walker ● 133 (1858–1938) set up a studio here and ended up staying for several years (and having a street named after him). The quay, completed in 1855, gives a breathtaking view of Quebec.

SAINT-LAURENT AND SAINT-JEAN. The history of these two rural communities reflects the close links between their former inhabitants and the river. Around 1830, Saint-Laurent was home to approximately 20 rowboat manufacturers. One of these firms, the CHALOUPERIE GODBOUT, has opened a museum celebrating the work of these craftsmen ● 80, on the site of the old Saint-Laurent shipyards (1905–67). The village of Saint-Jean boasts not only a splendid church (1732) but also a string of pilots' houses dating from the 19th century. The MAUVIDE-GENEST MANOR, an elegant 19th-century house, perpetuates the memory of two illustrious families. Jean Mauvide, born in Tours (France) in 1701, settled in the Île d'Orléans in 1726 to work as a surgeon. Eight years later, he married Marie-Anne Genest and commissioned a stone house on land donated by his father-in-law; over the years, he added several extensions to the house.

SAINTE-FAMILLE. The oldest parish on the island has preserved its stone church, built between 1743 and 1748. One of the finest examples of traditional, religious rural architecture ● 113, it is distinguished by its exceptional façade and its three bell towers. The interior decoration includes numerous paintings, including five produced by François Baillairgé ▲ 255 between 1801 and 1805.

SAINT-PIERRE. Saint-Pierre's church, built between 1717 and 1719, is the oldest on the island. In 1955, it was taken over by the Government, which has been at pains to maintain this jewel of ecclesiastical architecture from the French regime. It was in this village that the poet and singer Félix Leclerc ▲ 241 spent the last years of his life.

Below: *The Morning Milk* by Horatio Walker (1925)

ÎLE D'ORLÉANS CHEESE
Up until the first half of the 20th century, the inhabitants of the Île d'Orléans lived off the land. They made cheese according to a traditional method. First they curdled the milk by applying pressure. The cheese was then left to dry on a layer of rushes, and the resulting pieces were wrapped in a linen cloth before being placed in a wooden trunk to mature.

▲ Devotions to Saint Anne

Sainte-Anne-de-Beaupré has been attracting pilgrims since the second half of the 17th century, including sailors, Native Americans and, in the 19th century, devotees from the US. They are all drawn by the 'wonders' attributed to Saint Anne which are recorded on numerous commemorative plaques. Work started on the present basilica in 1927 to replace a sanctuary burnt down in 1922, and no expense was spared to create a grandiose building comparable to European cathedrals. The million pilgrims who visit every year are greeted by enormous naves, a mixture of neo-Roman and neo-Gothic styles and sumptuous décor.

DEVOTION TO SAINT ANNE
In 1680, Mgr de Laval ▲ 265 evoked 'the special devotion that Saint Anne bears for all the inhabitants of this country – a devotion that, we can guarantee with certainty, distinguishes them from other people'. The first French colonists bestowed the Saint's name on several places and associations: churches, parishes, the Sainte-Anne Fort, and carpenters' guilds of 'Madame Sainte Anne'. In Sainte-Anne-du-Petit-Cap (the original name of Saint-Anne-de-Beaupré), a gilt wooden statue from France has been venerated since the early 1660s.

SAINT ANNE OF THE NATIVE AMERICANS
When indigenous communities began to convert to Christianity, they showed a particular devotion to Saint Anne. Their great respect for the ancestors led them to consider her as a forebear who had initiated them into their new faith. The Micmacs and Montagnais have placed several of their towns under her protection.

THE INTERIOR OF THE BASILICA
The opulent decoration is the work of renowned artists from both Quebec and overseas. They used precious materials to create arresting forms inspired by biblical and historical themes.

THE 'WONDERS'

The priest Thomas Morel wrote *The story of the wonders that occurred in the church of Sainte-Anne du-Petit-Cap, on the Côte de Beaupray, in Nouvelle-France*, which was reproduced in the *Report of the Jesuits* in 1667. He completed his account three years later with a further 25 'wonders'. These favors ensured the popularity of the pilgrimages. They are celebrated by countless commemorative plaques of great symbolic value, some of which date back to the 17th or 18th century.

THE PILGRIMAGE

The biggest crowds are found on Saint Anne's feast day (July 26) and during the Great Novena leading up to it. These ceremonies broadened their scope in 1930, coinciding with improvements in transport links. Pilgrims arrived from all over North America to ask Saint Anne for temporal or spiritual favors (cures or conversions, respectively), or simply to express their devotion. Native Americans used to set up camp alongside the basilica.

SOUVENIR du PELERINAGE de STE. ANNE DE BEAUPRÉ

PROVINCE de QUÉBEC

Sainte Anne de Beaupré

GRANDE Neuvaine

A LA SAINTE ANNE JUILLET 1947

The Côte-de-Beaupré

The Côte-de-Beaupré is a narrow strip of terraced farming land that has been inhabited since the early 17th century. The arable lands of the first parishes were quickly claimed, so newcomers settled in the hinterland (Saint-Féréol-les-Neiges and Saint-Tite-des-Caps) and in the neighboring region of Charlevoix.

CHÂTEAU-RICHER. At the entrance to this village, which once occupied a strategic position in the center of the seigneury of Beaupré, the OLD MILL OF PETIT-PRÉ (1695) houses a museum that focuses on the economic and social development of the Côte-de-

Beaupré. Between L'Ange-Gardien and Sainte-Anne-de-Beaupré – famous for its basilica ▲ *278* – the picturesque Royal Way winds past numerous examples of traditional Quebecois farms and rural houses, vegetable stores and procession chapels. A few miles further on, the GRAND CANYON OF THE SAINTE-ANNE FALLS offers a great view of the waters of the Sainte-Anne-du-Nord River, which crash from a height of almost 200 feet (60m) into a narrow, rocky gorge.

SAINT-JOACHIM. The church of Saint-Joachim stands not far from the nature reserve of Cap Tourmente ▲ *282*. Built in 1779 then enlarged in 1860, it is generally considered one of the foremost examples of religious architecture built in Quebec after 1760 ● *113*. The interior decoration is the work of the architects François and Thomas Baillairgé ▲ *255*. For over three centuries, priests from the seminary in Quebec City farmed vast tracts of land in this region. The GREAT FARM, a long house overlooking the Saint Lawrence dating from 1866, now serves as a heritage museum.

Petite-Rivière-Saint-François

FROM THE SEA TO THE MOUNTAIN, FROM THE MOUNTAIN TO THE SEA. The year 1675 marked the foundation of the first settlements in Charlevoix – the beautiful coastal villages of Petite-Rivière-Saint-François and Baie-Saint-Paul. The former, tucked between the mountain and the river, entranced the novelist Gabrielle Roy ● *156*, who came here to write every summer. Away from the main road, the ski resort of Le Massif (2,520 feet/770m) benefits from the longest gradient east of the Canadian Rockies.

Baie-Saint-Paul

This little town, surrounded by awe-inspiring promontories, has truly been blessed by Nature. Snuggling in the bottom of the Gouffre River valley, it is surrounded by extraordinary scenery. The painter Clarence Gagnon (1881–1942) ● *133* was one of the first to celebrate its beauties, leading the way for several other well-known Canadian artists, such as Marc-

Aurèle Fortin, Alexander Young Jackson and Jean-Paul Lemieux ● *132*. On either side of the church, rues Saint-Jean-Baptiste and Falard have preserved their charm, largely due to their attractive houses ● *112*. The town contains several art galleries and shops, as well as two exhibition halls.

Saint-Joseph-de-la-Rive ★

The delightful village of Saint-Joseph-de-la-Rive, accessible from the spectacular Highway 362, stretches alongside the Saint Lawrence River. The (extremely hilly) road leading to the village offers exhilarating views of the Île aux Coudres and the Saint Lawrence, with a few schooners stranded on its banks as mementos of the area's nautical past. The SAINT-GILLES PAPETERIE, founded by Mgr Félix-Antoine Savard, uses traditional techniques to manufacture a sophisticated, mottled paper unique to Canada. Saint-Joseph-de-la-Rive is the departure point for a ferry service to the Île aux Coudres.

Île aux Coudres

When Jacques Cartier dropped anchor to the southeast of this island in September 1535, he gave it a name that reflected its abundance of hazel trees (*coudriers*). Settlement began in 1720 and the first inhabitants devoted themselves to farming, building rowboats and schooners, fishing and craftwork. The MILLS OF THE ÎLE AUX COUDRES, set close to a stream, provide a glimpse of life from times gone by. It is possible to visit a watermill (1825) and a windmill (1836), both in working order ● *66*. The VOITURES D'EAU museum, set on a schooner, presents exhibitions about navigation on the Saint Lawrence ● *80*.

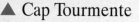

Every spring and fall, the muddy foreshore extending along the foot of Cap Tourmente receives the entire population of the *Atlanticus* sub-species of the snow goose. The geese stop off here for a few weeks to feed, interrupting their migratory flight between the Arctic (where they nest) and the marshes on the east coast of America (where they spend the winter). Their population was reduced to around 2,000 birds a century ago, but it recovered to reach 70,000 by the early 1970s. Thanks to various protective measures (hunting restrictions, conservation of feeding areas), their numbers have now shot up to 700,000.

FLIGHT OF GEESE IN FALL
As a result of their recent population boom, the geese now use several stopovers on the south bank of the Saint Lawrence, from Lake Saint-Pierre to Rimouski.

FLIGHT OF GEESE IN SPRING
When the high tide prevents the geese from reaching the rhizomes of bulrushes, it is not unusual to see them nibbling young shoots on farmland.

AMERICAN BULRUSH
This is the only intertidal plant in the area. Geese feed on its rhizomes by plunging their beaks into the silt.

The geese can be seen on the cape from mid-April to late May, and from late September to early November.

Adult

Young

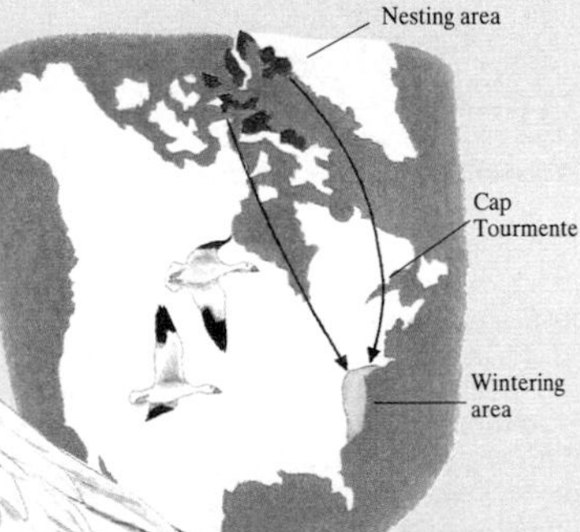

Nesting area

Cap Tourmente

Wintering area

MIGRATORY ROUTE
Geese often migrate in one single flight, from the Arctic in fall and from the Atlantic coast in spring.

THE SNOW GOOSE

Some years, when there is too much snow on the ground, the geese cannot make their nests and so fail to reproduce.

There are two species of snow goose – the white and the blue. The plumage of the former is an unbroken white, apart from the remiges, which are black (*above*); the less common blue goose has a slate-gray back and underbelly. The head acquires a reddish tinge after contact with the iron oxide in the substrates where the birds rummage for food. This phenomenon is more frequently seen in fall than in spring.

BREATHTAKING LANDSCAPES
There are spectacular views from Highway 362 as it shadows the Saint Lawrence from Baie-Saint-Paul to La Malbaie. Even in the 19th century, wealthy tourists came to this area to enjoy the dazzling scenery and the abundance of fish.

Les Éboulements

This little village sprawls across a plateau overlooking the Saint Lawrence. The area once suffered from a gigantic landslide after an earthquake (1663). At the entrance to the village, the SALES-LATERRIÈRE MANOR, with its outhouses and communal mill, conjures up a picture of rural life under the seigneurial system.

Saint-Irénée ★

The village of Saint-Irénée, perched on a mountainside, was founded in the early 19th century and went on to serve as a microcosmic model for research into the traditional peasant family. Two famous studies were carried out here. The first (1861) was conducted by Charles Gauldrée-Boilleau, the French consul in Quebec and disciple of Frédéric Le Play,

Above: Les Éboulements

RODOLPHE FORGET
The high-flying Montreal financier Rodolphe Forget ▲*184* regularly visited the region, where he owned a house (Gil'Mont). In 1904, as Charlevoix's member of the federal parliament, he managed to endow the region with a railroad link between La Malbaie and Quebec.

while the second (1921) was conducted by Léon Gérin, Canada's first sociologist. The FORGET ESTATE, once the property of Sir Rodolphe Forget (1861–1919), one of the first French-Canadian millionaires, boasts a music and dance school, and plays host to an international classical music festival every summer. Saint-Irénée also offers a fine beach that attracts summer holidaymakers, despite the uninviting temperature of the water.

Pointe-au-Pic

Pointe-au-Pic, a pioneer in Canada's tourist industry, has been welcoming visitors for almost two centuries. Some used to stay in the Manoir Richelieu, a luxury hotel built in 1899 for the Richelieu and Ontario Navigation Company; others, such as William Taft, built themselves elegant villas with views of the sea. Modern tourists still appreciate the chance to play golf or tennis, or go fishing, horse riding or skiing (on Mont Grand Fonds), as well as enjoying the recent addition of a casino in the Manoir Richelieu.

The village of Pointe-au-Pic also contains the CHARLEVOIX MUSEUM, dedicated to the region's history, ethnology and popular art, which is worth a visit.

La Malbaie

This town owes its name to Champlain who, when he ran aground in 1608 because the bay did not provide sufficient anchorage for his ship, exclaimed '*La malle baye!*' ('the wretched bay!'). After the Conquest, the settlement became known as Murray Bay; in 1761, John Nairne and Malcolm Fraser, two Scottish officers in the British army, obtained a seigneury from Governor James Murray spread over both sides of the Malbaie River. From 1849 onwards, the area attracted numerous tourists arriving on steamboats from Quebec City, as well several Canadian painters in search of inspiration. Quebec's first female novelist, Laure Conan (1845–1924), was born in La Malbaie and remained there for most of her life.

THE HINTERLAND. Between Baie-Saint-Paul and La Malbaie, Highway 138 reveals a land of hills and plateaus dotted with villages, set against the spectacular wooded backdrop of the Laurentides. The Clermont pulp mill is the only major industrial plant in the area. The Charlevoix hinterland is also the setting for the ecological reserves of the Park of the Grands-Jardins and the Park of the Hautes-Gorges-de-la-Rivière-Malbaie ▲ 286, to the north of Saint-Aimé-des-Lacs.

Around Tadoussac

After the picturesque resort of Cap-à-l'Aigle (to the east of La Malbaie), the countryside, although still extremely beautiful, becomes less hospitable and villages are few and far between.

SAINT-FIDÈLE.
This small hamlet, situated on a plateau looking down over the Saint Lawrence, is particularly renowned for its excellent cheeses – on sale *in situ* – and the Port-au-Saumon ecological station ▲ 287.

SAINT-SIMÉON. This village, the departure point for a ferry service to Rivière-du-Loup ▲ 292, on the south bank of the Saint Lawrence, is an important crossroads. Travelers can take the road to Chicoutimi ▲ 322 or continue on to Tadoussac and the North Shore ▲ 328.

THE MANOIR RICHELIEU
On September 12, 1928, the original manor house was destroyed by fire. The very next day, the construction of a new, even more spacious hotel was announced. The architect John S. Archibald was commissioned to draw up a building (*above*) in the Château style ● *118*, which was extremely popular at the time.

ILLUSTRIOUS VISITORS
In the late 19th and early 20th centuries, Charlevoix had an irresistible allure for countless American tourists. Steamboats traveled along the river from Quebec City, dropping off passengers on the way. Some visitors, such as William Howard Taft (1857–1930), the president of the US from 1909 to 1913 (*above*, with his 10 grandchildren), came here to relax with their families.

The Charlevoix region is much appreciated by visitors for its artistic traditions and welcoming hostelries, but it also boasts unspoilt scenery of astonishing beauty. Its range of natural parks is guaranteed to appeal to both ecologists and geologists; ornithologists are also in their element, as the conditions for bird watching are ideal on Cap Tourmente (Côte-de-Beaupré) ▲ *282*, on the beach of Saint-Irénée and the banks of the Île aux Coudres.

Les Grands-Jardins

A DISTINCTIVE ECOSYSTEM. The Park des Grands-Jardins, situated to the north of Baie-Saint-Paul ▲ *280*, is devoted to the conservation of vegetation not found anywhere else at this latitude. This phenomenon can be explained by the height of the mountains (up to 3,300 feet/1000m) that make up the heart of the Laurentides massif ▲ *216*. Nordic vegetation proper to the boreal forest, or taiga ■ *32* dominates the landscape, although in the valleys it gives way to dense spruce-fir forests. The wildlife is also specific to the taiga: the blackpoll warbler, the gray jay and Bricknell's thrush (which has recently been elevated to the rank of a species, albeit an endangered one). A flock of caribou was introduced around 30 years ago, and the abundance of lichen has enabled them to adapt very well ▲ *232*. The staggering panoramic views from the top of Mont du Lac-des-Cygnes, taking in the Gouffre Valley and the Massif des Éboulemonts, reveal the indentation created by the impact of a meteorite 350 million years ago. The Park des Grands-Jardins also offers tours with a naturalist for a guide, as well as campsites and sporting activities such as canoeing and rock climbing.

Gorges of the Rivière Malbaie ★

RUGGED TERRAIN. The Park des Hautes-Gorges-de-la-Rivière-Malbaie contains one of the most spectacular glacial valleys on the eastern side of the continent. This vast park (90 sq miles/233 sq km) is close to La Malbaie ▲ *285* but access is difficult: it can only be reached by a tortuous, unpaved road. Once there, visitors are regaled by breathtaking 2,600-ft (800m) escarpments framing a magnificent trough (*above*). It is possible to take a boat trip on one section of the river. Les Hautes-Gorges are

distinguished by diversified vegetation, ranging from huge elms in the valley to Arctic-Alpine flowers on the peaks. This tiered vegetation is matched by an array of birds: the black-throated blue warbler and the pileated woodpecker nest in the maple groves in the valley, while the fox sparrow and the American pipit keep themselves to the high plateaus. The walk up the narrow footpaths winding through the sides of the valley is amply rewarded by the awesome views from the top. The park is perennially popular with aficionados of rock climbing, canoeing and mountain biking.

Port-au-Saumon

AN ECOLOGICAL CENTER. This center is tucked into the mountain backing the bay of Port-au-Saumon, 13 miles (20km) to the east of La Malbaie ▲ 285. It controls 235 acres (95ha) of land covered with forests and rivers and offers visitors to Charlevoix their first contact with the estuary. It is justly proud of its conservation policy: it is strictly forbidden to pick fruit or flowers or to stray from the footpaths. Hikers are accompanied by a guide who will reveal the secrets of the vegetation and wildlife surrounding the well-tended trails. The tour starts in a small canyon and ends up at the foot of a cove replete with marine animals like sea urchins and starfish. In the distance, it is sometimes possible to spot alcids (such as murres), eiders and divers (loons), as well as the occasional seal or beluga whale.

Les Palissades

A FOREST CENTER. Six miles (9km) to the north of Saint-Siméon ▲ 285, the educational center of Les Palissades lies under the shadow of a 1,000-ft (300m) escarpment bounding a broad, glacial valley. After crossing the Pont des Soupirs, one of the footpaths leads to the top of the valley. Down below, a mass of ice remains throughout the year, impeding the development of plant life. Birds like the boreal chickadee, the northern parula and the pileated woodpecker thrive in this forest of poplars, pines, firs and silver birches.

MOOSE
This large mammal ● 84 is particularly well suited to the Quebecois forest environment. Its long legs and large hooves allow it to move freely in both snow and marshes. In winter, a thin down grows under its long fur and its antlers fall off to facilitate its search for young shoots and branches.

BLACKPOLL WARBLER
When the blackpoll warbler returns in springtime from its long migration right down to South America, its shrill 'tit tit tit' once again echoes through the boreal forest and the Parks des Grands-Jardins and des Hautes-Gorges.

A GLACIAL VALLEY
Les Hautes-Gorges-de-la-Rivière Malbaie is an impressive example of a deep-trough glacial valley. In this region, the action of glaciers has left several, sometimes spectacular geomorphological phenomena, including cirques and hanging valleys.

⏱ 4 days

🚌 250 mi/400km

THE GROSSE-ÎLE QUARANTINE STATION
In 1832, the authorities acted against the threat of a cholera epidemic by

setting up a quarantine station on Grosse-Île, on the Saint Lawrence River. Hundreds of thousands of immigrants, mainly from the British Isles, were housed and cured here, but tens of thousands failed to survive. In 1847 alone, for example, 106,000 immigrants, mostly Irish fleeing famine, arrived here hungry and weak, crammed into ships; 8,000 of these did not live to see any more of the New World than this island.

Nomadic Native Americans had been roaming the South Shore for thousands of years when the first seigneurial concessions were granted in 1630. Agriculture was only introduced in 1672, but another century would pass before it extended along the entire coastal plain up to Kamouraska. Intensive settlement of the Lower Saint Lawrence area only began in the early 19th century, with the development of the lumber industry. It was not long before the delightful scenery and accessible coastline attracted tourists to Bellechasse, Kamouraska, Cacouna and Métis. The enchanting maritime landscape of Le Bas-du-Fleuve more than fulfils its promise of tranquility and relaxation.

The South Shore

A drive or walk through the area's old villages, whether nestling in coves or gazing out from headlands, reveals an active rural life and a landscape full of interest.

BEAUMONT. After passing through the heart of the old village, travelers encounter the SEIGNEURIAL MILL OF THE MAILLOU FALLS. Built in 1821 to card wool, it has since acquired millstones and a saw. It still produces flour, to the delight of the visitors who savor the bread and brioches baked in its log-fired oven.

SAINT-MICHEL-DE-BELLECHASSE. With its main street lined with tall trees, its maze of narrow streets, its clusters of small, old boatmen's houses and its charming buildings in the church square, Saint-Michel (*below*) is best explored on foot. This is the best way to appreciate the harmony of the local houses and the diversity of their finely chiseled wooden décor. The influence of the river is all-pervading, as evidenced by the weather vanes and scale models of boats and lighthouses adorning the gardens.

MONTMAGNY. This town experienced a boom in the early 20th century, as sawmills, foundries and factories (making agricultural machinery) formed a solid infrastructure that still dominates the landscape today. In fall, hundreds of thousands of birds descend on the sand bars ■ *24* and the surrounding fields. The MIGRATIONS CENTER contains exhibitions about the great white goose and other migratory species, such as the mallard and the teal.

> 'But here we are, newly arrived at the Port-Joli River [...]
> With its pretty banks covered with wild roses,
> its woods of firs and spruces and its alder suckers.'
>
> Philippe Aubert de Gaspé, 1864

As Grosse-Île is visible from the coast, the Center also puts on an audiovisual presentation explaining the organization of its quarantine station. The MANOIR DE L'ACCORDÉON, set in the Couillard-Dupuis manor (part of which dates back to 1764), is not only an accordion museum and documentation center but also still manufactures instruments today, keeping alive a cherished tradition ● *91*.

L'ISLE-AUX-GRUES. Montmagny provides access to the only island in this chain that has been inhabited without interruption since the 17th century. A seigneurial manor house and estate, several centuries-old cabins and a few self-catering cottages punctuate the magnificent unspoilt scenery.

L'ISLET-SUR-MER. This village bears witness to the nautical culture of the riverside settlements: a charming procession chapel dating from 1835 is dedicated to Saint Joseph the Helper of Sailors, while the BERNIER MARITIME MUSEUM displays models of boats, as well as sailing accessories and equipment. Outside, an icebreaker and a hydrofoil are also on show. One of the rooms is devoted to Captain Joseph-Elzéar Bernier (1852–1934, *left*), who roamed the Nordic seas and helped to awaken interest in the Arctic region. The CHURCH OF NOTRE-DAME-DE-BONSECOURS, built in 1770, boasts an altarpiece that covers the entire apse, as well as several sculptures.

SAINT-JEAN-PORT-JOLI. The longstanding traditions of river transport, boatbuilding, carpentry and sculpture require technical woodworking skills. This heritage is reflected by the subtlety of the chiseled wooden décor in the old houses, as well as by the craftwork being produced today on the South Shore, particularly in Saint-Jean-Port-Joli. The family name of Bourgault constantly crops up in this context: this dynasty of sculptors and decorative artists has been practicing its trade in the village since the 1930s. The local woodwork is on display in several stores.

THE BOURGAULT DYNASTY (1897–1967)
Médard Bourgault, born in Saint-Jean-Port-Joli, sailed on the Saint Lawrence for several years before learning boatbuilding from his father. In order to feed his extensive family, he started sculpting small figurines and other objects to sell to passing tourists in the summer of 1930. The success of this venture led him to teach his relatives – and more besides, as he ended up opening a sculpture school in 1940. Hundreds of craftspeople have perpetuated the tradition of the Bourgaults.

PHILIPPE AUBERT DE GASPÉ (1786–1871)
The last seigneur of Saint-Jean-Port-Joli published two books that proved landmarks in 19th-century Canadian literature: *The Old Canadians* (1863), a comedy of manners evoking seigneurial life at the time of the British Conquest ● *38*, and his *Memoirs* (1866), which recount his childhood and bring to life the places and events of the South Shore.

LAKE TROIS-SAUMONS. This lake, lying inland from Saint-Pamphile amidst natural scenery, is ideally suited to water sports. A 75-mile (125km) network of trails has also been set up for the benefit of hikers.

LA SEIGNEURIE DES AULNAIES. This old estate, about 3 miles (5km) east of the village of Saint-Roch, has been converted into a museum of the seigneurial system, which was officially abolished in 1854. The picturesque, recently restored manor house opens onto gardens and the river; it is open to the public, as is the watermill, which has been refitted with new machinery ● 66 so that it can once again produce wheat and buckwheat flour.

Kamouraska County

This region marks a transition between the South Shore and the Lower Saint Lawrence. The landscape changes drastically: after the low terrace of Kamouraska, the coast rears up in a string of narrow, rugged terraces that herald the meeting of the mountains and the sea.

LA POCATIÈRE. This industrial and trading town is also an academic center. The cleric and teacher Abbott François Pilote (1811–86) became interested in agricultural education in the 1850s, when he was the head teacher of the classical college in La Pocatière. In 1859, he founded Canada's school of agriculture here, and his mission as a teacher and researcher is continued today by an agricultural technology institute and some experimental farms. The FRANÇOIS PILOTE MUSEUM displays, over a series of rooms, collections of winter vehicles, such as carioles; scientific instruments, such as sound meters; and stuffed specimens of the local fauna, such as moose, bison, turtledoves and partridges.

SAINT-PACÔME. In the exceptional surroundings of one of the most beautiful gorges of the Ouelle River, and in one of the 40 pits that bound it, it is possible to witness the sight of salmon making their way upriver ● 87. The fish leap out of

the water and demonstrate the power of their instincts
as they endeavor to pass over obstacles.

RIVIÈRE-OUELLE. The quay is the prolongation of a
small cove shrouded in dog roses, with a view of the
Charlevoix coast in the distance. The village is off the
beaten track, but its villas, beaches, inn and mid-19th
century hotel offer an inviting foretaste of the Gaspésie
region ▲ 298.

SAINT-DENIS. The ABOITEAU DE KAMOURASKA museum,
near Saint-Denis, explains the creation (1823) and
functioning of the longest polder in Quebec, spread along
38 miles (60km) of the county's coastline. It was built to
drain the marshy shores and regulate the spring tides that
used to destroy crops. Saint-Denis is also the site of the
MAISON CHAPAIS, once owned by Jean-Charles Chapais
(1811–85), one of the fathers of the 1867 Confederation ● 41.

KAMOURASKA. This village overhanging the sea is one of the
oldest (1790) and one of the most beautiful in the region. It
flaunts two strips of elegant villas and luxurious residences,
which give way to the old sailors' houses on the quayside,
complete with their impeccable gardens. It is tempting to
enter it on tiptoes, for fear of disturbing its gentle charm.
There is a sly, slightly malicious, local saying that 'Charlevoix
is the most beautiful part of Quebec... seen from
Kamouraska'. The village has served as a county town, seat
of justice, port and trading center, and it has been attracting
tourists ever since 1815. Its ART AND HISTORY CENTER provides
an overview of its settlement, local history and genealogy,
while the KAMOURASKA MUSEUM focuses on ethnography,
with a selection of 19th-century domestic objects and
furniture.

SAINT-ANDRÉ-DE-KAMOURASKA. The HALTE ÉCOLOGIQUE
DES BATTURES DU KAMOURASKA provides information on the
fragile ecosystem of the salt marshes and the wildlife of the
riverbank. The CHURCH OF SAINT-ANDRÉ, built in 1806, is the
oldest in the region: its sculpted, gilt décor is restrained but
nevertheless reflects the affluence of the riverside parishes.
LA BOUCANERIE, in the heart of the village, offers smoked
salmon, sturgeon and herring, as well as the subtle smells
associated with this Native-American preservation method.

Pour Information Sadresser au
PACIFIQUE CANADIEN

FISH SMOKEHOUSES
The smoking of fish
and venison – long
practiced by the
Native Americans,
who had no
knowledge of the use
of salt – involves
exposing their flesh to
the dehydrating
action of fumes.
Numerous
smokehouses can be
found in Lower Saint
Lawrence, from
Saint-André-de-
Kamouraska to
Matane ▲ 299,
passing through the
Île-Verte, which is still
dotted with several of
these buildings.
Salmon, sturgeon and
herring are the
preferred dishes of
smoked-fish
connoisseurs.

THE DAMSON PLUM
The purple damson, originally brought to Europe by the Crusaders, was introduced into Nouvelle-France in the 17th century. It moved from Quebec City with the establishment of new settlements and became a feature of orchards on both sides of the Saint Lawrence. It became scarce in the 1950s but has now found its way back into Quebecois kitchens thanks to the efforts of the Maison de la Prune in Saint-André.

PEAT BOGS
Lower Saint Lawrence still exploits several peat bogs that use harvesting techniques such as aspiration and harrowing to ensure the renewal of plants. Glacial constrictions or bad drainage created these atrophied expanses of water thousands of years ago. The decomposed vegetal matter and bog moss that colonize them are used for horticultural purposes, as a filtration agent, or by health practitioners for their curative properties.

To the east of the village, the MAISON DE LA PRUNE is dedicated to the revival of a regional tradition – the cultivation of damson plums. The orchard here boasts some extremely old and rare plum trees. On the ground floor of the adjoining museum – used as a general store between 1853 and 1875 – the harvested fruit is put on sale: damson plums, blueberries, crab apples and *amélanches* (small purplish berries with a delicate taste), as well as various homemade jams.

The Bas-du-Fleuve ★

In the Bas-du-Fleuve, the Saint Lawrence Valley gives way to the Gaspésie coastline. The terrain becomes more rugged, the wind more gusty and the climate somewhat harsher, although this is tempered by the influence of the sea. Forestry and fishing gradually take over from agriculture and livestock farming; tourism has been a major seasonal activity for over 150 years.

RIVIÈRE-DU-LOUP. The seigneury granted in 1673 to the fur trader Charles-Aubert de La Chesnaye received a significant boost in the early 19th century when it began exporting its wood. The economy was subsequently further strengthened by the introduction of light industry, commerce and tourism. The LOWER SAINT LAWRENCE MUSEUM, specializing in the region's art and history, puts on exhibitions of an ethnological nature.

CACOUNA. Its name means 'home of the porcupine' in Algonquin. In the early 20th century, it was one of the province's most renowned spas. Many middle-class families came here to spend the summer, including that of the poet Émile Nelligan. A 28-stage architectural circuit takes in old villas, chapels, a general store and a church. The latter two are open to the public.

ÎLE VERTE. This island (*below*) has a wealth of treasures: agricultural landscapes, a lighthouse dating from 1809, rocky outcrops, small coves, untouched beaches, birds (both nesting and predatory) and, offshore, seals and whales. A mere 50 years ago, the island could boast hundreds of residents living there all year round, but these numbers have now dwindled to around 30 hardy souls. The small museum set up in an *école de rang* (a type of rural school) ▲ *220* concentrates on eelgrass and herring smokehouses.

ÎLE-AUX-BASQUES. This island contains prehistoric remains dating from the 8th century BC. Much later, in the 16th century, it was occupied by Basques intent on catching whales and trading with the Native Americans. The ovens they used to melt whale fat can still be seen ● *46*. In the 19th century, agriculture and logging came to the fore. In 1929, the island was bought by the Canadian Provancher Society of Natural History, which declared it a protected heritage site and a refuge for migratory birds. In summer, the Society organizes day trips to the island from Trois-Pistoles.

TROIS-PISTOLES. The village's name comes from a 17th-century story of a sailor who lost a goblet with three *pistoles* (gold coins) here. THE PARK OF THE BASQUE ADVENTURE IN

VICTOR-LÉVY BEAULIEU
Victor-Lévy Beaulieu, born in 1945 in Saint-Paul-de-la-Croix near the Rivière-du-Loup, is a novelist, dramatist, essayist, publisher and journalist who has explored a wide range of literary genres, from short stories to laments and humorous epics. He has won a number of awards, including the Governor General's Prize for *Don Quichotte de la démanche*. He has published criticism on forgotten Quebecois authors, as well as on Victor Hugo and Jack Kerouac. He has also scripted soap operas that are distinguished by their great literary merit: *Race de monde*, *L'Héritage* and *Montréal, P.Q.* His characters, such as Xavier Galarneau in *L'Héritage*, are remarkable for their intensity.

AMERICA chronicles and commemorates the history of the Île-aux-Basques. In the heart of the village, the MAISON VLB is an imaginative museum devoted to the work of the writer Victor-Lévy Beaulieu. It contains not only his manuscripts, novels and studies of local parishes, but also sets from his soap operas, an audiovisual room and a café.

LE BIC. Legend has it that the little angel entrusted with the decoration of the earth at the time of the Creation mislaid all his treasures in Le Bic, accidentally giving it beautiful wild beaches, lofty headlands, reefs, caves, islets, sheltered coves and a river amply stocked with salmon. Le Bic is indeed an impressive sight, whether viewed from the sea or from Saint-Fabien, tucked into the foot of the Pic Champlain mountain.

The Saint Lawrence is undoubtedly one of the world's greatest river. It may not be the longest, or the widest, or the most heavily populated, or the oldest, but it stands out on account of its awe-inspiring landscapes, its abundant and diversified wildlife and its history. With a watercourse of these dimensions, the issue of human responsibility for the environment comes to the fore. Just as the present inevitably bears traces of the past, so nothing that occurs upstream can be disassociated from its effects downstream.

THE BELUGA, ECOLOGICAL SYMBOL OF THE RIVER
This small white cetacean feeds on the fish and invertebrates in the estuary. It is thought that there were several thousand of them when the first Europeans arrived, but there are now no more than 500. They have been affected by the chemical pollution emitted by the upstream industrial zones.

UNDERWATER LIFE
Life takes on surprising shapes and colors against the river's rocky walls and bed. The organisms permanently lodged there benefit from a constant renewal of their food supply, while crustaceans and small fish play hide and seek, providing a fascinating spectacle for divers. The river's depths also supply food to large fish, seals and belugas.

A VARIED HABITAT
Over the course of its journey, the river changes its character, from choppy to leisurely, from expansive to constrained by steep banks. This variability allows it to create habitats favorable to the different species of fish, birds and mammals that feed and reproduce in it or use it as a break during migration. When the sea waters mix with those of the river, the fauna diversifies and gains new riches.

RIMOUSKI. This town expanded rapidly in the mid 20th century, mainly because of the lumber industry, although the postwar recovery and the subsequent development of the service sector and the North Shore mines ▲ *330* were also major contributing factors. There has also been an upsurge in seafaring activities. The town's old school is now used as a regional museum; in Rimouski-Est it is possible to visit the stone and timber MAISON LAMONTAGNE, built in the 18th century and enlarged in the 19th. Further east lie the MUSEUM OF THE SEA and the POINTE-AU-PÈRE NATIONAL HISTORIC SITE, containing exhibitions on navigation and the wrecking of the *Empress of Ireland*.

SAINTE-LUCE. Here, the riverbank is lined by a watermill, a church with striking interior decoration and picturesque late-19th-century villas, their bright colors setting off the older, neoclassical houses. A sandy beach stretches out to the east of the town.

MÉTIS GARDENS ★. These gardens at the mouth of the River Métis extend over 197 acres (88ha), around a fifth of which are cultivated, and benefit from a microclimate created by the humid atmosphere engendered by the salty waters. The land was originally purchased by a rich industrialist in 1887 as a salmon fishing ground. After it passed into the hands of his niece, Elsie Meighen Reford, she gradually transformed it into a sumptuous getaway surrounded by gardens designed in the English style. These were created between 1926 and 1959 as a series of distinct settings – including the Rockery, the Royal Alley, the Rhododendron Garden, the Primrose Garden and the Apple-Tree Garden – punctuated by running water, ponds, undergrowth, indigenous plants, botanical d floral compositions. The villa rves as a restaurant, local museum l crafts store, as well as offering icnic areas for the use of visitors. he Métis Gardens provide an atable finale to a tour of the Fleuve.

TRAGEDY
When the *Empress of Ireland* left the shipyards in 1906, it was acclaimed for its speed and comfort. Designed to hold 1,550 passengers, it had 1,477 onboard when it left Quebec City for Liverpool on the night of May 28, 1914. At 1.50am, near Rimouski, it spotted a ship about to cross its bows. The sudden appearance of a fog bank and the resulting loss of visibility forced both vessels to make maneuvers and in the confusion, it proved impossible to avoid a collision. A hole in the *Empress'* hull measuring 20 by 25 ft (6 by 7m) let almost 800,000 gallons (3 million l) of water enter the ship per second; it sank in 14 minutes, taking 1,012 passengers to their death.

Gaspésie and the Îles-de-la-Madeleine

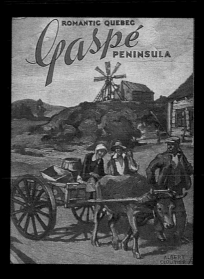

Matane, *299*

Saint-Anne-des-Monts, *300*

From Tourelle to Gaspé, *301*

The Coast from Gaspé to Percé, *303*

Forillon Park, *304*

Baie des Chaleurs, *307*

Matapédia Valley, *309*

A chain of islands in the Gulf of
Saint Lawrence, *310*

Île du Cap aux Meules, *313*

Île d'Entrée, *314*

Île du Havre Aubert, *314*

Île du Havre aux Maisons, *316*

From Pointe-aux-Loups
    to Grande Entrée, *316*

▲ Gaspésie

1. MATANE 2. SAINTE-ANNE-DES-MONTS 3. GASPÉSIE PARK 4. LA MARTRE 5. MONT-SAINT-PIERRE 6. MURDOCHVILLE 7. L'ANSE-AU-GRIFFON 8. CAP-DES-ROSIERS 9. FORILLON PARK 10. GASPÉ

⏱ 7 days
🚌 675 mi/1000km

GEOLOGICAL FORMATION

Gaspésie forms the last link in the Appalachian chain. Its land formation is ancient – 400–500 million years old – mainly sedimentary and strikingly molded by erosion. In its widest section, the peninsula is an immense, raised plateau covered with a network of valleys. The Baie des Chaleurs is flanked by more recent formations (350 million years old), made up of sandstone, shale or limestone.

Gaspésie is a peninsula the size of Switzerland that protrudes into the Gulf of Saint Lawrence toward the Atlantic Ocean. Most of its villages are scattered around the coastline, while the interior remains wild and largely uninhabited. For generations of Quebecois, the 'tour of Gaspésie' constitutes a pilgrimage that must be undertaken at least once in a lifetime.

The history of Gaspésie

Archeologists have unearthed numerous prehistoric sites, and some of these indicate that human occupation of the region dates back to the very distant past. Some seven or eight thousand years ago, as the ice packs retreated, Plano hunters started to inhabit Gaspésie. This prehistoric people, who were dispersed all over North America, adapted to the peninsula's environment. Over the course of the following millennia, they were succeeded by other groups, such as the Iroquois ● 44, the Montagnais ▲ 329 and the Micmacs ▲ 308. In 1534, Jacques Cartier landed in Gaspé ▲ 303 and took possession of the area; a century later, fishermen began to settle in Mont Louis, Gaspé, Percé and Pabos. The French paid little attention to the colonization of Gaspésie, however, but after the Conquest the 'Gaspé

11. PERCÉ **12.** ÎLE BONAVENTURE **13.** CHANDLER **14.** NEWPORT **15.** PASPEBIAC **16.** BONAVENTURE **17.** MIGUASHA PARK **18.** HISTORIC SITE OF LA BATAILLE-DE-LA-RISTIGOUCHE **19.** MATAPÉDIA **20.** CAUSAPSCAL

Landscape near Percé

'What do you want, this is cod country! Through your eyes and nostrils, through your tongue and throat, as well as through your ears, you will soon be convinced that, on the Gaspésie peninsula, cod forms the basis of nourishment and amusement, business and conversation, regrets and hopes, fortune and life – I would dare to say, of society itself.'
Abbot Jean-Baptiste-Antoine Ferland (1836)

Coast' was subjected to a more sustained development and population drive. Demobilized English soldiers made their homes here, followed by waves of Acadians uprooted from their homeland ▲ *308* and Loyalist colonists ■ *18*. From 1766 onwards, businessmen from Jersey began to set up shop here, and they attracted significant numbers of manual workers to the region. Charles Robin ▲ *308*, John LeBoutillier ▲ *302* and John Fauvel, among others, established powerful empires based on cod, by combining exploitation of fishermen's labor with a monopoly over the sale of cod as a foodstuff. At the end of the 19th century, reduced catches, a serious banking crisis and a fishermen's revolt led the Jersey entrepreneurs to withdraw, to the benefit of Canadians. In the 20th century, the local fishermen organized themselves as cooperatives. Fishing became increasingly industrialized and, meanwhile, the regional economy diversified, firstly through logging, mining and paper production and then through tourism. The total depletion of cod reserves in the estuary over the last few years has dealt a severe blow to fishermen and obliged them to resort to other species (such as lobster, crab and queen scallop) ■ *28*.

Matane

This town, known as the 'shrimp capital', plays an important role in the local economy. It boasts a modern port that guarantees a year-round ferry connection ▲ *355* with the North Shore (Godbout and Baie-Comeau ▲ *330*). With the decline in fishing, both the town and the surrounding area have increasingly drawn on the resources of their forests.

THE *BARACHOIS*
After Matane, the coast takes the form of a broad plain that climbs upward along gently sloping terraces. Many villages have grown up at the mouths of the major rivers, in a configuration reflecting a nautical

tradition that is now partially lost: in order to accommodate their boats and fishing facilities, many of these villages were built near *barachois* (from the Basque *barra choa*) – shallow expanses of water that form behind sandbanks at the mouth of a river.

AN ENDANGERED SPECIES?
Gaspésie once had an ample population of caribou. Now, Gaspésie Park shelters and protects the last herd in the region. It also plays host to other cervids, such as the white-tailed deer (*below*), known locally as the Quebec roe deer.

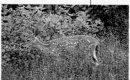

Matane soon acquired a large paper mill. In the town center, a migratory channel, set close to a dam, provides a good opportunity to watch the powerful leaping of the salmon as they attempt to travel upriver to breed ● *87*. The rivers in the hinterland are rich in salmon and are protected as natural reserves. A stroll along their banks can bring some delightful discoveries, such as 'salmon pits' nestling in the coolness of the forest.

MATANE RESERVE. Matane's famous salmon river leads to a wildlife reserve set in the heart of the Appalachians, an extensive boreal forest with large plantations of white birch trees. A network of forest trails makes it possible to penetrate the habitat of the hazel grouse, the beaver, the bear and, above all, the moose, which can be spotted in summer around wetland areas (near Lake de la Tête and the trout pond, for example). Lake Matane, situated in the hollow of a glacial valley, is a haven of tranquility, where walkers can admire a number of different birds, including loons, barn swallows and, increasingly rarely, royal eagles.

Sainte-Anne-des-Monts

This village at the mouth of the Sainte-Anne River is popular with fishermen. Most of its original buildings were destroyed by a fire in 1915, but some superb houses have survived, particularly the MAISON LAMONTAGNE, a fine example of the Regency style that was built around 1872 by an important logging magnate.

GASPÉSIE PARK. Highway 299, which leaves Sainte-Anne-des-Monts and crosses the peninsula from north to south, provides access to Gaspésie Park; this covers part of the Chic Choc Mountains, which include Mounts Albert and Jacques-Cartier, the highest peaks in Quebec. Partly spared from the action of the glaciers in the last glaciation ▲ *298*, they are endowed with a totally distinctive flora and provide a refuge for an isolated population of caribou. In the McGerigle Mountains area, visitors may stumble on the exceptional sight of woodland caribous, moose and white-tailed deer ▲ 332 together on the same spot. The top of Mount Albert, as flat as a pancake, is a veritable grassy tundra that serves as the southernmost mating ground for Arctic birds such as redpolls and pipits. Well-kept footpaths lead to the highest spots in the park, where there are peaks of

over 1,000 feet (305m), with stunning views of an endless sea of steep-sided valleys, stark ridges and abrupt depressions. (The paths require a moderate level of fitness.) The park has excellent accommodation facilities (a hotel and high-quality campsites), as well as a fine restaurant in the Gîte du Mont-Albert.

From Tourelle to Gaspé

Beyond Sainte-Anne-des-Monts, the Chic Chocs are more tightly packed and the villages squeeze in between the mountains and the sea. After Tourelle, which is distinguished by an impressive natural monolith near the harbor, the coastal road climbs, weaving its way round capes and mountains before crossing numerous valleys and coves. The rivers open on to the sea almost at a right angle to create one of the prettiest stretches along this coast; this delightful picture is further enhanced by the charming little villages strung out along the side of the road.

LA MARTRE. This hamlet nestling on a cape boasts a wooden-framed lighthouse dating from 1906 that now serves as a museum focusing on all the region's lighthouses. Further on, the peaks looming over MONT-SAINT-PIERRE are a mecca for fans of paragliding and hang-gliding. Every year, the village organizes an international hang-gliding festival. A track turns away from the coast to ANSE-PLEUREUSE, a village tucked in the valley with easy access to Lake Anse-Pleureuse, a magnificent expanse of water bounded by wooded mountains that attracts few visitors.

NORDIC LANDSCAPE
The Chic Choc Mountains provide the backbone of Gaspésie. These mountains, eroded by glaciers and shaped by geological folding and faults, soar to heights of over 4,000 feet (1,220m). Some of them have vegetation similar to that of the Great North of Quebec.

BETWEEN THE SKY AND THE SEA
Three launching ramps have been set up for hang-gliders on the summit of Mont-Saint-Pierre, and their colorful wings have become an integral part of the local environment.

MURDOCHVILLE. In the early 20th century, Alfred Miller was the first to discover traces of copper on the bed of the River York, close to Gaspé. He made several further investigations, along with his brothers, before finding a rich seam at the source of the river. The brothers then sold their concession to Noranda Mines, which built a town right next to the mine in the early 1950s. Situated 25 miles (16km) from the coast, amid splendid natural scenery, it was named Murdochville, in honor of the company's first chairman, James Y. Murdoch. Noranda Mines decided to process the mineral in situ and so installed the technology to convert the ore into a metallic form. This operation requires abundant electricity, forcing the company to build its own hydroelectric power station ● 68 at the end of the 1950s. A museum offers visitors the opportunity to go down into the (still operating) mine and visit one of the galleries.

TOWARD POINTE DE FORILLON. Going back to the coast, the terrain is again extremely striking. Around GROS-MORNE and MANCHE-D'EPÉE, the capes plunge right into the sea, squashing the road against the shoreline. Bold slashes in the rocky façades reveal their twisted entrails, folded countless times by the shuddering of the Earth's crust. The road goes through several villages, including the former fishing stations of CLORIDORME, L'ANSE-À-VALLEAU and RIVIÈRE-AU-RENARD.

MANOIR LEBOUTILLIER. This house, built between 1936 and 1938 with a cargo of pine rescued from a shipwreck, is situated in the small village of L'Anse-au-Griffon. It presents an exhibition covering the life of John LeBoutillier, one of the important Jersey businessmen who contributed to the development of the Gaspésie peninsula.

CAP-DES-ROSIERS LIGHTHOUSE. The village of Cap-des-Rosiers, the gateway to Forillon Park ▲ 304, contains the tallest lighthouse in the country (121 feet/37m). It was built in 1858 in response to the numerous shipwrecks that had occurred off this part of the coast. In April 1847, the *Carrick*, a ship carrying Irish immigrants, crashed into the rocks of Fortillon. Barely half the

WOMEN AND CHILDREN FIRST! Gaspésie is 'a land of tempests and shipwreck', according to Abbott Ferland, the 19th-century missionary and traveler.

> 'And there we found a strange tide, [...] We had to stay
> close to the land, between the aforesaid cape and
> an island to its east [...] And there we dropped anchor...'
>
> Jacques Cartier

passengers survived the terrible storm, and those that did decided to settle on the coast between Cap-des-Rosiers and Rivière-au-Renard. In summertime, the Cap-des-Rosiers lighthouse opens its doors to the public and there is a guided tour explaining the role and development of lighthouses in the region.

The coast from Gaspé to Percé

GASPÉ. Jacques Cartier's point of disembarkation in 1543 owes its name to the Micmac word *gespeg* ('end of the land'). Six steles overlooking the bay commemorate this sailor's voyage from Saint-Malo in Brittany. Before the Conquest, there had been various fruitless attempts at colonizing Gaspé. English immigrants, led by Felix O'Hara, joined forces with Loyalists toward the end of 18th century to establish the foundations of the town, taking advantage of its natural harbor to exploit the resources of the sea (with cod and salmon fisheries, shipbuilding, whaling and international trade). The cathedral contains a superb stained-glass window and a fresco marking the 400th anniversary of Cartier's arrival. Gaspé has also preserved some older buildings, such as the OLD SEMINARY (1926), SAINT PAUL'S ANGLICAN CHURCH (1940) and the ASH INN, an eccentric stone house built for William Wakeham (1845–1915). This doctor and sailor led an expedition to the Hudson Strait in 1897 in order to proclaim Canada's sovereignty over its Arctic territory. THE GASPÉSIE MUSEUM presents a permanent exhibition ('A People of the Sea') exploring the history of the peninsula. Other exhibitions are regularly organized around

more specific themes, such as art, heritage, history, craft or Native Americans traditions. To the west of the River York lie the buildings of the GASPÉ FISH FARM (1875–1938), the oldest of its kind in Quebec. This complex was created by the Government to encourage the spawning of trout and salmon.
BARACHOIS DE MALBAIE. This *barachois* ▲ 300, situated inside a bay which was known as Bayc-des-Morues under French rule, is the most spectacular in the whole Gaspésie region. After passing through COIN-DU-BANC, the road to Percé offers drivers a series of spectacular panoramic views as it traverses a succession of abysses, curves and dizzying climbs.

Jacques Cartier left Saint-Malo on April 20, 1534, and took about three weeks to cross the Atlantic. After other explorations, he and his crew finally landed in Gaspé on July 24.

COD FISHING
In former times, the Gaspésie fisherman worked alone onboard his traditional barge. His main accessory was his fishing line, with a lead ballast attached to the hook. Sometimes three men would join forces on bigger barges to

trawl: using a sleeping line fitted with several hundred hooks, they caught squid, cod and small fish. The cod would be gutted and decapitated, then salted and left exposed to air and sunlight on the shingly beach or on *vigneaux* – stalls covered by a grill that allowed air to circulate.

Forillon Park, with its high cliffs, wooded mountains and string of bays, constitutes a miniature replica of Gaspésie. Several ecosystems rub shoulders here: immense forests, Arctic and Alpine plants, the flora of the Penouille dunes and that of the marshes. This peninsula provides a haven for a wide range of animals and is an ideal spot for observing birds of prey and passerines during the migration season. Other attractions include sea mammals and the buildings in the historic sector, vestiges of fishermen's lives a hundred years ago.

THE *ALCIDAE*
The black guillemot and the razorbill (which resembles the Emperor penguin of the southern hemisphere) are seabirds that live on the Forillon cliffs. While razorbills organize themselves in tightly knit communities, black guillemots tend to form loose groups and some even nest in isolation. Less pelagic than the other members of the *Alcidae* family, they stay close to the coast and pass the winter near water that remains free from ice.

ARCTIC VEGETATION

For the last 10,000 years, the limestone cliffs of the north face of Forillon have been home to around 30 rare plant species. Swept along by the glaciers, they are of Arctic and Alpine origin: some come from the Great North, others from the Rocky Mountains.

THE KITTIWAKE

The kittiwake is the most numerous of all the seabirds that nest on the Forillon cliffs: 10,500 pairs were counted in 1989. They have been steadily increasing in number over the last 30 years as an indirect result of intensive deep-sea fishing in the area. The large fish caught in this way are the main predators of the smaller fish that form the bulk of the kittiwake's diet.

THE MAMMALS

Black bears, porcupines, beavers, marmots, hares, foxes and moose are among the mammals most often seen in the park's forests. From May to November, the coastal waters provide sustenance for passing colonies of seals and whales.

GRAND-GRAVE, AN OLD FISHING STATION

The historic site of Grand-Grave, situated to the south of the Forillon headland, comprises a handful of restored and furnished buildings (*above*). The different processes of cod fishing ▲*303* are explained here, as well as the methods by which it is salted and dried and the repercussions of the cod industry on international trade.

THE SEALS

Three species of seal are found off the coast of Forillon Park. The gray seal – also known as the sea wolf on account of its howling – is a large mammal (750 lb/ 340kg) with a long muzzle. Common seals (*below*) appear at the foot of the Forillon cliffs from mid-May to mid-June and can be easily observed until mid-November. Since 1993, schools of Greenland seals have occasionally been spotted swimming along the coast.

PERCÉ. The village of Percé is famous for its
scenery. It lies close to a splendid rock molded by the sea,
while the nearby mountains and capes are seemingly scattered
at random by some antediluvian upheaval. The village is
divided into two large coves, one backed by Mount Joli, the
other by its prolongation, the Percé Rock. The Micmacs
considered this to be a sacred site (as well as an excellent
fishing ground). Around the end of the 16th century,
European fishermen also came here to cast their nets. It was
not until the mid-17th century, however, that a more stable
settlement began to take shape, defying British incursions
bent on evicting its inhabitants. In 1781, the Jersey
businessman Charles Robin ▲ *308* set up a fishing station in
Percé that went on to become the most important center for
cod production in Gaspésie. The village has preserved some
fine architectural mementos of this past,
particularly on the quayside. The
CHAFAUD and the SALINE were both used
to process cod. The BELL HOUSE, the so-
called PIRATE'S HOUSE, the old barn-
turned-art center and the general store
now occupied by the fishermen's
cooperative are all vestiges of buildings
owned by the Robin Company. In the
second half of the 19th century, Percé
became a prized tourist destination, with
naturalists, writers and holidaymakers
flocking to revel in its charms.

THE ÎLE BONAVENTURE. Percé looks
out onto a lush island lined with red cliffs
that evoke the shape of a whale and
provide a nesting place for an array of
seabirds. This ornithologist's paradise is
hard to match anywhere else in Quebec.
A visit to the Île Bonaventure allows
visitors to enjoy a close-up view of a
colony of gannets. The kittiwake,

razorbill and guillemot all take refuge in the crevices of the cliffs on the east coast of the island; they can be observed from a footpath, living and breeding in their colonies according to time-honored rituals. When they arrive in springtime, these birds set about gathering the seaweed and plants required to build their nest. Each species has its own particular nesting ground, which they return to year after year. They are skilful fishers and feed themselves from the nearby sea, but when winter approaches they make their way to more southerly climes.

THE *TURLUTTEUSE*
Born in Newport of an Irish father and Acadian mother, Mary Travers (1894–1941), better known as La Bolduc, was one of Quebec's great singer-songwriters ● 92. From 1928 until her death, she recorded nearly 80 songs inspired by local traditions and working-class life. Her songs, punctuated by *turluttes* (hummed refrains), evoked the experience of humble folk with extraordinary vitality.

Baie des Chaleurs

The name 'Bay of Heats' was coined by Jacques Cartier, who was struck by the high temperatures prevailing in July 1534. The region's financial development has been based on forestry resources, agriculture and fishing. Its towns are alternately anglophone and francophone, bearing witness to the various waves of colonists that have made their homes here. Loyalist and Acadian communities can also be found.

Gaspésie is remarkable for its small, brightly colored rural houses. Their architecture reflects the various waves of immigrants who have settled on the peninsula.

CHANDLER. This town was the first in Gaspésie to be endowed with a pulp mill (1910), and even today it revolves around the paper industry. The waters of its port are deep enough to receive the large ships that load up with the paper used to print the *New York Times*.

GRAND-PABOS. Archeological excavations have unearthed a fishing station dating back to the period of French rule; its remains are on show in a futuristic structure on the *banc* (strand) of Grand-Pabos. A few miles further west, NEWPORT commemorates the life and career of one of its daughters, Mary Travers (La Bolduc) ● 92.

ROBIN OF THE COAST
In the late 18th century, Charles Robin (1743–1824) teamed up with other immigrants from Jersey to create Charles Robin, Collas & Co. (CRC). From its base in Paspébiac, the company controlled an enormous fishing infrastructure that squeezed the lifeblood out of fishermen: CRC set the price of both fresh cod and the processed end-product sold to the fishermen, who had no alternative but to buy from the company.

ACADIANS IN GASPÉSIE
In 1713, France gave Acadia to England under the terms of the Treaty of Utrecht. This territory, which now forms part of the Maritime Provinces, was inhabited by French speakers. In 1755, when the threat of war loomed in the colonies, the Governor of Nova Scotia took the precaution of deporting all Acadians. A good number of these ended up in Gaspésie. By the end of the 18th century, three-quarters of Gaspésie's population was Acadian.

HISTORIC SITE OF THE BANC DE PASPÉBIAC. A cluster of buildings on the strand of Paspébiac dates from the era of the great Jersey merchants and reflects their commercial activities. An old office, a powder store and the Robin boathouse are grouped around a large warehouse (the 'BB', after LeBoutillier Brothers), where cod was prepared for delivery. There are also some sumptuous residences, such as the manor that once belonged to the Robin family (1815), now a thalassotherapy center called the Auberge du Parc.

ACADIAN MUSEUM OF QUEBEC. The village of Bonaventure, set at the mouth of a beautiful river, is a bastion of Acadian culture. The museum built near the church tells the story of this people, who were marked by their uprooting in 1755. It organizes exhibitions on the history and culture of the Acadians that settled in Quebec in the 18th century. A few miles inland, enthusiasts of caves and ancient life forms can make an appointment to visit the underground grotto in SAINT-ELZÉAR, the oldest excavation of its kind in Quebec. The bones of extinct species, such as the wolverine, have recently been discovered here.

NEW RICHMOND. This little village steeped in Loyalist tradition bears witness to the duality of the region's culture. A reconstruction of an old hamlet, the BRITISH HERITAGE CENTER, charts the history of the British colonists who left the US to settle in Gaspésie.

MARIA MICMAC RESERVE. Up until the 16th century, the Micmacs occupied a vast territory that stretched from Gaspésie all the way to the Maritime Provinces. The arrival of the Europeans led them to settle along the coast of Baie des Chaleurs. Alcohol, disease and a sedentary lifestyle had devastating effects on their development. Today, the Micmacs are concentrated in Gaspé, Maria and Restigouche.

MIGUASHA PARK. This park, long recognized internationally as a paleontological site of major importance, is endowed

with a modern museum that sets off the remarkable collection of fossilized plants, fish and amphibians. A tour of the park includes a visit to the foot of the cliffs, where systematic excavations have been undertaken over the last 25 years. Fossils up to 365 million years old have been found.

BATTLE OF THE RISTIGOUCHE HISTORIC SITE ★. This center near Pointe-de-la-Croix commemorates the last military episode in the British conquest of Canada. In 1760, almost a year after their defeat on the Plains of Abraham ▲ *253*, the French sent a fleet to recapture Quebec City. The ships, commanded by Admiral François Chenard de La Giraudais, were unable to enter the Gulf of Saint Lawrence and so took refuge in the Baie des Chaleurs, at the mouth of the Ristigouche River, where they came under enemy fire and were all sunk. One of these ships, the *Machault*, has been the subject of extensive archeological excavations. Numerous items, remarkably preserved from the ravages of time, have been rescued from the seabed and are now on display.

RENÉ LÉVESQUE (1922–87)
René Lévesque, born in New Carlisle, started his career as a war correspondent before becoming a highly respected television presenter. In 1962, he put the finishing touches to the nationalization of electricity as a minister for the Liberal Party. He broke ranks in 1968 to form the Parti Quebecois. He was elected Prime Minister of Quebec in 1976 and remained in office until 1983. This man of dazzling intelligence and irresistible charisma advocated the independence of Quebec and has had a lasting impact on its subsequent development.

The Matapédia Valley

MATAPÉDIA. Situated at the confluence of two major rivers (the Ristigouche and the Matapédia), this village has long been famous for its salmon fishing. After passing through the village, the road crosses the Matapédia Valley, leaving the coast behind to enter a densely wooded mountain region where the natural scenery is wild and breathtaking.

CAUSAPSCAL. This village is dominated by the activity associated with its sawmills but it also contains an old salmon 'fishing camp' ● *87*, the DOMAINE MATAMAJAW, which now serves as a museum familiarizing visitors with all aspects of the once-exclusive sport of salmon fishing. As the road continues onward, the landscape gradually becomes more subdued, giving way first to a region of lakes – including the spectacular Lake Matépedia, which borders on Amoul, Val Brillant and Sayabec – and then to rolling countryside largely occupied by impressive dairy farms and their livestock.

309

▲ A chain of islands in the Gulf of Saint Lawrence

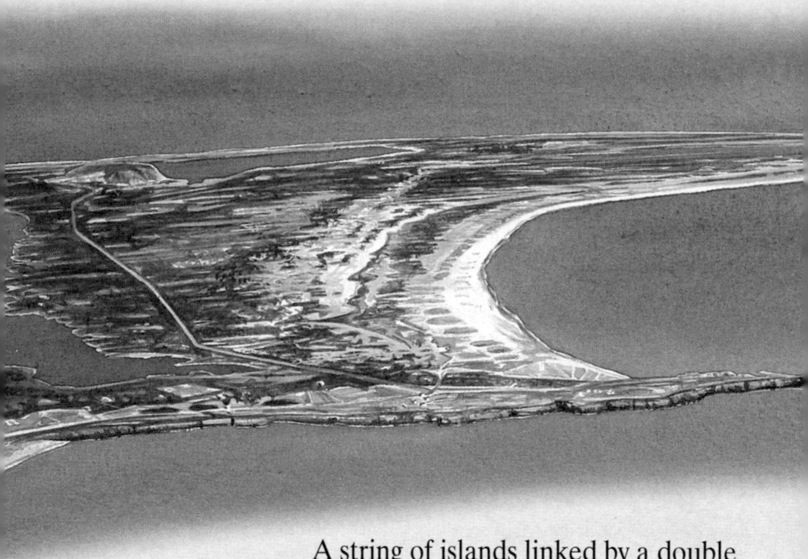

A string of islands linked by a double cordon of sand dunes is scattered far from the coast of Gaspésie. The Îles-de-la-Madeleine take the shape of a crescent indented with lagoons and generously covered with beaches, complemented by Île Brion, with its ecological reserve, Île d'Entrée, with its lush hills, and a sprinkling of islets that serve as bird sanctuaries. The wind and the waves have sculpted their friable sandstone cliffs, molded their sand dunes and battered the few trees that survived the axe of the first inhabitants.

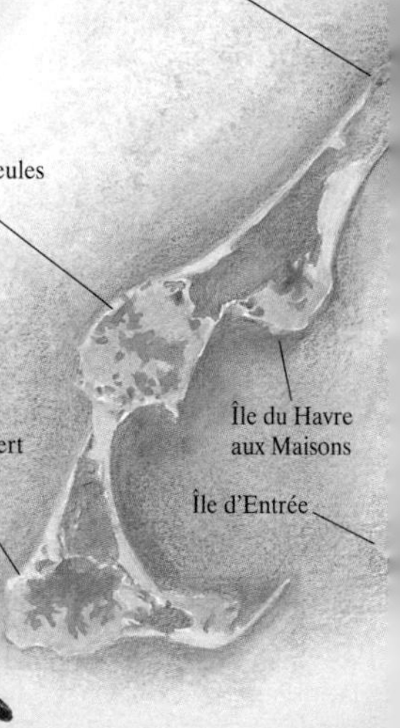

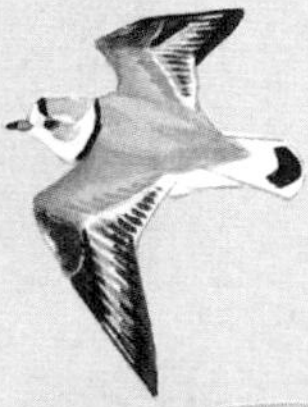

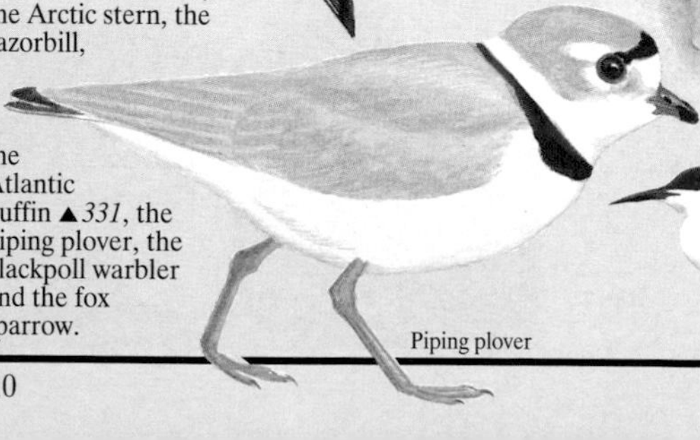

Île aux Loups
Île du Cap aux Meules
Île du Havre aux Maisons
Île du Havre Aubert
Île d'Entrée

A REFUGE FOR BIRDS
Île Brion and the Rocher-aux-Oiseaux play host to significant bird colonies comprising a wide range of species: the horned grebe, the gannet, Leach's storm-petrel, the black guillemot ▲*304*, the whimbrel, the kittiwake ▲*305*, the Arctic stern, the razorbill, the Atlantic puffin ▲*331*, the piping plover, the blackpoll warbler and the fox sparrow.

Piping plover

Dougall's stern

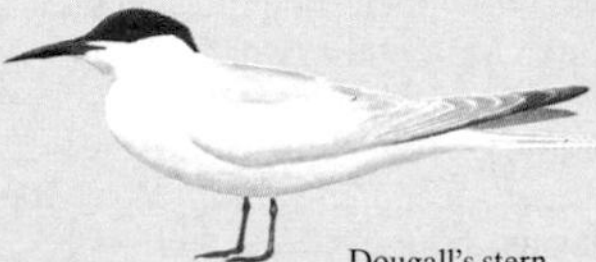

THE ECOLOGY OF THE ISLANDS

The islands are the outgrowths of an underwater platform containing vast deposits of salt. The visible parts are composed of friable sandstone the color of red brick, with occasional splashes of gypsum and clay. Ceaselessly eroded by the wind and the waves, the sandstone on the shore breaks up into dramatic capes. The oxides that color them are rinsed out before blending into the water and going on to nourish the white sand dunes.

Île Brion

Grosse Île

Île de la Grande Entrée

- water
- beach/dune
- prairie
- woodland

A HISTORY OF FISHING

Life on the Îles-de-la-Madeleine has always revolved around fishing, even more so than in Gaspésie. Since 1880, fishermen have taken advantage of the shallows around the islands (as well as their distinctive maritime ecosystem) to net their traditional catches cod, mackerel, herring and lobster. The numerous lagoons are also a boon to fish farmers.

SEALS

Around the end of February, a sizeable school of Greenland seals leaves the Arctic to give birth on the ice floes off the island. Seal culling has been forbidden since the 1970s but local fishermen would like to stabilize their population in the gulf, as they consider them largely responsible for the reduction in the numbers of cod.

A FRAGILE LIFE

The Îles-de-la-Madeleine constitute a fragile environment that often has difficulty in maintaining its precarious equilibrium. The vegetal cover is weakened, the springs of drinking water are under threat and the demand for fresh water is extremely high in summer, when tourists swell the population to twice its normal size.

311

The cliffs of Belle Anse

AN EASY CATCH
Right up to 1914, whales were hunted down in the Gulf of Saint Lawrence (especially beyond Gaspé) and their fat subsequently turned into oil. Way back in the 17th century, an eye witness reported that at 'some times of the year these great cetaceans are so

The Îles-de-la-Madeleine are made up of a dozen islands, most of which are linked by sand dunes and lagoons. They were originally populated by fishermen and today's inhabitants still depend on the resources of the sea for their livelihood. Cod, mackerel and lobster are the traditional catches of the local fishermen, who exploit the islands' distinctive ecosystem ▲ *310* and the shoals that surround them. The breathtaking scenery of cliffs and lagoons, along with the long golden beaches, has made the islands a popular summer destination for tourists, including windsurfers, for whom the windswept conditions are ideal.

A slow growth

Several thousand years ago, the Micmacs ▲ *308*, who were skilled sailors, came to fish in the waters around the islands, which they called *Menagoesenog* ('islands beaten by the backwash'). In the late 16th century, these seas began to attract European fishermen in search of walruses and 'sea wolves' (seals), as well as a place to dry their cod. Despite a few unsuccessful attempts at settling (led by Nicolas Denis in 1654, followed by Sieur Doublet de Honfleur, the Comte de Saint-Pierre and the Pascaud brothers), it was not until the Conquest of 1760 that tenable conditions for sustained occupation could be established. In 1762, some Acadians who had been chased out of their homeland ▲ *308* finally managed to lay the foundations of a permanent settlement. This nucleus was joined by another

numerous that they can be killed with a blow from an oar'.

contingent of Acadians expelled from Saint-Pierre and Miquelin during the French Revolution (due to their support for the Church) and Scottish immigrants who arrived around the same time. In 1787, the seigneury of the Îles-de-la-Madeleine passed into the hands of Isaac Coffin.

The Coffin family maintained a fierce grip over the local economy until 1902 by exploiting the workforce and systematically opposing any demands for property rights. Furthermore, the fishermen suffered not only from the domination of the Jersey businessmen (like their counterparts in Gaspésie) ▲ *299*, but also from overfishing by the Americans, until the government introduced fishing regulations in the 19th century. The abolition of the seigneurial system, closer contact with the mainland and the creation of a number of cooperatives enabled the islanders to improve their lot in the 20th century. Since the 1970s, however, the lack of demand for some fish species, the exhaustion of the stocks of cod and the banning of seal culling have all been severe blows to the livelihoods of islanders. The recent development of tourism and salt mining has injected a welcome diversification into the local economy – notwithstanding the dangers they pose to the environment ▲ *310*.

Île du Cap-aux-Meules

CAP-AUX-MEULES. Traveling by sea to the Îles-de-la-Madeleine, whether onboard a ferry from the Île-du-Prince-Édouard or a cargo ship from Montreal, inevitably entails docking in the port of Cap-aux-Meules, on the island of the same name. This center is the most densely populated island in the chain and the hub of local commerce and administrative services.

L'ÉTANG-DU-NORD. This little village boasts one of the island's most important fishing ports. The area around the harbor, graced with a splendid sculpture celebrating the strenuous work of fishermen, is the starting point for a stroll along the beach to the Cape du Phare, half a mile to the north. Further inland, a climb up the BUTTE DU VENT (525 feet/160m) is rewarded by a panoramic view of the whole chain of islands. A network of short paths links up the delightful old houses that reveal why the islands were – and still are – famous for their inhabitants' bold sense of color. From the Cap du Phare, magnificent landscapes unfurl, especially between Belle Anse and Cap au Trou, along a coastline that has been shredded by the sea to create a series of capes.

THE WORK OF THE DEVIL?
The Lavernière church, close to L'Étang du Nord, was partially built with a cargo of lumber rescued from a shipwreck. The timber was originally transferred to another vessel, but this also sunk in a storm. The owner finally gave the wood to the islanders, who used it to build this church. Shortly after it opened, however, a fierce wind blew up and knocked the building down as if it were a house of cards. Legend has it that, before he drowned, the first captain was heard to cry: 'I leave my cargo to the Devil!'

Île d'Entrée

The Île d'Entrée, with only a skimpy layer of grass for vegetation, is isolated from the other islands and stands out due to the fact that it is entirely populated by immigrants of Scottish descent. It has a lighthouse, a small Protestant church, a few houses, delightful footpaths leading to the cliffs and plenty of quiet charm. The population is concentrated on a plateau that forms the lower part of the island. The landscape to the west, dotted with hillocks and crowned by the Big Hill (570 feet/ 174m), is perfect hiking country. Long footpaths wind through verdant valleys and around the cliffs, providing access to an occasional, isolated creek. There are daily ferry crossings from Cap-aux-Meules to the Île d'Entrée, as well as special trips to the island in summer.

Île du Havre-Aubert

HAVRE-AUBERT. This is the oldest village on the Îles-de-la-Madeleine. Acadian fishermen settled here in 1762 under the leadership of Richard Gridley, a former British army officer who was granted ownership of the island. They put down roots at the foot of hills known as the Collines de la Demoiselle, near a natural harbor tucked between Cape Gridley and the majestic outcrop of Sandy Hook. After passing through the heart of the village, the road leads to the GRAVE (strand) area, a shingle beach once occupied by a tightly packed string of *chafauds* (salting tubs with accommodation for a fisherman on top), stores and warehouses, all connected with fishing to some extent. All that remains now is an old store converted into a café, two *chafauds*, a hardware store, a handful of houses and a large saltworks near the quay. A later addition is the AQUARIUM, which gives visitors a chance to view the local marine fauna (crustaceans, molluscs and a range of fish). The MUSEUM OF THE SEA, on the headland of Pointe Shea, offers various collections that illustrate the island's past by describing the numerous shipwrecks that have marked its history, the evolution of fishing techniques and the vagaries of navigation in the gulf.

BUILDING A CASTLE
A sandcastle competition is organized every year on the beach of Havre-Aubert.

TRADITIONAL HOUSES

The island's traditional domestic architecture, with its hybrid roof forms, borrows from several styles: the Acadian, the Loyalist, the neocolonial, the neoclassical, and so on. These influences reflect the islanders' prolonged contact with the Maritime Provinces. The houses are generally built out of wood and, although white is a constant element, the landscape is distinguished by the array of vivid colors used to provide the finishing touches.

Île du Havre aux Maisons

The Île du Havre aux Maisons is connected to Cap aux Meules by a bridge stretching over the lagoon. LA POINTE is endowed with a marina and harbor, but its large herring smokehouses of yesteryear have now given way to facilities devoted either to culture or to mussel processing. Like Île de l'Entrée, Havre aux Maisons is almost barren, apart from the north coast, which is home to the island's airport. After leaving La Pointe, the road steers away from the sea and passes two beautiful buildings: an old wooden presbytery (deprived of its church, which burnt down in 1973) and the old Convent of Notre-Dame-des-Flots, the only freestone building on the islands (1915). POINTE-BASSE sports an impressive fishing harbor that once used to specialize in processing herring.

From Pointe-aux-Loups to Grande Entrée

GROSSE-ÎLE. Pointe-aux-Loups provides access to two of the island's prettiest beaches (those of the Dune du Nord and the Pointe-aux-Loups) and to Grosse-Île. The Pointe-de-l'Est area has a National Wildlife Reserve surrounded by magnificent beaches that seem to stretch as far as the horizon. The island's population, of Scottish descent, lives off fishing, agriculture and, until recently, the exploitation of a salt mine dug into the dune. OLD HARRY was once the site of a boathouse from which local men would embark on expeditions to hunt walruses. The village has a small museum devoted to recording the island's English-speaking heritage.

GRANDE ENTRÉE. The last island to be inhabited (in 1870), Grande Entrée is flanked to the south by the Bassin des Huitres, an isolated pool detached from the sea. The port by the Pointe de la Grande Entrée is one of the most important in the Îles-de-la-Madeleine and specializes in lobster fishing. The island also has a Seal Interpretation Center that explains the ecology of this mammal and its role in the history and traditions of the islanders.

Saguenay-Lac-Saint-Jean

Métabetchouan, *319*

Ghost village of Val-Jalbert, *320*

Mashteuiatsh, *320*

Saint-Félicien Zoological Garden, *320*

Dolbeau, *320*

Péribonka, *321*

Alma, *321*

Jonquière, *322*

Chicoutimi, *322*

Saguenay Fjord, *324*

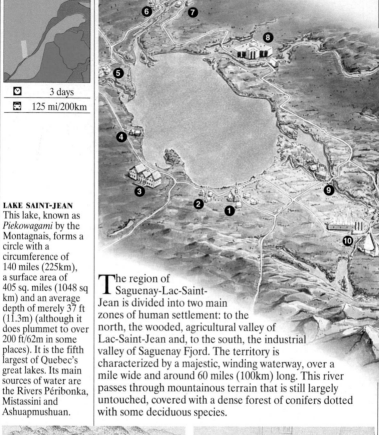

🕐   3 days

🚗   125 mi/200km

LAKE SAINT-JEAN
This lake, known as *Piekowagami* by the Montagnais, forms a circle with a circumference of 140 miles (225km), a surface area of 405 sq. miles (1048 sq km) and an average depth of merely 37 ft (11.3m) (although it does plummet to over 200 ft/62m in some places). It is the fifth largest of Quebec's great lakes. Its main sources of water are the Rivers Péribonka, Mistassini and Ashuapmushuan.

The region of Saguenay-Lac-Saint-Jean is divided into two main zones of human settlement: to the north, the wooded, agricultural valley of Lac-Saint-Jean and, to the south, the industrial valley of Saguenay Fjord. The territory is characterized by a majestic, winding waterway, over a mile wide and around 60 miles (100km) long. This river passes through mountainous terrain that is still largely untouched, covered with a dense forest of conifers dotted with some deciduous species.

THE KINGDOM OF SAGUENAY
The locals call this region the 'Kingdom of Saguenay'. The name was attributed to Jacques Cartier, who enthusiastically wrote that 'the Kingdom of Saguenay' is a fabulous land 'where there is infinite gold, rubies and other riches'.

History of Saguenay-Lac-Saint-Jean

Although discovered by Jacques Cartier in 1535, this region remained uncolonized for over three centuries, during which time the banks of the Saguenay were roamed by Native American hunters ● *46*. The year 1652 ushered in a new era, in which hunting monopolies were granted ● *48*, trees were felled, exploratory expeditions were organized and trading took place between Europeans and the indigenous peoples. In 1676, when the fur trade had diminished the reserves of animals in Tadoussac ▲ *328*, companies moved to this region and set up trading posts in Chicoutimi, Métabetchouan,

1. MÉTABETCHOUAN
2. DESBIENS
3. VAL-JALBERT
4. MASHTEUIATSH
5. SAINT-FÉLICIEN
6. DOLBEAU
7. MISTASSINI
8. PÉRIBONKA
9. ALMA
10. JONQUIÈRE
11. CHICOUTIMI
12. LA BAIE
13. L'ANSE-SAINT-JEAN
14. TADOUSSAC

Chamouchouane and Mistassini. In 1838, when the monopoly on furs expired, the Englishman William Price (1789–1867) set up a series of small sawmills along the Saguenay and established the first isolated settlements in L'Anse-Saint-Jean, Grande-Baie and Chicoutimi. Colonists made their homes close to the sawmills, clearing plots so that they could live off the land ■ *18*. At the end of the 19th century, timber merchants grew rich as a result of the ever-growing demand for paper pulp all across the Western world. So began the age of the great logging industry, complemented, in 1922 by those of electricity and aluminum ● *72*.

Saguenay Fjord ▲ *324* has some of the most breathtaking scenery in the whole of Quebec.

Métabetchouan

This village is situated at the mouth of the River Métabetchouane, a name which means 'water that comes groaning from the mountain' in Montagnais. Although records show that this trading post was established in 1676, archeological excavations undertaken 50 years ago revealed that the site had been frequented and inhabited for at least 3,000 years by the Montagnais, the Iroquois, the Abenakis and the Hurons. A museum in nearby Desbiens guides visitors through the history of Saguenay and its fur trade, with the help of findings from archeological expeditions and a reproduction of a trading post.

GENERATIONS OF CHEESEMAKERS Although Cheddar originated in England, the Perron family from Saint-Prime, near Mashteuiatsh, have passed down the art of making it for over 100 years with the utmost respect for tradition. The cheese factory, built in 1895, is the only one of its kind in Quebec. It recalls the vital importance of cheese- and butter-making in the region in the early 20th century. When the old factory was turned into a museum, the cheese began to be made in a modern factory, although still using the traditional techniques. The museum explains how Cheddar is made and prepared for export – 75% of the 1,000 tons plus of Saguenay Cheddar produced every year are exported, almost exclusively to the UK.

Ghost village of Val-Jalbert

This village, built at the foot of a magnificent 235-ft-high (72m) waterfall, is the prime historical landmark of the logging and paper industries. It was founded in 1900 in the heart of the forest by Damase Jalbert, who set about exploiting the hydraulic force of the falls to drive a modern pulp mill, as well as bestowing prosperity and the modern innovations of electricity and asphalt roads on the village. The collapse of the pulp market in 1927 led to the total abandonment of Val-Jalbert, but in 1960 its remains were restored and its historical importance reappraised. It has been equipped with an observation tower that allows visitors to enjoy the stunning landscapes all around (*left*).

Mashteuiatsh

The 1,500 strong population of this Montagnais village, officially founded in 1856, can trace their roots back to the Kakouchack nation, and their presence on the territory dates back over 6,000 years. The Montagnais were nomads who lived from hunting, fishing and gathering and met up every year at the mouth of the great rivers to barter with each other. They have now successfully integrated into the modern world but remain fiercely proud of their autonomy and traditions. The Montagnais have succeeded in turning their folklore to profit by organizing *pow wows* (festivals) and running the AMERINDIAN MUSEUM OF MASHTEUIATSH, which displays handmade clothes and craft items such as snowshoes.

Saint-Félicien Zoological Garden

This zoo lies to the west of Lake Saint-Jean, on the edges of the area's inhabited land. Created in 1962 on the Île aux Bernard, at the mouth of the River Ashuapmushuan, the zoo concentrates on animals from North America, with a special mission to promote the conservation of endangered species such as the wolverine and the eastern cougar. The animals live in semi-freedom and can be observed in their natural habitat on visits in barred trucks along trails spanning the 1,000-acre (400 ha) site.

Dolbeau

This small town, created in 1927, owes its prosperity to the lumber industry, the production of bluebottle wine and its astronomy observatory. Magnificently situated in a wooded park running alongside the River Mistassini, the ASTRO CENTER is distinguished by the beauty and tranquility of its facilities and their setting in the heart of the countryside. The locals from the area around Sean-Jean go 'bluebottling' (*see right*) in August in large fields known locally as *bleutières*, including one in Mistassini, near Dolbeau.

Péribonka

In 1912, the Brest-born Louis Hémon (1880–1913) took advantage of a stay on the farm of the pioneer Samuel Bédard to write his novel *Maria Chapdelaine* (*below*, a plate from an edition illustrated by Clarence Gagnon ● *133*). This masterpiece paints a vivid fresco of the life of the first colonists of Lake Saint-Jean. Its success caused Bédard's house (1903) to be quickly converted into a place of pilgrimage. Since 1938, it has served as the LOUIS HÉMON MUSEUM, dedicated not only to the writer and his work but also to the heroism of the area's first settlers. This building, which was restored in 1987, is one of the few colonist houses that has survived with all its original architectural elements intact: log walls, an undivided interior, dry-stone foundations and a steeply sloping roof clad with shingle. Apart from this old house, two other buildings present a collection of artworks, archives and ethnological artefacts, as well as exhibitions on the art and culture of Quebec and beyond.

Alma

Alma, founded in 1893, is essentially an agricultural village, but it was industrialized with the establishment of a hydroelectric plant that supplies the ALUMINERIE ALCAN. (The factory offers guided tours of its premises for those who are interested.) The MUSEUM OF THE HISTORY OF LAKE SAINT-JEAN displays an interesting exhibition on the history of the region.

THE BLUEBOTTLES OF LAKE SAINT-JEAN
The bluebottle (*bleuet*) is a shrub that produces small berries similar to the myrtle. It grows in suckers and particularly thrives around rocks and in woods ravaged by fires. It has been present in the area for thousands of years and was used by Native Americans to garnish their dried meat. Nowadays, it is especially prized in pies, jams or on its own with a little milk. It also serves as the base for a liqueur and a wine. Harvesting in the *bleutières* yields about a quarter of a ton per acre (a ton per hectare) and takes place in August, when 'the fields are blue'. Although the bluebottle berries are usually small, those found around Lake Saint-Jean are so big that it is said that only three are required to make a pie! The bluebottle has therefore become the emblem of the region, so much so that its inhabitants are affectionately known throughout Quebec as *Bleuets*.

Jonquière

Jonquière was founded in 1847, and for five decades its inhabitants devoted themselves to agriculture. In 1899, however, a group of French-speaking businessmen opened a pulp mill there. In 1911, William Price (1867–1924), the grandson of the industrialist of the same name, built a second mill nearby and founded the town of Kénogami. In 1925, a consortium from the United States, the Aluminium Company of America, decided to exploit Saguenay's hydroelectric potential and built the largest aluminum plant in the world ● 72, the Alcan, creating the town of Arvida in the process. In 1975, Jonquière, Kémogami and Arvida were united to form the large industrial conurbation of Jonquière.

ANGLO-PROTESTANT NEIGHBORHOOD OF KÉNOGAMI. This residential area, created between 1910 and 1920, is distinguished by its mock-Tudor architecture ● 118, an echo of the vogue for this style in late-19th-century England. The neighborhood was designed to house the managers of the paper mill, and its élitist pretensions are reflected in the incorporation of landscaped gardens. The houses are remarkable for their expressive

forms; their supporting structures are open to view and they use a wide range of building materials, particularly red and brown bricks, stucco, shingle and wood.

ARVIDA. The MANOIR DU SAGUENAY is an imposing hotel built in 1939 by Alcan ● 124. The company closed it in 1985 and converted it into their office building (opened in 1990). The CHURCH OF NOTRE-DAME-DE-FATIMA ● 127, built in 1963, is famous for its modern design based on Native American wigwams. Near the Shipsaw hydroelectric plant, which serves the region's aluminum plants and offers visits to its installations, the ALUMINUM BRIDGE, dating from 1948, proudly bears witness to the advantages of this metal: the same bridge built with steel would have weighed at least twice as much.

William Price

Peter McLeod

Chicoutimi

Chicoutimi means 'up to where it is deep' in Montagnais. The action of the tides in the fjord when they meet the currents of the Chicoutimi River form a natural basin surrounded by steep slopes. It was here, on the western bank of the river, that one of the area's main trading posts ● 48 was founded in 1676.

It was the nerve center of Saguenay's fur circuit throughout the 18th century. It was near here that William Price (1789–1867) and the half-Montagnais Peter McLeod (c.1810–52) built, in 1843, the region's largest hydraulic sawmill, an impressive complex that accounted for half the local lumber production. In 1896, the French Canadian Alfred Dubue founded the Compagnie de Pulpe de Chicoutimi. Five years later, after the closure of the sawmill, the quays of the old trading post became the starting point for expeditions made by the Chicoutimi pulp mill in search of timber.

SAGUENAY-LAC-SAINT-JEAN MUSEUM. The region's history is illustrated by exhibitions describing the lifestyle of the pioneers and the manufacturing processes for paper pulp and aluminum.

OLD PULP MILL. At the confluence of the Rivers Saguenay and Chicoutimi, the evocative remains of the pulp mill (1896) celebrate the enterprising spirit of the Quebecois and their mastery of the forest. The mill is one of the most important historic industrial sites in Canada, both for the forbidding dimensions of its buildings and its rich heritage. The complex is made up of five huge, freestone buildings, set off by a series of locks and arches that supported the channels feeding water into the mechanical mills. The site was restored in 1980 and offers guided tours. It has also been embellished by a cultural center that gives visitors the opportunity to enjoy open-air concerts in an amphitheater hollowed out of the rock.

JULIEN-ÉDOUARD-ALFRED DUBUC
The founder of the Chicoutimi paper mill, whose striking premises can still be seen today, was one of French-speaking Quebec's greatest entrepreneurs.

HOME OF THE PAINTER ARTHUR VILLENEUVE
This house, built in the late 19th century, was inhabited by Arthur Villeneuve (1910–90) and his family from 1950 to 1993. A barber by trade, this artist unleashed his talent as a naive painter on the walls of his own home during 1957 and 1958, creating a thrilling fresco of the region's history, traditions and popular legends (*see left*). In order to protect this masterpiece from the rigors of the climate, the whole house was relocated in 1994 inside one of the buildings of the old pulp mill. It was opened to the public in 1996, along with a museum devoted to the mill, as part of the latter's centenary celebrations.

▲ Saguenay Fjord

Plunging capes, unfathomable depths, gigantic terraces and immense fir forests add up to spectacular views around the Saguenay Fjord, a formidable mass of fresh water on top of a layer of salt water. Throughout the summer, it is the feeding ground for fascinating sea mammals. The creation of the Saguenay National Park in 1983 has not only conserved this untouched wilderness but also made it more accessible, via boat trips and a network of footpaths.

HEAVY TRAFFIC
This waterway, which was already in use long before the arrival of Jacques Cartier, is now frequented by large ships. The maritime termini of the Baie des Ha! Ha!, Grande-Anse and Chicoutimi primarily serve the aluminum, paper ● 72 and oil industries.

LARGE AND SMALL ANIMALS
The fjord's ecosystem, highly attractive to sea creatures from the Arctic, is constantly enriched by the swirling of its waters and the effects of the tides on the estuary. The fjord boasts 250 species of invertebrates, 54 species of fish, such as the Atlantic salmon, and 16 of seals and whales, including schools of belugas (*right*), now threatened with extinction. The fjord's soaring walls play host to many birds, including peregrine falcons and ravens (*above*).

ON FOOT, BY BIKE, BY CAR OR BY BOAT
The network of footpaths provides a series of both long and short hikes that give visitors the chance to discover the fjord's majestic scenery, from the sand bars to the peaks. The belvedere of Anse de Tabatière, accessible by car via the covered bridge of Anse-Saint-Jean ▲ 326, offers an unbeatable view of the fjord. A number of boat trips along the fjord's steep sides are available, along with excursions into the Saint Lawrence estuary to observe sea mammals.

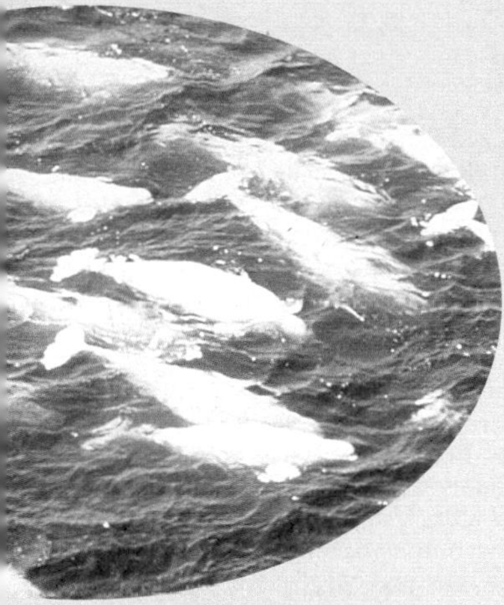

FRESH AND SALT WATERS

Saguenay has one of the most powerful flows of fresh water in the world: from 14,000 to 32,000 sq. ft (1300 to 3000 sq m) per second. Its tides can reach heights of 15 to 22 ft (4 to 6m). The shallowness of the sill at the mouth of the River Saguenay, 2½ miles (4km) from Tadoussac, causes sea water to rise up from the lower depths following the rhythm of the tides in an oceanographic phenomenon that is unique in the world.

IN THE LAND OF GIANTS

The Saguenay Fjord, deeply incised into the massif of the Laurentides, is 65 miles (104km) long and has an average width of 1½ miles (2.5km). Its average depth is 690 feet (210m), although it can go down as far as 900 feet (275m).

The origin of its formation lies in the rocky escarpments of granitic and syenitic gneiss, whose peaks rise up to 1,500 feet (457m). The most impressive of these are Éternité and Trinité ▲ 326, the 'wall' of Sainte-Rose-du-Nord and the 'Blackboard' (visible from Saint-Basile), a gigantic, unbroken sheet of rock.

THE SAINT-FULGENCE 'SPIRE'
This strange rock formation, perpendicular to the coast, advances for almost half a mile (1km) into the fjord at the foot of the Cap des Roches in Saint-Fulgence. It marks the boundary between the deep waters of the fjord to the east and the broad strands of Anse des Foins to the west.

THE OUANANICHE
This freshwater salmon, which thrives in the deep, extremely cold waters of the Saguenay Fjord, is more slender than the Atlantic salmon. The ouananiche has recently been declared an emblem of Saguenay-Lac-Saint-Jean.

NOTRE-DAME-DU-SAGUENAY ON CAPE TRINITÉ
Halfway between Tadoussac and Chicoutimi, the sculpture of Our Lady of Saguenay stands on an immense, spectacular rock wall that plunges 660 feet (200m) down into the chasm of the fjord. This monumental, 28-feet-high (8.5m) figure sculpted by Louis Jobin was built in 1881 on the first of the three plateaus on this famous cape by a traveler who, on the verge of drowning, had vowed to put up a monument to the Virgin Mary if he was saved.

Saguenay Fjord

LA BAIE. Saguenay-Lac-Saint-Jean is famous for its wide, open spaces, its harsh climate and the lush boreal forest that engulfs it. At the end of December, when the fjord is covered by a thick layer of snow and ice, the locals apply their attention to 'white fishing'. In Sainte-Rose-du-Nord, La Baie and Anse-Saint-Jean, villages of multicolored shelters (*above*) spring up, almost overnight, to accommodate fishermen with an eye on the cod, smelts, rockfish and Greenland sharks that lurk in this mixture of fresh water and Atlantic salt water.

SAGUENAY GROTTOS. Between the Baie des Ha! Ha! and the small harbor of Tadoussac, the rugged wall of the splendid Saguenay Fjord ▲ *324* hides four grottos that are only accessible to more adventurous visitors. These natural cavities, formed by the tides and old glaciers, were inhabited by Native Americans in pre-Columbian times. They were discovered around 1880 by fishermen, who found the remains of an old birch-bark canoe, pieces of basketwork, tools fashioned from bone and stone and hundreds of other objects left by their original owners. Although these grottos are accessible from the fjord, they had remained untouched for all these centuries thanks to the hostile environment and the abundant vegetation that, even now, hides them from the view of both hikers and boats on the Saguenay.

COVERED BRIDGE OF ANSE-SAINT-JEAN. This covered bridge spanning the River Saint-Jean has become celebrated all over North America. The Saguenay region can lay claim to several structures of this type, but the representation of this particular bridge on the back of the Canadian 1,000-dollar bill (*above*) has made it especially famous. Although it was built in 1929, its 112-foot-long (34m) wooden structure recalls the architecture of the 1820s. In 1986, following a spectacular flood caused by the springtime rise in the water level, the bridge was removed from its base and placed on the bank of the River Saguenay, a mile (1.5km) downstream. The structure was saved *in extremis*, restored and then returned to its foundations ten months later.

North Shore

Tadoussac, *328*

Manicouagan, *329*

Sept-Îles, *330*

La Minganie, *331*

Anticosti, *332*

Lower North Shore, *334*

1. TADOUSSAC
2. BERGERONNES
3. BAIE-COMEAU
4. MANIC 5
5. POINTE-DES-MONTS
6. SEPT-ÎLES
7. MINGAN
8. ÎLE D'ANTICOSTI
9. BAIE-SAINTE-CLAIRE
10. PORT-MENIER
11. HAVRE-SAINT-PIERRE
12. BAIE-JOHAN-BEETZ
13. NATASHQUAN
14. HARRINGTON HARBOR
15. BLANC-SABLON

H ighway 138 hugs the north bank of the Saint Lawrence for over 400 miles (670km), along a series of a hills and valleys, often interrupted by steep cliffs that loom over the river. Smaller rivers surge out of the rocks, while inviting beaches of fine sand seem to belie the hardships of the northern climate.
The Saint Lawrence plateau

⏱ approx. 10 days
🚌 700 mi/1,120km

is covered with spruce trees right until New Quebec. In olden times, Native Americans opened up trails through these vast forests generously endowed with water and underground mines. The spirit of Native American ways is all-pervasive in this region.

Tadoussac ★

The glaciers that covered part of North America thousands of years ago sculpted the rocks and earth and left stunning scenery in their wake. Rocky, wooded and rounded hills, known by the Montagnais as *Tatoushak* ('breasts'), flank the western side of this village.

MAISON CHAUVIN. In 1600, Pierre Chauvin de Tonnetuit built Canada's first-ever trading post in Tadoussac. In 1942, the owner of the Tadoussac Hotel built a replica with squared beams on

The old chapel in Tadoussac, built in 1747.

THE LITTLE SALTY LAKE
At high tide, salt water enters this lake near the banks of the Saint Lawrence via an opening in the river. In former times, Native Americans steered their boats down this channel to escape from the view of their pursuers.

the probable
site of the
original post.
It is used to display
a range of archeological
and historical exhibitions.
OLD CHAPEL. This chapel,
built in 1747, is thought to be the
oldest in Canada (*bottom left*). It contains
a fine collection of religious objects, such as a
Way of the Cross sculpted in wood, a banner of the
Holy Cross (1671) and an image of the Infant Jesus
that was reputedly given to the Native Americans by
Louis XIV. The bell was also a gift from the Sun King.
SEA MAMMAL RESEARCH UNIT. The merging
of the river and the fjord creates an
environment rich in the plankton
favored by finbacks, blue whales,
belugas and humpback whales. The
center presents an interactive exhibition
and organizes boat trips in summer to
observe whales in their natural environment.

Manicouagan

BERGERONNES. In 1603, Champlain named this spot
Bergeronnettes, after the terns that flock to the bank at
low tide ■ 24. The CAP-DE-BON-DÉSIR was originally known
as Pipouanapi, 'the place where there is winter water', by
the Montagnais, and, as the name suggests, it is unusual
to find frozen water in this cove. THE CAP-DE-BON-DÉSIR
INTERPRETATION CENTER displays objects found in
archeological digs that bear witness to the local presence
of Native Americans at least 4,000 years ago ● 44. The
collection includes arrowheads, scrapers and fragments
of pottery and bones. Sea mammals can be observed from
the shore.

**THE MONTAGNAIS
NATION**
The Montagnais
arrived from Asia
via the Bering Strait
and established
themselves on the
North Shore over
8,000 years ago.
These nomads of
Algonquin origin
were hunter-
fishermen who lived
in small groups.
They were highly
religious, believing
in a pantheon of
supernatural beings,
and dreams played
a key role in their
culture. They thought
that animals had a
soul and were afraid
of offending them.
They were among the
first Native
Americans to
fraternize with the
Europeans. By 1850,
they were living in
wigwams made of
birch bark. They now
live in nine villages,
seven of which are
dispersed along the
north bank of the
Saint Lawrence.
Although some still
hunt and fish, they all
try to adapt to
modern life, caught
between two worlds
that are often difficult
to reconcile.

MANIC 5
The Daniel-Johnson dam (Manic 5), 135 miles (215km) from Baie-Corneau, could claim, for many years, to be the biggest in the world. Over 700 feet (214m) tall, it is a series of concrete vaults and buttresses. Its reservoir, with a surface area of 770 sq miles (2000 sq km), serves to regularize the supply of water to plants built downstream, on the Manicouagan.

'IF YOU ONLY KNEW HOW BORING IT IS'
Inspired by the inaccessibility and isolation of the Manic, the poet Georges Dor (1931–2001) expressed the feelings of the men who built these great dams: 'If you knew how boring it is, on the Manic, you would write to me much more often, on the Manicouagan. If you have nothing much to say to me, write one hundred times the words "I love you", that will be the most beautiful of poems.'

BAIE-COMEAU. The majestic scenery beckons travelers to stop and admire. In 1936, Robert McCormick, the publisher of the *Chicago Tribune*, founded the town by building a pulp mill destined to supply his journal with paper. He named the town after Napoléon-Alexandre Comeau, a local trapper,

geologist and naturalist. The CHURCH OF SAINT-AMÉLIE, built in 1940 in the Dom-Bellot style ● *124*, is worth a visit to see its frescos and brightly colored stained-glass windows. At the entrance to the town, by the mouth of the River Manicouagan (the name means 'the place where there is birch'), stands Manic 1. Built in 1964, it was the first of a series of five dams installed by Hydro-Québec along the river. Guided tours of the MANIC 2 plant are available and it is also possible to walk on the famous, titanic MANIC 5 dam.

Sept-Îles

Built on an almost circular bay, this town is blessed with an incomparable setting. Its port is accessible all year round to the enormous ships that come here to load up with iron ore extracted from the mines in Labrador.
LE VIEUX-POSTE. The Montagnais were already passing through this area when the French set up a sizeable trading post here in the early days of colonization. This post was rebuilt in 1967 according to plans dating from the 18th century. A reconstruction of the Hudson Bay Company's store and an exhibition space trace the stories of the Montagnais and of the trading post.
NORTH SHORE REGIONAL MUSEUM. This museum was founded in 1975 by André Michel, a painter who specializes in depictions of Native American life. An exhibition explains how the North Shore came to be populated; other galleries are devoted to the region's contemporary art.

SEPT-ÎLES REGIONAL PARK. The seven islands after which the town is named now form a park ideally suited to the observation of birds such as the puffin (*below*) and the stern, as well as sea mammals such as whales and seals. The Île de la Grande-Basque is endowed with campsites and numerous hiking trails.

La Minganie

LONGUE-POINTE. The ÎLES DE MINGAN RESEARCH STATION studies the sea mammals found in the Gulf of Saint Lawrence, including the common finback, the beluga and the killer whale. It organizes educational programmes and boat trips ▲ *348* that provide a closer look at the local wildlife, including a colony of Arctic puffins ■ *24*.

MINGAN. The village church, built in the early 20th century by

POINTE-DES-MONTS
This village near Baie-Corneau has a lighthouse dating from 1830, which has now been converted into an inn.

John Maloney, was decorated by Montagnais artists.

HAVRE-SAINT-PIERRE. This town was founded by fishermen from the Îles-de-la-Madeleine in 1857, but industrialization did not follow until 1948, when the local seams of ilmenite (a natural oxide of iron and titanium) began to be mined.

MINGAN ARCHIPELAGO NATIONAL PARK RESERVE ★.
This park, which stretches from Longue-Pointe to Aguanish, comprises around 40 islands with bizarre landscapes made of sedimentary rocks formed five million years ago. The weight of the glaciers, the pressure of the ice and the thaw, combined with the action of the waves, fashioned these islands and their characteristic monoliths. The icy currents from Labrador, the various sedimentary soils and the humidity have created a unique bioclimate that encourages the growth of a wide range of plants. These include conifers, ferns, mosses, lichens, orchids and Minganie thistles, which are native to these islands and were classified by Brother Marie-Victorin in 1924. Large colonies of birds nest in the park, making it the most significant winter sanctuary in the whole Gulf of Saint Lawrence. The puffins are the most appealing to visitors but the Arctic sterns, black guillemot and common eider should not be overlooked. The waters are home to several species of seals, including the Greenland seal.

THE MONOLITHS OF MINGAN
The monoliths of Mingan, made of stratified limestone, gradually emerged as the waves and sea currents sculpted extraordinary shapes out of this soft stone.

The 'island before the coast' (*anti costa* in Basque), situated in the mouth of the Saint Lawrence River, measures 136 by 35 miles (220 by 56km), thus representing a considerable obstacle to traffic down the waterway's central corridor. In 1895, Henri Menier (1853–1913), a fabulously wealthy French chocolate manufacturer, bought the island as his own private hunting ground. Several large mammals, such as the black bear, the moose and the roe deer were introduced as suitable quarries. The roe deer are still there to attract hunting enthusiasts today, while fishermen come to catch salmon. Less sporty types can simply revel in the majestic scenery, complete with bird colonies and a variety of plants.

THE BALD EAGLE
Anticosti attracts the greatest concentration of nesting birds in the whole of Quebec. Visitors come from far and wide to admire the magnificent bald eagle (the species that has become the emblem of the United States). The bald eagle specializes in catching dead fish and finds ample sustenance in the nearby rivers laden with salmon. It takes four years to acquire its definitive plumage.

STEEP-SIDED CANYONS
Quebec is not greatly blessed with limestone deposits, making those of Anticosti (400–500 million years old) all the more exceptional. They abound in fossils of brachiopods and gastropods (shelled aquatic animals), along with coral reefs that are sometimes completely intact. Numerous infiltrations of water in the subsoil have propitiated the formation of chasms, caves, potholes and dolines. Over time, the great torrents of water have hollowed out the vertical walls and created several canyons. Those of the River Vauréal and the River Jupiter are particularly spectacular. The Vauréal waterfall (in the island's central northern area) plunges down from a height of 245 feet (75m).

THE HISTORY OF ANTICOSTI
A sailor's nightmare, Anticosti has provided the setting for hundreds of shipwrecks, as well as serving as a hideout for pirates. It was occupied by Native Americans before being discovered by Jacques Cartier in 1534. In 1680, the explorer Louis Jolliet ▲258 became the island's first seigneur. After his death in 1700, Anticosti passed through the hands of several owners, including Henri Menier, and many of them made attempts to exploit its natural resources. In 1974, it was taken over by the Quebecois government and turned into a wildlife reserve (complete with a historical museum), although a few families still live on the island.

THE ORCHIDS
The limestone soil is particularly favorable to around 25 varieties of orchids (over half the species found in Quebec). The diversity and coloring of their flowers are spectacular.

THE ROE DEER
Of all the animals introduced onto the island by Henri Menier, the roe deer is the one that has acclimatized most successfully. With a population more than 100,000 strong, this mammal thrives on the absence of natural predators and the suitable winter conditions. Such a high concentration (over 4 per sq mile/12 per sq km) has, however, made an impact on the vegetation: several trees and leafy shrubs have virtually disappeared, and the regeneration of the fir tree is under threat.

THE CAVES
Expeditions undertaken over the last 30 years have revealed the presence of numerous underground waterways and several caves. One of the most accessible caves is that of the River à la Patate, with its 33-feet-high (10m) entrance.

SEABIRDS
The cliffs of Anticosti are teeming with nesting seabirds. The puffin ▲ *331*, the guillemot ▲ *304*, the great cormorant, the razorbill and the northern gannet ▲ *306* are particularly drawn to the northeast of the island for their nesting. The Goélands cliff plays host to almost 25,000 pairs of kittiwakes ▲ *305*, making it one of the biggest colonies in North America.

'THE PEOPLE OF MY COUNTRY'
The husky-voiced Gilles Vigneault extols the simplicity of the people from his homeland, 'the snowy desert where scattered villages never fail to spring up'. Apart from his political activism, Vigneault has fought for the survival of French culture in America: 'There is not a single song of mine that is not entirely made of your words, your steps, your music.'

'THE BIRDS OF AMERICA'
In this work, Audubon set out to produce life-size illustrations of well-known birds – so all four volumes had to be over three foot high to accommodate the pelican, turkey or flamingo. The publication of this book, made up of 435 sheets in all, was spread from 1831 to 1839. All 300 copies were painted by hand.

Lower North Shore

ON THE TRAIL OF AUDUBON. From June to August 1833, the famous American naturalist Jean-Jacques Audubon (1785–1851) sailed along the North Shore from Natashquan to Brador (near Blanc-Sablon). He had come to this barely explored region to observe and draw the local birds for his masterwork *The Birds of America*, undoubtedly the most famous book on ornithology ever published. Modern visitors can follow in Audubon's wake on a boat trip down the Lower North Shore (the 15 villages dotted along the 300-mile/480km coastline between Natashquan and Blanc-Sablon are only accessible by boat and airplane).

'THE LAND GOD GAVE TO CAIN'. The landscape here is flat,

rugged and almost barren – hence its derogatory nickname. In places, it is bordered by a maze of rocky islets, through which launches have to weave their way to reach the villages on the bank. Just as in Audubon's day, these tiny islands are inhabited by huge numbers of puffins, kittiwakes, sterns and guillemots (*below*). The main activity in the region is fishing for crabs, lobster or queen scallops. Foggy days are not uncommon and, apart from rare exceptions, summer temperatures are on the cool side.

NATASHQUAN. The birthplace of the poet and singer Gilles Vigneault (1928) ● *92*, is the most heavily populated village on the Lower North Shore. It was here that Audubon discovered the then-unknown Lincoln's sparrow, on June 27, 1833. This is excellent hiking country, particularly along the River Natashquan, with its many waterfalls.

HARRINGTON HARBOUR ★. This village has a character all its own. Its wooden houses, painted in a variety of colors, are set on rocks and linked by sidewalks that cross over crevasses, hollows and waterways.

BLANC-SABLON. Some years, immense blocks of ice float slowly past the village right up until the summer, before merging with the waters in the gulf.

Nunavik

Inuit history, *336*
Inuit traditions, *338*
Inuit myths, rituals and beliefs, *340*
Inuit art, *342*
The Inuits of Nunavik today, *344*

The first inhabitants

The area's first settlers, some 4,000 years ago, were the Paleoeskimos, of Asian origin. Their culture developed in Alaska until they migrated eastward via the Arctic islands and Baffin Land in response to a warming of the climate. They lived by

hunting caribou and seals. About 1,500 years later, this people was superseded by the Dorset culture, which introduced technological innovations such as the kayak, the lamp, the soapstone cooking pot, the partially subterranean house reinforced by peat and the use of hunting dogs. The Dorset people demonstrated an artistic sense, making miniature sculptures from ivory and wood. Toward the end of the 12th century, the Thule culture emerged in Alaska and spread throughout the Arctic region. The highly mobile Thules possessed not only the kayak but also the *umiaq*, a large crewed boat made of skin, and sleds drawn by dogs. They were very well equipped for hunting sea mammals, including the right whale, which was then abundant in Arctic waters (they have become colder since then). The Thules were the direct ancestors of today's Inuits, and it was the latter who witnessed the arrival of the first European explorers.

The first contact with Europeans (1610–1850)

The first European description of the Inuits of Nunavik was written after the expedition by Henry Hudson who, in his quest for a passage to Asia, penetrated the sea now known as Hudson Bay in 1610. The French captain Pierre LeMoyne d'Iberville left a second account. By bartering with the Inuits at the entrance to Hudson Bay during a naval campaign against the English, d'Iberville defied the monopoly on fur granted by the British Crown to the Hudson Bay Company in 1670. France only recognized this monopoly in 1713, through the Treaty of Utrecht. The first trading posts were established on the region's southern coast, particularly in the Richmond Gulf (1750–6) and Fort-Chimo (1830–42). They were rapidly abandoned, due to difficulties with supplies and poor relations with the Inuits. The advent of the steamship allowed them to be reopened in 1851. Every year, the Inuit traveled long distances in sleds to barter their furs in these posts.

> 'We can say that the notion of winter and the notion of summer are the two poles around which the Eskimos' [Inuits'] system of ideas revolve.'
>
> Marcel Mauss

Competition between the French and the English

THE GREAT FUR RUSH (1903–36)

The transfer of Rupert Land (around Hudson Bay) to Canada in 1870 opened this territory up to commercial competition. In 1903, the French company Revillon Frères set itself up as a rival to the Hudson Bay Company. Trading posts mushroomed until the stock market crash of the 1930s caused the price of fox fur to plummet, with the subsequent closure of the Révillon posts. This marked the beginning of a difficult period for the Inuits, who were left to fend for themselves in their camps.

THE BATTLE FOR SOULS

From the late 1930s onward, it was common for most Inuit to be baptized by itinerant Protestant pastors. Seven Catholic missions were opened in the Great North, however, between 1936 and 1948 – only to close quickly for lack of a congregation.

Political rivalry

In 1960, Quebec decided to take on the administration of the territory granted to it by the federal government in 1912. A two-pronged administrative system was introduced into all the Inuit villages. In 1971, when the Inuit cooperative movement was making real progress in trying to set up a regional government, a breakaway group created the Northern Quebec Inuit Association to oppose this move. Constituted on an ethnic basis, it obtained the support of the federal government and asserted itself as the sole representative of the Inuits in Quebec, coinciding with the announcement of the James Bay hydroelectric project. The political rivalry between the federal and provincial governments only ceased when, along with the Inuit, they signed the James Bay Agreement of 1975. This agreement required the Inuit to renounce certain territorial rights; in exchange, they received financial compensation and full responsibility for managing economic municipal affairs. They also gained partial control of healthcare and education, while Quebec could exploit the energy of the region's rivers ● 68.

The annual cycle of activities followed the rhythm of the seasons. In winter, families gathered together on the shore, in camps of about ten igloos. The extremely short days, intense cold and scarcity of game made hunting unreliable, so the Inuit lived off reserves of meat conserved since the fall in stone hideaways. The shamans led communal sessions in large igloos, involving games, dancing and singing. In springtime, families moved into tents and spread out along the coast in order to obtain the maximum returns from their hunting. At the end of the summer, the Inuit set out for the hinterland, in *qajaq* and *umiaq* (types of canoe), in order to hunt caribou on their migration routes.

THE INUIT HOUSE

Inuits have risen to the formidable challenge of settling in a country with no trees. For their winter dwellings, they created the snow igloo with ice windows, and the semi-underground house made with peat, stones and whalebones. In summer, they lived in sealskin tents supported by poles cut from floating logs. The indispensable oil lamp served as a source of heat and light, as well as a means of cooking. The bedding consisted of mats made of dwarf birch tied together with tendons, caribou or bear skins, and caribou sleeping bags.

MEANS OF TRANSPORT

The sled drawn by dogs harnessed in a fan-shape formation suited the rugged terrain of the coasts, where blocks of ice were often dislodged by the strong tides. The kayak was used to hunt sea mammals. The *umiaq* (*above*) was used to transport entire families in summer, enabling them to reach the far end of the fjords. From there, they continued on foot to the caribou hunting grounds, where they would lie in wait for the migrating herds.

HUNTING AND FISHING

The hunting of sea mammals – like that of the caribou – was essentially a man's job and it occupied most of his year. The Inuit had traps at their disposal, including *timijjivit*, small coves that became lakes at low tide. Although women could sometimes replace men in a hunt, they tended to concentrate on gathering food in the bays and catching small fish on the ice fields.

CLOTHING

Winter clothing comprised two sets of caribou skins. One was worn indoors, close to the skin, with fur lining on the interior. The other had its fur on the outside and was put on top of the other to go outdoors. On the islands that had no caribou, duck skin was used instead. In summer, the Inuit opted for a double layer of seal skin, which was lighter, not so hot, hard-wearing and waterproof. Boots and gloves were made along the same lines.

WEAPONS, TOOLS AND UTENSILS

A hunter's arsenal was made up of bows, arrows, spears and articulated harpoons. The bow drill and adze served to fashion other tools: knives made of horn or ivory to cut snow or with a half-moon, double-edged blade; bone needles; leather thimbles; thread from caribou sinews; and pouches with flint and pyrites for making fires. The everyday Inuit utensils included buckets, goblets and gourds made from skins, wooden plates edged with whalebone, wooden clothes driers, plaited sinews and soapstone cooking pots ▲ *342*.

To Westerners, the world of the Inuits seems to be no more than a vast, white desert; to the Inuits themselves, it is nothing of the sort, as all the natural elements are inhabited by spirits. The Inuit respect, cajole and beseech not only the spirits of animals but also those that govern the movements of the universe. The shamans – intermediaries between the living and the dead, as well as between humans and their quarries – are responsible for overcoming misfortunes like disease or particularly foul weather, interpreting unforeseen events, accidents or setbacks and interceding with the great spirits.

THE SHAMANS
Shamans, who could be either men or women, had to help the members of their community from their birth until their passing to the celestial or underwater afterlife.

COLLECTIVE BELIEFS AND RITUALS
The coasts of Nunavik are dotted with caves known as *tuurngatuuq*. This term evokes the presence of the *tuurngait*, protective spirits of shamans but also powerful and mythical spirits capable of making themselves invisible. Traditionally, the old camps were adjoined by circles of large stones called *qaggiq*, used to hold celebrations and collective rituals linked to the catching of a large whale or a visit from a neighboring camp.

THE SUN AND THE MOON

Legend has it that a young, blind man was deceived by his mother and committed incest with his sister. He went to join her in Heaven, where they became the Sun and the Moon. This Inuit myth establishes a link between the cosmic and the social order, which condemns incest and endogamous marriage.

MYTHS AND PLACE NAMES

Myths still play a part in Inuit life as they are inscribed in both the collective memory and the topography of Nunavik. Several sites in the region have direct associations with mythology; for example, the steep-sided valley of the River Kuuktaq, between Puvirnituq and Inukjuak, was said to be the result of a giant striking the mountain with an axe.

RELIGIOUS MOVEMENTS AND MESSIANISM

After the first wave of conversions to Christianity in the 20th century, religious movements combining ancestral beliefs and Christian doctrines have emerged among several groups in Nunavik. In the 1920s, the Inuit announced the end of the world and killed all their dogs to be ready to welcome Christ.

TUNNITUARRUIT

These mythological creatures resemble flying heads covered with tattoos. Their hair serves as wings, while their chin sprouts two bird's legs and genital organs.

▲ Inuit art

Inuit art, in the form of sculpture and engraving on soapstone (a compact stone made of talc) has experienced an ever-growing international reputation since the 1960s. It started to be commercialized in 1948, when the Puvirnituq and Inukjuak cooperatives were formed at the instigation of the Canadian artist James A. Houston. This art is, however, rooted in a long tradition that goes back to prehistoric times. The Inuit dependence on hunting has made them acute observers of nature, as well as skilled craftsmen. Moreover, in the past their imagination was constantly being fuelled by stories and shamanic rituals.

PREHISTORIC ART
Small figurines sculpted in ivory have been found on almost all the prehistoric sites, particularly those of the Dorset culture ▲ 336. The wall engravings in Qajartalik (*above*), situated on an island off the south bank of the Hudson Strait, dates from this period. It is thought that this art was connected to religion and shamanistic rituals.

TRADITIONAL CRAFTS

As they lived exclusively from hunting and fishing, early Inuit men and women had to be able to make their own tools and everyday utensils. Although tasks were divided according to sex and individual talents, all Inuit nevertheless needed to know how to be self-sufficient. Everyone was an artist and knew the secrets of working with stone, wood, bone, ivory, skins, and other materials. The most gifted craftworkers were universally acclaimed. The first explorers and sailors who came into contact with the Inuit showed a keen interest in their decorative figurines and craftwork utensils. Demand was such that they began making miniatures of kayaks, animals and human beings to exchange for goods imported by the Europeans.

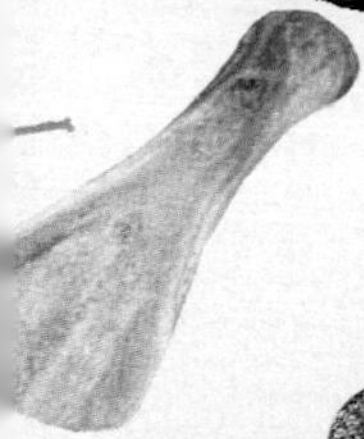

FROM SCULPTURE TO ENGRAVING ON SOAPSTONE

The Inuit continued to sell or barter their craftwork in trading posts but in the 1960s they began to focus their attention on the art market, particularly further south, where there was a great demand for their statuettes depicting animals and everyday scenes. This artistic production, initially confined to a few villages in Arctic Quebec, quickly extended to all the central Arctic area. Canadian artists were encouraged by dealers and cooperatives to teach the Inuit how to engrave soapstone, and their art branched out to embrace etching, appliqué, screen-printing and acrylics.

MODERN ARTS AND CRAFTS

The international success of several traveling exhibitions of Inuit art has increased the demand for this work, to such an extent that galleries entirely devoted to its promotion have started to emerge.

343

▲ The Inuit of Nunavik today

'THE HUMANS'
The term 'Inuit' means human being. It has replaced the ethnic classification of Eskimo ('eaters of raw meat'), of Algonquin origin, which was common parlance during the three centuries of colonial domination.

A project for political autonomy

Three villages in which the cooperative movement was particularly strong have refused the conditions of the James Bay Agreement (1975) ▲ 337 and have created a dissident association known as 'The Inuit who stand upright on their own land'. These implacable activists have refused to give up their territorial rights. Their influence has been positive and their concept of a non-ethnic territorial government has been taken up by the Inuit as a whole in a recent draft constitution that would recognize a political autonomy conferred by the National Assembly of Quebec.

ᑕᑯᕇᐊᒋᑐᐅᕐᓂᖅ ᑕᑯᐊᐅᕝᑎᕐᓂᕐᐅᖃᑦᒐᐃᐅᓪᐋᕐᓗ ᐱᓕᐅᒦᑎᕐᓂᐅᑎᒐ

The Makivik Company

Since 1975, the Inuit company Makivik has handled their people's funds and intervened in important areas of Inuit economic, social and cultural life. It has several subsidiaries, including two airlines, Air Inuit and First Air. In 1986, the Inuit of Arctic Quebec rechristened their territory Nunavik (which means 'our land'). Their leaders are involved in new negotiations with the Canadian government to win recognition of their ancestral rights over the coastal islands and territorial waters surrounding Nunavik.

INUIT SCRIPT
The syllabic alphabet was perfected in the mid-19th century by English missionary James Evans. It is now used alongside the Roman alphabet in Nunavik. Books by Inuit authors in syllabic script have been published by the Université Laval de Québec since 1980 and the Avatak Cultural Institute publishes *Turnivut* magazine in syllabic script with French and English translations.

Tradition and modernity

The 7,000 Inuit of Nunavik, spread over 14 villages, now live in houses with all modern conveniences. They travel around by snowbike, car or motorboat and work in a variety of jobs, although unemployment and the social problems associated with it affect them more deeply than the Quebecois further south. They still mainly eat the produce of hunting and fishing. Apart from Inuktitut and its syllabic script, young Inuit learn French and English in school and some further their education in the universities and colleges of Quebec.

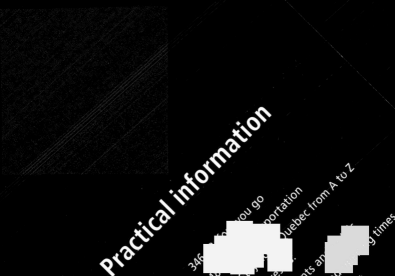

Practical information

346

Quebec from A to Z

transportation

...before you go

...g times

USEFUL ADDRESSES

→ IN THE US
Canadian Embassy
501 Pennsylvania
Avenue, NW
Washington, DC
20001
Tel. (202) 682-1740
canada@canadian
embassy.org

→ IN THE UK
**Canadian High
Commission:**
Macdonald House,
1 Grosvenor Square,
London W1X
Tel. (020) 7258 6600
www.canadianembassy
.co.uk

→ TOURIST INFORMATION
Bonjour Quebec
www.bonjourquebec.
com
Tel. 1-877-bonjour
Daily 3–11pm (from
4pm on Wednesdays)

→ SPECIALIST BOOKSTORES
**The Double Hook
Book Shop**
1235A Greene Ave,
Westmount,
Montreal H3Z 2A4
Tel. (514) 932-5093
info@doublehook.com
www.doublehook.com
**La Maison Anglaise
Bookstore**
Place de la Cité
2600, bd Laurier
Sainte-Foy,
Quebec G1V 4T3
Tel. 1-800-228-5818
www.lamaisonanglaise
.com

MONEY

Canadian dollar (CA$)
CA$1 = US$1.23
CA$1 = £0.42
CA$1 = €0.60
at the time of going
to press.

INSURANCE

Taking private
medical insurance
is strongly
recommended.
Contact your travel
agent or insurance
broker for details.
However, be sure to
avoid any pointless
duplication and
check beforehand

what your credit
cards may offer as
some companies
have their own
insurance,
healthcare and
repatriation scheme.

TO QUEBEC BY PLANE

→ FROM THE US
■ **NEW YORK TO MONTREAL**
Direct flights from
New York to
Montreal take just
under 1½ hours, and
can be found for
under US$200 on
American Airlines,
Continental, Delta,
and Air Canada. US
Airways offers flights
from New York to
Montreal with a

connection in
Philadelphia.
■ **LOS ANGELES TO MONTREAL**
Nonstop flights from
Los Angeles to
Montreal take just
over 5 hours on Air
Canada or United
Airlines. Flights with
layover cost around
US$350.
■ **NEW YORK TO QUEBEC CITY**
Flights from New
York to Quebec City
take just over
1½ hours, and can be
found for less than
US$350. Continental

offers nonstop
flights from Newark,
and United and
Air Canada offer
connecting flights
from New York via
Toronto or Montreal.
American Airlines,
Continental, Delta,
United Airlines, US
Airways, Air Canada
and others offer a
frequent service to
Quebec from most
major American
cities.
Air Canada
Tel. 1-888-247-2262
www.aircanada.com
Delta
Tel. 1-800-241-4141
www.delta-air.com
Continental
Tel. 1-800-231-0856
www.continental.com

United Airlines
Tel. 1-800-538-2929
www.united.com
US Airways
Tel. 1-800-428-4322
www.usairways.com
**Other useful
websites**
www.orbitz.com
www.travelocity.com
www.cheapflights.com

→ BY PLANE FROM THE UK
The average length
of the flight from
the UK is 6½ hours.
■ **Air Canada**
Tel. 0871 220 1111
www.aircanada.com

■ **Canadian Affair**
This travel operator
offers discounted
flights on several
airlines flying to
Canada, as well as
special rates on car
rental.
Tel. (020) 7616 9184
in London
www.canadian-
affair.com
■ **TIME DIFFERENCE**
There is a difference
of (at least) six hours
from the UK. From
early April to late
October, eastern
Canada adopts
summer time and
moves the clocks
forward by one hour.

TO QUEBEC BY TRAIN

The railroad
companies Via Rail
(Canadian) and
Amtrak (American)
connect Quebec with
the rest of Canada
and the US.
INFORMATION
■ **Via rail**
www.viarail.ca
Tel. 1 888 842-7245
■ **Amtrak**
www.amtrak.com

TO QUEBEC BY BUS

Greyhound is the
principal bus
company offering a
service between
American and
Canadian cities.
INFORMATION
■ **Greyhound
Canada**
Tel. (800) 661-TRIP
www.greyhound.ca
■ **Greyhound USA**
Tel. 1-800-231-2222
www.greyhound.com

CUSTOMS

Individuals aged
over 18 have the
right to import
into Quebec 200
cigarettes, 50 cigars
and 14oz (400g) of
tobacco, 114 cl of
wine or liquor (1
bottle), or 24 bottles
of beer (12oz/355ml)
as well as gifts of a
value not exceeding
CA$60. It is
forbidden to bring
in perishable

foodstuffs; and the carriage of certain other products (plants, firearms) and pets is tightly controlled. Returning from Canada to the US, visitors who are at least 21 years of age may bring 200 cigarettes (1 carton), 50 cigars or 4.4lb (2kg) of tobacco, plus 1 liter of alcohol and gifts to the value of US$100.

INFORMATION
www.adrc.qc.ca
or 1 800-668-4748 (free call within Canada).

CLIMATE
Describing the Quebecois climate as temperate would be a comforting euphemism. In fact, the climatic variations are very marked, both between the north and the south and also from one day to the next. In January, the temperature can go from $-4\,°F$ ($-20°C$) to $32\,°F$ ($0°C$) in 24 hours. In summer, the heat is sometimes accompanied by heavy humidity, especially in the cities. Spring and fall are unpredictable, and winter, though often dry and sunny, is characterized by an average of 10 feet (3m) of snow.

→ WHEN TO GO
The high season traditionally begins on June 24, Saint John the Baptist's Day, and ends in early September. The period from mid-September to mid-October is particularly suited to nature watching. The long, harsh winter (November to March–April) does, however, have the advantage

of offering a wide variety of winter sports ◆355.

→ CLOTHING
Spring and fall: take a raincoat, light woolen garments and a windcheater. Summer: often warm, so opt for cotton and other light fabrics, with a jacket or pullover for the evenings. Winter: be prepared for the cold. Woollen pantyhose or long johns, double-layer waterproof boots, gloves, hat covering the ears, knitwear, scarf and warm blanket.

Note
◆ *A good insecticide is recommended at the late spring to summer to provide relief from mosquitoes.*
◆ *Camera: in winter, stock up with spare batteries and a plastic bag for protection; reckon on an overexposure of 1 or 2 notches.*

ELECTRICITY
In Quebec, the current is 110 V and the plugs have two flat pins. An adapter

and transformer are needed to use electrical equipment conforming to UK and US regulations.

FORMALITIES
→ PASSPORTS AND ID CARDS
Europeans need a passport that is still valid three months after the return journey; a visa is required for stays of over three months. A return ticket and proof of means are sometimes demanded. US citizens only require an ID card with photograph and proof of US citizenship.

→ DRIVING LICENCE
The driving licence of a UK or US citizen over 21 is sufficient to allow them to drive for six months. To obtain an international licence (valid for a year), contact the AA:
■ **American AA**
Tel. 1 800 564 6222
www.aaa.com
■ **British AA**
Tel. 0870 550 0600
www.theaa.co.uk

HEALTH
No vaccinations or special precautions

are needed. Don't forget to bring prescription medicines. Pack moisturizing creams, lip balm in winter and sun cream in summer.
Note
Make sure you have the required level of physical fitness before undertaking any intensive open-air activity.

TELEPHONE
■ **To call Quebec from the US**
Dial the province number followed by the 7-digit number. For city codes see Telephone ◆ 357.
■ **To call Quebec from the UK**
00 + 1 (Canada) + province code + number
■ **International Directory Enquiries**
3212

CELL PHONES
A cell phone must be compatible with the American GSM1900 or IDEN 800 standards to be usable in Canada. It is possible to rent a phone of this type.
INFORMATION
Cellhire
Tel. 0 810 610 610

INTERNET
■ www.montreal.com
The website of Montreal Island.
■ www.vieux.montreal.qc.ca
Information about the old city.
■ www.pc.gc.ca
Information about Canadian parks.
■ www.quebec vacances.com
Information for organizing a trip to Quebec.
■ www.ville.quebec.qc.ca
Official website of Quebec City.
■ www.pleinair-quebec.com
Open-air activities.
■ www.britainin canada.org

◆ LOCAL TRANSPORTATION

Prices given in the following pages are in Canadian dollars

AIRPLANE

Airplanes are more expensive than trains or buses but they nevertheless have the advantage of covering Quebec's long distances more quickly.

■ **AIR CANADA JAZZ**
Tel. (514) 393-3333
www.flyjazz.ca

■ **AIR CANADA**
Tel. (514) 393 3333
www.aircanada.com

Note
Discounts are available on flights reserved 14 days before departure.

BOAT

→ FERRYBOATS ('TRAVERSIERS')
Ferryboat routes include the following:

■ **YEAR-ROUND ROUTES**
Sorel–Saint-Ignace-de-Loyola
10 minutes; $2
Tadoussac–Baie-Sainte-Catherine
10 minutes, free
Quebec–Lévis
10 minutes; $2.50
Île aux Coudres–Saint-Joseph-de-la-Rive
15 minutes; free
Matane–Baie-Comeau–Godbout
2 h 20 mins; $10.85

■ **SEASONAL ROUTES**
Trois-Pistoles–Les Escoumins
(May–Oct.)
1 ½ hours; $11.50
Saint-Siméon–Rivière-du-Loup
(Apr–Jan)
1 ¼ hours; $11.30
Prince Edward Island–Îles-de-la-Madeleine
$35

■ **Information**
Société des Traversiers du Québec
Tel. 1-877-562-6560
www.traversiers.gouv.qc.ca

→ TO THE ÎLES-DE-LA-MADELEINE
The CTMA Vacancier, with a seating capacity of 400,

makes the trip from Montreal every week from April–Dec. Book in February for July–Aug.
■ **Duration**
Two days.
■ **Information**
Tel. 1 888 986 3278
www.ctma.ca

→ TO LOWER NORTH SHORE
The Nordik Express leaves Rimouski, stops off in Sept-Îles, Port-Menier (Anticosti), Havre-Saint-Pierre and

docks in Blanc-Sablon. Minimal comfort but plenty of atmosphere!
■ **PRICE**
Approx. $745 return.
■ **Information**
Relais Nordik
205, rue Léonidas Rimouski, G5L 2T5
Tel. (418) 723-8787

BUS

→ MONTREAL
The bus network offer 163 daytime routes and 20 at night, covering the entire island and even beyond (Laval to the north and Longueuil to the south). The stops are clearly indicated, and positioned on street corners.

■ **Tickets**
Tickets (also valid for the subway) are sold in subway stations, *tabagies* (tobacconists) and *dépanneurs* (convenience stores). A single ticket costs $2.50, a book of six tickets $11.50, a monthly travel card $59 and a fortnightly one $18. There is also a tourist card available for $8 for a day and $16 for three days. It is on sale in the Infotouriste center ◆*371*, tourist information kiosks and some hotels.
■ **Connections**
To transfer from the subway to the bus on the same trip, or vice versa, take a connection ticket from the ticket machine or from the bus driver. It is valid for 1½ hours.
Note
If you don't have a ticket, exact change is required to take a bus.
■ **Information**
Tel. (514) 288-6287, Mon–Fri 7am–8.30pm, weekends and public holidays 8am–4.30pm.
www.stcum.qc.ca

→ QUEBEC
Buses pass less frequently than in Montreal. A map of the network is displayed in the telephone directory and at the sales points for tickets.
■ **Tickets**
A single ticket costs $2.50 (exact change only) and a day pass $5.45. They are sold in *dépanneurs*, *tabagies* and pharmacies.
■ **Timetable**
Buses run daily from 6am to 12.30pm.
■ **Information**
Tel. (418) 627-2511
www.stcuq.qc.ca

LONG-DISTANCE BUS

These are more popular than trains in Quebec and go virtually everywhere.
■ **TERMINUS**
Montreal
505, bd de Maisonneuve Est
Tel. (514) 842-2281
Quebec
320, rue Abraham-Martin
Tel. (418) 525-3000
■ **FARES**
Students and over-65s benefit from discounts. In all cases, the price is cheaper with a day return. Packages are on offer in the major towns; they comprise a return journey plus a pass for a boat trip or bus excursion.
■ **ROUTEPASS**
From May to October, this grants 7 days of travel in both Quebec and Ontario. It costs $278.
Note
If buying a routepass in Europe you will be offered a further six days' travel.

SUBWAY

→ MONTREAL
There are 65 stations spread over four lines along the north–south and east–west axes.

The entrances are indicated by a white arrow pointing downward against a blue background.

■ **Timetable**
All year round, Sun–Fri 5am–12.30am, Sat 5.30am–1am.

■ **Tickets**
Same price as the bus.

TRAIN

Although the railroad network is fairly limited in Quebec, the Via Rail company serves most regions.
www.viarail.ca

■ **STATIONS**
Montreal
895, rue La Gauchetière Ouest
Tel. (514) 989-2626
Quebec
450, rue de la Gare-du-Palais
Tel. (418) 692-3940

■ **FARES**
Discounts are available for students and senior citizens. It is also cheaper to buy tickets 10 days in advance and avoid traveling on Friday, Sunday and public holidays.

Note
'Canrailpass' is a one-month travel pass available in both Quebec and the rest of Canada: $472 to $757 depending on the season. Sold in travel agencies in Europe. Tel. 1 888 842-7245 (9am–7pm).

TAXIS

→ **MONTREAL**
The basic fare is $2.75 (starting price) + $1.30/km.

→ **QUEBEC**
Taxis are harder to find in Quebec, except around the big hotels. It is best to book in advance by telephone.

■ **Information**
Tel. (418) 525-5191, (418) 525-8123 (418) 522-2001

Note
The phone numbers of local taxi companies can be found in the Yellow Pages.

SHARED CARS

This is a convivial and cheap means of transportation. Passengers and drivers are put in touch by the Allô-Stop company.

■ **PRICE**
The annual membership card costs $6 and the price of the trip depends on the starting point and destination, but it's sure to be cheaper than a taxi.

■ **OFFICES**
Offices in Montreal, Quebec, Baie-Comeau, Sept-Îles, Sherbrooke, Rimouski, Gaspé, Chicoutimi, Jonquiere, La Baie, Hull, Ottawa, and Edmundston.

■ **Information**
www.allostop.ca
Allô-Stop Montréal
4317 rue Saint-Denis
Tel. (514) 985-3032
Allô-Stop Québec
665 rue Saint-Jean or 2360 chemin Sainte-Foy
Tel. (418) 522-0056

CAR

As in all of North America, the car is the most popular means of transport. Quebec has a very extensive road network, except in the Lower North Shore and the far north.

→ **ROAD MAPS**
Maps published by the Quebecois Ministry of Transportation are available in the local ATR or the tourist information offices ◆ *370.*

Note
There is no toll payable on the freeways in Quebec and the gasoline is roughly half the price that it is in Europe (similar to the US).

→ **DRIVING IN WINTER**
Before setting off, heat up the car, clear away the snow and defrost the windows. Drive slowly, never brake abruptly and reckon on twice the normal stopping distance. Beware of patches of ice that may be scarcely visible. Finally, when there is freezing rain, do as the Quebecois do and use public transportation.

→ **CAR RENTAL**
A plane-hotel-car package purchased before departure works out cheaper than hiring a vehicle on the spot. In the latter case, reckon on at least $50 a day for a first-class car. Good packages are available at weekends, often with unlimited mileage.
The main companies (Avis, Budget, Discount, Hertz, Thrifty, Via Route) have branches in stations, airports and the main cities.

■ **CONDITIONS**
Minimum age of 21 and possession of credit card.

→ **USEFUL NUMBERS**
■ **Traffic information**
Montreal
Tel. (514) 873-7781
Quebec
Tel. (418) 643-1911
■ **Weather information**
Montreal
Tel. (514) 283-3010
Quebec
Tel. (418) 648-7766
■ **In case of accident**

Sûreté du Québec (police)
Tel. 1 800 461-2131
■ **Canadian Automobile Association**
A simple phone call is enough to bring assistance to car drivers in difficulty. This service is not free, however.
Montreal
Tel. (514) 861-1313
Elsewhere in Quebec
Tel. 1 800 222 4357
www.caaquebec.com

→ **SAFETY**
Canada's speed limit is 100 km/hr (62 mph) on the freeway, 70, 80 or 90 km/hr (43, 50, 56 mph) on side roads and 50 km/hr (31 mph) in urban areas. Wearing a safety belt is compulsory for all passengers.

Note
Be alert after seeing a signpost with the silhouette of a moose or deer. These animals can cause real damage to your car.

→ **PARKING**
To avoid any fines – expensive in Quebec – or, even worse, the towing away of a vehicle, respect the signs indicating the permitted parking days and times. Parking meters can be found on the main shopping streets of the big cities.

■ **PRICE**
Montreal
The cost of parking meters varies from $0.50 to $1.50 an hour, depending on the location. Parking has to be paid for until 9pm on Thursdays and Fridays, but it is free on Sundays.
Elsewhere in Quebec
The city centers have numerous parking lots, with a wide range of prices.

Useful addresses	350
Airports	350
Money	350
Getting around in Montreal	351
Public holidays	351
Festivals and events	351
Accommodation	351
Alcohol	352
Food	353
Shopping	353
Hunting and fishing	353
Nature watching	354
Parks and reserves	355
Sports and leisure	355
Mail	356
Media	357
Internet	357
Going out	357
Taxes	357
Tipping	357
Telephone	357
Emergencies	357

USEFUL ADDRESSES

→ ATR (ASSOCIATION DU TOURISME RÉGIONAL)

Each tourist region (●14) has its own Regional Tourist Association (ATR) answerable to Tourisme Québec. These bodies can provide information on a wide range of subjects (hotels, activities, transport…). For a full list of ATRs *see pages 370–1.*

→ EMBASSIES AND CONSULATES

■ US EMBASSY
1155 rue St Alexandre, Montreal H3B 1Z1
For passport, citizenship or other American Citizen Services:
Tel. 800 529 4410
Montreal-ACS @state.gov

■ US CONSULATE GENERAL
2 Place Terrasse Dufferin, behind Château Frontenac (mailing address: BP 939, Quebec City, Quebec G1R 4T9)
Tel. (418) 692 2095

■ BRITISH CONSULATE-GENERAL
1000 De La Gauchetière St Ouest Suite 4200
Montreal H3B 4W5
Tel. (514) 866 5823
montreal@britainin canada.org
www.britainincanada. org

■ BRITISH HONORARY CONSUL
Le Complexe St Amable 700-1150
Claire-Fontaine
Quebec City
Quebec G1R 5G4
Tel. (418) 521 3000
Fax (418) 521 3099

AIRPORTS

Both Pierre-Elliott-Trudeau (Montreal) and Jean-Lesage (Quebec) receive international flights.

→ FROM TRUDEAU TO MONTREAL

Pierre-Elliott-Trudeau airport is situated 12½ miles (20km) from Montreal city center.
Tel. (514) 394-7377
1 800-465-1213
www.admtl.com

■ TO THE CITY CENTER BY AEROBUS
The Aerobus runs daily between the airport (departures every 20 minutes 7am–2am) and Montreal Bus Central Station (departures 4am–11pm), at the corner of Maisonneuve Est and Berri.
One-way ticket: $13. The Aerobus stops en route at Marriott Château Champlain, Delta Centre-ville, Fairmont the Queen Elizabeth, Sheraton and Delta Montréal. Information tel. 1 800 465-1213

■ TO THE CITY CENTER BY LIMOUSINE
Approx. $48 (for four passengers). Hire on the spot.

■ TO THE CITY CENTER BY TAXI
Approx. $31. Can be hired on the spot.

■ TO THE CITY CENTER WITH A RENTED CAR
Alama, Avis, Budget, Hertz and Thrifty all have branches in the airport.

→ FROM JEAN-LESAGE TO QUEBEC CITY

The airport is 12.5 miles (20km) from the center of Quebec City.
Tel. (418) 640-2700
www.admtl.com

■ TO THE CITY CENTER BY LIMOUSINE
Approx. $100 (for four passengers). Information tel. (418) 523-5059

■ TO THE CITY CENTER BY TAXI
Approx. $27. Can be hired on the spot.

■ TO THE CITY CENTER WITH A RENTED CAR
Budget, Hertz, National and Thrifty all have branches in the airport.

MONEY

The Canadian dollar (CA$) is divided into 100 cents. Bank notes come in demoninations of 5, 10, 20, 50 and 100 dollars, the coins in 1, 5, 10 and 25 cents, as well as 1 and 2 dollars. The $1 coin is known as a 'loonie' after the bird on one face.

→ BANKS

Open from 10am to 3pm Mon–Wed and until 6 or 8pm Thu–Fri.

■ CURRENCY EXCHANGE OFFICES
In airports and exchange bureaux located in tourist areas. They charge less commission than the banks. There are also currency exchange machines, particularly in the Desjardins Complex in Montreal. Note that US dollars are widely accepted although it's often on a one-for-one basis. For exchange rates, *see page 346.*

→ TRAVELERS' CHEQUES

These are honored on presentation of a passport in big hotels and some restaurants. It is advisable to obtain travelers' cheques in Canadian dollars if you are not visiting the United States.

→ CREDIT CARDS

The most well-known (Visa,

MasterCard and American Express) are accepted everywhere.

→ **CASH DISPENSERS**
It is possible to withdraw Canadian currency with a credit card (Visa or MasterCard) or a debit card from any banking network that is affiliated with the international Cirrus, Delta or Plus networks. Fixed commission is charged for each withdrawal.

GETTING AROUND IN MONTREAL
By dividing their city into west and east from the axis of the Boulevard Saint-Laurent, the citizens of Montreal flout the basic laws of geography. With their back to the river, they claim to be facing 'north', when in fact they are looking north-west. The streets are numbered from the river towards the 'north'. The streets laid out 'east–west' are numbered upwards on either side of the Boulevard Saint-Laurent and unfurl in a symmetrical fashion.

PUBLIC HOLIDAYS
• January 1 and 2
• Good Friday
• Easter Monday
• Penultimate Monday of May: feast of Dollard and Queen Victoria
• June 24: Quebec's national holiday (Saint John the Baptist)
• July 1: Canada's main national holiday
• First Monday of September: Labor Day
• Second Monday of October: Thanksgiving
• December 25–26

FESTIVALS AND EVENTS
There are several hundred festivals throughout Quebec. To obtain a complete list, contact:
Société des Fêtes et Festivals du Québec
4545, Av. Pierre-de-Coubertin
CP 1000, succ. M, Montreal, H1V 3R2
Tel. (514) 252-3037
Fax (514) 254-1617
www.festivals.qc.ca
■ **QUEBEC CITY CARNIVAL**
For eleven days in February, the Quebecois capital is adorned with snow sculptures and a spectacular ice castle. Activities include parades, canoe racing on the river, thematic evenings...
www.carnaval.qc.ca
■ **AIR CANADA MOTOR RACING GRAND PRIX**
First week in June in Montreal.
www.thegrandprixclub.com
■ **MONTREAL INTERNATIONAL JAZZ FESTIVAL**
The biggest in North America and one of the five most important in the world. More than

400 concerts, a good many free and in the open air. For ten days, late June–early July.
www.montrealjazzfest.com
■ **JUST FOR LAUGHS**
Montreal's comedy festival 'Juste pour rire' is unique in its field. A launching pad for tomorrow's stars, it attracts comedians from all over the world, who perform in over 300 shows spread across the city, some of them in the open air. 10 days, mid-July.
www.hahaha.com
■ **TOUR DE L'ÎLE**
A bicycle race over a 45-mile (72km) circuit running through the city of Montreal. In June.
www.velo.qc.ca
■ **MONDIAL DE LA BIÈRE**
An annual festival in Montreal where you can taste from a selection of more than 340 beers and ciders from around the world. Early June.
www.festivalmondialbiere.qc.ca
■ **INTERNATIONAL FIREWORKS COMPETITION**
The largest display

of pyrotechnics in the world. In Montreal from mid-June to the end of July, every year.

ACCOMMODATION
→ **HOTELS**
These come in all categories, for all budgets.
◆ **Information**
www.quebecreservation.com
www.tourisme.gouv.qc.ca.

→ **MOTELS**
Typically American, highly practical and cheaper than hotels, these can be found by the sides of roads and on the outskirts of big cities.

→ **AUBERGES**
Although the term 'auberge' means an inn, it is sometimes applied to hotels with over 100 rooms. The most charming examples are rural houses that serve sophisticated food. Booking is compulsory. Seek out the guidebook *Auberges et relais de campagne du Québec* (published by Les Guides du Jour), which is updated every year.

→ **HÔTELLERIE CHAMPÊTRE**
The small country hotels in this network offer packages of activities for all four seasons (golf, horse riding, tennis, skiing, snowbiking, etc.) in idyllic settings.
◆ **Information**
455, rue St-Antoine Ouest, office 114, Montreal, H2Z 1J1
Tel. 1 800 861-4024
Fax 1 800 861-4032
www.hotelleriechampetre.com

→ **RELAIS DE SANTÉ**
These inns offer leisure and health activities; their prices vary according to

351

the options chosen ($125 to $310 per person).

◆ **Information**
Association des Relais de Santé du Québec
Tel. (514) 842-1556 or 1 800 788-7594
www.sparelaissante. com

→ **BED & BREAKFAST**
For anybody seeking the intimate warmth of a private house, in either the city or the country, bed and breakfasts (*gîtes du passant*) provide the perfect answer. Affiliation to the Federation des Agricotours du Québec is an indicator of quality.

◆ **Information**
Fédération des Agricotours du Québec
4545, avenue Pierre-de-Coubertin
CP 1000, succ. M
Montreal H1V 3R2
Tel. (514) 252-3138
Fax (514) 252-3173
www.agricotours. qc.ca

And also
www.canadianbandb guide.ca
http://bbcanada.com
Both sites have a comprehensive section on Quebec B&Bs.

Note
Credit cards are not always accepted in B&Bs.

→ **YOUTH HOSTELS**
There are 18 in Quebec. No age limit. From $16 to $20 per person (cheaper for members).

◆ **Information**
Fédération Québécoise de Tourisme Jeunesse
4545, av. Pierre-de-Coubertin, CP 1000, succ. M,
Montréal H1V 3R2
Tel. (514) 252-3117
www.tourismej.qc.ca

Also
www.hostelling montreal.com

→ **CAMPING**
Quebec boasts over 800 campsites with a total of 72,000 spaces. Although some are located near cities, the most attractive ones are in parks and wildlife reserves. North American comfort prevails: showers, electricity, laundry, sports facilities ($15 to $27 per day).

◆ **Information**
• Fédération Québécoise de Camping-caravaning
Tel. (514) 252-3333
www.campingquebec. com

• Camping Québec
Tel. 1 800 363 0457
www.campingquebec. com

Note
Mosquitoes can disrupt or spoil an outdoor excursion. They are very numerous from June to August around Montreal, but further north they appear later in the year. There is no miracle recipe or 100%-effective protection against mosquito or black-fly bites. A few tips, however:
• The mosquito nets fitted in many tents are ineffective. They should be replaced by netting with a finer mesh.
• Perfumed soap and shampoo should be avoided.
• Do not wear dark clothes.

■ **RUSTIC CAMPING**
This is practiced in a dozen parks, both Quebecois and national. However, you can't just pitch a tent anywhere you feel like out in the wild: platforms, refuges and natural settings are designed for this purpose. It is advisable to book beforehand (it can be free or up to $20 per day).

◆ **Information**
• Parcs Québécois Société des Etablissements de Plein Air du Québec
Tel. 1-800-655-6527
www.sepaq.com
• Parcs nationaux Parcs Canada
Tel. (418) 648-4177 or 1 888 773-8888
www.parcscanada. qc.ca

■ **WINTER CAMPING**
A complement to cross-country skiing and snowshoeing, winter camping is not only exciting and exotic but also mosquito-free. The Forillon, Gaspésie, La Mauricie and Mont-Tremblant parks and the Saint-Maurice wildlife reserve all supply brave souls with campsites, dry toilets, fireplaces, wood and even sometimes heated refuges.

Note
• Any tent can be used, provided that it is fitted with a double roof and a ground sheet. Pitch the tent away from the wind, use the snow as insulation and take a good portable stove.
• Your sleeping bag must provide protection at – 40 °F (– 40 °C).
• Wear as few clothes as possible, because perspiration is the worst enemy. Polypropylene underwear and good woolen socks are sufficient.

ALCOHOL
Alcoholic drinks are readily available in branches of the Société des Alcools du Québec (SAQ), in the Maisons des Vins and in *dépanneurs* (convenience stores) before 11pm.

→ **BEERS**
The major brewers, Labatt and Molson-O'Keefe, face stiff competition from a large number of smaller companies. Some bars also make their own beer. Many bars and restaurants serve draft beer (*bière en fût*).

→ **LIQUEURS AND OTHER ALCOHOLIC DRINKS**
The SAQ sells a mulberry liqueur called *chicoutai*. Mead and cider are

also available from independent producers.

→ WINES

Some 15 vineyards in Estrie offer tours and tastings.

◆ **Information**
From the Eastern Provinces ATR (*see page 371*).

■ BRING YOUR OWN WINE

Wine is very expensive in restaurants and some have no licence to sell it. A number of restaurants – generally those in the medium price range – will let you bring your own bottle to dinner, which you can buy more cheaply from Société des Alcools (SAQs). Ask when you make your reservation.

FOOD

→ BACKGROUND

Quebecois cuisine was first inspired by French cooking but has also assimilated the Anglo-Saxon influence. Today's chefs base their dishes on local produce but add their own distinctive innovations. Montreal, Quebec and many tourist resorts are famous for their elaborate food, while elsewhere home cooking is predominant.

■ TRADITIONAL SPECIALTIES

There are plenty of hearty dishes that make it possible to endure the hardships of the long winter!
• Pea soup or *soup aux gourganes* (with broad beans)
• *Tourtière* (meat pie)
• *Cretons* (potted meat)
• *Fèves au lards*

(broad beans with bacon)
• *Gibelotte*: a kind of bouillabaisse
• *Cipaille* (see page 98)
• Pies, whether with sugar, blueberries, or *à la ferlouche* (with raisins and molasses)

■ LOCAL CURIOSITIES

• *Poutine*: French fries with brown sauce and fromage fraîs
• *Guedille*: hot-dog bun filled with various garnishes, typical of the region around Quebec City.

Note
The Guide Debeur *(published by Thierry Debeur) and the* Repertoire des bonnes tables au Québec, *revised annually, are distributed free in branches of the Société des Alcools du Québec (SAQs).*

→ MEALS

In Quebec, breakfast is served in the morning, lunch at midday and dinner from any time after 5.30 pm. On Sundays, brunch is popular in some places.

→ SUGAR PARTIES

(*see page 82*)
These take place in the sugar cabins in springtime. The menu includes ham cured with maple wood, pork rinds, eggs with maple syrup and the famous taffy-on-the-snow.

SHOPPING

→ OPENING HOURS

Stores are usually open Mon–Wed 10am–6pm, Thu–Fri 10am–9pm, Sat 10am–5pm and Sun noon–5pm.

→ CONVENIENCE STORES

These food stores (known as *dépanneurs,* from the verb *dépanner,* to help out) are widespread in Quebec. They stay open late at night (some never close at all), seven days a week. Although they are more expensive than supermarkets and grocery stores, they have a wide range of produce on offer. They are forbidden by law to sell alcoholic drinks after 11pm.

HUNTING AND FISHING

→ INFORMATION

■ CANADIAN WILDLIFE SERVICE

Service Canadien de la Faune, 1141, route de l'Église CP 10100, 9th floor Sainte-Foy, Quebec, Canada G1V 4H5 Tel. (418) 648-7225 Fax (418) 649-6475 quebec.scf@ec.gc.ca

→ EQUIPMENT

■ HUNTING

According to the species and the time of year, hunters can track down their prey using: a shotgun, a rifle, a crossbow or a longbow. A permit is compulsory all year round.

■ FISHING

Anglers can use lures, hooks or flies, but the use of live bait is restricted. Fishing from boats with a longbow, crossbow or harpoon is only authorized under certain conditions. Each salmon river has its own regulations, depending on the specific characteristics of the fish.

→ ANNUAL PROVINCIAL PERMIT

Compulsory for both hunting and fishing (except fishing in ponds and in the Saint Lawrence). Sold on hunting and fishing sites, in *pourvoiries* ◆354 and equipment stores.
◆ **Price**
Fishing
$ 45 (or $20 for three days), $99 (salmon).
Hunting
From $63 (small game) to $250 (caribou and moose).
Note
To hunt migrating birds, a federal

permit is required (on sale in post offices).

→ WHERE TO HUNT AND FISH
■ THE POURVOIRIES
This term refers to inns offering facilities for hunting and fishing. Guests are not only supplied with comfortable lodging and delicious food but also with equipment, boats, 4-wheel-drive vehicles and guides. After a successful expedition, the cooks prepare the fish or game. The qualified staff supervises the storage and dispatch of catches. Some *pourvoiries* also offer activities like hiking, cycling, sledging with dogs and snowbiking.
◆ **Information**
Fédération des Pourvoyeurs du Québec
5237, bd Hamel,
270,
Quebec, G2E 2H2
Tel. (418) 877-5191
or 1 800 567-9009
Fax (418) 527-6638
www.fpq.com

■ THE ZEC
Quebec is divided into several controlled exploitation zones (ZECs). These unspoilt territories are entrusted to wildlife conservation associations. They offer few services, apart from camping sites and the rental of boats.

■ PARKS AND WILDLIFE RESERVES
Although fishing is permitted in Quebecois and Canadian parks, hunting is forbidden. In the wildlife reserves, some hunting activities are reserved for residents of Quebec on the basis of a quota system. Fishing and small-game hunting are open to all, however.
◆ **Price**
Approx. $25 for a day's fishing in a boat. Both parks and wildlife reserves also offer accommodation.

→ FISHING IN WINTER
All that is required to fish in winter is a hole in the ice and a line to put in it.

■ SAINTE-ANNE-DE-LA-PÉRADE
This village is the main center for the highly popular smelt fishing. Several cabins are erected right on the river for enthusiasts, all in a carnival atmosphere.
◆ **Price**
From $20 to $24 per day, including equipment.
◆ **Information**
Association des Pourvoyeurs de la rivière Sainte-Anne
8, rue Marcotte,
Sainte-Anne-de-la-Pérade GOX 2J0
Tel. (418) 325-2475
www.laperade.qc.ca/pourvoyeurs

NATURE WATCHING
→ SEA BIRDS
The islands on the Saint Lawrence constitute one of the biggest sanctuaries for sea birds in all the Americas.
◆ **Information**
From ATRs (*see pages 370–1*)

→ SEAL CUBS
In March, millions of females give birth to cubs to the north of the Îles-de-la-Madeleine and special trips are arranged where you can see them without disturbing them.
◆ **Price**
Package for three or four nights from $1,370, including the airplane from Montreal, accommodation, protective clothing, breakfast and transport by helicopter to the ice floes.
◆ **Information**
In travel agencies.

→ WHALES
From June to September, the Saint Lawrence Gulf and Estuary are home to one of the largest and most varied display of sea mammals in the world ■26. They can be observed from dry land from the North Shore and in some parks (Forillon and Mingan Archipelago, or the Saguenay marine park). The most spectacular sights, however, are to be found on trips in a dinghy, schooner or sailboat.
◆ **Information**
ATRs of Charlevoix, Manicouagan, Duplessis, Bas-Saint-Laurent, Gaspésie (*see pages 370–1*).

■ THE MINGAN ISLANDS RESEARCH CENTER
This offers excursions in a dinghy ($80) and stays of one or two weeks. All profits finance research into whales and their protection.
◆ **Information**
378, Bord-de-la-Mer, Longue-Pointe-de-Mingan, G0G 1V0
Tel. (450) 465-9176
www.rorqual.com

→ DEER
Gaspésie is the only place in North America where white-tailed deer, moose and caribou can be seen together in the same habitat. Organized hikes from May to September.

■ DESTINATION CHIC-CHOCS
96, bd Sainte-Anne Ouest,
CP 280, Sainte-Anne-des-Monts
G0E 2G0
Tel. (418) 763-9020

■ ON THE CARIBOU TRAIL
A herd of 150 caribou live in the Grands-Jardins Park. In winter, a weekend of observation combined with a 30-

mile (48km) cross-country skiing route costs $215 (chalet, meal and transport for luggage).
◆ **Information**
Tel. (418) 890-6527
Fax (418) 528-6025
www.sepaq.com

PARKS AND RESERVES
→ **PARKS**
Quebec has four national parks (run by the federal government) and 17 provincial parks devoted to conservation and recreation. They all have a reception area and infrastructures for outdoor pursuits, such as canoeing, camping, nature watching, hiking, fishing, as well as other activities, depending on the individual characteristics of the park.
◆ **Price**
The entrance fee varies from $5 to $7 per car; that of a camping spot, from $5 to $20 per night. Some parks offer other types of accommodation (chalets, inns or refuges).

→ **WILDLIFE RESERVES**
These cover larger territories than the parks and were created to conserve their natural habitats. Some, however, allow certain open-air sports.
◆ **Information**
National parks:
Parcs Canada
3, rue Buade,
CP 6060, G1R 4V7
Tel. (418) 648-4177, (514) 283-2332 or 1-800-463-6769
www.parcscanada. qc.ca
Quebec parks:
Réserves Fauniques
Service Canadien
de la Faune
1141, Rte de l'Église

CP 10100
9th floor
Sainte-Foy (Quebec)
G1V 4H5
Tel. (418) 648 7225
Fax (418) 649 6475
quebec.scf@ec.gc.ca
Bookings:
1 800 665-6527
www.sepaq.com

SPORTS AND LEISURE
→ **CANOEING**
Paddle for a few hours in a park or embark on an expedition in the heart of the forest.
◆ **Information**
Fédération
Québécoise du

Canot et du Kayak
Tel. (514) 252-3001
Fax (514) 252-3091
www.canotkayak.qc.ca

→ **HORSE RIDING**
It is possible to rent a horse by the hour, but nothing beats galloping for several days across Quebec or enjoying life on a ranch!
◆ **Information**
Fédération Québec
à Cheval
Tel. (450) 434-1433
Fax (450) 434-8826
www.cheval.qc.ca

→ **ROCK CLIMBING**
For experienced climbers who want

to reach the best peaks the region has to offer.
◆ **Information**
Fédération
Québécoise de la Montagne et de l'Escalade
Tel. (514) 252-3004
or 1 866 204-3763
Fax (514) 252-3201

→ **MARINE KAYAKS**
Kayaks are ideal not only for exploring the Saguenay Fjord and the Saint Lawrence Estuary but also for viewing whales and seals at close range or observing sea birds.

■ **L'ÉCOLE MER ET MONDE**
This school organizes expeditions for beginners and experts.
◆ **Price**
About $95 for a day-long excursion, with equipment (kayak, thermal clothing, etc.) and meals included. Expedition of two days and one night in a fjord from $228.
◆ **Information**
405, rue de la Mer
Les Bergeronnes
Québec G0T 1G0
Tel. (418) 232-6779
or freephone

1 866 637 6663
Fax (418) 232-1007
www.mer-et-monde.qc.ca

→ **SNOWBIKING**
Snowbiking originated in Quebec ●*89* and is very popular, with a grand total of over 20,000 miles (36,000km) of pistes.
■ **ESSENTIALS**
Rental agencies demand a driving licence (car or motorbike) and a credit card to cover the cost of the deposit (approx. $500).
◆ **Price**
Rental by the hour, day or week. The basic package ($100–$200 per day) includes a permit to drive on the trails, gas, insurance, ski suit, boots, gloves and helmet. Packages are available from $230 per day, including guide, meal, night in an inn or *pourvoirie*.
◆ **Information**
From the ATR (*see pages 370–1*) or the Fédération Québécoise des Motoneigistes
Tel. (514) 252-3076
Fax (514) 254-2066
www.fcmq.qc.ca
Note
• Although there is no speed limit, the Fédération Québécoise des Motoneigistes advises its members not to exceed 44mph (70km/h). Driving a snowbike is more difficult than it looks and any damage can involve costly repairs.
• Wear jogging clothes rather than jeans under the ski suit. Also take good woolen socks.
• Always go out in a group (never on your own) and make sure you know the route thoroughly.

→ RAFTING

The rivers run particularly fast in spring, but summer also offers some exhilirating descents. No experience is required, but you must weigh at least 100lb (45kg).

■ **EQUIPMENT**

This is provided, and isothermal suits can be rented in situ. Take a towel, running shoes, warm underwear, a nylon jacket and spare clothes.

■ **PACKAGES**

Packages of half a day (three hours), a whole day (five to six hours) or several days.

◆ **Information**

From ATRs (see page 370)

→ HIKING

Way-marked footpaths are available for both short and long hikes.

◆ **Information**

Fédération Québécoise de la Marche Tel. 1 866 252-2065 Fax (514) 254-5137 www.fqmarche.qc.ca

■ **ESTRIE TRAIL**

This is one of the longest hikes in Quebec (95 miles/150km); it stretches from Kingsbury to the American border. Reckon on at least ten days to cover it in its entirety. Camp sites are on offer every 5 or 6 miles (8–10km).

◆ **Information**

Les Sentiers de l'Estrie 5182, bd Bourque Sherbrooke (Quebec), J1N 1H4 Tel. (819) 864 6314 www.lessentiersde lestrie.qc.ca

■ **CHARLEVOIX CROSSING**

Once reserved for skiers and hikers, this route (six days, 60 miles/100km) is now accessible to walkers. There is spectacular scenery in the Hautes-Gorges-de-la-Rivière-Malbaie.

◆ **Price**

From $80 (camping, no other services supplied) to $250 (transport for luggage, chalet).

◆ **Information**

www.charlevoix.net/ traverse/imraid/raid 841, rue St-Édouard, CP 171, Saint-Urbain G0A 4K0 Tel. (418) 639-2284 Fax (418) 639-2777

→ SNOWSHOEING

Some hiking trails are open to snowshoers.

◆ **Information**

Fédération Québécoise de la Marche Tel. 1 866 252-2065 Fax (514) 252-5137 www.fqmarche.qc.ca

→ CROSS-COUNTRY SKIING

Although the mountains of Quebec are modest in height, they offer first-rate ski runs. The season lasts from mid-November to mid-April, depending on the area. Several ski resorts are fitted with lighting to allow night-time skiing. Quebec boasts about a hundred winter sports resorts, several of them within easy reach of big cities (Quebec City region, Estrie and Laurentides).

■ **SKI RESORTS**

The most important are Mont-Tremblant (2,133 ft/650m), north of Montreal, and Mont-Sainte-Anne (2,051 ft/625m), east of Quebec City.

◆ **Price**

Approx. $51 per day (including ticket for ski-lift) for Mont-Sainte-Anne, $55 for Mont-Tremblant. Some resorts offer packages (half-day, etc.).

◆ **Information**

From ATRs (see page 370)

→ SKIING HIKES

Several cross-country ski resorts also offer hiking trails suitable for skiers. Mont-Sainte-Anne is well endowed, with 200 miles (360km) of well-maintained trails.

◆ **Price**

Approx. $10 per day.

■ **CROSS-COUNTRY SKIING CENTERS**

Around 40 specialist centers offer pistes (long or short), skating trails and cross-country or woodland tracks. Association des centres de ski de fond Tel. (450) 436-4051 Fédération Québécoise de la Marche Tel. 1 866 252-2065 Fax (514) 252-5137 www.fqmarche.qc.ca

→ SPORT IN THE CITY

Ski hiking, ice skating, tobogganning, etc. can also be enjoyed in city centers, or close by.

→ SLEDDING

The traditional sledding team comprises 6 to 12 dogs (Siberian huskies, malamutes or samoyeds) which can cover 20 to 40 miles (30–60km) in a day at a speed of about 6 mph (10km/h). Driving a sled (taught in situ) demands physical exertion, especially when making turns. The handling of the team can also be entrusted to a *musher* (dog master).

◆ **Information**

From ATRs (see page 370)

→ CYCLING

In Quebec, more than 1250 miles (2000km) of bicycle paths run alongside rivers, old railroad tracks and through picturesque villages.

◆ **Information**

Maison des cyclistes 1251, rue Rachel Est, Montreal, H2J 2J9 Tel. (514) 521-8356 or 1 800 567-8356 Fax (514) 521-5711 www.velo.qc.ca

MAIL
Poste Canada offices (indicated by red signs) are open Mon–Fri 8am–5.45pm.
Note
Some convenience stores (dépanneurs) and pharmacies offer similar services to post offices.
◆ **Price**
Letters to the US cost $0.85. Letters and postcards to Europe are $1.45

MEDIA
→ **RADIO AND TELEVISION**
The Canadian Broadcasting Corporation (CBC) has a Francophone radio and television network that broadcasts throughout the country.

→ **PRESS**
■ **DAILY NEWSPAPERS**
Five daily newspapers are published in French in Quebec: *La Presse, Le Devoir, Le Soleil* (Quebec), *Le Journal de Montréal, Le Journal de Québec.*

■ **WEEKLY**
Voir is a weekly magazine available free in cafés, bars and elsewhere. It lists cultural events in Montreal and Quebec.

INTERNET
Internet cafés are concentrated in the big cities.
◆ **Price**
$5 on average for one hour of connection.

GOING OUT
To find out what's on, consult *La Presse* (Montreal), *Le Soleil* (Quebec) or *Voir*.
■ **MONTREAL**
It is possible to book tickets for shows by telephone if you have a credit card.

Réseau Admission
Tel. (514) 790-1245
Place des Arts
Tel. (514) 842-2112

TAXES
There are quite a few hidden costs to take into account when traveling in Quebec. Tips and service are usually not added to restaurant bills. The 7% federal tax on products and services (TPS), plus the 7.5% Quebec sales tax (TVQ), is applied to most purchases, including meals.

Warning
These taxes are not usually included in the price marked on goods.

→ **REIMBURSEMENT**
Tourists can claim a reimbursement of ceratin taxes (accommodation and purchases such as souvenirs, clothes and gifts). Keep the receipts and ask for a brochure from Canadian customs.
◆ **Information**
Agence des Douanes et du Revenu du Canada Programme de remboursement

aux visiteurs Green (information) number:
1 800 668-4748 or (902) 432-5608 (from outside Canada)
www.ccra-adrc.gc.ca/visiteurs

TIPPING
Service is not included in restaurant bills in Canada. The normal practice is to leave 15% of the total cost (the equivalent of taxes). Other tips – for taxi drivers, gas service attendants, bar staff, hotel porters and hairdressers, etc. – are left to the discretion of customers.

TELEPHONE
Phone numbers consist of seven digits, always preceded by the regional code

→ **CODES**
■ **Montreal (city)**
514
■ **Region of Montreal**
450
■ **Quebec City, Gaspésie and the eastern regions**
418

■ **Estrie, Hull and the northern regions**
819

→ **CHARGES**
■ **LOCAL CALLS**
These are free from a private telephone but cost $0.25 from a call box.
■ **INTERCITY CALLS**
Charges vary according to the distance, time and length of call.
■ **800 NUMBERS**
Calls to numbers starting with 1-800, 1-866, 1-877 or 1-888 are free within both Canada and the United States.
■ **INTERNATIONAL**
From Quebec dial 011 + country code (44 for the UK, + the number The prepaid Allô! card is on sale in tourist information offices and Bell Teleboutiques; it can be used for calls all over the world.

→ **USEFUL NUMBERS**
■ **Operator**
Dial 0
■ **Directory enquiries**
411
■ **International directory enquiries**
dial 0
■ **'Green numbers' for information**
1-800-555-1212

EMERGENCIES
■ **Police, fire service or ambulance**
911
■ **Traffic conditions**
Montreal
(514) 873-7781
Quebec
(418) 643-1911
■ **Weather**
Montreal
(514) 283-3010
Quebec
(418) 648-7766
■ **In case of accident**
Sûreté du Québec
1 800 461-2131
■ **Anti-intoxication center**
1-800-463-5060

◆ RESTAURANTS AND HOTELS

◆ *In Quebec,* table d'hôte *means set menu or à la carte* ◆ CP *means* casier postal *(postal box)* ◆ *Hotel prices are for a double room with double occupancy* ◆ *The addresses below are listed per touristic region (white names on black backgrounds) – see page 14.*

Abitibi-Témiscamingue	358
Chaudière-Appalaches	358
Bas-St-Laurent	358
Charlevoix	358
Mauricie	359
Estrie	359
Gaspésie	360
Îles-de-la-Madeleine	360
Laurentides	361
Manicouagan	361
Montérégie	361
Montreal	362
Outaouais	365
Quebec region	366
Saguenay-Lac-St-Jean	369

ABITIBI-TÉMISCAMINGUE

VAL-D'OR (▲ 230)

HOTELS

★ AUBERGE DE L'ORPAILLEUR
104, rue Perreault, J9P 2G3
Tel. (819) 825-9518
Fax (819) 825-8275
www.aubergeorpailleur.com
Former gold-miner's bunkhouse, which is tucked into the heart of the mining village Bourlamaque within Val d'Or, once the center of the Abitibi gold rush. The auberge is within walking distance of the historical Cité de l'Or goldmine (now a museum) and over 60 inhabited log houses that comprise a protected historical site. Hearty breakfasts are included and often contain local blueberries. One-to six-day adventure tourist packages are available for snowmobiling, snowshoeing, dogsledding, canoeing, kayaking, and trekking. There are just seven rooms, so reservations are a must.
🖥

GÎTE LAMAQUE
119, Perry Drive
Val-d'Or, J9P 2G1
Tel. (819) 825-4483
www.gite-lamaque.com
Quaint, comfortable, English-style home built in 1936 in the heart of the Vallée de l'Or historical site, converted into a threpe-room smoke-free B&B serving continental breakfast. Within 5 miles (8km) of many outdoor activities, including golf, hiking, downhill and cross-country skiing,

LA MUSE

snowmobiling and ice-skating. Also close to the Cité de l'Or mining museum, a fitness center, a cinema, and a restaurant district. Reservation recommended.
🖥

CHAUDIÈRES APPALACHES

LÉVIS (▲274)

HOTEL-RESTAURANT

LE ROSIER
473, rue St-Joseph, G6V 1G9
Tel. (418) 833-6233
or 1-877-778-8977
www.bbkerosier.com
With terrace views of the Saint Lawrence River, Mont Ste-Anne, and Île d'Orléans, this old Victorian home is inviting and smoke-free. Its four rooms are spacious, each with a private bathroom, and decorated with antique furnishings and floral bedding. Guests can play the piano or relax on antique couches in a cozy wine-colored living room with a chandelier and regal velvet curtains. Breakfast included,
served on the lovely terrace in warmer months.
🖥

MONTMAGNY (▲288)

HOTEL-RESTAURANT

MANOIR DES ÉRABLES
220, bd Taché, E G5V 1G5
Tel. (418) 248-0100
or 1 800 563-0200
Fax (418) 248-9507
www.manoirdeserables.com
An elegant 1814 stone manor with 23 modern rooms/suites with simple wood furniture, many in
an attached new pavilion. The stylish dining room, with chandeliers, original woodwork, and a roaring fireplace, serves excellent cuisine showcasing local cheeses and wines, and there's a cigar room with an open fireplace, period furniture, and board games. Winter packages include dogsledding, snowmobiling, and also old-fashioned snowmobiling (in an old Bombardier B-12 snowcat). In the summer there is golfing, a river cruise to Grosse Île, or sea kayaking on the St-Lawrence River. A Snow Goose festival is held every October; guided bird-watching tours at Île-aux-Grues are year-round.
🖥

LOWER ST LAWRENCE

NOTRE-DAME-DU-PORTAGE

HOTEL-RESTAURANT

AUBERGE DU PORTAGE
671, route du Fleuve, G0L 1Y0
Tel. (418) 862-3601
Fax (418) 862-6190
www.aubergeduportage.qc.ca
Located 7 miles (11km) west of Rivière-du-Loup ▲ 292, this turn-of-the-century Victorian manor on the shore of the Saint Lawrence River offers comfortable rooms, in-house dining, and extensive spa and beauty salon services. Come here to enjoy the beach, a heated outdoor salt-water pool, indoor and outdoor whirlpools, the sauna, and view the area's spectacular sunsets from one of the auberge's

several verandas. Easy access to golfing (18-hole), tennis, shuffleboard, bicycles (free), and kayaks.
▣

LE BIC (▲ 293)

HOTEL-RESTAURANT

★ **AUBERGE DU MANGE-GRENOUILLE**
148, rue Ste-Cécile, G0L 1B0
Tel. (418) 736-5656
Fax (418) 736-5657
www.aubergedumange grenouille.qc.ca
Originally Le Bic's general store, this 28 room D&B is a striking piece of architecture: a majestic wine-red manor covered with white gingerbread detailing, verandas, turrets and window boxes. Once inside, the theme is warmth and romance, with luxurious decoration including rich, heavy curtains, walls painted a range of warm colors, and beds and couches littered with overstuffed pillows, this place predisposes guests to relax and enjoy. Welcoming owners, spectacular gardens, and an excellent restaurant (table d'hote $24–34).

CHARLEVOIX
BAIE-ST-PAUL (▲ 280)

HOTEL-RESTAURANT

LA MAISON OTIS
23, rue St-Jean-Baptiste, G0A1B0
Tel. (418) 435-2255
www.quebecweb.com/ maisonotis/accueil.htm
With 30 rooms scattered throughout three neighboring villas, living quarters come in all shapes and sizes at La Maison Otis, all uniquely and tastefully decorated.

Guests can enjoy four-star dining, a well-stocked wine cellar, a lively fireplace bar, and attractive gardens and terraces in the warmer months. Packages of special interest include golf, spa services, skiing on Le Massif, and salmon fishing on the Gouffre River.
▣

LA MALBAIE (▲ 285)

HOTEL-RESTAURANT

★ **MANOIR RICHELIEU**
181, av. Richelieu, G5A 1X7

MANOIR RICHELIEU

MANOIR HOVEY

Tel. (418) 665-3703
ou 1 800 257-7544
Fax (418) 665-3093
This storybook French-style castle ▲285, built in 1928, is a spectacularly elegant 405-room hotel against the magnificent backdrop of Charlevoix's natural beauty. Find old-world charm combined with first-class service and all the amenities of a 5-star hotel: luxurious common spaces, attentive staff, extensive spa services, numerous restaurants, and an

in-house casino. This is one of Quebec's crown jewels, part of the famous Fairmont Hotels family, an hour and a half's drive east of Quebec City.
▦

MAURICIE
GRAND-MÈRE (▲ 241)

HOTEL-RESTAURANT

AUBERGE LE FLORÈS
4291, 50e Avenue, G9T 1A6
Tel. (819) 538-9340
or 1 800 538-9340
Fax (819) 538-1884
www.leflores.com

Enchanting country bed-and-breakfast with 34 bedrooms (many smoke-free), surrounded by welcoming walkways, gardens, and an outdoor pool. Rooms are tastefully decorated and the common spaces are cozy and chock full of Quebecois antiques. Extensive spa services include Swedish massage, hot stone treatment, reflexology therapy, and even a chocolate body wrap treatment.

Creative cuisine is served, with both a standard ($23) and gourmet ($40) table d'hote each evening.
▣ ▦

GRANDES-PILES

HOTEL

CAPITAINERIE DU PASSANT
740, 3e Avenue, G0X 1H0
Tel. (418) 266-2165
or 1 877 778-8977
Fax. (418) 266-1535
www.capitaineriedu passant.com
Modest turn-of-the-century country home converted into a welcoming four-room bed-and-breakfast overlooking the picturesque Saint-Maurice River. Spacious sleeping quarters, private access and large decks allow you to get comfortable yet maintain your privacy, even within the charming home of your hosts. Full breakfast served daily, cozy fireplace lounge, internet access. Located halfway between Montreal and Quebec City, with snowmobile trails beginning right across the street and La Mauricie National Park just 15 minutes away.
▣

ESTRIE
KNOWLTON (▲ 211)

HOTEL-RESTAURANT

★ **AUBERGE LAKEVIEW INN**
50, rue Victoria, J0E 1V0
Tel. (450) 243-6183
ou 1 800 661-6183
Fax (450) 243-0602
www.aubergelakeview inn.com
A charming historical villa located in the center

◆ RESTAURANTS AND HOTELS

of the Victorian village of Knowlton near Lake Brome, built in 1874 by Loyalists who fled the US. Now a grand 28-room inn, which has been designated a heritage site. There's a very attractive dining room with original woodwork, tin ceiling, and vintage oil lamps, where they serve regional specialties such as Lake Brome duck and Quebec lamb. It also boasts a well-stocked wine and port cellar, reading room, fireplace lounge, and heated outdoor pool.
▦

MAGOG (▲ 212)

HOTEL-RESTAURANT

AUBERGE CHÂTEAU DU LAC
85, rue Merry Sud, J1X 3L2
Tel. (819) 868-1666 or 1 888 948-1666
Fax (819) 868-9989
www.auberge chateaudulac.com
Built near the majestic Lake Memphremagog by a wealthy financier in 1867, this lovely inn was fully gutted and rebuilt in 1999 by the current owner, who purchased it in a state of complete disrepair. All eight rooms are spacious and tidy, and bathrooms are newly renovated, some of them with bidets and whirlpool baths. Fine French and European cuisine is served, with reasonably priced five-, seven-, or nine-course dinners, live piano music, and occasional after-dinner dancing. Full breakfast is included.
▦

GASPÉSIE
BONAVENTURE

HOTEL-RESTAURANT

LE CHÂTEAU BLANC
98, av. Port-Royal, CP 880, G0C 1E0
Tel. (418) 266-2165 or 1 877 778-8977
Fax (418) 266-1535
www.quebecweb.com/riotelchateau
Built in 1906 and reconstructed in 1961 after a fire, the Château Blanc is located in the heart of the picturesque Bonaventure village, close enough to the water's edge for you to hear the waves from your room. Thirty-two rooms vary in price and style from B&B ($50-60 per night), to motel, hotel, and luxury suites ($120-160 per night); all have access to a private beach. Historically a summer resort for Quebec's business élite and American salmon anglers, Bonaventure still perpetuates the Acadian tradition of hospitality. Activities include canoeing, sea kayaking, biking, golfing, salmon fishing, horseback riding, dog sledding, or snowmobiling. Local artists are known for their work with sea leather. The restaurant is known for its excellent local seafood dishes.
▣

PERCÉ (▲ 306)

HOTEL-RESTAURANT

AUBERGE LES TROIS SŒURS
77 B, route 132 G0C 2L0
Tel. (418) 782-2183 ou 1 800 463-9700
Fax (418) 782-2610
www.gaspesie.com/les3soeurs

Open May 15– October 15
Seaside B&B and motel facing a majestic rock jutting up offshore. Rustic Victorian building with five cute rooms with hardwood floors, decorated with antiques; one room is tucked up under the roof, with a slanted pine ceiling. The all-wood original living room with piano makes for a comfortable relaxation spot. Next-door a modern motel has 63 rooms, decorated sparsely, some with kitchenettes. Rooms in both establishments are between $109 and $119 a night, but breakfast is only included for B&B guests. In the B&B is the quaint and cozy Restaurant Mathilde, open to all guests for breakfast and dinner. Decorated with original artwork by local artists, it serves a variety of local seafood specialties, and its table d'hote menu is in the $20 range.
▣

SAINTE-ANNE-DES-MONTS (▲ 300)

HOTEL-RESTAURANT

AUBERGE-GÎTE DU MONT-ALBERT
2001, route du Parc, G4V 2E4
Tel. 1 866 727-2427
Fax (418) 763-7803
www.parcsquebec.com.
Closed mid-Oct–mid-Feb except chalets
Reputed since 1950 for its fine cuisine and warm hospitality, this establishment serves up excellent meals in a comfortable,

outdoorsy atmosphere. The beautifully designed main chalet offers magnificent views of Mont Albert. All 48 rooms and 15 nearby picturesque chalets can be reserved with full breakfast and dinner included in the price. It's a convenient spot from which to cross-country ski, hike, and enjoy the natural beauty of Gaspésie.
▣

ÎLES-DE-LA-MADELEINE
CAP-AUX-MEULES
(▲313)

HOTEL-RESTAURANT

CHÂTEAU MADELINOT
323, route 199, CP 265, G0B 1B0
Tel. (418) 986-3695
Fax (418) 986-6437
www.ilesdelamadeleine.com/hotels/chateau/
A sprawling seaside resort hotel built in 1972, Château Madelinot has 120 modern and comfortable rooms, an indoor pool, sauna, whirlpool, internet access, and even a theater, all within walking distance of the port village of Cap-aux-Meules. Ecotourism packages (for three to six days) are available in March, to observe adult seals and their new pups sprawled as far as the eye can see. Other local attractions include dog sledding, sea kayaking, ice fishing, and – for those seeking an adrenaline rush – power-kiting with a tandem buggy.
▣

RESTAURANTS
■ < CA$ 20
■ CA$ 20–40
■ > CA$ 40

HAVRE AUBERT

HOTEL-RESTAURANT

AUBERGE CHEZ DENIS À FRANÇOIS
404, chemin d'En-Haut, CP 183,
G0B 1J0
Tel. (418) 937-2371
www.aubergechezdenis
.ca
Built in 1874 with lumber salvaged from a shipwreck, this B&B has eight smoke-free rooms tastefully decorated in a rustic style. The cheerful and sunny dining room serves a full breakfast to guests and then becomes a public restaurant for lunch and dinner, specializing in local seafood specialties. Located at the entrance of historical site La Grave, near Sandy Hook beach, with easy access to Havre-Aubert's aquarium, museum, marina, craft boutiques, and cafés.
■

HAVRE-AUX MAISONS

HOTEL-RESTAURANT

AUBERGE DE LA PETITE BAIE
187, route 199,
G0B 1K0
Tel. (418) 969-4073
www3.sympatico.ca/
auberge.petitebaie
Well-preserved turn-of-the-century customs station tastefully converted into a four-room B&B with unimpeded views of the Baie de la Plaisance and the Petite Baie. Rooms are decorated with antiques; each has a private bath. Breakfast is included. Dining room with unpainted original wood trim seats 24 and serves local

seafood specialties (starting at $29) such as lobster, salmon in smoked herring butter, seal with cranberry sauce, mussels with Pernod, and maple syrup tarts.
■

LAURENTIDES
MONT-TREMBLANT

HOTEL

AUBERGE LE LUPIN B&B
127 Pinoteau,
J8E 1G2
Tel. (819) 425-5474
or toll free
1-877-425-5474
Fax (819) 425-6079
www.lelupin.com
An Alpine chalet-type log cabin built in 1945 as a private residence, now a charming nine-room B&B. Décor is rustic, walls are mostly pure white, most rooms have hardwood floors, one has a fireplace. Living quarters are welcoming, with plump duvets and special touches like fresh flowers and chocolates on pillows. Located directly on a bicycle and in-line skating path, nearly a mile (1.5km) from the Mont Tremblant ski resort and village, and with access to a private beach on Lac Tremblant. Includes full breakfast, with choices such as apple pancakes or goat cheese and tomato omelets.
■

HOTEL-RESTAURANT

HÔTEL CLUB TREMBLANT
121, rue Cuttle,
J0T 1Z0
Tel. (819) 425-2731
or 1 800 567-8341
Fax (819) 425-9903
www.clubtremblant.
com
Built in the 1930s as a private retreat

across the lake from the Mont Tremblant ski resort, Club Tremblant has grown to become a world-class, year-round resort with 122 suites, a private beach, indoor/outdoor pool, tennis courts, and full service spa. Suites are decorated in a rustic yet luxurious style, each containing a living room with a fireplace and patio door leading to a private balcony or terrace. Three excellent on-site restaurants provide a selection of typical Quebecois countryside cuisine as well as an assortment of Atlantic delights.*
■

MANICOUAGAN
POINTE-DES-MONTS
(▲ 331)

HOTEL-RESTAURANT

★ **GÎTE DU PHARE DE POINTE-DES-MONTS**
Chemin Vieux-Phare,
G0H 1A0
Summer tel. (418) 939-2332. Winter tel. (418) 589-8408
www.pointe-des-monts.com
A series of rustic seaside cabins scattered along the beach between ½ and 2 miles (1–4km) from the Pointe-des-Monts lighthouse. Built in 1830, the picturesque red-and-white lighthouse is a designated heritage site, a seven-story museum, and the home base of this ecotourism B&B. Lodgings come with or without kitchenette; three meals a day available (for guests only) in the former chapel. Packages available for whale/seal-watching, salmon/ trout fishing and sea

fishing, as well as duck, moose, or bear hunting.*
■

TADOUSSAC (▲ 328)

HOTEL-RESTAURANT

HOTEL BELUGA
191, rue des Pionniers,
G0T 2A0
Tel. (418) 235-4784
Fax (418) 235-4295
www.fortune1000.ca/
beluga
Attractive seaside hotel-motel located in the heart of Tadoussac. Steps away from the local tourist office, find a three-story green clapboard villa with 39 rooms, all painted a stark white and simply decorated. Next door to Restaurant Auberge du Lac, a sunny dining room with courteous service and plenty of reasonably priced seafood specialties. Popular spot for snowmobiling and whale watching (the beluga is the only marine mammal that lives permanently in the Saint Lawrence River).
■

MONTÉRÉGIE
SAINT-SIMON

HOTEL-RESTAURANT

GÎTE À CLAUDIA
923, 4ième Rang Ouest,
J0H 1Y0
Tel: (450) 798-2758
or (450) 798-2334
www.domaine-st-simon.qc.ca
Homey three-room B&B in picturesque countryside near a maple grove, horse stables, and a traditional Quebec maple sugar shack. Rooms are decorated with antiques; one has a private bath. Hearty breakfast of

◆ RESTAURANTS AND HOTELS

★ the editors' choice

local products in a country-style sunroom with a wood-burning oven/range. Grounds include a pond, an in-ground pool, and roaming horses. Affiliated with a charming rustic bring-your-own-wine sugar shack (open March–April), which is a true Canadian tradition visitors simply must not miss if here in season.
🔲

CHAMBLY

HOTEL

LA MAISON DUCHARME
10, rue de Richelieu,
QC J3L 2B9
Tel: (450) 447-1220
or 1-888-387-1220
Fax (450) 447-1018
www.maisonducharme
.ca
Remarkable 1814 stone house, originally a Fort Chambly officer barracks, and subsequently a hospital, a brewery, a bakery, a saddle shop, garage, private residence, and now a fabulous B&B. Four rooms, each with private bath and a great view. Half an hour from Montreal, located at the foot of the rapids and overlooking the Chambly basin. Beautiful grounds, pleasant terraces, swimming pool, and access to nearby private clay-court tennis club.
🔲

MONTREAL (▲ 164)

RESTAURANTS

L'ACADÉMIE
4051 St Denis,
H2W 2M7
Tel. (514) 849-2249
Popular Mediterranean-atmosphere restaurant with a lively ambiance and

hearty, well-priced food. Spread over three stories, connected by an impressive spiral staircase, with modern décor, mood lighting, and staff who allow diners to linger despite the line-up outside. House specialties include nine varieties of mussels, cannelloni, and veal scaloppini; pastas come in particularly generous portions. Bring your own wine, available from SAQ liquor store or convenience store, both nearby. Reservations only possible Mondays through Wednesdays, so expect a wait if arriving after 7pm.
🔲

BINERIE MONT-ROYAL
367, avenue du Mont-Royal Est
Tel. (514) 285-9078
Traditional Quebecois home cooking in a family-run 1940s diner with 11 stools and 4 tables. Very inexpensive, unrefined, but hearty food; it's impossible to leave here hungry. House special ($5.99) is baked beans with bread, sausage optional. Other favorites are 'tourtière', 'ragoût de boulettes', and 'cretons'. Famous for its 'pudding chomeur' (pudding for the unemployed) dessert. Most expensive meal is $8.95. Cash only, no liquor license, closed weekend evenings.
🔲

EDUARDO'S
404 Duluth Street
Est
Tel. (514) 843-3330
Charming Italian restaurant off the trendy strip of St-

Denis Boulevard. Two cozy exposed brick rooms (one smoke-free) pack in a boisterous clientele coming for affordable, carefully prepared meals preceded by generous baskets of warm focaccia. Favorites include several variations of veal scaloppini, and fettuccini alfredo. Bring your own wine, available from SAQ liquor store or convenience store, each a few doors away. There are no reservations taken Fri & Sat, so expect a short (but worthwhile) wait if arriving after 6pm.
🔲

LE PETIT EXTRA
1690, rue Ontario
Est
Tel. (514) 527-5552
www.aupetitextra.com
Large, lively French-bistro-style restaurant with courteous service and creative cuisine. Simple black tables with starched white tablecloths, neatly arranged in view of the blackboard containing the day's specials. Excellent value, with three-course menus starting at $10 for lunch and at $13 for dinner. Tempting specials include rabbit pie, braised duck, and Quebec lamb. Well-rounded wine list to accompany your meal.
🔲

ST-VIATEUR BAGEL SHOP & CAFE
263 St Viateur Ouest,
H2V 1Y1
Tel. (514) 276-8044
www.stviateurbagel.
com
Originally opened in 1957 by an East European baker, and a contender for Montreal's best

bagels ever since. Still hand-rolled and baked in a wood-burning oven, bagels dominate the menu, which also has numerous salads and many specialty coffees. The current owner began working here aged 14, in 1962. Located on a café-lined shopping street in the trendy Plateau neighborhood. Very popular with locals for weekend brunch.
🔲

★ **SCHWARTZ**
3895, Saint-Laurent
Tel. (514) 842-4813
Famous Jewish smoked meat deli serving up huge portions of lean, medium, or fatty smoked meat accompanied by rye bread, with side orders of fries and pickles. Expect a wait outside, as the interior is impossibly small, crammed tight with tables that are filled up with whoever is next in line. Sometimes gruff service is moderated by the joviality of the diners enjoying a tried-and-true, great-tasting plate of meat.
🔲

★ **TOQUÉ!**
900, place
Jean-Paul Riopelle,
H2Z 3B2
Tel. (514) 499-2084
www.restaurant-toque.com
A trendy, high-end yet casual restaurant with an innovative menu that changes frequently. Tempting main courses may include roasted British Colombia white sturgeon with hedgehog mushrooms and caramelized onions, or venison with potato purée and

oyster mushrooms.
Dinner is à la carte,
or there is a nightly
6-course 'mystery
menu' of seasonal
foods crafted by the
chef and co-owner
Normand Laprise for
a cost of $131,
which includes four
glasses of wine.
Extensive wine list,
with over 20 wines
available by the
glass. Make
weekend
reservations three
weeks in advance.
🏨

HOTELS

XIXE SIÈCLE
262, rue St-Jacques,
H2Y 1N1
Tel: (514) 985-0019
or 1-877-553-0019
Fax (514) 985-0059
www.hotelxixsiecle.
com
Impressive French
Second Empire
building, constructed
in 1870 as the head
office of the
Montreal City and
District Savings Bank,
and converted in
2001 to a 59-room
boutique hotel. The
beautifully restored
main lobby with
ceiling friezes is now
a library and reading
room for guests.
Elegant, spacious
rooms have very
high ceilings, tall
windows, and Louis-
Philippe-style period
furniture. The
courteous and
knowledgeable
concierge is helpful
in planning your
stay; the hotel is also
well located for
exploring Old
Montreal and its
port. A generous
breakfast (not
included) is served in
an elegant, all-white
dining room, with
fresh croissants,
pâté, local cheeses,
and home-made
jams (very tasty, and
they are available
for purchase).
🏨

LE GERMAIN
2050, rue Mansfield,
H3A 1Y9
Tel: (514) 849-2050
or 1-877-333-2050
Fax (514) 849-1437
A trendy 101-room
boutique hotel that
achieves a mixture of
superb comfort
within minimalist
décor. Rooms are
large, featuring
luxurious beds with
down comforters
and well-cushioned
wicker easy chairs.
Special touches in
every room include
freshly cut orchids, a
basket of fresh fruit,
bottled water, and a
selection of Aveda
bath products.
The buffet breakfast
is served in the
lobby, with
unlimited fresh
croissants and cafés
au lait, and an
assortment of
newspapers.
🏨

**★ LES PASSANTS
DU SANS-SOUCY**
171, rue St-Paul
Ouest, H2Y 1Z5
Tel. (514) 842-2634
Fax (514) 842-2912
www.lesanssoucy.com
A gorgeous 1723
fur warehouse
transformed into a
6-room, smoke-free
bed-and-breakfast.
The rooms are truly
stunning, each with
exposed stone walls,
wooden floors,
French Canadian
antiques, wrought-
iron or brass beds,
faux fireplaces, and
Jacuzzi tubs.
The lobby doubles
as an art gallery
featuring local
artists; the sitting
room has an open
fireplace and daily
newspapers are
supplied. The
copious breakfasts
on offer include
fresh-baked
croissants, omelets,
French toast, fresh
fruit and good
coffee.
🏨

**PETITE AUBERGE LES
BONS MATINS**
1401, avenue
Argyle,
H3G 1V5
Tel: (514) 931-9167
or 1-800-588-5280
Fax (514) 931-1621
www.bonsmatins.com
Charming family-run
bed-and-breakfast in
a row of
magnificently
restored turn-of-the-
century townhouses.
Refined décor,
vibrant colors in the
rooms, and walls
adorned with 75
works of art by a
local artist (who also
happens to be a
family member).
Guest kitchen open
24 hours, stocked
with black, herbal,
and ice teas, coffee,
hot chocolate, and
cookies. There are
seven rooms and
nine suites, each very
different, with the
suites containing
whirlpools and
fireplaces. The
courteous hosts pay
special attention to
detail, with fresh
flowers and fruit
baskets in rooms and
common areas. The
sumptuous breakfast
(which is included in
the room rate) will
rule out lunch,
tempting guests
with made-to-order
waffles, French
toast, eggs benedict,
omelets, local
cheeses, smoked
salmon, café au lait,
and fresh-squeezed
juice.
🏨

LE SAINT SULPICE
414 rue St-Sulpice,
Old Montreal,
H2Y 2V5
Tel: (514) 288-1000
Fax (514) 288-0077
www.lesaintsulpice.
com
High-end boutique
hotel in a renovated
heritage building
with European flair
and superb attention
to detail. Well
located in the heart

of Old Montreal,
behind the Notre
Dame Basilica. Every
amenity imaginable,
from fine dining to a
luxurious fitness
center. A total of 108
spacious suites range
from 550–1,500
square feet (51–140
sq m), many with
fireplaces and views
of the private
terrace courtyard.
In-house dining at
S Le Restaurant,
which specializes in
regional cuisine such
as Quebec lamb and
pheasant, and
provides 24-hour
room service.
🏨

HOTEL-RESTAURANTS

**★ CHÂTEAU ET
HOTEL VERSAILLES**
1659, rue
Sherbrooke Ouest,
H3H 1E3
Tel. (514) 933-3611
or 1 888 933-8111
Fax (514) 933-6867
www.versailleshotels.
com
Chic and artsy
65-room boutique
hotel spread across
several elegant
interconnected row
houses. Vibrantly
painted interiors
mixed with rich,
textured fabrics
make for an intimate
atmosphere
punctuated with
original architectural
details, tasteful
antiques, and
original art by
local artists. Le
Boudoir fireplace
lounge is for hotel
guests only and has
a private club
atmosphere. Rooms
are modern and
come with
funky lighting,
evening bed
turndown, and
complementary
continental
breakfast. No
elevator. French
cuisine in the
restaurant
Les Champs-Élysées.
🏨

◆ RESTAURANTS AND HOTELS

★ THE RITZ-CARLTON

1228, rue
Sherbrooke Ouest,
H3G 1H6
Tel. (514) 842-4212
Fax (514) 842-3383
www.ritzcarlton.com
Built in 1912 by the
New York architects
Warren and
Wetmore, who also
built NY's Grand
Central Station, the
Ritz-Carlton is a
Montreal landmark,
and a truly classy
and luxurious place
to stay. All 229
rooms are spacious,
decorated with
antiques, and many
have been upgraded
with marble baths
and goose-down
pillows. Guests can
also meander
through several
drawing rooms, a
ballroom, a cocktail
bar, and even a
garden restaurant
with a duck pond.
The famous Café de
Paris is known for its
tasty breakfasts,
daily High Tea, and
a superb Sunday
brunch, all worth
trying even if you're
not staying there.
⊞

CAFÉS AND BARS

BEAVER TAILS
127, de la Commune
Est, Old Montreal
Port, H2Y 1J1
Tel. (514) 392-2222
www.beavertailsinc.
com
First popularized in
Ottawa, Beaver Tail
pastries have a cult
following in
Montreal. This
piping hot specialty,
which has become a
Canadian classic ,
comes in several
variations, from the
standard Cinnamon
Sugar to the more
daring Hazelnut and
Reese's Pieces. Meet
a friendly talking
beaver mascot when
you enter this cozy
five-stool snack bar
along the Old Port
waterfront.

JAVA U
191 rue St-Paul
Ouest
Tel. (514) 849-8881
Trendy daytime
coffee shop that
morphs into a
nighttime lounge
with live bands and
DJs. Daytime bistro-
inspired fare consists
of creative versions
of panini
sandwiches, salads,
and tasty desserts,
accompanied by a
broad selection of
coffees. There's
tapas-type dining in
the evenings: a
range of appetizers
is complemented by

HÔTEL CHÂTEAU MONTEBELLO

full bar service and
delicious martinis.
The décor is very chic
and modern, with
lots of glass design
elements and
furniture primarily in
white leather.
There's a good
people-watching
vantage point from
the second level
balcony tables. Also
have six other
locations around
town.

MOOZOO
133, de la Commune
Est, Old Montreal
Port, H2Y 1J1
Tel. (514) 392-2222
www.moozoo.com

Very funky purveyor
of divine and
decadent yogurts
and juices. First
popularized by their
delectable
smoothies, Moozoo
also offers fresh,
made-on-the-
premises yogurts
that are great on
their own or in any
of the smoothies.
Tantalizing flavors
like honey-ginger or
chocolate-Toblerone
– you may never
look at yogurt the
same way again.
Chocolate therapy
bars with names like
'Success' or 'Amour'
come with words of
wisdom inside the
wrapper. Bar service,
with funky seating
for 15 people.

NEWTOWN
1476 Crescent St
Tel. (514) 284-6555
www.newtown.ca
Classy bar-club-
lounge and
restaurant on the
trendy night strip
of Crescent Street.
Owned by the
Canadian Formula 1
driver Jacques
Villeneuve
(translates as 'New
Town'), this is a
spacious four-level
complex, including a

four-season terrace
on top, affording
diners a spectacular
view of the area.
Although the food
is tasty, this place
picks up after the
dinner hour. DJs
play the full gamut
of R&B, disco,
groove, hip-hop,
and more. Décor
is modern yet
classy, with a distinct
aura of decadence.
Expect a line-up
outside on
weekends.

SHOPPING

HENRY BIRKS ET FILS
1240, Phillips Square,
H3B 3H4
Tel. (514) 397-2511
www.birks.com
Perhaps Canada's
most respected
jeweler. Located in a
beautifully ornate
Victorian-era store,
with carved wood
display cases, marble
floors, stone pillars,
and impeccable
service. In 1879, the
first Henry Birks
store was opened by
a Canadian-born
Englishman whose
family had been in
the business since
1564. The product
line has grown to
include timepieces,
pens, desk
accessories, leather
goods, glassware,
and china. Relatively
new to the market,
Canadian-mined
diamonds are
available here,
laser-engraved
with the Birks name,
a maple leaf, and an
authenticity
certificate number.

HOLT RENFREW
1300, rue
Sherbrooke Ouest
www.holtrenfrew.com
Founded by an
Irishman as a hat
shop in Quebec City
in 1837, Holt
Renfrew (storefront
just says Holts) has
grown to become
one of the world

RESTAURANTS
🔲 < CA$ 20
🔲 CA$ 20–40
🔲 > CA$ 40

leaders in fashion and shopping. Carries top name brands such as Giorgio Armani, Gucci, Prada, and Chanel. Don't expect any bargains, but there is no compromise on quality, and you will certainly get a look at some swanky Montreal shoppers. Elevator operated by a real person!

L'ESSENCE DU PAPIER
4160, rue Saint-Denis
The famous Saint-Gilles paper (100 percent cotton) made in Saint-Joseph-de-la-Rive.

LA BAIE
585, rue Sainte-Catherine Ouest
A large store renowned for its blankets, rugs and coats in the colours of the Hudson Bay Company..

LE BARON
8601, bd Saint-Laurent
www.lebaron.ca/
Clothes to be seen in for the outdoorsy/ adventurer type.

LES AILES DE LA MODE
677, rue Sainte-Catherine Ouest
www.lesailes.com
A large store, known as much for its Art Deco restaurant, Le 9ᵉ, as for the goods it sells.

OGILVY
1307, rue Sainte-Catherine Ouest
In this elegant Victorian-style building since 1912, Ogilvy is perhaps best known for its mechanically enhanced Christmas windows. Also known for quality men's and women's wear, with 50+ in-store boutiques such as Rodier Paris,

Anne Klein, Aquascutum, and Guy Laroche. Specials are announced by a kilt-wearing bagpiper, who roams the store all day, piping out the occasional festive tune. There are elegant chandeliers, plush carpets, and quality merchandise.

OUTAOUAIS

HULL (▲ 228)

RESTAURANT

CAFÉ HENRI BERGER
69 Laurier St,
Tel. (819) 777-5646

CHÂTEAU FRONTENAC

Long one of the national capital area's most recognized and respected names in high-end French cuisine, this is a restaurant for special occasions (count on a bill of $75 per person). Warm ambiance, an unrushed environment and exquisite food are complemented by a well-rounded wine list and courteous service. Lovely views of the famed and unusual Museum of Civilization and the

Ottawa cityscape across the river.
🔲

MONTEBELLO (▲224)

HOTEL

FAIRMONT LE CHÂTEAU MONTEBELLO
392, rue Notre-Dame,
J0V 1L0
Tel. (819) 423-6341
www.chateaumonte bello@fairmont.com
This massive Swiss-Alps-inspired château was built in 1930 from 10,000 giant cedar logs. The main hall contains all of the

guest rooms and features a 3-storey atrium and magnificent six-sided fireplace, which can be enjoyed from an array of cozy seating nooks. Renowned for its fabulous Sunday brunch, which attracts day-trippers from Ottawa and Montreal. Offers a multitude of activities including golf, hiking, cross-country skiing, horseback riding, canoeing, and even hunting and fishing

(the latter two at their adjacent wilderness resort). A member of the famed luxury chain of Fairmont Hotels.
🔲🔲

OTTAWA (▲ 227)

RESTAURANTS

DOMUS CAFÉ
89 Murray Street,
K1N 5M5
Tel. (613) 241-6007
Fax (613) 241-5032
www.domuscafe.ca
Located in the Byward Market, Domus offers a delectable and imaginative selection of Canadian, regional, and seasonal foods, from local area producers whenever possible. Dine here and you will not be surprised to hear that Domus is a member of the international Slow Food Movement, dedicated to the appreciation of food without the rush. The owner has developed a Canadian cellar of age-worthy and exceptional wines, making this a great place to try some of Canada's best wines. Reservations a must.
🔲

VITTORIA TRATTORIA
35 William Street,
K1N 6Z9
Tel: (613) 789-8959
www.vittoriatrattoria. com
A cozy Byward Market restaurant with exposed brick walls, hardwood floors, intimate seating and contemporary lighting. Italian-inspired cuisine is coupled with one of the city's most extensive wine lists (35 pages), with offerings from around the globe and no fewer than 70 Canadian wines.

★ *the editors' choice*

Tempting main dishes include porcini-dusted grilled Alberta strip steak with white truffle oil, or fettuccine with shrimp and Prince Edward Island mussels in a marinara sauce. ⊠

HOTEL

AUBERGE DU MARCHÉ
87, Guigues,
K1N 5H8
Tel. (613) 241-6610
ou 1 800 465-0079
www.aubergedumarche
.ca
Turn-of-the-century row house renovated to create a comfortable, smoke-free, and exceptionally clean B&B with one suite (private bath) and three tastefully decorated rooms (shared bath). Very conveniently located in the Byward Market area, near the National Gallery, Parliament, and perhaps the city's best collection of restaurants and nightlife establishments. Full breakfast (included) served in a family dining room. ⊡

HOTEL-RESTAURANT

FAIRMONT CHÂTEAU LAURIER
1, Rideau,
K1N 8S7
Tel. (613) 241-1414
Fax (613) 241-2958
www.fairmont.com
Stunning granite and limestone French-Renaissance-style building with a turreted copper roof, opened in 1912 by the Grand Trunk Pacific Railway, now a part of the luxurious Fairmont Hotels chain. Located next to the Parliament buildings, along the

Rideau Canal, overlooking the Ottawa River, and one block from the Byward Market, it offers excellent access to bike paths, canal and river boat tours, shopping and dining out. Award-winning Wilfrid's Restaurant overlooks the Parliament buildings and Rideau Canal locks. Zoe's Lounge is famous for its Cocktail Hour and Afternoon High Tea, the latter worth booking even if not staying here. ⊞

NIGHTLIFE

THE COLLECTION & BAR 56
56 Byward Market Square
K1N 7A2
Tel. (613) 562-1120
Fax (613) 562-2384
www.collectionbar56.
com
These co-located establishments offer a funky, modern atmosphere for dancing or lounging. Good service and an extensive mixed drink menu, although they are best known for their martinis. Open seven nights a week until 2am, with each night featuring a DJ and different music (e.g. Saturday: dance floor jazz, funk, soulful house; Thursday: hip hop, house, funk).

HOTEL

LES TROIS ERABLES
801 Chemin Riverside,
J0X 3G0
Tel. (819) 459-1118
or toll free
1-877-337-2253
www.lestroiserables.
com

A turn-of-the-century neo-Queen-Anne Victorian mansion with original stained glass windows and remarkable woodwork, now converted to a five-room smoke-free B&B. Located on two acres (0.8ha) in the heart of the charming village of Wakefield, along the Gatineau River. Gracious hosts serve a full breakfast and are helpful in planning trips (even packing box lunches) to nearby Gatineau Park, local ski resorts, or Ottawa (35 minutes away). Guests are welcome to relax with a beverage or a board game in the dining room, salon, parlor, library, on the veranda, or in the garden.

RESTAURANTS

★ **LA MAISON GASTRONOMIQUE SERGE BRUYERE**
1200, rue Saint-Jean
Tel. (418) 694-0618
Fax (418) 694-2202
With three restaurants under one roof, this place can accommodate all types of budgets. La Grande Table serves high-end French cuisine adapted to the Quebec palate and is famous for its 'discovery menu' ($95) featuring eight courses of delectable specialties. Famous dishes include roasted duck with foie gras, and Charlevoix veal loin with Parma ham. Le Bistro Chez Livernois is less formal and less expensive, but

benefits from sharing the same kitchen. Le Pub St-Patrick in the exposed stone cellar serves pub fare accompanied by Irish beers and live folk music. ⊠

★ **AUX ANCIENS CANADIENS**
34, rue Saint-Louis,
Tel. (418) 692-1627
www.auxanciens
canadiens.qc.ca
In one of the city's oldest houses (1677) and one of the best places to taste cuisine reminiscent of the earliest years of New France. Despite its central location, meals are prepared with care and are reasonably priced, especially before 6pm. Generous portions of meat pie, sugar pie and Lake Brome duck; caribou and maple syrup figure in many dishes. Enjoy a true Quebecois meal served up by waiters in period costume in one of five dining rooms, each decorated differently – one has a fireplace and showcases a collection of antique dishes, another is ringed with wooden bas-reliefs of historical Quebec scenes. ⊠

★ **BUFFET DE L'ANTIQUAIRE**
95, rue Saint-Paul
G1K 3V8
Tel. (418) 692-2661
Probably the most economical spot to taste local fare on the antique row of Rue St-Paul. Open daily 7am–11pm and frequented mainly by locals, this buffet has full bar service and serves Quebec standards such as pea soup, 'poutine'

(fries topped with cheese curds and gravy), and 'feves au lard' (broad beans with bacon), in addition to a range of sandwiches, salads, and pastries. Dinette atmosphere upgraded by exposed brick wall décor.
▣

CAFÉ DU MONDE
84, rue Dalhousie,
Tel. (418) 692-4455
Open 11.30am–11pm
www.lecafedumonde.com
Delicious French-inspired international cuisine in a jovial atmosphere with impromptu live piano music provided by waiters and customers alike. The creative menu features local cheeses, pâtés, quiches, roasted lamb knuckle, duck confit, and a classic combo of fries and mussels (with a variety of sauces). Extensive imported beer selection, and a comprehensive wine list, with 15 varieties available by the glass, for those who wish to sample. Many tables have a view of the river.
▣

★ **COCHON DINGUE**
46, bd Champlain,
Tel. (418) 692-2013
www.cochondingue.com
The first location in a small local chain operating since 1979, the 'Crazy Pig' restaurant has sidewalk seating and indoor dining areas serving local must-haves such as mussels, steak-frites (steak with fries), and homemade desserts topped with maple cream. Housed in a charming 1860

building, formerly a police station (café side) and butcher (bar side), exposed stone walls blend tastefully with modern checkered tile floors and thoughtful décor.
▣

★ **LE MARIE-CLARISSE**
12, rue Petit-Champlain,
G1K 4H4
Tel. (418) 692-0857
One of the coziest restaurants in town, housed in a 340-year-old building in one of the oldest merchant districts in North America (Quartier Petit Champlain), at the foot of the famous 1893 iron stairway Escalier Casse-Cou ('Breakneck Steps'). Specializing in creative seafood and game dishes, the 'menu du jour' changes frequently and offers such enticing meals as halibut with pistachios flavored with orange and vanilla, or venison and beef duo with berries and sweet garlic. Table d'hote four-course meals from $38.
▣

HOTELS

★ **AUBERGE SAINT-ANTOINE**
8, rue Saint-Antoine,
G1K 4C9
Tel. (418) 692-2211
Fax (418) 692-1177
www.saint-antoine.com
Attractive boutique hotel in an 1830 maritime warehouse has a fabulous lobby with original beams and stone floor, fireplaces, a library, a bar, and 95 tastefully decorated modern rooms. Living quarters are outfitted with luxurious linens, goose-down duvets

and pillows, Bose sound systems, high-speed internet access, heated bathroom floors, and countless other creature comforts. Some rooms have private terraces, including one with a private three-hole putting green. Buffet breakfast and afternoon cheese and wine are served in the lobby for enjoyment by the fireplace. Gastronomic packages (1–3 nights of dinners) are available for true foodies.
⊞

HOTEL DOMINION 1912
126 rue St-Pierre,
G1K 4A8
Tel. (418) 692-2224
or 1-888-833-5253
Fax (418) 692-4403
www.hoteldominion.com
Originally built as a warehouse in 1912, now a sophisticated boutique hotel with 60 rooms overlooking either the Saint Lawrence or the Old Town. Spacious rooms have goose-down duvets and pillows and sleek, custom-designed furniture. As the owners pride themselves on attention to detail, travelers enjoy special touches such as bathrobes, guest umbrellas, fresh fruit, bottled water, and a newspaper delivered every morning. Couples may want to book one of four 'Romantic Escape' packages available: the 'Chocolate Escape' involves a chocolate oil massage, chocolate body wrap, and a box of chocolates, while the 'Rose Escape' promises a bed of rose petals and vase of long-

stem roses upon arrival.
⊞

ICE HOTEL QUEBEC-CANADA INC.
143 route Duchesnay,
Pavillon l'Aigle
Ste-Catherine-de-la-Jacques-Cartier,
G0A 3M0
Tel: (418) 875-4522
Fax (418) 875-2833
www.icehotel-canada.com
First opened in 2000, the Ice Hotel is located 30 minutes from downtown, covers an area of 30,000 feet (3,000m), has 4 foot-thick (1.5m) walls, and is a true marvel to see. Each of the hotel's 32 rooms is uniquely crafted by local ice sculptors, and guests sleep on ice beds lined with animal skins. Other amenities include a cinema/theatre, chapel, art gallery, Absolut Ice Bar, the N'ice Club, where drinks are served in – you guessed it – ice glasses. Temperatures inside remain between 28° and 23° Fahrenheit (–2° and –5° C). At $500 per night (double occupancy), a night's rest doesn't come cheaply, but there is a 30-minute $15 tour well worth a curious traveler's while. Open January to April.
⊞

LE MANOIR D'AUTEUIL
49, rue d'Auteuil,
G1R 4C2
Tel. (418) 694-1173
Fax (418) 694-0081
www.quebecweb.com/dauteuil/introang.html
Originally a luxurious private residence built in 1835, this lavish manor is now a charming 16-room B&B. Each room is unique, so do not

◆ RESTAURANTS AND HOTELS

hesitate to ask to see what is available. One room used to be a chapel, one has a quirky staircase up to a loft bathroom, and another has an expansive turquoise-tiled bathroom that is as large as a bedroom. Off-season and fourth-floor room rates are reduced. Continental breakfast is included.
▪▪

HOTEL-RESTAURANTS

CHÂTEAU FRONTENAC
1, rue des Carrières, G1R 4P5
Tel. (418) 692-3861 or 1 800 441-1414
Fax (418) 692-1751
www.fairmont.com/frontenac
The city's most remarkable landmark, the Château Frontenac was built as a luxury hotel in 1893 by New York architect Bruce Price. It underwent numerous expansions over the years, now has 618 rooms and is a member of the Fairmont family of hotels. High on a bluff and overlooking the Saint Lawrence River, the view is as breathtaking as the luxurious interior décor and impeccable service. Five in-house restaurants serve a delicious selection of local and international dishes. Afternoon tea in Le Champlain restaurant is a tried and true Quebecois tradition; there is also a special afternoon tea for children, including a lesson in manners and the etiquette of taking tea.
▪▪▪▪

★ **HOTEL CLARENDON**
57, rue Sainte-Anne, G1R 1X4
Tel. (418) 692-2480 or 1 888 554-6001
Fax (418) 692-4652
www.quebecweb.com/clarendon
www.hotelclarendon.com/en/index.asp
The oldest family hotel in the province of Quebec, this elegant building dates back to 1866 and is one of the city's most renowned examples of Art Nouveau/Art Deco. Priding itself on attention to detail, rooms are first class, spacious, and decorated with simple lines. The sunny, soothing lobby showcases impressive wrought iron work. Breakfast is served overlooking the Old City. In-house Le Charles Baillairgé has a fine international menu featuring seafood dishes, guinea fowl, game, vegetables from their own garden, local cheeses, and a broad selection of wines and ports. Also in the hotel is café-bar l'Emprise, an icon in the Quebec City jazz scene and a great place to listen to some fabulous blues.
▪▪

SHOPPING

LA MAISON SIMONS
20, cote de la Fabrique (Upper Town),
Tel. (418) 692-3630
One of the city's first department stores when it opened here in 1840, Simons continues to be a trendy spot for designer apparel (Tommy Hilfiger, Hugo Boss, Donna Karan, plus other biggies), household

linens, and home décor. Two newer stores in town are less centrally located but are each 60,000 sq feet (5580 sq m) and have a greater selection.

Areas not to miss
Rue du Trésor is famous for its local art scene. Started in the 1960s by an ambitious group of young artists, this open-air gallery continues to be a draw for artists and art lovers alike. Preview this charming alley at: http://ruedutresor.qc.ca/

Rue St-Paul, near the Old Port, has become the antique district, with literally dozens of shops of all shapes and sizes specializing in French-Canadian, Victorian, and Art Deco furniture, as well as stemware, flatware, porcelain, and countless other collectibles.

Quartier Petit Champlain is a charming old shopping district known for its excellent selection of local arts/crafts, tasteful souvenirs, and designer clothing tucked into small boutiques along picturesque, narrow streets. Plenty of cafés and bistros regenerate weary shoppers. Preview this must-see area at: www.quartier-petit-champlain.qc.ca

NIGHTLIFE

COSMOS CAFÉ
575, Grande Allee Est, G1R 2K4
Tel. (418) 640-0606
www.lecosmos.com
Lively restaurant and nightclub with exposed brick walls,

funky sci-fi décor, custom barstools, and quirky, energetic personnel. Open from 7 or 8am every day until midnight (1am on weekends), Cosmos serves creatively presented gourmet meals all day and transforms into a wine-cellar atmosphere nightclub by turning the lights down and the tunes up. Lunch specials are particularly well priced, at $7–15; patio seating is available in warmer months.
▪▪

VOODOO GRILL
575 Grande Allee Est,
G1R 2K4
Tel: (418) 647-2000
www.voodoogrill.com
Billing itself as the 'house of all pleasures', there are actually three establishments under one roof here: restaurant, nightclub, and cigar lounge. Voodoo Grill has African-inspired décor and live, somewhat distracting, drummers moving about the room. Creative cuisine with roots in the Pacific Rim and Southeast Asia. The atmosphere is loud, intense, and casual; the clientele is young and trendy. Maurice Nightclub is an ultra-hip club with dazzling lights, funky décor, and a spacious dance floor; cover charge waived with proof of dining at Voodoo. At the Société Cigar, guests can sample over 200 types of cigars and 30 types of Scotch while listening to jazz, blues, and swing.
▪▪/▪▪

RESTAURANTS

- ▣ < CA$ 20
- ▣ CA$ 20–40
- ▣ > CA$ 40
- ▣ > CA$ 80

L'INOX
L'Inox Maîtres
Brasseurs
37, Quai St-André,
Vieux-Port de
Québec, G1K 8T3
Tel. (418) 692-2877
Fax (418) 692-5347
www.inox.qc.ca
Combination beer
museum and brew
pub, with a sunny
outdoor terrace and
a welcoming indoor
pub with an
exposed brick
backdrop to a
stainless steel bar
area and billiard
tables. Ten beers are
brewed on site, five
of which are
seasonal. For
example, Viking
beer is available in
February, is brewed
according to an
ancient Swedish
recipe, and would
have been a choice
brew in the days of
Hagar the Horrible.
Food is relatively
uninspired, which is
made up for by a
good selection of
Quebec cheeses.
Reserve ahead for a
$5 tour and taste-
test.

BEAUPRÉ

HOTEL-RESTAURANTS

★ AUBERGE
LA CAMARINE
10947, bd Sainte-
Anne,
Tel. (418) 827-1958
www.camarine.com
Built 120 years ago,
this former grand
home has lost some
of its character since
becoming a 31-room
inn in 1985. Rooms
are simple, some
have balconies, and
luxury suites may
have a fireplace,
whirlpool bath, or
stationary bike.
Auberge La
Camarine is actually
better known for its
restaurant, which is
considered one of
the best in the
province. Inspired by
French, Italian, and

Asian cuisine, chefs
are creative and
enjoy whimsical,
often vertical, food
presentation. An
award-winning wine
list accompanies
your meal. The table
d'hote changes
frequently and runs
$45–60. Smoke-free,
open for dinner
only, with breakfast
and lunch available
to hotel guests.
▣

CHÂTEAU
MONT SAINTE-ANNE
500, bd Beau-Pré,
G0A 1E0
Tel. (418) 827-5211
or 1 800 463-4467
Fax (418) 827-3421
www.chateaumont
sainteanne.com
Opened at the base
of Mont Ste-Anne in
1979, this sprawling
ski resort has grown
to 240 rooms and
185 suites, condos
and cottages on an
adjacent plateau.
Living quarters are
comfortable and
modern. All rooms
have a/c, balcony,
fridge, and coffee
machine; 42 rooms
have fireplaces.
The focus is on
drawing guests
out of their rooms
to enjoy what the
resort has to offer:
three in-house
dining areas, two
chalets at the
summit (serviced
by cable cars),
downhill skiing
(sometimes until
mid-May), cross-
country skiing,
ice skating,
snowmobiling,
and dog sledding.
Summer rates are
up to 45% reduced,
and activities
include golfing,
horseback riding,
cycling, and even
a circus school day
camp for children
run by the École de
Cirque de Québec.
▣

SAGUENAY-LAC-
SAINT-JEAN

LA BAIE

HOTEL

★ AUBERGE DES 21
621, rue Mars,
G7B 4N1
Tel. (418) 697-2121
or 1 800 363-7298
Fax (418) 544-3360
www.aubergedes21.
com
Large family inn
across from the
Saguenay Fjord and
Marine Park, named
for the 21 settlers
who founded La
Baie in 1838.
Spacious rooms with
views of nearby
cliffs or hotel
gardens; one room
has a fireplace. The
chef-owner runs the
restaurant, which
gives preference to
local produce and
incorporates wild
edible plants such as
bulrushes, pimbina,
chicoutees, wild
violets and
mayflowers in
cuisine inspired by
local and
Amerindian recipes.
No less than 620
miles (1000 km) of
snowmobile trails
nearby.
Comprehensive spa
offers California or
Swedish massage,
and an intriguing
Canyon Love Stone
Therapy treatment.
▣

MÉTABETCHOUAN
(▲ 319)

HOTEL

AUBERGE LAMY
56, rue Saint-André,
CP 396,
G0W 2A0
Tel. (418) 349-3686
or 1 888 565-3686
www.bbcanada.com/la
maisonlamy
Charming Victorian
doctor's mansion
built in 1926, now
converted to a
romantic six-room
inn. Rooms are

tastefully decorated
with antiques;
bedding is in
cheerful florals.
Each room has a
sink, three rooms
have antique
bathtubs, and some
rooms share a
washroom. Walking
distance to a
beautiful beach
on Lac St-Jean.
Breakfast included.
▣

SACRÉ-CŒUR

HOTEL

HOTELLERIE
BARDSVILLE
Route 172,
G0T 1Y0
Summer
tel. (418) 236-1222.
Otherwise
tel. (418) 236-4604
www.arsm.qc.ca
A scattering of very
rustic cabins along
the Ste-Marguerite
River, run by the
Ste-Marguerite River
Association (ARSM).
Attractive to the
adventurous
traveler who wants
a true escape, or the
curious traveler who
wants to take a shot
at salmon or trout
fishing. Novices
should pre-book a
four-hour $50
salmon fishing
lesson and enquire
about fishing
seasons and licenses.
Get specifics on your
booking, as some
are quaint log
cabins, others are
actually glorified
tents, and some are
only accessible by
ATV (all terrain
vehicle).

◆ REGIONAL TOURIST ASSOCIATIONS

Telephone numbers starting with 1-8 are freephone numbers

GENERAL

TOURISME QUÉBEC
CP 979, Montreal, H3C 2W3
Tel. (514) 873-2015 or 1-877 266-5687

www.tourisme.gouv. qc.ca

REGIONAL TOURIST ASSOCIATIONS (ATR)

ATR OF THE ABITIBI-TÉMISCAMINGUE

170, av. Principale (office 103)
Rouyn-Nouranda, J9X 4P7
Tel. (819) 762-8181 or 1-800-808-0706
www.48nord.qc.ca

Open Mon–Fri 8.30am–noon and 1–4.30pm.

ATR JAMES BAY

166, bd Springer, CP 1270,
Chapais, G0W 1H0
Tel. (418) 745-3969 or 1-888 745-3969
Fax (418) 745-3970

Open Mon–Fri 8.30am–noon and 1–4.30pm.

ATR LOWER SAINT LAWRENCE

148, rue Fraser
Rivière-du-Loup, G5R 1C8
Tel. (418) 867-1272 or 1-800-563-5268
www.tourismebas-st-laurent.com/

Open Mon–Thu 8.30am–4.30pm, Fri 8.30am–4pm in season;
Mon–Thu 8.30am–5pm, Fri 8.30am–4.30pm out of season.

ATR CENTRE-DU-QUEBEC

20, bd Carignan O
Princeville, G6L 4M4
Tel. (819) 364-7177 or 1-888 816-4007
www.tourismecentreduquebec.com

Open Mon–Fri 8.30am–noon and 1–4.30pm.

ATR CHARLEVOIX

495, bd de Comporté
La Malbaie, G5A 3G3
Tel. (418) 665-4454 or 1-800-667-2276
www.tourisme-charlevoix.com

Open Mon–Fri 9.30am–9pm, Sat-Sun 9am–9pm in season;
Mon–Fri 8.30am–4.30pm, Sat–Sun 9am–5pm out of season.

ATR CHAUDIÈRE-APPALACHES

800, autoroute J.-Lesage
Saint-Nicolas, G7A 1E3
Tel. (418) 831-4411 or 1-888 831-4411
www.chaudapp.qc.ca.

Open daily 8am–7pm in season;
daily 8.30am–4.30pm out of season.

ATR DUPLESSIS

312, av. Brochu
Sept-Îles, G4R 2W6
Tel. (418) 962-0808 or 1-888 463-0808
www.tourismecote-nord.com

Open Mon–Fri 8.30am–noon and 1–5pm.

ATR OF THE GASPÉSIE

357, route de la Mer
Sainte-Flavie, G0J 2L0
Tel. (418) 775-2223 or 1-800 463-0323
www.tourisme.gaspesie.qc.ca.

Open daily 8.30am–4.30pm.

ATR ÎLES-DE-LA-MADELEINE

128, rue Principale, CP 1028
Cap-aux-Meules, G0B 1B0
Tel. (418) 986-2245 or 1-877 624-4437
www.ilesdelamadeleine.com

Open daily 7am–8pm in summer; Mon–Fri 9am–5pm in winter. In season, the locals open up their home to visitors. To rent a room, a chalet or a house, consult the ATR from March to September.

ATR OF LANAUDIÈRE

3643, Queen Rawdon, J0K 1S0
Tel. (450) 834-2535 or 1-800 363-2788
www.tourisme-lanaudiere.qc.ca/'

Open Mon–Fri 8.30am–noon and 1–4.30pm;
Sat–Sun 9am–4pm.

ATR OF THE LAURENTIDES

14142, rue de la Chapelle
Mirabel, J7J2C8
Tel. (450) 436-8532 or 1-800 561-6673
Fax (450) 436-5309

Open Mon–Thu 9am–5pm.

ATR LAVAL

2900, bd Saint-Martin O
Laval, H7T 2J2
Tel. (450) 682-5522 or 1-877 465-2825
Fax (450) 682-7304
www.tourismelaval.com

Open Mon–Fri 9am–5pm.

ATR OF MANICOUAGAN

337, bd La Salle
(office 304)
Baie-Comeau, G9N1H1
Tel. (418) 294-2876 or 1-888 463-5319
Fax (418) 294-2345
www.tourismecote-nord.com

Open daily 9am–5pm.

ATR OF MAURICIE

777, 4e Rue
Shawinigan, G9N1H1
Tel. (819) 536-3334 or 1-800 567-7603
Fax (819) 536-3373
www.icimauricie.com

Open daily 9am–5pm.

ATR OF THE MONTÉRÉGIE

11, chemin Marieville
Rougemont (Quebec), J0L 1M0
Tel. (450) 469-0069 or 1-866 469-0069
Fax (450) 469-1139
www.tourisme-monteregie.qc.ca

Open daily 9am–5pm in summer (10am–5pm in winter).

ATR MONTREAL

Infotouriste
1555, rue Peel (office 600)
Montreal, H3A 3L8
Tel. (514) 844-5400 or 1-877 266-5687
Fax (514) 844-5757
www.tourisme-montreal.org

Open Mon–Fri 8.30am–7.30pm in season; Mon–Fri 9am–6pm out of season.

ATR NUNAVIK

CP 779, Kuujjuaq,
J0M 1C0
Tel. (819) 964-2876 or 1-888 594-3424
Fax (819) 964-2002
www.nunavik-tourism.com

Open Mon–Fri 9am–5pm (may vary).

ATR OF THE OUTAOUAIS

103, rue Laurier
Hull, J8X 3V8
Tel. (819) 778-2222 or 1-800 265-7822
Fax (819) 778-7758

Open mid-June–Aug: Mon–Fri 8.30am–8pm, Sat–Sun 9am–5pm; Mon–Fri 8.30am–5pm, Sat–Sun 9am–4pm out of season.

ATR SAGUENAY-LAC-SAINT-JEAN

455, rue Racine (office 101),
Chicoutimi (Quebec), G7H 1T5
Tel. (418) 543-3536 or 1-800 463-9651
Fax (418) 543-1805
www.tourismesaguenay
lacsaintjean.qc.ca

Open daily 8am–5pm.

TOURIST OFFICE OF THE URBAN COMMUNITY OF QUEBEC

399, rue Saint-Joseph
2nd floor,
Quebec, G1K 8E2
Tel. (418) 641-6654 or 1-800 641-6407
www.quebecregion.com

Open June–Aug: daily 8.30am–8pm; Sep–mid-Oct: daily 8.30am–5.30pm; mid-Oct–April: daily Mon–Fri 9am–5pm.

TOURISM FOR THE EASTERN PROVINCES (ESTRIE)

20, rue Don-Bosco S,
Sherbrooke, J1L 1W4
Tel. (819) 820-2020
or 1-800-355-5755
www.cantonsdelest.com

Open daily 10am–6pm in season; daily 9am–5pm out of season.

◆ PLACES TO VISIT

Cities and towns are listed alphabetically, followed by the name of the tourist region to which they belong and the telephone number of the tourist office when there is one. The letter and number (for example E7) refer to the front endpaper map. The symbol ▲ refers to the Itinerary section.

PLACES TO VISIT

ALMA	SAGUENAY-LAC-SAINT-JEAN TEL. (418) 669-5030/5043	▲321
MUSEUM OF LAKE SAINT-JEAN 54, rue St-Joseph S Tel. (418) 668-2606 www.sagamie.org	*History of the area.* *Open daily 9am–6.30pm.*	E7

AMOS	ABITIBI-TÉMISCAMINGUE TEL. (819) 6727-1242	B7
REFUGE PAGEAU 4241, ch. Croteau Amos (Quebec), J9T 3A1 Tel. (819) 732-8999 Fax (819) 732-9989 www.refugepageau.ca	*Open end June–Aug: Tue–Fri 1–5pm, Sat–Sun and public hols 1–9pm; Sep: Sat–Sun 1–4.30pm. Groups by appointment.*	

ANGLIERS	ABITIBI-TÉMISCAMINGUE	▲231
TUGBOAT T.-E. DRAPER CP 82 Angliers (Quebec), J0Z 1A0 Tel. (819) 949-4431	*Open summer season June 24–Labor Day: daily 10am–5pm;* *spring and fall: groups by appointment.*	A8

ANSE-AU-GRIFFON	GASPÉSIE	▲301
MANOIR LEBOUTILLIER Route 132 Tel. (418) 892-5150	*Open mid-June–mid-Oct: 9am–5pm.*	IJ6

AYLMER	OUTAOUAIS TEL. (819) 685-1823	▲229
THE SYMNES HOTEL 1, rue Front Tel. (819) 685-5033	*Old inn built in 1831, once the haunt of trappers and fur traders.*	C10

BAIE-COMEAU	MANICOUAGAN TEL. (418) 589-5319	▲330
HYDRO-QUEBEC MANIC 2 135, bd Comeau Tel. (418) 294-3923	*Dam and hydroelectric power station.* *Open mid-June–Aug: daily 9–11am and 1–3.30pm. Information and bookings: 1-866 526-2642*	H6

BAIE-SAINT-PAUL	CHARLEVOIX TEL. (418) 6435-4160	
EXHIBITION CENTER Tel. (418) 435-3681	*Open July–Aug: daily 9am–7pm; 9am–5pm out of season. Museum-gallery for Charlevoix artists.*	▲280
DOMAINE CHARLEVOIX Route 362 Tel.(418) 435-2626	*Park open daily 9am–11pm. Belvedere, well-maintained footpaths, cross-country skiing in winter. Bicycle rental service.*	
GRANDS-JARDINS PARK Tel. (418) 846-2057 or (418) 435-3101	*At 42km on freeway 381. An oasis of vegetation from the Grand Nord in Charlevoix.*	▲286
POURVOIRIE OF LAKE MOREAU Tel. (418) 665-4400 Fax (418) 665-4400 www.lacmoreau.com	*Via freeway 381, then a 6-mile (10km) forest road. Hunting and fishing stopovers.*	

BAIE-SAINTE-CATHERINE	CHARLEVOIX	G7
DUFOUR CROISIÈRES Route 138 Tel. 1-800 463-5250 www.croisiresbaleines.com	*To observe whales or explore the Saguenay Fjord (by motor boat or schooner).*	

BATISCAN	MAURICIE	E9
OLD PRESBYTERY 346, rue Principale Tel. (418) 362-2051	*Open end May–mid-Oct: Tue–Sun 10am–5pm.*	▲249

BEAUMONT	CHAUDIÉRE-APPALACHES	F9
MILL OF THE MAILLOU FALLS 2, route du Fleuve RR1, G01 1C0 Tel. (418) 833-1867	*Open end June–Aug: Tue–Sun 10am–4.30pm; May 15–June 24 and Sep–Oct: Sat–Sun only 10am–4.30pm.*	▲288

BEAUPORT	QUEBEC REGION	F9 ▲276
MONTMORENCY FALLS 2492, av. Royale Tel. (418) 663-3330 www.chutemontmorency.qc.ca	*Waterfall plunging 270 ft (83m), with walkways, cable cars, belvederes and museum.*	

BEAUPRÉ	QUEBEC REGION	F8 ▲280
GRAND CANYON OF STE-ANNE FALLS CP 104, 206, route 138 E Beaupré (Quebec) Canada G0A 1E0 Tel. (418) 827-4057 Fax (418) 827-2492	*Open May–June 23 and Sep–Oct: daily 9am–5pm; June 24–early Sep: daily 8.30am–5pm.* *Waterfall plunging 200 ft (60m), signposted circuit, restaurant. Visits without charge.*	

BERGERONNES	MANICOUAGAN	G7
ARCHÉO-TOPO 498, rue de la Mer Tel. (418) 232-6286	*Prehistory museum.*	▲329
THE CAP-DE-BON-DÉSIR INTERPRETATION CENTER 13, chemin du Cap-de-Bon-Désir Tel. (418) 232-6751 or 1-800 463-6769	*Open mid-June–mid-Sep: daily 9am–8pm. Observation of sea mammals and museum.*	▲329

BERTHIERVILLE	LANAUDIÈRE	TEL. (450) 836-7336	D9 ▲221
GILLES-VILLENEUVE MUSEUM 960, av. G.-Villeneuve Tel. (450) 836-2714 or 1-800 639-0103 www.villeneuve.com	*Open daily 9am–5pm.*		

BONAVENTURE	GASPÉSIE	I7 ▲308
ACADIAN MUSEUM OF QUEBEC 95, av. Port-Royal Tel. (418) 534-4000 www.ville.bonaventure.qc.ca	*Open end June–mid-Oct: daily 9am-8pm; mid-Oct– June 23: Mon–Fri 9am–noon and 1–5pm, Sat–Sun 1–5pm.*	

BROMONT	ESTRIE	TEL. (450) 534-2006	E10 ▲213
BROMONT TOURIST CENTER 150, rue Champlain Tel. (450) 534-2200 or 1-866 276-6668 www.skibromont.com	*Skiing in winter and mountain biking in summer.*		

CAP-AUX-MEULES	ÎLES-DE-LA-MADELEINE	TEL. (418) 986-2245	
CTMA TRAVERSIER 313, chemin du Quai CP 245 Tel. (418) 986-3278 or 1-888 986-3278 www.ilesdelamadeine.com	*Sea link with Souris (Prince Edward Island).*		▲313
SEA EXCURSIONS 236, chemin Pointe-basse, Marina Tel. (418) 986-4745 www.excursionsenmer.com	*Daily departures for the observation of grottos and cliffs, demonstration of lobster fishing.*		

CAP-DES-ROSIERS	GASPÉSIE	J7 ▲302
CAP-DES-ROSIERS LIGHTHOUSE 1127, bd de Cap-des-Rosiers Tel. (418) 892-5577	*Lighthouse open June–Sep: daily 9am–7pm.*	

CARILLON	LAURENTIDES	D10 ▲223
ARGENTEUIL REGIONAL MUSEUM 44, route du Long-Sault Tel. (450) 537-3861 www.parccanada.gc.ca/caserne carillon	*Regional museum open March–mid-Dec: Tue–Sun noon–6pm.*	

◆ PLACES TO VISIT

CHAMBLY	MONTÉRÉGIE	D10 ▲208
FORT CHAMBLY NATIONAL HISTORIC SITE 2, rue Richelieu Tel. (450) 658-1585 or 1-800 463-6769 www.parcscanada.gc.ca/fort chambly	*Open mid-May–Aug: daily10am–5pm; April–mid-May and Sep–Oct: Wed–Sun 10am–5pm; by appointment for groups Nov and March. Closed Dec–Feb.*	

CHARLESBOURG	QUEBEC REGION	TEL. (418) 641-6654	F9
NATIONAL PARK OF THE RIVER JACQUES-CARTIER Route 175 (km 74) Tel. (418) 848-3169 or 1-800 665-6527 www.sepaq.com/jacquescartier	*Open Mon–Fri 8.30am-4.30pm. Nature watching, canoeing camping, hiking.*	

CHÂTEAU-RICHER	QUEBEC REGION	F8-9 ▲280
CÔTE-DE-BEAUPRÉ INTERPRETATION CENTER 7976, av. Royale, CP 40 Tel. (418) 824-3677 www.culture-quebec.qc.ca/cicb	*Open June–mid-Oct: daily 10am–5pm. Groups by appointment. Geomorphology, history, heritage and economic development of the Côte-de-Beaupré.*	

CHICOUTIMI	SAGUENAY-LAC-SAINT-JEAN	TEL. (418) 698-3167	F7 ▲322
OLD PULP MILL OF CHICOUTIMI AND HOME OF ARTHUR VILLENEUVE 300, rue Dubuc Tel. (418) 698-3100 or 1-877 998-3100 www.pulperie.com	*House-museum of the painter Arthur Villeneuve. Open June–mid-Oct: daily 10am–4pm.*	

COTEAU-DU-LAC	MONTÉRÉGIE	D10 ▲209
NATIONAL HISTORIC SITE 308 a, chemin du Fleuve Tel. (450) 763-5631 www.parcscanada.gc.ca	*Open mid-May–Aug: Wed–Sun 10am–5pm; Sep–mid-Oct: Sat–Sun 10am–5pm.*	

DESBIENS	SAGUENAY-LAC-SAINT-JEAN	E7 ▲319
MUSEUM OF THE HISTORY AND ARCHEOLOGY OF MÉTABETCHOUANE 243, rue Hébert Tel. (418) 346-5341 www.chamans.can	*Open daily 10am–5pm.*	

DESCHAMBAULT	QUEBEC REGION	TEL. (418) 641-6654	E9 ▲250
OLD PRESBYTERY 117, rue Saint-Joseph Tel. (418) 286-6891 www.multimania.com/ deschambaultpat	*Open daily 10am–5pm.*	

DRUMMONDVILLE	MAURICIE	TEL. (819) 477-5529	E9-10 ▲245
VILLAGE QUÉBÉCOIS D'ANTAN 1425, rue Montplaisir Drummondville, J2B 7T5 Tel. (819) 478-1441 or 1-877 710-0267 www.villagequebecois.qc.ca	*Open June–Sep: daily 10am–5.30pm Reconstruction of a 19th-century Quebecois village with a farm and craftwork center.*	

ÉTANG-DES-CAPS	ÎLES-DE-LA-MADELEINE	
LA CHEVAUCHÉE DES ÎLES 42, chemin des Arpenteurs Tel. (418) 937-5453	*Open May-Oct: daily 9am–dusk Horse riding in the wood or on the beach.*	

GASPÉ	GASPÉSIE	TEL. (418) 368-6335	J7
BAY OF GASPÉ CRUISE Forillon Park Tel. (418) 892-5500 or 1-866 617-5500 www.baleines-forillon.com	*Open mid-June–mid-Sep: daily cruise for observing whales and seals (one to three departures a day).*	

GASPÉSIE MUSEUM 80, bd Gaspé Tel. (418) 368-1534	Open Tue–Fri 9am–noon and 1–5pm, Sat–Sun 1–5pm.	▲303
FORILLON PARK 122, bd Gaspé Tel. (418) 368-5505 www.parcscanada.gc.ca	Hiking. Visit to an old cod-processing company. Sea excursion. Camping. Diving.	▲304

GODBOUT	MANICOUAGAN	H6
AMERINDIEN AND INUIT MUSEUM 134, rue P.-Comeau Tel. (418) 568-7306 www.vitrine.net/gobout	Open June–mid-Sep: daily 9am–10pm.	

GRANBY	ESTRIE TEL. (450) 372-7273	E10
LAKE BOIVIN INTERPRETATION CENTER 700, rue Drummond Tel. (450) 375-3861	Open daily 8.30am–7pm in summer and 8.30am–4.30pm out of season. Footpaths plus information on nature (especially birds). Exhibitions.	
YAMASKA RECREATIONAL PARK 950, 8e rang O Tel. (450) 372-3204 Tel. (450) 776-7182 (swimming) Tel. (450) 777-5557 (ski)	Open May–Oct: daily 8am–sunset. Swimming, watersports, fishing.	
GRANBY ZOO 525, Saint-Hubert Autorue 10, sortie 68. Tel. 1-877 472-6299	Open May–Aug: daily 10am–6pm; May, Sep–Oct: Sat–Sun 10am–6pm.	▲210

GRAND-MÉTIS	GASPÉSIE	H7 ▲296
MÉTIS GARDENS Route 132 Tel. (418) 775-2221 www.jardinsmetis.com	Open June–mid-Oct: daily from 8.30am. Museum, restaurant, picnic areas, English gardens.	

GRANDE-ENTRÉE	ÎLES-DE-LA-MADELEINE	▲316
SEAL INTERPRETATION CENTER Route 199 Tel. (418) 985-2833	Open daily 10am–6pm.	

GRANDES-PILES	MAURICIE	E9 ▲241
BÛCHERON LUMBERJACK VILLAGE 780, 5e Av. Tel. (819) 538-7895 or 1-877 338-7895	Open mid-May–mid-Oct: daily 10am–5pm.	

GROSSE ÎLE	ÎLES-DE-LA-MADELEINE	
POINTE DE L'EST NATIONAL WILDLIFE RESERVE 377, route 199, CP 59 Tel. (418) 985-2833 www.bonjourquebec.com	Observation of the fauna. The beach is over 6 miles (10km) long.	▲316

HAVRE-AUBERT	ÎLES-DE-LA-MADELEINE	
AQUARIUM OF THE ISLANDS 982, chemin de la Grave Tel. (418) 937-2277	Open June 15 –Sep 15: Mon–Fri 10am–6pm, Sat–Sun 11am–5pm Impressive range of aquatic species.	▲314
L'ISTORLET NAUTICAL CENTER CP 249 Tel. (418) 937-5266 or 1-888 937-8166 www.istorlet.qc.ca	Open Mon-Sat 9am–5pm. Sailing, windsurfing, surfing, kayaks, diving. Classes, rental of equipment. Excursions.	
MUSEUM OF THE SEA 1023, route 199, CP 69 Tel. (418) 937-5711 www.ilesdelamadeleine.com/ musee	Open June 24–Aug: Mon–Fri 9am–6pm, Sat–Sun 10am–6pm; Sep–June 23: Mon–Fri 9am–noon and 1–5pm, Sat–Sun 1–5pm.	▲314

HAVRE-SUR-MER	ÎLES-DE-LA-MADELEINE	
LES EXCURSIONS DE LA LAGUNE CP 173, Havre-aux-Maisons Tel. (418) 969-4550	*Daily departures 11am, 2pm and 6pm, June–Sep,* *in a glass-bottomed boat.* *Tastings of shellfish and other seafood.*	
HULL	**OUTAOUAIS** **TEL. (819) 778-2222**	**C10**
CENTRALE DES RAPIDES-FARMERS Route 307 Gatineau Tel. 1-800 365-5229	*Mid-May–end June: visits 9am, 10.30am, noon,* *1.30pm, 3pm; end June–Aug: 9.30am, 11am,* *12.30pm, 2pm, 3.30pm.*	
CANADIAN MUSEUM OF CIVILISATIONS 100, rue Laurier Tel. (819) 776-7000 www.civilisations.ca	*Open all year; hours vary.*	▲229
THÉÂTRE DE L'ÎLE 1, rue Wellington Tel. (819) 595-7455	*Typical 19th-century architecture.*	
ÎLE AUX COUDRES	**CHARLEVOIX**	**F8**
MILLS OF THE ÎLE AUX COUDRES 247, chemin du Moulin, Saint-Louis Tel. (418) 438-2184	*Open end May–June 24: daily 10am–5pm;* *June 25–end Aug: daily 9am–7pm;* *Sep–mid-Oct: daily 10am–5pm.*	▲281
MUSÉE LES VOITURES D'EAU 203, chemin des Coudriers Saint-Louis Tel. (418) 438-2208 1-800 463-2118	*Sea transport. Open mid-June–mid-Sep: daily* *9am–6pm; June 1–15 and Sep–mid-Oct: Sat–Sun* *only 9.30am –5.30pm.*	▲281
TRAVERSIER SAINT-BERNARD 3, rue du Port Tel. (418) 438-2743	*Daily crossing to St-Joseph-de-la-Rive 7am–11pm;* *8 to 24 daily departures according to season.* *Free.*	
JOLIETTE	**LANAUDIÈRE** **TEL. (450) 759-5013**	**D9**
JOLIETTE ART GALLERY 145, rue Wilfrid-Corbeil Tel. (450) 756-0311 www.bw.qc.ca/musée.joliette	*Open July–Aug: Thu–Fri 11am–7.30pm;* *Wed–Sun noon–5pm out of season.*	▲220
JONQUIÈRE	**SAGUENAY-LAC-SAINT-JEAN** **TEL. (418) 548-4004**	**F7**
CENTRALE DE SHIPSHAW 1471, route du Pont Tel. (418) 699-4111	*Hydroelectric power station.* *Visits June–Aug; Mon–Fri 1.30–4pm .* *Booking advised tel. 1-800-561-9196.*	▲322
KAMOURASKA	**LOWER SAINT LAWRENCE**	**G8**
KAMOURASKA MUSEUM 69, av. Morel Tel. (418) 492-9783	*Open June–end Aug: daily 9am–5.20pm;* *Nov–May; Mon–Fri 9am–5pm and Sat–Sun by* *appointment.*	▲291
KNOWLTON	**ESTRIE**	**E10**
BROME COUNTY HISTORICAL MUSEUM 130, Lakeside Tel. (450) 243-6782	*Open mid-May–mid-Sep: Mon–Sat 10am–4.30pm* *and Sun 11am–4.30pm*	▲211
L'ACADIE	**MONTÉRÉGIE**	**D10**
ONCE UPON A TIME THERE WAS A SMALL COLONY 2500, route 219 Tel. (450) 347-9756	*Interactive museum. Visits 11am, 1.30pm, 3.30pm.* *Store open 10am–5pm.*	▲209
L'ASSOMPTION	**LANAUDIÈRE**	**D9**
THE OLD PALACE OF JUSTICE 255, rue Saint-Étienne Tel. (450) 589-3266 or 1-866 559-3266	*Open July–Aug: daily 9am–5pm.* *The tribunal's main hall has remained unchanged* *since 1925.*	▲221
L'ISLET-SUR-MER	**LOWER SAINT LAWRENCE**	**F8**
BERNIER MARITIME MUSEUM 55, chemin Pionniers E Tel. (418) 247-5001	*Open June–Sep: daily 10am–4pm;* *Oct–May: Tue-Fri 10am–4pm.*	▲289

LA MALBAIE	CHARLEVOIX	TEL. (418) 665-4454	**F8** ▲286
HAUTES GORGES PARK Tel. (418) 439-1227	Via St-Aimé-des-Lacs and a 21-mile (34km) forest road. The highest rock faces in eastern Canada.		
LA MARTRE	GASPÉSIE		**I6** ▲301
LIGHTHOUSE INTERPRETATION CENTER 10, av. du Phare Tel. (418) 288-5698	Open June–first Mon in Sep: daily 9am–5pm.		
LA POCATIÈRE	LOWER SAINT LAWRENCE		**FG8** ▲290
FRANÇOIS-PILOTE MUSEUM 100, 4ᵉ Av. Tel. (418) 856-3145	Open June–Aug: Mon-Sat 9am–5.30pm, Sun 10.30am–5.30pm; Aug–mid-Oct: by appointment. www.kam.qc.ca		
LA TUQUE	MAURICIE		**E8** ▲241
PARC DES CHUTES DE LA PETITE-RIVIÈRE-BOSTONNAIS 3701, bd Ducharme Tel. (819) 523-6111 www.mrchsm.org	Nature research center. Hiking paths, picnic zones, 115-ft (35m) high waterfalls.		
LAVAL	MONTÉRÉGIE	TEL. (514) 682-5522	**D10**
COSMODÔME 2150, autoroute des Laurentides Tel. (450) 978-3600 or 1-800 565-5567	Open 10am–6pm. Closed Mon in Sep-June. Introduction to aerospace science. Courses.		
LE BIC	LOWER SAINT LAWRENCE		**G7** ▲293
PARC DU BIC 3382, route 132 O Tel. (418) 736-5035 or 1-800 665-6527 www.sepaq.com/bic	Nature research center. Walking, cycling sea excursions, camping.		
LES ÉBOULEMENTS	CHARLEVOIX		**F8** ▲284
SALES-LATERRIÈRE MANOR 159, rang Saint-Joseph Tel. (418) 635-2666 www.camplemanoir.qc.ca	Open by appointment.		
LÉVIS	CHAUDIÈRE-APPALACHES	TEL. (418) 838-6026	**F8**
MARTINIÈRE FORT 9805, bd de la Rive S Tel. (418) 833-6620 www.membres.lycos.fr/ pierre13/index/html	Open 9am–4pm. Guided tours noon–4pm.		▲274
FORTS-DE-LÉVIS NATIONAL HISTORIC SITE 41, chemin Gouvernement Tel. (418) 835-5182 or 1-800 463-6769 www.parcscanada.gc.ca/levy	Open mid-May–Aug: daily 10am–5pm; Sep: Sat–Sun 1–4pm; April–mid-May by appointment.		▲274
MAISON DESJARDINS 6, rue Mont-Marie Tel. (418) 835-2090 or 1-866 835-8444	Open Mon–Fri 10am–noon and 1–4.30pm, Sat–Sun noon–5pm.		▲274
LOUISEVILLE	MAURICIE		**E9** ▲248
LAKE SAINT-PIERRE 75, lac Saint-Pierre E Tel. (819) 228-8819 Fax (819) 228-8819 www.geocities.com/ doMaynelacsaintpierre	Eco-tourism excursions, boat trips. In winter, excursions in sleds.		
MALARTIC	ABITIBI-TÉMISCAMINGUE	TEL. (819) 762-8181	**B7** ▲230
MUSEUM OF MINES 650, rue de la Paix Tel. (819) 757-4677	Open mid-June–mid-Sep: daily 9am–5pm; mid-Sep–May: Mon–Fri 9am–noon and 1–5pm, Sat–Sun by appointment.		

MANAWAN	LANAUDIÈRE	D8
POURVOIRIE OF LAKE KEMPT 596, chemin N.-Dame-des-Mères Tel. (819) 846-2663	*Fifty miles (80km) from the Atikamek community.* *Fishing, bear and moose hunting. Five chalets.*	▲220

MASHTEUIATSH	SAGUENAY-LAC-SAINT-JEAN	E7
AMERINDIAN MUSEUM 1787, rue Amishk Tel. (418) 275-4842 or 1-888 875-4842 www.autochtones.com/ musee_amerindien	*Open June–Sep: daily 9am–6pm;* *Oct–May: Mon–Fri 8am–noon and 1–4pm.*	▲320

MATANE	GASPÉSIE · TEL. (418) 562-1250	H7
ATLANTIC SALMON **OBSERVATION CENTER** 260, av. Saint-Jérôme Tel. (418) 562-7006	*Salmon fishing by appointment.*	▲300
SOCIÉTÉ DES TRAVERSIERS **DU QUEBEC** 1410, rue Matane-sur-Mer Tel. (418) 562-2500 or 1-877 562-6560	*Sea links with Baie-Comeau and Godbout.*	

MELOCHEVILLE	MONTÉRÉGIE	D10
BEAUHARNOIS **HYDROELECTRIC CENTER** 80, bd E.-Hébert Tel. 1-800 365-5229 www.hydroquebec.com/visitez	*Open mid-May–beg Sep: daily 9.30am–4.30pm;* *gudied tours 9.30am, 11.15am, 1pm and 2.45pm.*	▲209
ARCHEOLOGICAL PARK OF **POINTE-DU-BUISSON** 333, rue Emond Tel. (450) 429-7857	*Open mid-May–end Aug: Mon–Fri 10am–5pm,* *Sat–Sun 10am–6pm; Sep–Oct: Sat–Sun only* *10am–6pm (or by appointment).*	▲209

MONTEBELLO	OUTAOUAIS · TEL. (819) 778-2530	C10
LOUIS-JOSEPH PAPINEAU MANOR **NATIONAL HISTORIC SITE OF CANADA** 500, rue N.-Dame Tel. (819) 423-6965 or 1-800 463-6769 www.parcscanada.gc.ca/papineau	*Open July–Aug: daily 10am–5pm;* *mid-May–June and Sep–mid-Oct; Wed–Sun 10am–* *5pm.*	▲224
OMEGA PARK Route 323 N Tel. (819) 423-5487 www.parc-omega.can	*Open daily 9.30am–6pm in season;* *daily 10am–5pm out of season.*	

MONTMAGNY	CHAUDIÈRE-APPALACHES · TEL. (418) 248-9196	F8-9
MIGRATIONS CENTER 53, rue du Bassin N Tel. (418) 248-4565 www.centredesmigrations.com	*Open daily 10am–5pm in season;* *Thu–Sun 10am–5pm out of season.*	▲288
MANOIR DE L'ACCORDÉON 301, bd Taché E Tel. (418) 248-7927	*Open mid-June–Sep: Mon–Fri 9am–5pm, Sat–Sun* *10am–4pm; Sep–mid-Oct: Mon–Fri 9am–5pm;* *mid-Oct–mid-June: by appointment.*	▲289

MONTREAL		D10
CENTRE INFOTOURISTE 1001, rue Square-Dorchester H3B IG2 Tel. (514) 873-2015 or 1-877 266-5687 Fax (514) 864-3838 www.tourisme-montreal.org	*Open June–Aug: daily 8.30am–7pm;* *Sep–May: daily 9am–6pm.*	
NOTRE DAME BASILICA 110, rue Notre-Dame O (Place-d'Armes subway station) Tel. (514) 842-2925 www.basiliquenddm.org	*Open daily 7am–5pm.* *Visits start at 8am.*	▲168

BIODÔME 4777, av. Pierre-de-Coubertin (Viau subway station) Tel. (514) 868-3000 www.biodome.qc.ca	*Open July–Aug: daily 9am–6pm;* *Sep–June: Tue-Sun 9am–5pm.*	▲197
MARIE-REINE-DU-MONDE CATHEDRAL 1085, rue de la Cathédrale corner Mansfield (Bonaventure subway station) Tel. (514) 866-1661 www.cathedralecatholiquede montreal.org	*Open Mon–Fri 7am–5.30pm,* *Sat 8am–8pm, Sun 9.30am–5.30pm.*	▲175
CANADIAN CENTER FOR ARCHITECTURE 1920, rue Baile (Alwater or Guy-Concordia subway stations) Tel. (514) 939-7026 www.cca.qc.ca	*Open Wed–Sun 10am–5pm, Thu 10am–9pm.*	● 129
HISTORY CENTER 335, place d'Youville (Square-Victoria subway station) Tel. (514) 872-3207 www.ville.montreal.qc.ca/chm	*Open May–Aug: Tue–Sun 10am–5pm;* *Sep–mid-Dec: Wed–Sun 10am–5pm;* *end Jan–Aprll: Wed–Sun 10am–5pm* *Possible guided walk of Montreal: ask Guidatour* *(Tel. 514) 844-4021.*	▲171
CHAPEL OF N.-D.-DE-BONSECOURS 400, Saint-Paul E (Champ-de-Mars subway station) Tel. (514) 282-8670	*Open May–Oct: Tue–Sun 10am–5.30pm;* *Nov–Jan, March–April: 11am–3.30pm.* *Closed February.*	▲172
CHÂTEAU DUFRESNE 2929, av. Dufresne (Peel subway station) Tel. (514) 259-9201 www.chateaudufresne.qc.ca	*Open Tue and Thu–Sun 11am–6pm,* *Wed 11am–9pm.*	▲196
CHÂTEAU RAMEZAY 280, rue Notre-Dame E (Champ-de-Mars subway station) Tel. (514) 861-3708 www.chateauramezay.qc.ca	*Open June–Sep: daily 10am–6pm;* *Oct–May: Tue-Sun 10am–4.30pm.*	▲171
BOTANIC GARDENS AND INSECTARIUM 4101, rue Sherbrooke E (Pie-IX subway station) Tel. (514) 872-1400 www.ville.montreal.qc.ca/jardin	*Open June 24–Aug: daily 9am–6pm; Sep–June 23:* *daily 9am–5pm.*	▲196
LACHINE CANAL NATIONAL **HISTORIC SITE OF CANADA** 500, chemin des Iroquois, Lachine Tel. (514) 283-6054 or 1-800 463-6769	*Open May–Sep: Mon 1–6pm, Tue–Sun 10am–noon* *and 1–6pm.*	▲201
FUR TRADE INTERPRETATION CENTER 1255, bd Saint-Joseph, Lachine Tel. (514) 637-7433 or 1-800 463-6769 www.parcscanada.gc.ca/fourrure	*Open April–mid-Oct: daily 10am–12.30pm and* *1–6pm; mid-Oct–Nov: Wed–Sun 1–5pm.*	▲201
MUSEUM OF ARCHEOLOGY **AND HISTORY** 350, place Royale Pointe à Caillère (Place-d'Armes subway station) Tel. (514) 872-9150 www.pacmusee.qc.ca	*Open June–Aug: Tue-Fri 10am–6pm, Sat–Sun* *11am–6pm; Sep–June: Tue-Fri 10am–5pm, Sat–Sun* *11am–5pm.*	▲173
CONTEMPORARY ART MUSEUM 185, rue Sainte-Catherine O (Place-d'Armes subway station) Tel. (514) 847-6226 www.macm.org	*Open Tue, Thu-Sun 11am–6pm and* *Wed 11am–9pm.*	▲181
LACHINE TOWN MUSEUM 110, chemin Lasalle Tel. (514) 634-3471 (poste 346)	*Open Mon–Thu 9am–4.30pm, Fri 9am–9pm.*	▲201

MUSÉE DES BEAUX-ARTS 1380, rue Sherbrooke (South Pavilion) 1379, Benaiah Gibb (North Pavilion) (Guy-Concordia subway station) Tel. (514) 285-2000 www.mbam.qc.ca	*Open Tue, Thu–Sun and public holiday* *Mon 11am–6pm, Wed 11am–9pm.*	▲184
MCCORD MUSEUM OF **CANADIAN HISTORY** 690, rue Sherbrooke O (McGill subway station) Tel. (514) 398-7100 www.musée-mccord.qc.ca	*Open Tue–Fri 10am–6pm, Sat–Sun 10am–5pm.*	▲180
OFFICE NATIONAL **DU FILM DU CANADA** 1564, rue Saint-Denis (Berri-UQAM subway station) Tel. (514) 496-6887 or 1-800 267-7710 www.onf.ca	*Open Tue–Sun noon–9pm.* *Canada's national movie archive.* *Video-theater and 'cinérobothèque' where you* *can see more than 3,000 of the ONF's movies.*	
SAINT JOSEPH'S ORATORY 3800, chemin Queen-Mary métro Côtes-des-Neiges Tel. (514) 733-8211 www.saint-joseph.org	*Open daily 6.30am–9.30pm* *Christmas crib end Nov–early February.*	▲186
OLYMPIC PARK 4141, avenue Pierre- de-Coubertin Tel. (514) 252-8687 www.rio.gouv.qc.ca	*Open June–Aug: daily 10am–9pm;* *Sep–May: daily 9am–5pm.*	▲196

MONT-SAINT-HILAIRE	MONTÉRÉGIE	TEL. (450) 536-0395	D10

MONT-SAINT-HILAIRE NATURE **CONSERVATION CENTER** 422, chemin des Moulins Tel. (450) 467-1755 www.centrenature.qc.ca	*Open daily 8am–sunset.* *Nature watching and open-air activities (hiking,* *cross-country skiing, etc.).*	▲208

MONT-TREMBLANT	LAURENTIDES	TEL. (819) 425-2434	C9

CROISIÈRES MONT-TREMBLANT 2001, rue Principale Tel. (819) 425-1045 or (819) 425-8681	*History and legends of Lake Tremblant.* *Daily excursions 1pm, 2.30pm and 4pm,* *June–early Oct.*	
MONT-TREMBLANT PARK Tel. (819) 688-2281 or 1-800 665-6527 www.sepaq.com	*The doyen of Canadian parks (575 square* *miles/1490 sq km, 405 lakes, seven rivers). Wide* *range of sports and open-air activities.*	▲218

MURDOCHVILLE	GASPÉSIE	I7

COPPER INTERPRETATION CENTER 345, route 198 Tel. (418) 784-3335 or 1-800 487-8601 www.ccmurdochville.com	*Open mid-May–early Oct: daily 10am–4pm.* *By appointment otherwise.*	▲302

NEW RICHMOND	GASPÉSIE	I7

BRITISH HERITAGE CENTER **GASPÉSIEN VILLAGE** 351, Perron O Tel. (418) 392-4487 www.gbhv-vghb.com	*Open daily early June–early Sep.*	▲308

NOUVELLE	GASPÉSIE	I7

MIGUASHA PARK 270, Miguasha O Tel. (418) 794-2475 or 1-800 665-6527 www.sepaq.com	*Open June–Aug: daily 9am–6pm;* *Sep–mid-Oct: daily 9am–5pm.*	▲308

OKA	LAURENTIDES	D10
CISTERCIAN ABBEY R.R. 1, Oka Tel. (450) 479-8361 www.abbayeoka.com	*Open Mon 1–4.30pm, Tue–Fri 2–4.30pm,* *Sat 9.30am–4.30pm.*	▲223

ORFORD	ESTRIE	TEL. (819) 843-2744	E10
ARTS CENTER 3165, chemin du Parc Tel. (819) 843-3981 or 1-800 567 6155 www.arts.orford.org	*Open Mon–Fri 8.30am–5pm.* *Classes, festival of classical music.*		▲213
MONT-ORFORD RECREATIONAL PARK 3321, chemin du Parc Tel. (819) 843-6233 or 1-800 665 6527 www.sepaq.com/montorford	*Camping, cross country-skiing, cycling.*		▲212
STATION DU MONT-ORFORD 4380, chemin du Parc Tel. (819) 843-6548 or 1-866 673-6731	*Skiing in winter, golf, mountain biking* *in summer.*		▲213

OTTAWA	(ONTARIO PROVINCE)	C10
CANADIAN WAR MUSEUM 330, prom. Sussex Tel. (819) 776-8600 or 1-800 555-5621 www.civilization.ca	*Open Tue–Wed and Fri–Sun 9.30am–5pm,* *Thu 9.30am–8pm.*	
CANADIAN MUSEUM OF NATURE Angle Metcalfe et McLeod Tel. (613) 566-4700 or 1-800 263-4433	*Open May–Aug: Mon, Thu and Sun 9.30am–8pm,* *Tue–Wed and Fri–Sat 9.30am–5pm;* *First Tue in Sep–April: Mon–Wed and Fri–Sun* *10am–5pm, Thu 10am–8pm.*	▲228
NATIONAL GALLERY OF CANADA 380, prom. Sussex Tel. (613) 990-1985 or 1-800 319 2787 www.national.gallery.ca	*Open Mon–Wed and Fri–Sun 10am–5pm,* *Thu 10am–9pm.*	▲228
NATIONAL MUSEUM OF SCIENCE AND TECHNOLOGY 1867, bd Saint-Laurent Tel. (613) 991-3044 www.sciencetech.technomuses.ca/ francais/index.cfm	*Open May–Aug: Mon–Thu and Sat–Sun 9am–5pm,* *Fri 9am–9pm;* *Sep–April: Tue–Sun 9am–5pm.*	▲228
CANADIAN PARLIAMENT 111, rue Wellington Édifice de l'Est Tel. (613) 992-4793 Édifice du Centre Tel. (613) 239-5000 www.parl.qc.ca	*East building: open daily 9.35am–4.35pm in* *summer.* *Centre building: open Mon–Fri 9am–8.30pm,* *Sat–Sun 9am–5.30pm (end May–early Sep);* *daily 9am–4.30pm (early Sep–end May).*	▲227

PARC DE LA GATINEAU	OUTAOUAIS	TEL. (819) 227-2020	B9
BELVÉDÈRE CHAMPLAIN Tel. 1-800 465 1867	*Spectacular view of the Ottawa River and the* *Eardley Escarpment. Wooded park, hiking with* *guides.*		▲229
DOMAINE MACKENZIE-KING 75, chemin Barnes Tel. (819) 827-2020 or 1-800 465-1867 www.capitaleducanada.gc.ca/ gatineau	*Open daily 10am–6pm mid-June–mid-Oct ;* *mid-May–mid-June: Wed-Sun 11am–5pm.* *Park, hikes with guides.*		

PASPÉBIAC	GASPÉSIE	I7
HISTORIC SITE OF THE BANC-DE-PASPÉBIAC 3, route du Quai Tel. (418) 752-6229	*Open early June–mid-Sep: daily 9am–6pm.*	▲308

PERCÉ	GASPÉSIE	TEL. (418) 782-5448)	J7
ÎLE-BONAVENTURE PARK AND PERCÉ ROCK 4, rue du Quai Tel. (418) 782-2240 www.sepaq.com/ilebonaventure	*Open June–mid-Oct: daily 9.30am–4pm Major colony of northern gannets.*		▲306

PÉRIBONKA	SAGUENAY-LAC-SAINT-JEAN		E7
LOUIS-HÉMON MUSEUM 700, rue Maria-Chapdelaine (route 169) Tel. (418) 374-2177 www.destination.ca/museelh	*Open June–Sep: daily 9am–5pm; Oct–May: Mon–Fri 9am–4pm. The author of Maria Chapdelaine lived in this cabin.*		▲321

PETITE-RIVIÈRE-SAINT-FRANÇOIS	CHARLEVOIX		F8
LE MASSIF 1350, rue Principale Tel. (418) 632-5876 or 1-877 536-2774 www.lemassif.com	*Ski center.*		▲280

PLAISANCE	OUTAOUAIS		C10
HERITAGE MUSEUM 276, rue Desjardins Tel. (819) 427-6400 www.ville.plaisance.qc.ca	*Open end June–early Sep: daily 10am–5pm. Out of season by appointment.*		▲224
PLAISANCE FALLS 100, chemin Malo Tel. (819) 427-6400	*Picnic areas close by.*		
PLAISANCE NATIONAL PARK 2432, ch. de la petite Presqu'île Tel. (819) 427-5334 or 1-800 665-6527 www.sepaq.com/plaisance	*Open mid-April–mid-Oct Hiking, discovery of the regional fauna.*		▲224

POINTE-À-LA-CROIX	GASPÉSIE	TEL. (418) 775-2223	I7
BATTLE OF THE RISTIGOUCHE NATIONAL HISTORIC SITE Route 132 Tel. (418) 788-5676 or 1-800 463-6769 www.parcscanada.gc.ca/ristigouche	*Open June–mid-Oct: daily 9am–5pm.*		▲309

POINTE-AU-PÈRE	LOWER SAINT LAWRENCE		GH7
POINTE-AU-PÈRE NATIONAL HISTORIC SITE, MUSEUM OF THE SEA AND LIGHTHOUSE 1034, rue du Phare Tel. (418) 724-6214 www.museedelamer.qc.ca	*Open June–Aug: daily 9am–6pm; Sep–mid-Oct: daily 9am–5pm.*		▲296

POINTE-AU-PIC	CHARLEVOIX		FG8
CHARLEVOIX MUSEUM 10, chemin du Havre Tel. (418) 665-4411	*Open end June–early Sep: Tue-Fri 10am–5pm, Sat–Sun 1–5pm.*		▲285

POINTE-DU-LAC	MAURICIE		E9
TONNANCOUR MILL 2930, rue N.-Dame Tel. (819) 377-1396	*Open mid-June–mid-Sep: Tue-Sun noon–5.30pm.*		▲249

QUEBEC			D10
OFFICE OF TOURISM 399, Saint-Joseph E Tel. (418) 641-66540 www.quebecregion.com			
HOLY TRINITY ANGLICAN CATHEDRAL 31, rue des Jardins Tel. (418) 692-2193 www.ogs.net/cathedral	*Open May–Oct: Mon–Fri 8.30am–8pm, Sat 10am–8pm, Sun 11am–6pm; Nov–April: Mon–Sat 9am–6pm, Sun noon–6pm.*		▲261

CATHERINE-DE-ST-AUGUSTIN CENTRE 32, rue Charlevoix Tel. (418) 692-2492	*Open Mon-Sat 9am–5pm, Sun 2–5pm.*	▲268
PLACE ROYALE **INTERPRETATION CENTER** 27, rue Notre-Dame Tel. (418) 646-3167 or 1-866 710-8031 www.mcq.org	*Open Tue-Sun 10am–5pm.*	▲255
OLD-PORT-OF-QUEBEC **INTERPRETATION CENTER** 100, quai Saint-André Tel. (418) 648-3300 or 1-800 463-6769	*Open May–Aug: daily 10am–5pm;* *Sep–mid-Oct: daily 1–5pm;* *mid-Oct–April by appointment.*	▲258
JESUIT CHAPEL 20, rue Dauphine Tel. (418) 694-9616	*Open daily 11am–1.30pm.*	▲260
CHÂTEAU FRONTENAC 1, rue des Carrières Tel. (418) 691-2166	*Guided tours daily 10am–6pm (every hour)* *May–Oct 15; Sat–Sun only out of season.*	▲255
CHURCH OF NOTRE-DAME- **DES-VICTOIRES** Pl. Royale Tel. (418) 692-1650	*Open Tue-Sun 10am–5pm.*	▲264
ST ANDREW'S PRESBYTERIAN **CHURCH** 5, rue Cook Tel. (418) 694-1347	*Open July-Aug: Mon-Sat 10am–4.30pm,* *Sun 1–4pm; out of season by appointment.*	
CHURCH OF SAINT-JEAN-BAPTISTE 490, rue Saint-Jean Tel. (418) 525-7188	*Open May-Sep: Mon-Sat 1–5.30pm,* *Sun noon– 3pm. Oct-April: Mon-Sat 1–5.30pm.*	▲270
CHALMERS-WESLEY CHURCH 78, rue Sainte-Ursule Tel. (418) 692-2640	*Concerts every Sunday afternoon in summer.*	▲267
NATURE ADVENTURE Route 375 (Km 74) Tel. (418) 848-3169	*Open June-Oct.* *Jacques-Cartier River Park. Wildlife watching,* *moose safari, guided hikes in the forest.*	
NATIONAL ASSEMBLY 1045, rue des Parlementaires Tel. (418) 643-7239 or 1-866 337-8837 www.assnat.qc.ca	*Visits end June–early Sep: Mon–Fri 9am–4.30pm,* *Sat–Sun 10am–4.30pm;* *Sep–early June: Mon–Fri 9am–4.30pm.*	▲270
IMAX THEATER 5401, bd des Galeries Tel. (418) 627-4629 or 1-800 643-4629	*Open Tue-Sun noon–9pm.* *Movies shown on a giant screen.*	
L'ÎLOT DES PALAIS 8, rue Vallière Tel. (418) 641-6173 www.museocapitale.qc.ca	*Open end June–early Sep: daily 10am–5pm;* *out of season by appointment.*	▲259
MAISON CHEVALIER 50, rue du Marché Tel. (418) 646-3167	*Open Tue-Sun 10am–5pm.*	▲255
MAISON HENRY STUART 82, Grande-Allée O Tel. (418) 647-4347 www.cmsq.qc.ca	*Open mid-June-Aug: daily 11am–5pm;* *out of season Sun only 1–5pm.*	
MAISON FRANÇOIS-XAVIER- **GARNEAU** 14, rue Saint-Flavien Tel. (418) 692-2240 www.louisgarneau.com	*Open May–Jan: Sun 1–5pm.*	
MUSÉE BON-PASTEUR 14, rue Couillard Tel. (418) 694-0243 www.museocapitale.qc.ca/ 011.htm	*Open Tue–Sun 1–5pm.*	▲268
MUSEUM OF FRENCH AMERICA 2, côte de la Fabrique Tel. (418) 692-2843 www.mcq.org	*Open Tue–Sun 10am–5pm.*	▲265

MUSEUM OF CIVILISATION 85, rue Dalhousie Tel. (418) 643-2158 or 1-866 710-8031 www.mcq.org	*Open Tue–Sun 10am–5pm.*	▲256
AUGUSTINES MUSEUM **AND HÔTEL-DIEU-DE-QUEBEC** 32, rue Charlevoix Tel. (418) 692-2492	*Open Tue–Sat 9.30am–noon and 1.30–5pm,* *Sun 1.30–5pm.*	▲268
URSULINES MUSEUM 12, rue Donnacona Tel. (418) 694-0694 www.musee-ursulines.qc.ca	*Open May–Oct: Tue-Fri 9am–5pm, Sat–Sun 1–5pm;* *March–April: Wed–Sun 1–5pm; Nov–Feb: by* *appointment.*	▲269
MUSEUM OF THE FORT 10, rue Sainte-Anne Tel. (418) 692-2175 www.museedufort.com	*Open April–Oct: daily 10am–5pm;* *Nov, Feb–March: Thu–Sun 11am–4pm.*	▲261
MUSEUM OF QUEBEC Parc des Champs-de-Bataille Tel. (418) 643-2150 www.mdq.org	*Open June–Aug: daily 10am–6pm;* *Sep–May: Tue, Thu–Sun 10am–5pm,* *Wed 10am–9pm.*	▲270
QUEBEC EXPERIENCE 8, rue du Trésor - Suite 200 Tel. (418) 694-4000	*Open mid-May–mid-Oct: daily 10am–10pm; out of* *season: Mon–Thu, Sun 10am–5pm, Fri* *10am–4.45pm, Sat 10am–10pm. Son et lumière* *historical show.*	
NOTRE-DAME-DU-SACRÉ-CŒUR **SANCTUARY** 71, rue Sainte-Ursule Tel. (418) 692-3787 www.patrimoine-religieux.com	*Open daily 7am–8pm.*	▲267
TRAVERSIER LÉVIS 10, rue des Traversiers Tel. (418) 644-3704 www.traversiers.gouv.qc.ca	*Québec-Lévis river link. Departure every 30 mins by* *day and every hour at night.*	

RIMOUSKI	**LOWER SAINT LAWRENCE** TEL. (418) 723-2322	**G7**
MAISON LAMONTAGNE 707, bd du Rivage Tel. (418) 722-4038 www.Maysonlamontagne.com	*Open mid-May–mid-Oct: daily 9am–6pm.*	▲296

RIVIÈRE-DU-LOUP	**LOWER SAINT LAWRENCE** TEL. (418) 862-1981	**G8**
MUSEUM OF THE LOWER **SAINT LAWRENCE** 300, rue Saint-Pierre Tel. (418) 862-7547 www.mbsl.qc.ca	*Open end June–Aug: daily 10am–8pm;* *Sep–end June: Mon–Fri 10am–noon and 1–5pm,* *Sat–Sun 1–5pm.*	▲292
TRAVERSIER SAINT-SIMÉON 199, rue Hayward Traverse Rivière du loup Tel. (418) 862-5094 Traverse Saint-Siméon (418) 638-2856 www.travrdlstsim.com	*Times vary. Ask the tourist office.*	

ROUYN-NORANDA	**ABITIBI-TÉMISCAMINGUE** TEL. (819) 797-3195	**A7**
MAISON DUMULON 191, av. du Lac Tel. (819) 797-7125 www.Maysondumoulon.ca	*Open end June–mid-Sep: daily 9am–8pm;* *mid-Sep–end June: Mon–Fri 9am–noon, 1–5pm.*	▲231
AIGUEBELLE PARK 1737, rang Hudon par Saint-Norbert-de-Mont-Brun Tel. (819) 637-7322 www.sedaq.com	*Observation of the fauna and flora. Numerous* *sports activities.*	
LA VÉRENDRYE **NATURE RESERVE** R.R.1 Mont Cerf Tel. (819) 438-2017 www.sedaq.com	*Open in summer only. Hunting and fishing. Hiking* *(way-marked footpaths).*	▲230

SAINT-ANDRÉ-DE-KAMOURASKA	LOWER SAINT LAWRENCE	G8
HALTE ÉCOLOGIQUE DES BATTURES 273, route 132 O Tel. (418) 493-2604 www.sebkan.ca	Open end June–early Oct: Mon–Fri 10am–6pm, Sat–Sun 9.30am–8pm. Groups by appointment all year.	▲291
LA BOUCANERIE 111, rue Principale Tel. (418) 493-2929	Open mid-April–Dec 24: 9am–9pm. Smoked fish.	
MAISON DE LA PRUNE 129, route 132 E Tel. (418) 493-2616	Learn about damson plums. Open Sun 10am by appointment.	▲292

SAINT-BENOÎT-DU-LAC	ESTRIE	F10
ABBEY OF SAINT-BENOÎT-DU-LAC Tel. (819) 843-4080 www.st-benoit-du-lac.com	Open daily for Vespers at 5pm. Cheese on sale.	●125 ▲213

SAINT-CONSTANT	MONTÉRÉGIE	D10
CANADIAN RAILROAD MUSEUM 110, rue Saint-Pierre Tel. (450) 632-2410 www.exporail.com	Open May–early Sep: daily 9am–5pm; early Sep–mid-Oct: Sat–Sun 9am–5pm (groups by appointment during the week).	▲209

SAINT-DENIS-DE-KAMOURASKA	LOWER SAINT LAWRENCE	G8
MAISON CHAPAIS 2, route 132 E Tel. (418) 498-2353 www.kam.qc.ca	Open end June–mid-Oct: daily 10am–6pm. Out of season by appointment.	▲291

SAINT-DENIS-SUR-RICHELIEU	MONTÉRÉGIE	DE9
MAISON NATIONALE DES PATRIOTES 610, chemin des Patriotes Tel. (450) 787-3623 www.mndp.qc.ca	Open Tue–Fri 10am–5pm May–Sep and Nov. Groups by appointment all year.	▲205 ▲207

SAINT-EUSTACHE	LAURENTIDES	D10
LÉGARÉ MILL 236, rue Saint-Eustache Tel. (450) 974-5170 www.ville.saint-eustache.qc.ca	Open May–Oct: daily 9am–4.30pm; Nov: Mon–Fri 9am–4.30pm.	▲223
MUSEUM OF SAINT-EUSTACHE Manoir Globensky 235, rue Saint-Eustache Tel. (450) 974-5170 www.ville.saint-eustache.qc.ca	Open end April–mid-Nov: Mon–Fri 8.30am–4pm.	▲222

SAINT-FÉLICIEN	SAGUENAY-LAC-SAINT-JEAN	TEL. (418) 679-9888	E7
ZOOLOGICAL GARDEN 2230, bd du Jardin Tel. (418) 679-0543 or 1-800 667-5687 www.zoosauvage.qc.ca	Open end May–mid-Oct: daily 9am–5pm; daily 10am–3pm out of season (Sat–Sun Jan–March). Animals roam freely.	▲320

SAINT-FIDÈLE	CHARLEVOIX	G8
PORT-AU-SAUMON ECOLOGY CENTER 337, route 138 Tel. (418) 434-2209 www.sepas.qc.ca	Open July–mid-Aug: daily 10am–4pm . Guided tours.	▲287

SAINT-GABRIEL-DE-VALCARTIER	QUEBEC REGION	E8
VILLAGE DES SPORTS 1860, bd Valcartier G0A 4S0 Tel. (418) 844-2200 or 1-888 384-5524 www.valcartier.com	Summer aquatic activities: swimming pool with waves at 79 °F (26°C), pedal boats, diving demonstrations. In winter, skating, snow rafting, tobogganing, etc.	

SAINT-GEORGES	CHAUDIÈRE-APPALACHES	TEL. (418) 227-4642	F9
SAINT-GEORGES ART CENTER 250, 18e Rue O Tel. (418) 228-2027	Open Tue–Wed and Sat–Sun 1–5pm, Thu–Fri 1–8pm. Groups by appointment.	▲275

SAINT-IRÉNÉE	CHARLEVOIX	F8
THE FORGET ESTATE 5, rang Saint-Antoine Tel. (418) 452-3535 or 1-888 336-7438 www.domaineforget.com	*Courses with master classes (music and dance)* *June–Aug. Concerts Wed, Fri-Sat.*	▲284

SAINT-JEAN-SUR-RICHELIEU	MONTÉRÉGIE	TEL. (450) 359-4849	D10
HAUT-RICHELIEU REGIONAL **MUSEUM** 182, rue J.-Cartier N Tel. (450) 347-0649	*Open Wed–Sun 12.30–5pm.*	▲208

SAINT-JÉRÔME	LAURENTIDES	TEL. (450) 436-8532	D9
VIEUX-PALAIS EXHIBITION **CENTER** 185, rue du Palais Tel. (450) 432-0569	*Open Wed–Sun noon–5pm, Tue noon–8pm.*	▲217

SAINT-JOACHIM	QUEBEC REGION	
CAP TOURMENTE **NATURE RESERVE** 570, chemin du Cap-Tourmente Tel. (418) 827-4591 www.lavoieverte.qc.cc.qc.ca	*Bird watching.*	▲282

SAINT-JOSEPH-DE-BEAUCE	CHAUDIÈRE-APPALACHES	F9
MARIUS-BARBEAU MUSEUM 139, rue Sainte-Christine Tel. (418) 397-4039 www.museemariusbarbeau.com	*Open July–Aug: Mon–Fri 9am–5pm, Sat–Sun* *10am–5pm;* *Sep–June Tue–Fri 9am–4pm, Sat–Sun 1–4pm.*	▲275

SAINT-JOSEPH-DE-LA-RIVE	CHARLEVOIX	F8
PAPETERIE SAINT-GILLES 304, rue F.-A.-Savard Tel. (418) 635-2430 or 1-866 635-2430 www.papeteriessaintgilles.com	*Paper manufacture. Open all year.*	▲281

SAINT-LAMBERT-DE-LAUZON	MONTÉRÉGIE	D10
AVENTURE NORD-BEC 665, rue Saint-Aimé Tel. (418) 889-8001 www.aventures-nord-bec.com	*For driving a team of Alaskan malamutes.* *Excursions from campsite or chalet.*	

SAINT-LAURENT (ÎLE D'ORLÉANS)	QUEBEC REGION	F9
PARC MARITIME DE SAINT-LAURENT 120, ch. Chalouperie Tel. (418) 828-9672 www.iledorleans.qc.ca	*Open mid-June–early Sep: daily 10am–5pm;* *early Sep-mid-Oct: Sat–Sun by appointment.*	▲277

SAINT-PAUL-DE-L'ÎLE-AUX-NOIX	MONTÉRÉGIE	D10
THE LACOLLE BLOCKHOUSE 1, rue Principale, via road 223 Tel. (450) 246-3227 www.ile-aux-noix.com	*Open June–Aug: daily 9am–5pm; Sep: Sat–Sun* *only*	▲209
FORT LENNOX **NATIONAL HISTORIC SITE** 1, 61e Av. Tel. (450) 291-5700 or 1-800 463-6769 www.parcscanada.gc.ca/fortlennox	*Open mid-May–end June: Mon–Fri 10am–5pm,* *Sat–Sun 10am–6pm; end June–Aug: daily* *10am–6pm; Sep–mid-Oct: Sat–Sun 10am–6pm*	▲209

SAINT-PRIME	SAGUENAY-LAC-SAINT-JEAN	E7
CHEDDAR CHEESE MUSEUM 148, av. Albert-Perron Tel. (418) 251-4922 or 1-888 251-4922 (gratuit) www.museecheddar.org	*Open end June–early Sep: daily 9am–8pm.* *Groups by appointment all year.*	▲320

SAINT-ROCH-DES-AULNAIES	CHAUDIÈRE-APPALACHES	FG8
MUSEUM OF THE SEIGNEURIAL SYSTEM 525, rue de la Seigneurie Tel. (418) 354-2800 or 1-877 354-2800 www.laseigneuriedesaulnaies.qc.ca	*Open mid-May–early Sep: daily 9am–6pm; mid-Sep–mid-Oct: Sat–Sun 10am–4pm*	▲290

SAINT-SAUVEUR-DES-MONTS	LAURENTIDES	D9
STATION MONT-SAINT-SAUVEUR 350, rue Saint-Denis, J0R 1R3 Tel. (450) 227-4671 or 1-800 363-2426 (freephone) www.montsaintsauveur.com	*The largest spotlit ski run in North America. Sugar cabin, aquatic park.*	▲218

SAINT-SIMÉON	CHARLEVOIX	G8
TRAVERSIER RIVIÈRE-DU-LOUP 199, rue Hayward Tel. (418) 862-5094 www.travrdlstsim.com	*April–Jan. Up to five daily departures depending to season.*	▲285

SAINTE-ANNE-DE-BEAUPRÉ	QUEBEC REGION	TEL. (418) 641-6654	F8
SAINTE-ANNE-DE-BEAUPRÉ BASILICA 10018, av. Royale Tel. (418) 827-3781 www.ssadb.qc.ca	*Visits 1pm and 2.15pm early June–Aug.*		▲278

SAINTE-ANNE-DE-SOREL	MONTÉRÉGIE	TEL. (450) 469-0069	DE9
CROISIÈRES DES ÎLES DE SOREL 68, rue Saint-Maurice Tel. (450) 743-7227/7807 or 1-800 361-6420 www.croisieresrichelieu.com	*Open early May-mid Oct. 'Eco-nature' cruises for birdwatchers.*		▲204

SAINTE-ANNE-DES-MONTS	GASPÉSIE	I6
GASPÉSIE PARK Secteur Mont-Albert Route du Parc (route 299) Tel. (418) 763-7811 or 1-800 665-6527 www.sepaq.com/gasperie	*Nature research center (June–Sep). Hiking, mountain bikes, fishing, cross-country skiing, snowshoeing.*	▲300

SAINTE-MARIE	CHAUDIÈRE-APPALACHES	F9
MAISON J.-A.-VACHON 383, rue Coopérative Tel. (418) 387-4052 or 1-866 387-4052	*Open early April–end Sep:daily 9am–5pm; out of season by appointment.*	▲275

SEPT-ÎLES	DUPLESSIS	TEL. (418) 962-1238	HI6-7
TRADING POST MUSEUM 99, bd Montagnais Tel. (418) 968-2070 www.mrcn.qc.ca	*Open mid-June–early Sep: daily 9am–5pm; mid-Sep–mid-June; Tue-Fri 10am–noon and 1–5pm, Sat–Sun 1–5pm.*		▲330
MUSEUM OF THE NORTH SHORE 500, bd Laure Tel. (418) 968-2070 www.mrcn.qc.ca	*Open mid-June–early Sep: daily 9am–5pm; mid-Sep–mid-June: Tue-Fri 10am–noon and 1–5pm, Sat–Sun 1–5pm.*		▲330
RELAIS NORDIK 17, av. Lebrun Tel. (418) 723-8787 or 1-800 463-0680	*Crossings: Sept-Îles, Port Menier, Havre-St-Pierre and Lower North Shore.*		

SHAWINIGAN	MAURICIE	E9
ENERGY CITY MUSEUM 1000, av. Melville Tel. (819) 536-8516 www.citedelenergie.com	*Open July–early Sep: Tue–Sun 10am–6pm (evenings by appointment); June, Sep–Oct: Tue–Sun 10am–5pm.*	▲240
LA MAURICIE NATIONAL PARK 702, 5e rue Tel. (819) 538-3232 or 1-800 463-6769 www.parcscanada.gc.ca/mauricie	*Interactive museum. A 38-mile (60km) panoramic road. Outdoors activities: swimming, fishing, canoe- camping…*	▲241

◆ PLACES TO VISIT

SHERBROOKE	ESTRIE	TEL. (819) 821-1919	E10
MUSEUM OF NATURAL SCIENCES 225, rue Frontenac Tel. (819) 564-3200 www.mnes.qc.ca	*Open Tue-Sun 1–5pm, Wed 1–9pm.*		▲214
MUSÉE DES BEAUX-ARTS 241, rue Dufferin Tel. (819) 821-2115 www.mba.ville.sherbrooke.qc.ca	*Open Tue, Thu-Sun 1–5pm, Wed 1–9pm.*		▲215
SILLERY	**QUEBEC REGION**		F9
THE OLD JESUIT HOUSE 2320, ch. du Foulon Tel. (418) 654-0259 www.museocapitale.qc.ca	*Open Feb–May and Sep–Dec: Wed–Sun 1–5pm ; June–Sep: Tue–Sun 11am–5pm.*		▲271
TADOUSSAC	**MANICOUAGAN**	TEL. (418) 543-9778	G7
SEA MAMMAL RESEARCH UNIT 108, rue de la Cale-Sèche Tel. (418) 235-4701 www.baleinesendirect.net	*Open mid-June–mid-Sep: daily 9am–8pm; mid-May-mid-June and mid-Sep-end Oct: Mon–Fri noon–6pm, Sat–Sun 10am–6pm. Interactive exhibitions. Center of documentation on whales.*		▲329
LA MAISON DES DUNES Route du Moulin Baude Tel. (418) 235-4238	*Open early June–mid-Oct: daily 9am–5pm.*		▲328
OLD CHAPEL Bord-de-l'Eau Tel. (418) 235-4324	*Open daily mid-June–early Sep.*		▲329
POSTE DE TRAITE CHAUVIN 157, Bord-de-l'Eau Tel. (418) 235-4446	*Open mid-June–mid-Sep: daily 9am–8.30pm; end Sep–mid-Oct: daily 9am–noon and 3–6pm.*		▲329
TERREBONNE	**LANAUDIÈRE**	TEL. (450) 964-0681	D9-10
L'ÎLE DES MOULINS 900, place Île-des-Moulins Tel. (450) 471-0619 www.iledesmoulins.qc.ca	*Open end June–end Aug: Wed–Sat 10.30am– 8.30pm, Sun 10am–5.30pm.*		▲247
THETFORD MINES	**CHAUDIÈRE-APPALACHES**	TEL. (418) 335-2981	F9
FRONTENAC NATIONAL PARK 9, rue de la Plage Est Tel. (418) 486-2300 or 1-800 665-6527 www.sepaq.com/frontenac	*Picnic areas, hiking trails and beaches.*		
TROIS-PISTOLES	**LOWER SAINT LAWRENCE**		G7
THE BASQUE ADVENTURE IN AMERICA 66, rue du Parc Tel. (418) 851-1556	*Park open mid-June–mid-Oct.*		▲293
MAISON VLB 23, rue Pelletier Tel. (418) 851-6852	*Museum of Victor-Lévy Beaulieu. Open daily mid-June–mid-Sep.*		▲293
TROIS-RIVIÈRES	**CŒUR-DU-QUEBEC**	TEL. (514) 375-9628	E9
PULP AND PAPERS EXHIBITION CENTER 800, parc Portuaire Tel. (819) 372-4633	*Exhibition center about the paper industry. Open daily.*		▲239
CROISIÈRES M/S JACQUES-CARTIER 1515, rue du Fleuve, CP 64 G9A 5E3 Tel. (819) 375-3000 or 1-800 567-3737 www.croisiere.qc.ca	*Open daily 9am–8pm in summer; Mon–Fri 9am–5pm in winter. Discovery of the history of the 'drive' ● 77 on the River Saint-Maurice.*		
SAINT-MAURICE FORGES HISTORIC SITE 10000, bd des Forges Tel. (819) 378-5116	*Open Mon–Fri 8am–4.30pm.*		▲240

MANOIR BOUCHER-DE-NIVERVILLE 168, rue Bonaventure Tel. (819) 375-9628	*Open Mon–Fri 9am–5pm.*	▲239
URSULINES MUSEUM 734, rue des Ursulines Tel. (819) 375-7922 www.musee-ursulines.qc.ca	*Open May–Sep: Tue–Fri 9am–5pm, Sat–Sun 2–5pm; Nov–April: Wed–Sun 2–5pm.* *by appointment.*	▲239
OLD PRISON OF TROIS-RIVIÈRES – **MUSEUM OF FOLK CULTURE** 200, rue Laviolette Tel. (819) 372-0406	*Open June–Sep daily 9am–8pm;* *Oct–April: Tue–Sun 10am–5pm.* *Ask beforehand about the Museum of Folk Culture as it is possible it will close down.*	▲239
VALCOURT	**ESTRIE**	**E10**
J.-ARMAND-BOMBARDIER MUSEUM 1001, av. J.-A.-Bombardier Tel. (450) 532-5300 www.museebombardier.com	*Open end June–mid-Oct: daily 10am–5pm;* *mid-Oct–end June: Tue-Sun 10am–5pm.*	▲212
VAL-D'OR	**ABITIBI-TÉMISCAMINGUE** TEL. (819) 824-9646	**B7**
LA CITÉ DE L'OR 90, av. Perreault Tel. (819) 825-7616/5310 or 1-877 582-5367	*Mining village. Open daily 9am–6pm end June–early Sep. By appointment the rest of the year.*	▲230
WAWATÉ 347, chemin Val-du-Repos Tel. (819) 825-9518	*Trips downriver and camping with the Algonquins. In winter, sledding, snow biking.*	
VILLE-MARIE	**ABITIBI-TÉMISCAMINGUE** TEL. (819) 629-3355	**A8**
FUR TRADING POST NATIONAL **HISTORIC SITE** 834, ch. du Vieux-Fort Duhamel-Ouest Tel. (819) 629-3222 or 1-800 463-6769 www.temiscamingue.net/ fort_temiscamingue	*Open May–Sep (times vary);* *Oct–April by appointment*	▲231
GUÉRIN MUSEUM 932, rue Principale Nord Tel. (819) 784-7014 www3.sympatico.ca/musee-guerin	*Open mid-June–end Aug: daily 10am–6pm* *(7–9pm mid-July–early Aug);* *mid-May–mid-June and early Sep–mid-Oct: groups by appointment.*	▲231
WENDAKE	**QUEBEC REGION** TEL. (514) 682-5522	**E9**
AMERINDIAN VILLAGE 33, ch. de la Coulée Lac Beauport Tel. (418) 849-4252 www.cnhw.qc.ca	*Open Mon–Fri 8am–4pm.*	▲271

◆ BIBLIOGRAPHY

TRAVEL WRITING

◆ Armstrong, Julian: *A Taste of Quebec*, Hippocrene Books, 2001
◆ Dorion, Henri: *Living in Quebec*, Flammarion, 2004
◆ Ferguson, Will and Ian: *How to be a Canadian: Even if You Already Are One*, Douglas & McIntyre, 2003
◆ Gravenor (K. and J.D.): *Montreal: The Unknown City*, Arsenal Pulp Press, 2003
◆ Grescoe, Taras: *Sacre Blues: An Unsentimental Journey Through Quebec*, Macfarlane Walter & Ross, 2001
◆ Hustak, Alan: *Exploring Old Montreal: An Opinionated Guide*, Véhicle Press, 2003
◆ Lopez, Barry: *Arctic Dreams: Imagination and Desire in a Northern Landscape*, Vintage 2001
◆ Morris, Jan: *O Canada: Travels in an Unknown Country*, HarperCollins 1992
◆ *Streetwise Montreal*, Inc Streetwise Maps, 2000

NATURE

◆ Beland, Pierre: *Beluga: A Farewell to Whales*, Lyons Press, 1996
◆ Butt (C.), Marleau (J.): *Montreal/Laurentides*, Mussio Ventures, 2004
◆ Chandler, Richard: *The Facts on File Field Guide to North Atlantic Shorebirds*, Facts on File, 1989
◆ Callum, Kevin: *A Paddler's Guide to the Rivers of Ontario and Quebec*, Boston Mills Press, 2003
◆ Cooke, Tim: *The Saint Lawrence River*, Gareth Stevens Publishing, 2003
◆ Dykstra, Monique: *Alone in the Appalachians – a City Girl's Trek from Maine to the Gaspésie*, Raincoast Books, 2002
◆ Hanson, Charles: *25 Bicycle Tours in the Lake Champlain Region*, Countryman Press, 2004
◆ McCarthy (M.) ed.: *Ski Magazine's Guide to New England and Quebec*, Mountain Sports Press, 2003
◆ McGuffin (G. and J.): *Canoeing Across Canada*, Diadem, 1990
◆ McKay, Donald: *Anticosti: the Untamed Island*, McGraw-Hill Ryerson, 1979
◆ McKibben, Alan and Susan: *Cruising Guide to the Hudson River, Lake Champlain and the Saint Lawrence River*, Lake Champlain Publishing Company, 2001
◆ Villiers (M. de), Lewis (M.): *National Geographic Guide to America's Outdoors: Eastern Canada*, National Geographic, 2001
◆ Pelly, David F.: *Sacred Hunt: A Portrait of the Relationship between Seals and Inuit*, University of Washington Press, 2001
◆ Pielou, E.C.: *A Naturalist's Guide to the Arctic*, University of Chicago Press, 1995
◆ Watson, Lyall: *Sea Guide to Whales of the World*, Hutchison, 1981

HISTORY AND LANGUAGE

◆ Bélanger (J.), Desjardins (M.) and Frenette (Y.): *Histoire de la Gaspésie*, Boréal Express, Montréal, 1981
◆ Brown, Craig: *The Illustrated History of Canada*, Key Porter Books, 2003
◆ Champlain (S.), ed. Slafter (E.F.): *Voyages of Samuel de Champlain*, Prince Society, Boston, 1878
◆ Charbonneau (H.), Desjardins (B.) Guillemette (A.): *The First French Canadians: Pioneers in the St Lawrence Valley*, University of Delaware Press, 1993
◆ Chénier, Rémi: *Quebec: A French Colonial Town in America, 1660–1690*, National Historic Sites, Environment Canada, 1991
◆ Coverdale (W.H.): *Tadoussac, then and now: a History and Narrative of the Kingdom of the Saguenay*, Charles Francis Press, 1947
◆ Dickinson (J. A.) and Young (B.): *A Short History of Quebec*, McGill–Queen's University Press, 2000
◆ Donaldson (G.): *Battle for a Continent, Quebec 1759*, Doubleday Canada, Toronto, 1973
◆ Fahmy-Eid (N.) et Dumont (M.): *Les Couventines*, Boréal, Montréal, 1986
◆ Fortin (J.-C.) et Lechasseur (A.): *Histoire du Bas-Saint-Laurent*, Institut québécois de recherche sur la culture, Québec, 1993
◆ Gougeon, Gilles: *A History of Quebec Nationalism*, Lorimer Books, 1994
◆ Institut Quebecois de recherche sur la culture: *History of the Outaouais*, 1997
◆ Isajlovic (R.) and Martin (I.): *Quebecois–English, English–Quebecois Dictionary and Phrasebook*, Hippocrene Books, 2002
◆ Leacock, Stephen: *The Mariner of St-Malo: A Chronicle of the Voyages of Jacques Cartier*, Brook & Co, Toronot, 1915
◆ Linteau (P.-A): *Histoire de Montréal depuis la confédération*, Boréal, Montréal, 1992
◆ McNaught, Kenneth: *The Penguin History of Canada*, Penguin, 1991
◆ Morrissey (B.) and Hook (A.): *Quebec 1775: The American Invasion of Canada (Campaign 128)*, Osprey Publishing, 2003
◆ Mathieu (J.): *La Nouvelle-France. Les Français en Amérique du Nord (XVIe–XVIIIe siècle)*, Belin/Presses de l'université Laval, 1991
◆ Mathieu (J.) and Keld (E.): *Les Plaines d'Abraham. Le culte de l'idéal*, Septentrion, Québec, 1993
◆ Neary (P.) and O'Flaherty (P.): *Part of the Main: an Illustrated History of Newfoundland and Labrador*, Independent Publishing Group, 1986
◆ Newman (P. C.): *Caesars of the Wilderness*, Penguin, 1988
◆ Newman (P. C.): *Empire of the Bay. An Illustrated History of the Hudson's Bay Company*, Madison Press Books, Toronto, 1989
◆ Pouliot (J.-C.): *L'Île d'Orléans, glanures historiques et familiales*, Leméac, Montréal, 1984
◆ Proteau (L.): *La Parlure québécoise*, Proteau éd., Montréal, 1982
◆ Provencher (J.): *Chronologie du Québec 1534-2000*, Boréal, Montréal, 2001.
◆ Québec: *Itinéraires toponymiques du Québec*, Québec, Les Publications du Québec, Québec, 7 vol.
◆ Québec: *Noms et lieux du Québec*, Québec, Les Publications du Québec, 1994
◆ Reid, Stuart, Embleton, Gerry: *Quebec 1759: The Battle That Won Canada*, Osprey Publications, 2003
◆ Riendeau, Roger: *A Brief History of Canada*, Fitzhenry & Whiteside Ltd, 2000
◆ Ruddel (D.-T.): *Québec, 1765-1832. L'évolution d'une ville coloniale*, Musée canadien des Civilisations, 1991
◆ Taylor (J. H.): *The History of Canadian Cities: Ottawa, An Illustrated History*, James Lorimer & Co. et le musée canadien des Civilisations, Toronto, 1986
◆ Timmins, Steve: *French Fun: The Real Spoken Language of Québec*, John Wiley & Sons, 1995
◆ Vachon (A.): *Rêves d'empire, le Canada avant 1700*, Archives publiques du Canada, Ottawa, 1982

ARTS AND TRADITIONS

◆ Adam-Villeneuve (F.) et Fecteau (C.): *Les Moulins à eau de la vallée du Saint-Laurent*, Éditions de l'Homme, Montréal, 1978
◆ Arpin (R.): *Rencontre de deux mondes*, Musée de la civilisation, Québec, 1992
◆ Béland (M. sous la dir. de): *Restauration en sculpture ancienne*, Musée du Québec, Québec, 1994
◆ Chalifour (B.) et Germain (G.-H.): *Québec, Québec*, Art Global, Publications du Québec, Montréal, 1992
◆ Côté (L.), Tardivel (L.) et Vaugeois (D.): *L'Indien généreux*, Boréal, Montréal, 1992
◆ *Creative Canada: A biographical dictionary of 20th-century creative*

and performing artists, University of Toronto Press, 1971

◆ Dumond (D.): *The Eskimos and Aleuts*, Thames & Hudson, 1987

◆ Gagnon (F.-M.) : *Images du castor canadien, XVIIᵉ-XVIIIᵉ siècle*, Septentrion, Sillery, 1994

◆ Genest (B.), Bouchard (R.), Cyr (L.) and Chouinard (Y.) : *Les Artisans traditionnels de l'est du Québec*, Ministère des Affaires culturelles, Québec, 1979

◆ Giroux (R.) : *Le Guide de la chanson québécoise*, Triptyque, Montréal, 1991

◆ Hart (L.) and Sandell (G.): *Danse ce soir: Fiddle and Accordion music of Quebec*, Mel Bay Publications, 2001

◆ Johansson, Warren I.: *Country Furniture and Accessories from Quebec*, Schiffer Publishing 1997

◆ Lahoud (P.) and Dorion (H.): *Quebec from the Air – From Season to Season*, Les Editions de l'Homme, 2004

◆ Lessard (M.), Huot (C.) : *Quebec: City of Light*, Éditions de l'Homme, 2004

◆ McMillan, Alan D.: *Native Peoples and Cultures of Canada*, Douglas & McIntyre, 1995

◆ Musée de la Civilisation : *Objets de civilisation*, Broquet, Québec, 1990

◆ Pommerleau (J.) : *Les Coureurs de bois*, éd. Dupont, Montréal, 1994

◆ Porter (J. R.) and Trudel (J.) : *Le Calvaire d'Oka*, Galerie nationale du Canada, Ottawa, 1974

◆ Provencher (J.) : *Les Quatre Saisons dans la vallée du Saint-Laurent*, Boréal, Montréal, 1988

◆ Roy (G.-A.) and Ruel (A.) : *Le patrimoine religieux de l'île d'Orléans*, Ministère des Affaires culturelles, Québec, 1982

◆ Sainte-Marie (M.) : *Guide des antiquités québécoises*, Libre Expression, Montréal, 1981, vol. 2

◆ Saucier (C.) and Kedl (E.) : *Image inuit du Nouveau-Québec*, Fides, musée de la Civilisation, sl, 1988

◆ Seidelman (H.), Turner (J.): *The Inuit Imagination: Arctic Myth and Sculpture*, University of Alaska Press, 2001

◆ Simard (C.) and Noël (M.) : *Artisanat québécois, tome III, Indiens et Esquimaux*, Éditions de l'Homme, Montréal, 1977

◆ Simard (J.) : *Les Arts sacrés au Québec*, Éd. de Mortagne, Boucherville, 1989

◆ Soucy (C.) and Roy (J.-L.) : *Le Banc de Paspébiac, histoire, patrimoine et développement régional*, Centre de documentation et d'interprétation de Paspébiac, sl, 1983

◆ Turner (L.-M.), *Indiens et Esquimaux du Québec*, Desclez éd., Montréal, 1979

◆ Voisine (N. sous la dir. de) : *Histoire du catholicisme québécois* (en plusieurs vol.), Boréal, Montréal, 1984.

◆ Wallace, Mary: *The Inuksuk Book*, Maple Tree Press, 1999

ARCHITECTURE

◆ Chartrand, Rene: *French fortresses in North America 1535–1763*, Osprey Publishing, 2005

◆ Demchinsky (B.): *Grassroots, Greystones and Glass Towers: Montreal Urban Issues and Architecture*, Vehicule Press, 1989

◆ Dube, Philippe: *Charlevoix: Two Centuries at Murray Bay*, McGill–Queen's University Press, 1990

◆ Germain (A.) and Rose (D.): *Montreal: The Quest for a Metropolis*, John Wiley & Sons, 2000

◆ Kaldman (H.) and Roaf (J.): *Exploring Ottawa*, University of Toronto Press, 1983

◆ Moogk, Peter N.: *Building a House in New France*, Fitzhenry & Whiteside, 2002

◆ Noppen (L.): *Au musée des Beaux-Arts du Canada 'Une des plus belles chapelles du pays'*, Musée des Beaux-Arts du Canada, 1988

◆ Noppen (L.), Paulette (C.) and Tremblay (M.) : *Trois siècles d'architecture*, Libre Expression, 1979

◆ Noppen (L.), Jobidon (H.) and Trépanier (P.) :

Québec monumental : 1890-1990, Septentrion, Montréal, 1990

◆ Ordre des architectes du Québec: *L'Architecture de Montréal*, Libre Expression, Montréal, 1990

◆ Québec : *Les Chemins de la mémoire. Monuments et sites historiques du Québec*, tome 1, Québec, 1990 ; tome 2, Québec, 1991

◆ Richards, Larry (ed): *Canadian Centre for Architecture: Buildings and Gardens*, MIT Press, 1989

PAINTING

◆ Baker (V. A.) : *Images of Charlevoix, 1784-1950*, Musée des Beaux-Arts de Montréal, 1981

◆ Béland (M.) : *La Peinture au Québec, 1820-1850. Nouveaux regards, nouvelles perspectives*, musée du Québec, Québec, 1991

◆ Finkenstein, Maria von: *Celebrating Inuit Art, 1948–70*, Canadian Museum of Civilisation, Key Porter Books, 2000

◆ *Frontiers of our Dreams: Quebec Painting in the 1940s and 1950s*, Winnipeg Art Gallery, 1979

◆ Horik, Vladimir: *Charlevoix: A Quebec Treasury in Painting*, Horik Diffusion International, 2000

◆ Hubbard, R.H.: *Canadian Landscape Painting, 1670–1930: The Artist and the Land*, University Press of New England, 1973

◆ Karel (D.) : *La Collection Duplessis*, Musée du Québec, Québec, 1991

◆ Musée du Séminaire de Québec : *Les Maîtres canadiens de la collection Power Corporation du Canada, 1850-1950*, Musée du Séminaire de Québec, sl, 1989

◆ Musée du Québec : *Agenda d'art 1995. Les saisons*, Musée du Québec, Québec, 1994

◆ Nadeau (M.) : *Masterpieces of the collection*, Musée du Québec, Québec, 1991

◆ Noël (M.): *Art inuit*, Roussan, Pointe-Claire, 1992

◆ Reid, Dennis: *A Concise History of Canadian Painting*, Oxford University Press, 1973

◆ Roussan, Jacques de: *Quebec in Painting*, Roussan éditeur, 1989

◆ Swinton (G.), Hessel (I. and D.): *Inuit Art: An Introduction*, Douglas & McIntyre, 2003

LITERATURE

◆ Anahareo: *Grey Owl and I: a New Autobiography*, P. Davies, 1972

◆ Campbell Scott (D.): *The Green Cloister*, McLelland & Stewart, 1935

◆ Cohen, Leonard: *Beautiful Losers*, New Canadian Library, 1966

◆ Dickens, Charles: *American Notes for General Circulation*, Chapman and Hall, 1842

◆ Gerber (A.) : *Montréal Blues*, Lacombe/Table Rase, Montreal, 1992

◆ Grey Owl: *Collected Works*, Firefly Books, 2001

◆ James Henry: *Portraits of Places*, 1883

◆ Kapesh, An Antane: *Qu'as-tu fait de mon pays?*, Editions Impossible, 1979

◆ Klein (A.M.): *Complete Poems*, University of Toronto Press, 1990

◆ Lampman (A,): *The Poems of Archibald Lampman*, 1900

◆ Lopez, Barry: *Literary walks in Montreal*, Québec/Amérique, 1989

◆ Mair, Charles: *Dreamland*, Citizen Publishing, 1868

◆ Richler, Mordecai: *Oh Canada! Oh Québec! Requiem for a Divided Country*, Alfred A. Knopf, 1992

◆ Rooke, Constance: *Writing Home: a PEN anthology*, McLelland & Stewart, 1997

◆ Roy, Gabrielle: *The Tin Flute*, McLelland & Stewart, 1947

◆ Scott (F.R.): *Events and Signals*, Ryerson Press, 1954

◆ Thoreau (H.D.): *Excursions and Poems*, Houghton Mifflin, 1906

◆ Trollope, Anthony: *North America*, Harper and Brothers, 1862

◆ Warburton (G.D.): *Hochelaga*, Wiley and Putnam, 1846

◆ Weaver (R.) and Atwood (M.), eds: *New Oxford Book of Canadian Short Stories in English*, Oxford University Press, 1995

Abbreviations :
ACP: Archives of the Canadian Pacific
ANC: National Archives of Canada, Ottawa
ANF: National Archives of France
ANQM: National Archives of Quebec in Montreal
ANQQ: National Archives of Quebec in Quebec
AST-R: Archives of the Seminary of Trois-Rivières
ATR: Regional Tourist Association
BMM: Montreal City Library
BN: National Library, Paris
BNQM: National Library of Quebec in Montreal
CHM: Center for the History of Montreal
CMcMAC: Collection McMichael of Canadian Art
CPCC: Canada's Power Corporation Collection
CQ: Quebec Film Institute
FCNQ: Federation of the Cooperatives of New-Quebec
H-Q: Hydro-Québec
MBAC: Museum of Fine Arts, Ottawa
MBAM: Museum of Fine Arts, Montreal
MCC: Quebec Ministry of Culture and Communications
MCdesC: Canadian Museum of Civilization, Hull
MCQ: Museum of Quebec Civilization, Quebec
MG: Gaspésie Museum
MMcHC: McCord Museum of Canadian History, Montreal
MMcHC-AN: McCord Museum of Canadian History – Notman Photographic Archives
MQ: Quebec Museum
ONF: Canadian National Film Theater
PC-MPC: Canadian Parks-Ministry of Canadian Heritage
SCP: Canadian post-office company
SHS: Historical Society of Saguenay-Lac-Saint-Jean
TQ: Quebec Tourism
VM: City of Montreal
VM-GDA: City of Montreal – documents and archives

Front cover:
The Ice Rink, Dufferin Terrace, detail, R. Pilot, c.1960, CPCC
Back cover:
Sliding, château Frontenac, ph. B. Ostiguy

1: Fishing the ouananiche on the Métabetchouane River, ph. Livernois, c.1910, ANQQ
2-3: 'Sugar loaf', Montmorency waterfall, ph. W. Notman, 1876, MMcHC-AN
4-5: Montagnais people from Pointe-Bleue (Mashteuiatsh), ph. 1890, ANQQ
6-7: Rue Sainte-Catherine in Montreal, 1901, ph. W. Notman, MMcHC-AN
9: Lake Sauvage, Saint-Donas ph. S. Majeau
14: Manic 5 dam, ph. P. Lahoud; snowy owl, ph. G. Delisle
15: Agricultural landscape, ph. P. Lahoud; Forest, ph. B. Ostiguy; Saint-Jean-Baptiste in Montreal, ph. P. Quittemelle; Registration plate, ills D. Héron
18: The Saint-Lawrence River entering the city of Quebec in Canada, end 18th c., BN; Cabin in the woods, M. Chaplin, c.1839, ANC
19: Houses, drawing D. Héron; La pesche des Sauvages , detail in Codex Canadiensis, L. Nicholas, v.1650, BN; View in the Eastern Townships, Lower Canada, on the River St. Francis , Day & Hague, ANC; Port de Montreal, detail ph. J. A. Millar, 1920, ANC
20-21: Ill. J. Chevalier; Map P. Mérienne ph. A. Guerrier © Colibri
21: Photos J. M. Brunet © Colibri; P. J. Dubois © Gallimard; J. J. Blanchon
22-23: Ills G. Houbre, P. Robin, S. Nicolle, A. Larousse, J. Candiard; Map P. Mérienne; ph. P. Lahoud
24-25: Ills F. Desbordes, J. Chevallier, P. Robin, D. Mansion, C. Felloni; Map P. Mérienne; ph. N. David
26-27: Ills F. Desbordes, J. Chevallier, A. Larousse
28-29: Ills F. Desbordes, P. Robin, F. Place; Map P. Mérienne; photos P. Fradette, P. Lahoud
30-31: Ills F. Desbordes, C. Felloni, A. Larousse, J. Chevallier
32-33: Ills S. Nicolle, F. Desbordes, A. Larousse, C. Felloni; ph. P. Lahoud
34-35: Ills F. Desbordes, J. Chevallier, S. Nicolle, C. Felloni; Map P. Mérienne; ph. © J. M. Brunet/Colibri
36: Ills F. Desbordes,

C. Felloni, F. Place; ph. A. Larousse © Gallimard
37: Travelers at Dawn, F. Hopkins, v.1871, ANC
38: Eskimo Woman and Child, J. White, c.1589, British Museum; Iroquois Native, J. Laroque, ANC; Map on parchment paper, 1546, ANC
39: Inhabitant, M. Millicent, c.1840, ANC; View of Quarantine Station at Grosse-Île, oil, H. Delattre, 1850, ANC; The War of the Conquest, London Gazette, 1759, ANC
40: Louis-Joseph Papineau, detail, N. Bourassa, 1858, ph. P. Altman, MQ; Special class under the Union regime, 1855, ANC
40-41: View of the Champ-de-Mars, W. Lenny and A. Bourne, 1830, ANQQ
41: Poster, ANC; W. Rotté's Farm, ph. W. Notman, 1906, MMcHC-AN; Sketch illustrating rural life in Quebec, F. Back, 1950, priv. coll.
42: Large family in The Province of Quebec, A. Girard, 1905, ph. L. Rioux, BNQ; Inauguration of Manic 5 (R. Lévesque, J. Lesage, and D. Johnson), 1968, ph. H-Q; René Lévesque, ANQM
43: Pro-choice demonstration, ph. J. Daggett, 1970, ANC; The Saint-Jean-Baptiste National Day in Montreal, photos P. Quittemelle
44 Burial of a Savage and Cemetery of the Savages, 1715, in New Travels ... Lahontan; Prehistoric Native American Village, F. Girard, © Vidéanthrop
44-45: Frieze of the Main People of America, detail G. Saint-Sauveur, ANC; Dance of the Kutcha-Kutchi, A. Murray, ANC
45: Stone head, ph. M. Laberge, © Vidéanthrop
46: Oven in the Île-aux-Basques, ph. L. Turgeon, U. Laval; Algonquins BMM; pearl for trade, ph. L. Turgeon, U. Laval
46-47: Pesca del Merluzzo in Terra Nuova America, MG; Jacques Cartier meets Iroquois Indians in Stadaconé, M.-A. de Foy Suzor-Côté, 1907, ph. J.-G. Kérouac, MQ; Copper cauldrons, ph. B. Ostiguy, MCC
47: Whale hunting, 1592, in Portugaliæ monumenta cartographica, A. Cortesao and A. Teixeira, British Library
48: Algonquin silver crown, c. 1825, MCdesC
48-49: Various models of beaver hats, H. Matin,

1892, from Castorologia, ANC; Fur traders in Montreal, detail, G. A. Reid, c. 1875, ANC; 'Travelers' Through a Waterfall in a Canoe; oil, detail, F. Hopkins, 1869, ANC
49: Trading between a Native American and a White Man, anonymous, ANQQ; Earrings, MCdesC; Native American with wampum, ANQQ
50: Quebec As It Is Seen From the East, cartouche from Map of Septentrional America, J.-B.-L. Franquelin, 1699, BN; Map of the Land around Trois-Rivières, S. Catalogne, 1709, BN
50-51: Arrival of Champlain in Quebec, H. Beau, 1904, ph. P. Altman, MQ
51: Hunters with Snowshoes, detail, H. S. Murrell, c.1849, ANC; France bringing Faith to the Hurons of Nouvelle-France, anonymous, c.1670; detail, Ursulines monastery, Quebec
52: Montreal from the Indian Encampment, J. Duncan, c.1850, ANC; John Molson, stamp, SCP
52-53: Work in progress to enlarge the Lachine Canal, Canadian Illustrated News, 1877, ph. L. Rioux, BNQM
53: Portrait of James McGill, L. Dulongpré, 1813, MMcHC; Cover of Oh Canada ! Oh Quebec ! by M. Richler, Les éditions Balzac, Montreal; Leonard Cohen, ph. J.-F. Bérubé
54: Detail from catechism, Deschâtelets Archives, Ottawa, ph. F. Brault; Evening Prayer, c.Gagnon, 1928–33, CMcMAC; Recumbent figure of Mgr Bourget, ph. F. Brault
54-55: Cover of Refus global, ph. L. Rioux, BNQM, © Éditions de l'Hexagone
55: La Corpus-Christi in Quebec, J.-P. Lemieux, 1944, ph. P. Altman, MQ; Prime Minister M. Duplessis, clerics and military figures, ANC
56: Cover from Les Insolences du frère Untel, J. P. Desbiens, 1960, Les Éditions de l'Homme; Montreal transformed, ph. La Presse
56-57: Poster for the Liberal party, 1962, ph. H-Q
57: Pauline Julien, ph. Le Jour, ANQM; Official stamp, Expo 67, SCP; Poster, BNQM; Jean Lesage on the building site, ph. R. Picard, La Presse; Demonstration for independence, ph. La Presse
58: Innu symbol, coll. M. Noël; Demonstrations by

Native Americans, ANQM; Native American communities in Quebec, map Saintonge Vision
58-59: The Patriot, D. Williams, 1992, ph. L. Leblanc, coll. M. Noël; Attikamek Niquay family, ph. L. Leblanc
59: Three Indian Apples, D. Williams, ph. L. Leblanc; Alanis Obumsawin, ph. G. Picard, MCC
60: Photos D. Héron; the Virtues of the Anneda, H. Perrigard, ANC; Dog and sleigh, detail, L. Nicholas in Codex canadiensis, c.1650, BN
61: Excerpt from L'Opinion publique, album souvenir, 1871, CHM; Demonstration in favor of Law 101, ph. A. Trottier, La Presse; Street peddlers, ph. A. Desilets; Snow bank, ph. N. Morant, ACP
62: Road sign, ph. B. Normand, Quebec Ministry of Transportation
63: Farm in St. Ours, C. Jefferys, ANC; Signs LACS, ph. B. Normand, Quebec Ministry of Transportation; Coin-du-Banc, ph. ATR Gaspésie
64: Saint-Maurice, ph. P. Lahoud; Bay-without-a-name, ph. M. Saint-Amour; Road sign in Montagnais, ph. S. Majeau, TQ
65: Manic 2, ph. H-Q
66-67: Ills D. Héron and J.-O. Héron
68: Symbol of Hydro-Quebec, ph. H-Q
68-69: Ills D. Héron and J.-O. Héron
69: Building site equipment, ph. H-Q
70: Manic 5 dam, ph. H-Q
70-71: Ills D. Héron and J.-O. Héron
71: Manic 2 dam, ph. H-Q
72: Ills D. Héron and J.-O. Héron
73: Napoleon Laliberté Bring News to the Village, C. Gagnon, c.1930, CMcMAC
74: Handwoven belt, ph. MCQ; Ice-Skating the European Way, PC-MPC
74-75: Falling over a fence in snow-shoes, R. Rutherford, detail, c.1882, ANC
75: Sketch illustrating rural life in Quebec, detail, F. Back, 1950, priv. coll.; Fur company, PC-MPC; Boots and moccasins, E. Massicotte, BNQ; Canadian farmer, M. Chaplin, c.1839, ANC
76: Men building rafts, detail ph. W. Notman, 1871, MMcHC-AN
76-77: Loggers' Camp in Vermillion, C. Gagnon, 1928–33, CMcMAC; Men on rafts Long-Sault, ANC
77: Le Défrichage, C. Gagnon, detail, c.1929, CMcMAC; 'Driver' on the Saint-Maurice River, ph. Village du Bûcheron, Grandes-Piles; E. B. Eddys's Manufacturing and Lumbering, Hull, P. Q., c.1875–1920, Mortimer & Co., Ottawa, ANC
78: Chairs and benches, photos P. Soulard, MCQ; Wardrobe doors end of the 18th c., ph. B. Merett, MBAM; Dresser, MBAM
79: Grandfather clock by M.-H. Bellerose, MBAM; Seat and dressing, design J.-M. Gauvreau, MBAM; Baby-face by J.-F. Jacques, coll. Omni, ph. L. Noppen
80: Project for a bow for the Royal Edward, F. Baillargé, 1793, ph. P. Altman, MQ; Canoe des Algonquin, L. Nicholas in Codex canadiensis, c.1650, BN
80-81: A General view of Quebec from Point Levy, oil, R. Short, ANC
81: The Duchesse-de-York on the Lachine Rapids, detail ph. W. Notman, c.1908, MMcHC-AN; Ice-breaker on the Saint-Lawrence, ph. P. Quittemelle; Quebec from Point Levy, detail J. Coke Smyth, 1840, ph. Y. Lacombe, CPCC; Ice boat, C. Krieghoff, 1860, ph. J.-G. Kérouac, MQ
82: Old Man carrying wood, H. Julien, 1908, MBAM; Collecting the sap from the maple trees, ph. P. Quittemelle; Cooking outside on the fire, P. Bainbridge, ph. c.1837, ANC
82-83: My Sugar Shack in Saint-Antoine-sur-Richelieu, M. Tanobe, 1986
83: Sugar Times, M. Tanobe, 1977; Sugar shack, ph. P. Quittemelle.
84: Hunting the Canadian moose, ph. P. Bernier, Ministry of Leisure, Hunting and Fishing; Hunting the Canadian moose, M. Chaplin, 1842, ANC; Canadian Moose Hunters, 1642, ANQQ
84-85: Back from the Hunt, H. Sandham, 1877, MBAC
85: Hunting with bow and arrow, ph. La Presse; Trap for small game, ill. D. Héron; Hunting in a floating hide, ph. La Presse
86: Salmon, ill. P. Robin, © Gallimard; American Indian wishing with harpoon, ill. D. Héron; Fishing Camp, ph. Livernois, ANQQ; Hunter on ice, ph. La Presse;
87: Fish, ills P. Robin, © Gallimard; Flies, ill. F. Place, © Gallimard; Two men in a boat in Sept-Îles, © P. Bernier/ Publiphoto; Salmon fishing, ph. La Presse
88: Poster from 1927, ACP; lacrosse players, c.1869, MMcHC-AN
89: Women curling, ph. W. Notman, 1876, MMcHC-AN; Maurice Richard, 1946, ph. Archives du Forum; McGill hockey club, ph. W. Notman, 1902, MMcHC-AN; Snowmobiles, ph. F. Jessua; Patrick Roy with the Stanley Cup, ph. La Presse, 1993
90: The Dance, G. Heriot, ANC
90-91: The Storytellers, C. Gagnon, c.1930, CMcMAC
91: Boatbuilder, Accordion, Sculptor, ph L. Leblanc
92: Show for Saint-Jean-Baptiste Day, ph. R. Picard, 1976, La Presse; La Bolduc, vinyl cover, MG; Beau Dommage, ph. La Presse, 1975
93: Show for Saint-Jean-Baptiste Day, ph. La Presse; À soir on fait pour au monde, CQ; Richard Desjardins, ph. R. Mailloux, La Presse; Diane Dufresne, R.R., La Presse
94: Robert Lepage, ph. D. Winkler, ONF; La La La Human Steps, ph. É. Lock, 1995; Le Dortoir de Gilles Maheu, ph. Y. Dubé, 1989
94-95: Drawing of a choreography, Tangente; Saltimbanco, ph. D. Lavoie, Cirque du Soleil
95: Joe, by Jean-Pierre Perreault, ph. R. Etcheverry; Testimony of the Rose, by Margie Gillis, ph. M. Slobodian; Les Belles-sœurs, 1971, ph. D Kieffer
96: Entre la mer et l'eau douce, directed by Michel Brault, coll. CQ; Pour la suite du monde, directed by Pierre Perreault, ONF; Sigle de l'Office national du film du Canada; Still from Blinkity Blank, directed by Norman McLaren, ph. D. McWilliams, ONF; Semeurs de grains, from the book L'Homme qui plantait des arbres, directed by Frédérick Back, SRC
97: Poster from Le Déclin de l'empire américain, directed by Denys Arcand, coll. CQ; La Vraie Nature de Bernadette, directed by Gilles Carle, coll. CQ; cover TV- Hebdo
98: The Smoker, C. Krieghoff, R.R., ph. P. Altman, MQ
98-99: Ph. É. Guillemot
100: Photos D. Héron, É. Guillemot, F. Rivard
101-108: Sketch illustrating rural life in Quebec, F. Back, 1950, priv. coll.
109: Ill. D. Héron
110-111: Ills D. Héron; Façade of Saint-Louis castle, Chaussegros de Léry, ANF, Aix; Plan of the fortified walls of Quebec City, 1716, Chaussegros de Léry, ANF, Aix; Façade of a private mansion, C. Aubert de La Chesnaye, detail of a cartouche of a map of Quebec, J.-B. Louis Franquelin, 1688, ANF, Paris; Cut-out of a palace in Quebec, Lagner de Mouville, 1715, ANF, Paris
112-113: Ills D. Héron; Palais de l'Intendant, Chaussegros de Léry, ANF, Aix
114-115: Ills D. Héron; View of the Falls of Montmorency with General Haldimand's House, J. Peachey, c.1783, ANC; Place d'Armes, Quebec, detail of a model, c.1807, ANC
116: Ill. D. Héron; Architectural Orders, T. Baillairgé, 1833–4 (Nicolet), Berlinguet, LsTh, ph. L. Noppen; Church reredos, Hôtel-Dieu, 1829, T. Baillairgé, Quebec, ph. L. Noppen
116-117: Ill. D. Héron
117: Winter Morning in Baie-Saint-Paul, C. Gagnon, s.d., MQ; Portrait of T. Baillairgé, 1816, Musée de l'Amérique française, ph. L. Noppen.
118-119: Cathedral of Trois-Rivières, MQ, ill. D. Héron
120-121: Ills J.-B. Héron et D. Lavoie; churches of Holyoke and Saint-Casimir, ph. L. Noppen
122-123: Monstrance, G, Loir, MQ; Ciborium et chalice de F. Ranvoyze, MQ; Ill. D. Héron; altar cloth, C. Huot; Church of Islet-sur-Mer, ph. F. Brault
124: Elevation E. of the Burstall House, 1904, H. & E. Black Staveley, ANQQ
124-125: Ills J. Morin
126-127: Ills J. Morin; Mirabel airport, architect L.-J. Papineau
128-129: Ills J. Morin; Pointe-à-Callière, Montreal Archeology and History Museum of Montreal; Winter garden of the Édifice IBM-Marathon, © S. Poulain; Entrance hall of the Canadian Center for Architecture, ph. R. Paré; Entrance hall of Édifice 1000 de La Gauchetière, Lemay & Ass. Architectes
130: Faubourg-Quebec, ill.

◆ LIST OF ILLUSTRATIONS

P.-L. Dumas Architecte; Nouveau Forum, Lemay & Ass. Architectes; Parliament Hill, Gauthier-Guité-D'Aoust Architectes
131: The Village of Baie-Saint-Paul in Winter, detail, Clarence Gagnon, c.1910, ph. Y. Lacombe, CPCC
132: Percé, Gaspé, coast, Lorne H. Bouchard, c.1960, CPCC
132-133: The Sawyers, Horatio Walker, 1905, ph. Y. Lacombe, CPCC; Country Station, Jean-Paul Lemieux, c.1960, CPCC
134: Le Champ-de-Mars in Winter, William Brymner, 1892, ph. B. Merett, MBAM; The Ice Rink, Dufferin Terrace, detail, R. Pilot, c.1960, CPCC
134-135: Hyman's Tobacco Store, Adrien Hébert, 1937, MBAM
136-137: Zacharie Vincent and his Son Cyprien, Z. Vincent, c.1845, ph. P. Altman, MQ
137: Portrait of François Taillon, Marc-Aurèle de Foy Suzor-Côté, 1921, MBAM; The Woolsey Family, 1809, William Berczy, MBAC
138: Tall Elms, Sainte-Rose, detail, Marc-Aurèle Fortin, 1926, ph. Y. Lacombe, CPCC
138-139: Baie Saint-Paul, Quebec, Arthur Lismer, 1931, CPCC; Thaw, March Evening, Arthabaska, c.1913, Marc-Aurèle de Foy Suzor-Côté, ph. Y. Lacombe, CPCC
140: Légers vestiges d'automne, Paul-Émile Borduas, 1956, CPCC; Non, non, non, non, non, detail, Jean-Paul Riopelle, 1961, ph. Y. Lacombe, CPCC
141-142: Details of a map of a silver mine, Du Chesneau, BN
142: Jacques Cartier, MG
143: Map 'Parte incognita', 1556, ANC; Voltaire, © Gallimard
144: Native American, ANC; Leonard Cohen, ph. J.-F. Bérubé
145: Native Americans building a canoe in La Malbaie, detail, ph. A. Henderson, c.1868, MMcHC-AN; A. Gérin-Lajoie, BNQM
146: Immigrants onboard a steamer on the Saint-Lawrence, after M. Deville in Around the World, 1861, © Gallimard; Jack Kérouac, © Gallimard
147: Boreal Dawn, detail, R. Duguay, c.1934, MQ; Newsboy, c.1905, detail ph. W. Notman, MMcHC-AN; Robert Marteau, ph. J. Sassier, © Gallimard.
148: Ice Islands, Terre-Neuve, P. Huet after M. Deville in Around the World, 1861 © Gallimard.
148-149: Victoria Bridge, S. Russel, 1854, MMcHC; Réjean Ducharme, © Gallimard
149: Hugh McClellan, ph. L. Gareau-Des Bois
150: Michel Tournier, ph. J. Sassier, © Gallimard; Anne Hébert, ph. Kéro
150-151: La Chaudière Falls, details, ANC
152: View of Quebec, detail, Grandsire after M. Deville in Around the World, 1891, © Gallimard; View of the Citadel of Quebec, detail, W. H. Bartlett, c.1840, MQ; H. D. Thoreau, BNQM
153: Pierre Morency, ph. J. Sassier © Gallimard; Jules Verne, © Gallimard
154: Régine Robin, ph. r.r.; Toward the East leaving Drummond Street, Y. L'Espérance © Héritage Montreal
155: Gabrielle Roy, BNQM; Michel Tremblay, Agence Camille Goodwin
156: A. M. Klein's manuscript, ANC; A. M. Klein, ph. Garcia Studios, ANC; Staircase, in The Streets of Montreal, façades and fantasy, © E. Mather, 1977, Tundra Books
157: A Gentleman's Sleigh, C. Krieghoff, s. d., ph. P. Altman, MQ
158: Rue Viger, ph. S. Majeau
158-159: Sliding, Château Frontenac, ph. B. Ostiguy
159: Jazz festival, ph. S. Majeau
160: Pines covered in frost, ph. S. Majeau; Summit of the Chic-Choc Mountains in winter, ph. M. Saint-Amour
161: Fall, ph. S. Majeau; Parc Saguenay, © F. Klus/ Publiphoto; Fall, ph. S. Majeau
162: Pumpkins, ph. F. Rivard; logs, ph. P. Quittemelle; Silica mine, ph. F. Rivard
163: Clocktower, ph. P. Quittemelle
164: Plan of Montreal City, G.-J. Chaussegros de Léry, 1725, ANF, Aix; Maisonneuve stained-glass window, ph. A Tremblay, Photographex; Triptych on the Life of Marguerite Bourgeois, c.1925, S. R.-A. Dufresne, Congrégation Notre-Dame
164-165: Fur traders Montreal, G. Reid, detail, c.1887, ANC
165: Rue Notre-Dame in Montreal, J. Murray, 1850, ANC; The Port of Montreal, detail, R. Sproule, 1830, MMcHC
166: Fogarty & Bros. Boots & Shoes Wholesale, BNQM; The Bank of Montreal on the Place d'Armes, ANQ; Fun on the Slopes in Montreal, J. Duncan, 1856, ANC
167: Edifice Sun Life, c.1932, Collection of Canadian Architecture, U. McGill; Shopkeeper in Montreal, coll. CHM; Beaver of the Montreal Olympic Games, VM-GDA; Stabile by Calder, Terre des Hommes, ph. VM
168: Rue Notre-Dame, J. Murray, 1850, ANC; Notre-Dame organ, Casavant brothers, ph. Photographex
169: Statue commemorating Maisonneuve, detail, BNQM; Sulpicien in the 17th century, H. Beau, ANC; Alfred Building, ANQM
170: Rue Saint-James, ph. VM; Bank of Montreal, ph. B. Ostiguy; Old Law Courts, ph. P. Quittemelle
171: Montreal's coat of arms, VM-GDA; Market day, place Jacques-Cartier, ph. W. Notman, 1890, MMcHC-AN
172: Church of Bon-Secours, detail ph. É. Daudelin
172-173: Bonsecours, ph. P. Quittemelle
173: Vieux-Port, ph. S. Majeau; Port of Montreal, ANQ; Sister Grise of the Montreal's Hospital, H. Beau, ANC
174: Ice castle, ANQQ; Dorchester Square, ANQM
174-175: Dorchester Square, ph. J. Pallasse, VM
175: Marie-Reine-du-Monde, ANQM
176: Hall of the square Ville-Marie, ill. Schwartz, catal. Webb & Knapp, Ltée, 1960; Bibliothèque du métro, ph. A. Trottier, La Presse
176-177: Cross-section of La Gauchetière, ill. BDC, 1990
177: Square Ville-Marie, ill. Schwartz, catal. Webb & Knapp, Ltée, 1960; Christ Church, ph. B. Lenormand; Cathedral promenade, ph. P. Quittemelle
178: Windsor Station, 1923, H. R. Perrigard, ACP; Enlightened Throng, ph. A. Harris
178-179: The University McGill, VM-GDA
179: Campus, U. McGill, ph. A. Harris
180: Montreal building after a fire, ph. W. Notman, c.1888, MMcHC-AN; Fur shop window, ANQM; Le 9e, restaurant, ph. B.Ostiguy
181: Victoria Square, ANQM; Imperial movie theater, ph. B. Ostiguy
182: Mont Royal terrace, ph. Studio Neurdein, Paris, 1907, BNQM
182-183: Wood, L. Muhlstock, c.1942, MBAM
183: Mont Royal, W. H. Napier, 1870, ANC; Montreal, ph. S. Majeau; Cemetery in Côte-des-Neiges, ph. S. Majeau
184: The Diver, bronze, R. Tait McKenzie, 1923, MBAM; James Cross and his Family, ph. W. Notman, MMcHC-AN
185: Royal Victoria's Hospital, ANQM; The Congregation of Notre-Dame, 20th century, H. Beau, ANC; A house in Westmount, ph. S. Majeau
186: Côte-des-Neiges, ANQQ; Oratory Saint-Joseph, ph. S. Majeau
187: Montreal University, reception room at the Royal Academy of Arts of Canada, E. Cormier, 1933, MBAC, © CCA; Outremont Theater, ph. R. Gagnon; © City of Outremont; Maplewood, ph. R. Gagnon, © City of Outremont
188: Ill. D. Héron; The Day of Arrival, CHM, coll. Château Ramezay; Portrait of a Greek man, © N. Tsakalakis/ Publiphoto; Portuguese festival, detail © B.Carrière/Publiphoto; Shopwindow, Chinese quarter, © Zani/ Publiphoto
189: Jean-Talon market, © J.-Y. Derome/Publiphoto; Bagel shop in Outremont © Image actuelle/ Publiphoto
190: Rue du Plateau, ph. C. Guest, © Gallimard; Saint-Enfant-Jésus-du-Mile-End, ph. B. Ostiguy
191: Doors, ph. É. Daudelin; Monday we wash everything, M. Tanobe; Synagogue, rue Bagg, ph. C. Guest, © Gallimard
192: Squirrel, ph. P. Quittemelle; Lafontaine Park, ph. M. Bazinet
193: Staircase (from left to right and from top to bottom), photos A. Harris, M. Bazinet, M. Bazinet, P. Quittemelle, M. Bazinet, M. Bazinet, C. Guest, M. Bazinet
194: Viger hotel and station, ANQM; Jazz festival, ph. FIJM
194-195: Carré Saint-Louis, ph. M. Bazinet
195: Émile Nelligan, ANC; Stained glass, Saint-Sulpice Library, ph. C. Guest © Gallimard
196: Château Dufresne, the smoking room, ph. G. Rivest, Montreal Museum of Decorative Arts; Panoramic tower and

Chinese garden, ph. S. Majeau; Botanical garden, ph. B. Ostiguy;
197: The Woman Farmer, ph. R. Gagnon, VM; Baseball, ph. D. Clark, La Presse
198: Victoria Bridge, ANQQ; Montreal Casino, ph. S. Majeau; Jean Drapeau, ph. A. Desilets;
199: Montreal and the île Sainte-Hélène, P. J. Bainbridge, 1838, ANC; Jacques-Cartier Bridge, ph. P. Quittemelle
200: Lachine Canal, BNQM; Oscar Peterson, Archives Université Concordia; Saint-Henri, ph. W. Notman, 1859, MMcHC-AN
201: Rafting, priv. coll.; A tanner's workshop, ph. ONF, PC-MPC
204: The Richelieu, ph. P. Lahoud; Sorel, J. Lambert, 1810, ANC; Madeleine de Verchères, miniature on Ivory, G. Hayward, ANC
205: Making organs, ph. Casavant brothers; Rouville-Campbell Manor, ph. B. Ostiguy; Hunting Ducks on a Misty Morning, O. Leduc, c. 1924, ph. P. Altman, MQ
206: Saint-Denis, Lower Canada, P. Bainbridge, 1837, ANC
206-207: View of the Back of the Church of Saint-Eustache and breaking up of the rebellious forces, C. Beauclerck, 1840, MMcHC
207: Pied-du-Courant Prison, Montreal, J. Duncan, ANC; The Six Counties Assembly, MQ, ph. P. Altman; Heading in L'Écho du pays, 1833, BNQM; Rebels in Beauharnois, Lower Canada, 1838, K. Ellice, 1838, ANC
208: Apple trees in bloom, ph. F. Rivard; Stone Chinaware Co., St. Johns, P.Q. Haut-Richelieu Regional Museum; View of Chambly, W. Bartlett, ANQQ
209: The Seigneurie of Beauharnois, J. Ellice, ANC; Beauharnois hydroelectric power station, ph. H-Q; Belœil railway station, c.1900, ANQQ
210: Ph. S. Majeau
210-211: Country Landscape near Knowlton, detail, A. Robinson, 1930, MBAM
211: Folker DVII, Brome County Historical Museum; Vineyards in Estrie, ph. P. Quittemelle
212: Snow mobile 1922, J.-A.-Bombardier Museum, Valcourt; Lake Memphrémagog, ph. S. Majeau;

The Coming Storm, detail, A. Edson, 1800, ph. J.-G. Kérouac, MQ
213: Poster, ACP; Saint-Benoît-du-Lac Abbey, ph. S. Majeau
214: Sir John Coape Sherbrooke, Sherbrooke History Society; Round farmhouse, ph. P. Quittemelle
214-215: Sherbrooke, ANQM
215: Bishop University, ph. B. Ostiguy; Statue, St. Mark's Chapel, ph. B. Ostiguy
216: Sketch illustrating rural life in Quebec, F. Back, 1950, priv. coll.; Statue of Father Labelle, ANQQ
217: The River from the North, detail, M. Cullen, MBAM; The Rolland paper company, Saint-Jérôme, 1883, BNQM; Jean-Pierre Masson as Seraphin in Tales of the Highlands, SRC; Affiche, 1939, detail, ALP
218: Saint-Faustin, ph. P. Quittemelle; Rafting down the River Rouge, ph. S. Majeau, TQ; Snowboarding, detail, ph. H. Georgi, Mont-Tremblant
219: 'Bypass' on the road, detail ph. 1903, coll. C. Morissonneau; Lake Sauvage, Saint-Donat, ph. S. Majeau
220: Louis Cyr, CHM; Rural school, ph. B. Ostiguy; Hydravion; Lake Taureau, ph. S. Majeau, TQ
221: Arrow sash, ph. L. Landry, ATR Lanaudière; The Chasse-galerie, H. Julien, 1906, ph. J.-G. Kérouac, MQ; Monte-à-Peine Falls, ph. S. Majeau
222: Jos Montferrand, stamp SCP
222-223: First log raft on the Outaouais River, C. Jeffreys, 1806, ANC
223: Dollard des Ormeaux, stamp, SCP; Chapels of the Calvary in Oka, ills D. Héron; Saint Martin Giving his Coat Away, F. Guernon aka Belleville, c.1796, MQ, ph. P. Altman
224: Château Montebello, ph. S. Majeau; Louis-Joseph Papineau, N. Bourassa, 1858, MQ; Lady Aberdeen, ph. W. Notman, 1895, MMcHC-AN
225: Covered bridge, ph. B. Chalifour, TQ
226: Philémon Wright's Sawmill and Tavern by the Chaudière Waterfalls on the Outaouais River, Lower Canada, 1823, H. DuVernet, ANC
227: Sketch illustrating rural life in Quebec, F. Back, detail, 1950, priv. coll.; Ottawa's Parliament, ph. P. Quittemelle
228: Rideau Canal,

Ottawa, ph. P. Quittemelle; Playing Hockey, in Hull, H. Masson, 1907, MBAC
228-229: Tulip Festival, Ottawa, ph. P. Quittemelle
229: Naskapi powder bag, MCdesC
230: Seaplane, ph. S. Majeau
231: View of Amos, ANQM; The minor, Val-d'Or, ph. R. Jankowski, Aiguebelle Park, photos Mia et Klaus, ATR de l'Abitibi-Témiscamingue; Poster of the International movie festival of Abitibi-Témiscamingue
232: Ill. by F. Desbordes
233: Caribou skins for boot soles, Avataq; The old Way to Hunt the Caribou, H. Napartuk, 1973, Avataq, FCNQ; Traditional Scene, relief on a caribou skin, A. Grégoire; Hunter and caribou II, T. Etook, FCNQ
234: The Bestiary, details c. Pèsemapèo Bordeleau, coll. M. Noël; Aurora Borealis, R. Duguay, c.1934, ph. P. Altman, MQ; Caniapiscau River, Nouveau-Quebec, ph. S. Majeau
235: Pitoune in Grand-Mère, ph. P. Quittemelle
238-239: The Rabaska, AST-R; Ursuline Monastary in Trois-Rivières, ph. Pinsonneault, ANQQ; Logs, ph. F. Rivard.
239: Logs going down the Saint-Maurice, ph. Pinsonneault, ANQQ; Pierre Boucher, AST-R; Maurice Duplessis, ANC
240: Common mergansers, ph. B. Ostiguy; Old Saint-Maurice Forges, L. Cuvelier, 1933, ph. J.-G. Kérouac, MQ; Portage de la rivière cachée, P. Bainbridge, detail, 1837, ANC
241: The Foundry Workers, O. Leduc, ph. F. Brault; Nature reserve of La Mauricie Park, ph. B. Ostiguy; Félix Leclerc, ph. La Presse
242: Beaver Hunting in Canada, I. Taylor, ANC; In the Northern Wilds Trapping Beaver, Currier & Ives, ANC
242-243: A beaver's habitat, Castor Fiber canadensis, ills F. Desbordes
243: Dams, ill. F. Desbordes; Poster, ANC
244: Nicolet seminary, ANQQ
244-245: Winter Landscape, 1909, M.-A. de Foy Suzor-Coté, MBAC
245: Common merganser, J.-J. Audubon, ANC; Voltigeurs, G. Embleton, PC-MPC.
246: Victorian residences, photos B. Ostiguy; Statue

of Wilfrid Laurier, A. Laliberté, Musée Laurier
247: Detail of the Laurentian Flora, brother Marie-Victorin, BNQM; Asbestos strike, 1949, ph. La Presse
248: Yamachiche, ph. F. Rivard; Hamelin house, ph. F. Rivard; The presbytery's stonework 'refrigerator', Yamachiche, ph. F. Rivard
248-249: Saint-Lawrence River, P. Bainbrigge, c.1838, ANC
249: Wintertime fishing, R.R.
250: Regional road, Neuville, ANQM; Deschambault presbytery, ph. F. Rivard; Baldaquin, church of Saint-François-de-Sales, ph. F. Brault
251: Three-masted boat on the Saint-Lawrence River Quebec, E. W. Sewell, 1870, MBAM
252: Quebec (map-plan), anonymous, ANQQ; Monument to Wolfe and Montcalm, M. Chaplin, ANC
254: Abitation de Quebecq, plan by Champlain, ANC; Samuel de Champlain, A. Laliberté, c.1940, MMcHC; Notre-Dame-des-Victoires, ph. C. Huot; Anse-des-mères, detail, M. Cullen, 1904, MQ
255: Portrait of François Baillairgé, 1816, Museum of French America, ph. L. Noppen; Church of Notre-Dame-des-Victoires, ph. C. Huot
256: Goldilocks and the Three Bears, Auto Portrait, photos P. Soulard, MCQ
256-257: Ill. D. Héron
257: 1930s dress and cloche, photos A. Vézina, MCQ; cupboard and Danse Traction group, photos P. Soulard, MCQ
258: Jolliet, M.-A. de Foy Suzor-Coté, MQ; Street with funicular, coll. Y. Beauregard; Casse-Cou Steps, ph. J. Duncan, c.1890, ph. W. Notman, MMcHC-AN; Canoe races, ph. P. Quittemelle
259: Quebec as seen from the Saint-Lawrence River, E. Sewell, 1870, ANC; Quebec, the river in winter, ph. B. Ostiguy; A view of the Intendant's Palace, R. Short, c.1759, ANC
260: Frontenac on the Way to Cataraqui, J. Derinzy, ANC; Stained glass of the Château Frontenac, photos B. Ostiguy; Palm Court, Château Frontenac, photos B. Ostiguy; Details of the Château Frontenac, ph. B. Ostiguy
260-261: Poster, 1924, detail, ACP

261: Quebec conference, 1943, ph. ONF, ANC; Récollet, a Defunct Order, H. Beau, ANC;
262: Gaspard-Joseph Chaussegros de Léry (father), anonymous, 1750, ph. J.-G. Kérouac, MQ
262-263: The Citadel, ph. P. Lahoud
263: Gate of the Citadel, J. Cockburn, c.1828, MQ; St. Louis Gate, ANC; The Great Battery, ph. W. Notman, ANQQ
264: The Upper Town, ph. B. Ostiguy; The City Walls, Quebec, R. Pilot, 1949, MBAM; The Ice Palace in 1896, ph. J. Livernois, ANQQ
265: The Upper Town, detail ph. B. Ostiguy; Baldaquin of the basilica Notre-Dame, ph. B. Ostiguy; Monument for Mgr Laval, detail, ph. B. Ostiguy
266: Aux Anciens Canadiens, detail, ph. C. Huot; View of a Square in the Upper Town in Quebec, toward Cavalier-du- Moulin, anonymous, ANQQ; Cavalier-du-Moulin Park, ph. B. Ostiguy
267: Our House, M. Chaplin, c.1839, ANC; Gavazzi Riot, in L'Opinion publique, BNQM; Prison, rue Saint-Stanislas, J. Cockburn, c.1830, ANC
268: The Vocation of Catherine de Saint-Augustin, A. Pellan, detail, 1943, Augustine Monastery of Quebec City's Hôtel-Dieu; Ursuline Nuns Playing Croquet, 1867, ph. Livernois & Bienvenu, coll. Ursulines Monastery in Quebec; Rue Donnacona, ph. B. Ostiguy
269: Eternal Father, wood sculpture, P.-N. Levasseur, c.1768, ph. P. Altman, MQ; The post-office dog, coll. Y. Beauregard; The post-office, ph. B. Ostiguy
270: Quebec, Saint-Jean-Baptiste district, ph. B. Ostiguy; Capitole Theater, ph. B. Ostiguy; Parliament, ph. L.-A. Couturier
270-271: The Fire of Faubourg Saint-Jean as Seen from the West, J. Légaré, detail, c.1845, Art Gallery of Ontario
271: Saint Michael Defeating the Dragon, L. de Latour, c.1705, ph. P. Altman, MQ; Election of the New Commander of the Hurons, H. Thielcke, 1841, MQ
272-273: Map, Saintonge Vision
274: Sainte-Marie, ph. B. Ostiguy; Ice bridge, coll. Y. Beauregard
275: A. Desjardins, SCP; Vachon cakes, photos

P. Groulx
276: Château-Richer, ANQQ; Montmorency Falls, ph. S. Majeau
276-277: Sainte-Pétronille, M. Chaplin, c.1839, ANC
277: The Morning Milk, H. Walker, 1925, MQ
278: Capital of the Sainte-Anne-de-Beaupré Basilica, detail ph. Kedl; The interior of the basilica, ph. Kedl; The basilica on fire, 1922, coll. Y. Beauregard
278-279: Sainte-Anne de Beaupré, J. Morrice, 1897, MBAM
279: Ex-voto to those who drowned in Lévis, 1754, ph. Kedl; Souvenir of pilgrimage, coll. Y. Beauregard; Religious image, coll. J.-M. Lebel; Grande neuvaine, coll. J.-M. Lebel
280: Village of Saint-Joachim, ph. F. Rivard; The mountain range, ph. ATR of Charlevoix
280-281: Saint-Hilarion, A. Y. Jackson, c.1930, ph. Y. Lacombe, CPCC
281: Schooner in Saint-Joseph-de-la-Rive, ph. F. Rivard
282: Photos by J.-J. Blanchon, F. Rivard
282-283: Ills by F. Desbordes, A. Larousse, C. Felloni
283: Ph. N. David
284: Rodolphe Forget, Musée de Charlevoix
284-285: Les Éboulements, ph. F. Rivard
285: Manoir Richelieu, ph. ATR Charlevoix; William H. Taft and his grandchildren, Musée de Charlevoix
286: Barrows goldeneye (Bucephalaislandica), and fox sparrow (Passerella iliaca), ills S. Nicolle
286-287: Hautes-Gorges, ph. ATR Charlevoix
287: Moose, ph. S. Majeau; Blackpoll warbler (Dendroica stiata), ill. S. Nicolle; Hautes-Gorges, ph. ATR Charlevoix
288: Grosse-Île, J. Peachey, ANC; Saint-Michel-de-Bellechasse, ph. P. Lahoud;
289: White goose, ph. F. Rivard; Woman Farmer, J. Bourgault, Maison Musée Médard Bourgault, priv. coll.; Capitaine Joseph-Elzéard Bernier, Musée maritime Bernier; Philippe Aubert de Gaspé, SCP
290: Mill, seigneurie des Aulnaies, ph. B. Ostiguy; Bridge, Rivière-Ouelle, ph. P. Quittemelle; Experimental farm, Institut techno-agricole du Bas-Saint-Laurent, ph. S. Majeau

290-291: Ph. F. Rivard
291: Kamouraska, ph. S. Majeau; Poster, P. Ewart, 1942, ACP
292: Damson plum, ill. Bouliane, coll. P.-L. Martin; L'île Verte, ph. S. Majeau; Le Bic, ph. P. Lahoud
293: Seagull's eggs on the île-du-Pot-à-l'Eau-de-Vie, B. Ostiguy; Victor-Lévy Beaulieu, ph. J. Lambert; Hunting Seals in Trois-Pistoles, Jos. C. Morency, Musée du Bas-Saint-Laurent
294-295: The River with Great Waters, F. Back, © Gallimard
296: Empress of Ireland, 1910, Musée de la mer de Pointe-au-Père; Blue poppy in Métis, ph. B. Ostiguy; Métis gardens, ph. B. Ostiguy
297: Romantic Quebec, Gaspé peninsula, MG
298: Medallion Jacques Cartier, MG; Percé, ph. P. Quittemelle
299: Percé, ph. P. Quittemelle; Fisherman, ANQM
300: Plan of the barachois of Paspébiac, 1787, MCC; Caribou, ill. A. Deniau; White-tailed deer, ph. M. Saint-Amour
301: Trail in the Chic-Choc Mountains, ph. C. Dubois; Chic-Choc Mountains, ph. P. Lahoud; Hang-gliders, ph. S. Majeau, TQ
302: John Leboutillier, MG; Shipwreck, officier de l'Escarde Verte, ANQQ; Cloridorme, ph. P. Rastoul
303: Jacques Cartier Offering Mirrors to Indians, MG; Gaspésian Fishermen at Work, ANQM. Rivière-au-Renard, ph. P. Quitemelle
304: Black guillemot, ph. M. Saint-Amour
304-305: Ill. A. Larousse
305: Kittiwake, ph. M. Saint-Amour; Black bear, ph. M. Saint-Amour; Forillon National Park, ph. P. Quittemelle; Common seal, ph. M. Saint-Amour
306: Gannets, ill. A. Larousse; A View of the Pierced Island, ANQQ; Percé Rock, ph. P. Quittemelle
307: Les Maringouins, Mme Bolduc, musical score, MG; Percé region, Ph. © P.G. Adam/ Publiphoto
308: Seal from the Charles Robin Fishing Company, MG; Deportation of Acadians, ANC; Parc Mighasha, © F. Klus/ Publiphoto
308-309: Le Machault ship, ill., Centre d'interprétation de la Bataille-de-la-Ristigouche
309: René Lévesque, ph. Goupil, 1976, La Presse;

Salmon fishing on the Grande-Cascapédia, © F. Klus/Publiphoto; Covered bridge, rivière Matapédia, © P. Adam/ Publiphoto
310-311: Stern, ill. © Gallimard; Piping glover ill. S. Nicolle
310-311: Îles-de-la-Madeleine, detail ill. A. Larousse; Îles-de-la-Madeleine, ill. D. Héron
311: Grande Entrée island, ph. P. Quittemelle; Greenland seal (Pagophilus groenlandicus), ill. F. Desbordes; Boudreau island, Grande Entrée island, ph. P. Quittemelle
312: Belle-Anse, ph. P. Quittemelle; Whale, 1890, MG
312-313: Dune-du-Sud, ph. P. Quittemelle
313: Transporting hay, near Bassin, and baraque, photos coll. P. Rastoul, GRHQR; The Priest's Tornado, J.-C. Dupont, 1984
314: Mackerel processing (1910), Musée de la mer; Sandcastle, ph. S. Majeau
315: Houses, photos P. Quittemelle; Presbytery in Bassin, ph. P. Rastoul
316: Port d'Étang-du-Nord, ph. P. Quittemelle; Eskimo curlew, J.-J. Audubon, 1838, ANC; Fisherman with lobster, ph. P. Rastoul
317: Blueberries, ph. S. Majeau, TQ
318: Maps, Chicoutimi River, BN
319: The Saguenay, ph. F. Rivard; Burning Logs, C. Gagnon, c.1930, CMcMAC
320: Val-Jalbert, ph. P. Lahoud; Saint-Félicien Zoological garden, detail ph. É. Daudelin; Perron cheesemakers, Saint-Prime, beginning of 20th c., detail ph. coll. SHS
321: Blueberries, detail ph. É. Daudelin; Protecting the Herd, C. Gagnon, c.1930, CMcMAC
322: Chicoutimi, 1871, SHS; The Aluminerie Alcan in Jonquière, ph. P. Lahoud; William Price, SHS; Peter McLoed II, SHS
322-323: Sliding doors of the Arthur-Villeneuve house, Musée du Saguenay Lac-Saint-Jean
323: Julien-Édouard-Alfred Dubuc, coll. Pulperie de Chicoutimi; The old pulp mill, coll. Pulperie de Chicoutimi
324: The big crow, ill. © Gallimard; Saint-Basile-de-Tableau, ph. M. Savard
324-325: Belugas, ph. ATR Charlevoix; Baie Trinité, ph. J. Desbiens
325: Saguenay Fjord,

ill. A. Larousse
326: 'White fishing' on the Saguenay in La Baie, ph. P. Quittemelle; Thousand dollar bill, ph. D. Héron; Notre-Dame-du-Saguenay, detail, ph. SHS
327: Sainte-Marguerite River, Port Cartier, ph. S. Majeau.
328: Chapel in Tadoussac , ph. P. Quittemelle.
328-329: Tadoussac, ph. F. Rivard.
329: The Chauvin house, Tadoussac, ph. P. Quittemelle; Carrying the Wood, A. Michel
330: Pointe-des-Monts lighthouse, ph. S. Majeau; Puffins, J.-J. Audubon, 1838, ANC; Monolith, Grande-Île, Mingan, ph. M. St-Amour
331: Chicago Tribune, ph. P. Groulx; Manic 5 dam, ph. S. Majeau; Monolith Le Sorcier, ph. M. St-Amour
332: Bald eagle, ph. G. Delisle; Shipwreck in Anticosti, BNQM
332-333: The waterfall stream, ph. G. Delisle; La Vauréal waterfall, ph. G. Delisle
333: Calypso orchid, ph. G. Delisle; Roe deer, ph. S. Majeau.
334: Gilles Vigneault, ph. A Desilets; Flowers, ill. © Gallimard; Guillemots, J.-J. Audubon, 1838, ANC
335: Nanook of the North, R. Flaherty, coll. CQ
336: Inuk met on Baffin Island across from Nunavik, J. White, c.1589, British Museum; The Arrival in Hudson Bay, Musée Stewart
337: The Old Carpet, J. Talirunili, AVATAQ, FCNQ; Mission in Ivujivik, coll. AVATAQ; Northern sun, ph. P. Quittemelle; Woman of Nouveau-Quebec, ph. Mia & Klaus, TQ
338: Inuit family house, Nunavik, ph. B. Saladin d'Anglure, 1966
338-339: Summer journey inside the land at Puvirnituq, ph. B. Saladin d'Anglure, 1971
339: Umiaq arriving in Wakeham Bay, ph. P. A. Low, 1897, coll. B. Saladin d'Anglure; Transformation, T. Paningna, Avataq, FCNQ; Woman Fishing, D. K Tukala, Avataq, FCNQ
340: Woman playing drums, soapstone, N. Iyaituk d'Ivujivik, 1979
340-341: Transformation of Expressionist Animals, T. Paningna, AVATAQ, FCNQ
341: Study/Composition, L. Meeko, Avataq, FCNQ; Study/Composition, H. Napartuk, Avataq, FCNQ; Leaf River Eskimos With Flags, ph. McInnis, c.1931

342: Reconstitution of rupestrian art, D. Héron; Sculptor on soapstone in Kanqiqsujuaq, ph. B. Saladin d'Anglure, 1965
342-343: Traditional tools, ph. FCNQ
343: After Carrying Man the Giant dozes Off, L. Tukalak/C. Qumaluk, FCNQ; Mother with the First Goose Killed by Her Son, 1991, soapstone, M. Iyaituk of Ivujivik, FCNQ; Mother and Child, soapstone, J. Inukpuk d'Inoucdjouac, 1982, FCNQ
344: Plane, ph. Makivik; Inuk repairing his snow-mobile, soapstone, A. Niaqu of Povungnituk, 1988
345: Quebec's flag, ill. D. Héron
346: Saint-Irénée, DR; Montreal, ph. F. Rivard
347: Forillon Park, ph. P. Quittemelle; Saint-Fidèle, Charlevoix, DR
348: Traversier, Cap-aux-Meules, ph. P. Quittemelle; La Grande airport, ph. P. Quittemelle
350: Quebec, ph. B. Ostiguy
351: Seaplane, ph. S. Majeau, TQ; Hare, ph. M. Saint-Amour
352: House in Charlevoix, ph. F. Rivard; Chalet, ph. D. Héron
353: House on Île d'Orléans, ph. S. Mastelinck; Îles Manitounuk, ph. P. Quittemelle
354: Husky, ph. P. Quittemelle; Goose, ph. M. Saint-Amour
355: Rorqual, ph. P. Quittemelle; Original, ph. M. Saint-Amour
356: Rafting, ph. P. Quittemelle; Snow-shoes in the snow, ph. F. Rivard
357: The Hautes-Gorge, ph. F. Rivard; Crossing the Hautes-Gorges, ph. F. Rivard
360: Hôtel La Muse, R.R.
361: Manoir Hovey, ph. S. Majeau; Manoir Richelieu, ph. ATR Charlevoix
366: Château Montebello, © Château Montebello
367: Château Frontenac (detail), ph. B. Ostiguy

We wish to thank the following people for their invaluable help:
Nathalie Thibault
Pierre Lahoud
Brigitte Ostiguy
Mario Robert
Marie-Claude Saia
Carole Ritchot
Michel Godin
Richard Dubé
Christine Dubois
Yves Beauregard
Roanne Mohktar

Acknowledgments

Grateful acknowledgment is made to the University of Toronto Press Incorporated for permission to reprint an excerpt from "The Mountain" from THE COMPLETE POEMS by A. M. Klein. Reprinted by permission of the University of Toronto Press Incorporated.

We have been unable to locate the copyright holders and authors of certain images and documents before going to press. We will, however, acknowledge these sources in the next editions if and when we are made aware of their identity.

◆ THEMATIC INDEX

BARS AND NIGHTCLUBS

Beaver Tails (Montreal) 364
Collection & Bar 56 (Ottawa), 366
Cosmos Café (Quebec City), 368
Java U (Montreal), 364
L'Inox (Quebec City), 368
Moozoo (Montreal), 364
Newtown (Montreal) 364
Voodoo Grill (Quebec City), 368

HOTELS

Auberge Château du Lac (Magog), 360
Auberge Chez Denis à François (Havre Aubert),361
Auberge de la Petite Baie (Havre-aux-Maisons), 361
Auberge de l'Orpailleur (Abitibi-Témiscamingue), 358
Auberge des 21 (La Baie), 369
Auberge du Mange-Grenouille (Le Bic), 359
Auberge du Marché (Ottawa), 366
Auberge du Portage (Lower Saint Lawrence), 358
Auberge Lamy (Métabetchoauan), 369
Auberge Lakeview Inn (Knowlton), 359
Auberge le Florès (Grand-mère), 359
Auberge Le Lupin (Mont-Tremblant), 361
Auberge-Gîte du Mont-Albert (Sainte-Anne-des-Monts), 360
Auberge La Camarine (Beaupré) 369
Auberge les Trois Soeurs (Percé), 360
Auberge Saint-Antoine (Quebec City), 367
Capitainerie du Passant (Grandes-Piles), 359
Château et Hotel Versailles (Montreal), 363
Château Frontenac (Quebec City), 368
Château Madelinot (Cap-aux-Meules), 360
Château Mont Sainte-

Anne (Beaupré), 369
Fairmont Château Laurier (Ottawa), 366
Fairmont le Château Montebello (Montebello), 365
Gîte à Claudia (Montérégie), 361
Gîte du Phare de Pointe-des-Monts (pointe-des-Monts), 361
Gîte Lamaque (Abitibi-Témiscamingue), 358
Hotel Beluga (Tadoussac), 361
Hotel Clarendon (Quebec City), 368
Hôtel-club Tremblant (Mont-Tremblant), 361
Hotel Dominion 1912 (Quebec City), 367
Hotellerie Bardsville (Sacré-Coeur), 369
Ice Hotel Quebec-Canada Inc. (Quebec City), 367
La Maison Ducharme (Chambly), 361
La Maison Otis (Baie-St-Paul), 359
Le Château Blanc (Gaspésie), 360
Le German (Montreal), 363
Le Manoir d'Auteuil (Quebec City), 367
Le Rosier (Lévis), 358
Le Saint Sulpice (Montreal), 363
Les Passants de Sans-Soucy (Montreal), 363
Les Trois Érables (Wakefield), 366
Manoir des Érables (Lévis), 358
Manoir Richelieu (La Malbaie), 359
Petite Auberge Les Bons Matins (Montreal), 363
Ritz-Carlton (Montreal), 363
XIXe Siècle (Montreal), 363

PLACES

Alma 321
Amos 230
Amqui 309
Angliers 231
Anse-Pleureuse 301
Aylmer 229
Baie-Comeau 330
Baie-du-Febvre 244
Baie-Saint-Paul 280

Batiscan 249
Beaumont 288
Belœil 205
Bergeronnes 329
Berthierville 221
Blanc-Sablon 334
Bonsecours 211
Bromont 210
Bytown (Ottawa) 226
Cacouna 292
Cap-aux-Meules 313
Cap-de-Bon-Désir 329
Cap-de-la-Madeleine 249
Cap-des-Rosiers 302
Cap-Santé 250
Carillon 223
Causapscal 309
Chambly 208
Chandler 307
Château-Richer 280
Chicoutimi 322
Chissasibi 234
Coteau-du-Lac 209
Cowansville 211
Deschambault 250
Dolbeau 320
Donnacona 250
Drummondville 245
Gaspé 303
Gatineau 224
Granby 210
Grand-Mère 241
Grande Entrée 316
Grand-Pabos 307
Grosse-Île 316
Harrington Harbour 334
Havre-Aubert 314
Havre-Saint-Pierre 331
Hull 226, 228
Inverness 247
Joliette 220
Jonquière 124, 322
Kamouraska 291
Kingsey Falls 246
Knowlton 211
L'Acadie 209
Lachine 201
L'Étang-du-Nord 313
L'Île-aux-Grues 289
L'Islet-sur-Mer 289
La Malbaie 285
Lac-Brome 211
La Martre 301
La Pocatière 290
La Tuque 241
Le Bic 293
Lennoxville 215
Les Éboulements 284
Lévis 274
Longue-Pointe 331
Louiseville 248
Magog-Orford 212
Malartic 230

Manawan 220
Manicouagan 329
Mashteuiatsh 320
Maskinongé 248
Matagami 234
Matane 299
Matapédia 309
Métabetchouane 319
Mingan 331
Montebello 224
Montmagny 91, 288
Montréal 164-201
Mont-Saint-Hilaire 205
Mont-Saint-Pierre 301
Murdochville 302
Natashquan 334
Neuville 250
Newport 307
New Richmond 308
Nicolet 244
North Hatley 214
Odanak 245
Oka 223
Ottawa 227
Outremont 186
Paspébiac 308
Percé 306
Péribonka 321
Petite-Rivière-Saint-François 280
Plaisance 224
Plessisville 247
Pointe-au-Pic 284
Pointe-Basse 316
Pointe-des-Monts 331
Pointe-du-Lac 249
Pont-Rouge 250
Port-au-Saumon 287
Portneuf 250
Quebec 252-271
Radisson 234
Rawdon 220
Richmond 246
Rimouski 296
Rivière Chaudière 274
Rivière-du-Loup 292
Rivière-Ouelle 291
Rouyn-Noranda 231
Saint-André-de-Kamouraska 291
Saint-Denis 205, 291
Sainte-Adèle 218
Sainte-Agathe-des-Monts 218
Sainte-Anne-de-la-Pérade 249
Sainte-Anne-des-Monts 300
Sainte-Famille 277
Sainte-Luce 296
Saint-Elzéar 308
Sainte-Marie 274
Sainte-Pétronille 277
Sainte-Scholastique 223

Saint-Eustache 222
Saint-Fidèle 285
Saint-Gabriel-de-Brandon 220
Saint-Georges 275
Saint-Grégoire 244
Saint-Irénée 284
Saint-Jean 277
Saint-Jean-de-Matha 220
Saint-Jean-des-Piles 241
Saint-Jean-Port-Joli 289
Saint-Jean-sur-Richelieu 208
Saint-Jérôme 216
Saint-Joachim 280
Saint-Joseph-de-Beauce 275
Saint-Joseph-de-la-Rive 281
Saint-Jovite 218
Saint-Laurent 277
Saint-Michel-de-Bellechasse 288
Saint-Michel-des-Saints 220
Saint-Pacôme 290
Saint-Paul-de-l'Île-aux-Noix 209
Saint-Pierre 277
Saint-Raphaël 91
Saint Sauveur 218
Saint-Siméon 285
Saint-Zénon 219
Sayabec 309
Sept-Îles 330
Shawinigan 240
Sherbrooke 214
Sillery 271
Sorel 204
Tadoussac 328
Témiscaming 231
Terrebonne 221
Thetford Mines 247
Tourelle 301
Trois-Pistoles 293
Trois-Rivières 238
Val-Brillant 309
Valcourt 212
Val-d'Or 230
Val-Jalbert 320
Victoriaville 246
Ville-Marie 231
Warwick 246
Wendake 271
Westmount 182, 185
Yamachiche 248

RESTAURANTS

À la maison de Serge Bruyère (Quebec City) 366
Aux Anciens Canadiens (Quebec City) 367
Binerie Mont-Royal (Montreal) 362
Buffet de l'antiquaire (Quebec City) 366
Café du Monde (Quebec City) 367
Café Henri Berger (Hull), 365
Cochon Dingue (Quebec City) 367
Domus Café (Ottawa), 365
Eduardo's (Montreal), 362
L'Académie (Montreal), 362
Maison Gastronomique Serge Bruyère (Quebec City), 366
Le Marie-Clarisse (Quebec City), 367
Le Petit Extra (Montreal) 362
St-Viateur Bagel Shop and Café (Montreal), 362
Schwartz (Montreal) 362
Toqué (Montreal) 362
Vittoria Trattoria (Ottawa), 365

PEOPLE

Aberdeen, Lady 224
Abraham-Martin 258
Aiguillon, Duchess of 268
Allan, Sir Hugh 185
André, brother 186
Arcand, Denys 97
Archibald, John S. 285
Arnold, Matthew 151
Aubert de Gaspé, Philippe 266, 289
Aubert de La Chesnaye, Charles 111
Audubon, J.-J. 334
Back, Frédéric 97
Bagg, brothers 187
Baillairgé, Charles 255, 264, 265
Baillairgé, François 239, 250, 255, 265, 267, 277, 280
Baillairgé, Jean 255, 265
Baillairgé, Thomas 117, 244, 255, 265, 268, 280
Baillif, Claude 255
Barrott 169
Bartlett, William Henry 215
Beaugrand, Honoré 221
Beaugrand Champagne, Aristide 190
Beaulieu, Victor-Lévy 293
Bédard, Samuel 321
Beecher, Henry Ward 152
Bellerose, Michel 79
Bellot, dom Paul 125, 186, 213
Berczy, Williem von Moll 137
Berlinguet, François-Xavier 267
Bernier, Joseph-Elzéar 289
Bigot, François 266
Blackader 169
Bolduc, Mary Travers known as la 92, 307
Bombardier, Joseph-Armand 89, 212
Bonet, Jordi 205
Borduas, Paul-Émile 140, 205
Bouchard, Lorne 133
Boucher, Pierre 239
Bourassa, Napoléon 195
Bourgault, Médard 289
Bourgeau, Victor 118, 120, 169
Bourgeoys, Marguerite 173, 185, 201
Bourget, Mgr Ignace 55, 120, 175
Bouthilier, Louis-Tancrède 187
Brassard, father 220
Brault, Michel 96
Briand, Mgr Jean-Olivier 265
Briffa, Emmanuel 187
Brooke, Rupert 152
Brooke, Francis 153-4
Brunet, Émile 175
Brymner, William 135
Buade, Louis de 260
Bujold, Geneviève 97
By, Lieutenant-Colonel 226
Calvet, Pierre du 172
Campbell, Thomas Edmund 205
Campbell-Scott, Duncan 144
Canard, Pierre Renaud, known as 255
Cardinal, Douglas 229
Carle, Gilles 97
Carlu, Jacques 180
Carlu, Natacha 180
Caron, Louis 121, 246
Carr, Emily 228
Cartier, Jacques 38, 47, 142, 164, 252, 255, 276, 298, 303, 307, 318, 332
Casavant, Joseph 205
Catherine de Saint-Augustin 268
Cavelier de La Salle, Robert 201
Chaboulié, Charles 244
Chambly, Jacques de 208
Champlain, Samuel de 38, 46, 142 216, 252, 254, 260, 265, 276, 285, 329
Chapais, Jean-Charles 291
Charlebois, Robert 92
Charlevoix, François-Xavier 276
Charon, brothers 173
Chaussegros de Léry, Gaspard-Joseph 110, 262
Chauveau, Pierre-J.-O. 261
Chauvin de Tonnetuit, Pierre 328
Chenard de La Giraudais, Admiral 309
Chevalier, Jean-Baptiste 255
Chomedey de Maisonneuve, Paul 164
Churchill, Winston 261
Coffin, Isaac 312
Cohen, Leonard 53, 145, 191
Comeau, Napoléon-Alexandre 330
Conan, Laure 285
Cormier, Ernest 124, 170, 185
Courtens, A. 124
Cox, Palmer 210
Cullen, Maurice 254
Dawson, William 179
Demers, brother Louis 244
Demers, Jérôme 244
Denis, Nicolas 312
Deschamps, Yvon 92
Desjardins, Abbot Philippe-Jean-Louis 268
Desjardins, Alphonse 275
Desjardins, Richard 93
Desrochers, Urbain Brien known as 244
Dickens, Charles 149
Dion, Céline 93
Dollard des Ormeaux, Adam 223
Dor, Georges 92, 330
Doublet de Honfleur 312
Drapeau, Jean 198
Drummond, Lord 245
Dubé, Marcel 94
Dubuc, Julien-Édouard-Alfred 323
Dufferin, Lord 263

◆ THEMATIC INDEX

Dufort, Cajetan 197
Dufresne, Marius 196
Duguay, Rodolphe 214
Duplessis, Maurice 42, 239
Durham, Lord 40
Durnford, Elias Walker 263
Émond, Pierre 265
Empain, Baron 124
Fauvel, John 299
Ferland, Jean-Pierre 92
Ferron, family 248
Fitzbach, Marie 269
Footner, William 172
Forestier, Louise 93
Forget, Louis-Joseph 184
Forget, Sir Rodolphe 184, 284
Fornel, Louis 254
Fortin, Marc-Aurèle 139, 280
Fraser, Malcom 285
Frontenac, Louis de Buade, Count of 260
Fuller, R. B. 126
Gagnon, Clarence 133, 280
Gauldrée-Boilleau, Charles 284
Gaulle, Charles de 171
Gauthier, Claude 92
Gauvreau, Jean-Marie 79
Gavazzi, Alessandro 267
Gélinas, Gratien 94
Genest, Marie-Anne 277
George III 261
Gérin, Léon 284
Gérin-Lajoie, Antoine 146, 210
Gillis, Margie 95
Globensky, Marie-Louise 222
Globensky, Maximilien 222
Godin, Sévère 187
Granby, Marquis of 210
Grandbois, Alain 261
Gréber, Jacques 179
Gridley, Richard 314
Grignon, Claude-Henri 217
Guèvremont, Germaine 204
Haldimand, Gouverneur 114
Hanganu, Dan 173
Hébert, Adrien 135
Hébert, Anne 150
Hébert, Louis 208, 269
Hébert, Louis-Philippe 269
Hébert, Philippe 169, 175, 180, 247

Hémon, Louis 321
Héroux, family 248
Hill, George W. 175
Hitchcock, Alfred 261
Hocdeman, Co 97
Holgate, Edwin 135
Hopkins, Alfred 153
Houston, James A. 342
Hudson, Henry 336
Huot, Charles 123
Hyatt, Gilbert 214
Iberville, Captain of 336
Jackson, Alexander Young 139, 280
Jalbert, Damase 320
James, Henry 151
Jobin, Louis 275, 326
Joliette, Barthélemy 219
Jolliet, Louis 258, 332
Julien, Pauline 92
Jutra, Claude 97
Kapesh, An Antane 145
Kent, Duke of 266
Kipling, Rudyard 151
Kirby, William 269
Kirke, brothers 265
Klein, Abraham 147
Labelle, father 216, 218
La Chesnaye, Charles-Aubert de 292
Lafleur, Guy 89
La Joué, François de 111
Laliberté, Alfred 197, 217, 246, 247
Lampman, Archibald 155
Lanaudière, Charlotte de 219
Lanctôt, Micheline 97
Lanouguère, Thomas de 249
La Pérade, Pierre-Thomas Tarieu de 249
Larochellière, Luc de 93
Lartigue, Mgr 55
Laure, Carole 97
Laurier, Sir Wilfrid 175, 246
Laval, Mgr de 51, 265, 269, 277, 278
Laviolette, seigneur de 238
LeBer, Jacques 201
Leblond, Jean-Jacques Bloem known as 244
LeBoutillier, John 299, 302
Leclerc, Félix 92, 241, 277
Leduc, Ozias 205, 241
Leloup, Jean 93
Lemieux, Jean-Paul 133, 280
LeMoyne, Charles 201
Lepage, Robert 94, 258

Lesage, Jean 42, 56
Levasseur, Jean-Noël 268
Levasseur, Pierre-Noël 269
Léveillée, Claude 92
Lévesque, Raymond 92
Lévesque, René 42, 61, 309
Lévis, Chevalier François-Gaston de 274
Lismer, Arthur 139
Livernois, family 264
Lock, Édouard 94
Lorne, Marquis of 258
Macdonald, Sir John A. 175
Mackenzie King, William Lyon 229
MacPherson LeMoine, James 252
Mair, Charels 154
Maloney, John 331
Manners, John 210
Marchand, Jean-Omer 200
Marie-Victorin, Conrad Kirouac, known as brother 196, 247, 331
Marquette, Jacques 258
Marteau, Robert 147
Masson, Jean-Pierre 217
Mauvide, Jean 277
Maxwell, Edward 180
Maxwell, brothers 184, 185
McCormick, Robert 330
McGill, James 53, 179
McKim, Mead & White 170
McLaren, Norman 97
McLeod, Peter 323
Méloizes, Angélique de 266
Menier, Henri 332
Meredith, Henry 185
Messervier, family 91
Michel, André 330
Mies van der Rohe, Ludwig 127, 199
Miller, Alfred 302
Molson, John 81
Monk, James 185
Montcalm, Marquis of 60, 252, 253
Montferrand, Jos 222
Montgomery, General 171
Montmorency, Charles, Duke of 276
Moore, Henry 178
Morel, father Thomas 279
Morgan, Henry 180
Mountain, Jacob 261

Murdoch, James Y. 302
Murray, James 285
Nairne, John 285
Nelligan, Émile 292
Nelson, Admiral 171
Nincheri, Guido 187, 190, 196, 239
Notman, William 180
O'Bready, Mgr 210
O'Donnell, James 169
O'Hara, Felix 303
Obumsawin, Alanis 59
Olmsted, Frederick Law 182
Ostell, John 169, 173
Painter, Walter S. 270
Papineau, family 224
Papineau, Louis-Joseph 40, 222, 224
Pascaud, brothers 312
Payette, Eugène 195
Peachy, J.-F. 120, 270
Péan, madame de 266
Pei, I. M. 126, 178
Pelletier, Marie-Denise 93
Perrault, Pierre 96
Perreault, Jean-Pierre 95
Peterson, Oscar 53, 194, 200
Phipps, Admiral William 255, 262
Pilot, Robert 135
Pilote, Abbot François 290
Plamondon, Antoine 137, 250
Plamondon, Luc 93
Plessis, Mgr 244
Pozer, George 255
Price, Bruce 178, 184, 194, 260
Price, William 319, 322, 323
Provost, Théophile-Stanislas 219
Ramezay, Claude de 171
Ramsay, George 143
Reford, Elsie Meighen 296
Renaud, Pierre 255
Renaud, Toussaint-Xénophon 192, 197
Resther, father and son 192
Richard, Maurice 89
Richard-Lavallée, family 91
Richler, Mordechai 53
Riopelle, Jean-Paul 140
Robin, Charles 299, 302, 306, 308
Robinson, Albert Henry 211

Rolland, Jean-Baptiste 217
Roosevelt, Franklin D. 261
Ross, James 184
Ross, John Kenneth 184
Roy, Gabrielle 156, 280
Roy, Patrick 89
Safdie, Moshe 126, 228
Saint-Jean, Casimir 191
Saint-Pierre, Count of 312
Saint-Vallier, Mgr de 111, 269
Savard, Mgr Félix-Antoine 281
Scott, Francis Reginals 155
Sherbrooke, Sir John Coape 214
Siscoe, Stanley 230
Skead, Edward 229
Staveley, Harry 124
Steele, Sir John 170
Stephenson, Robert 199
Stewart, David M. 196
Suzor-Côté, Marc-Aurèle de Foy 137, 204, 215, 247
Taché, Eugène-Étienne 266, 270
Taft, William 284, 285
Tanobe, Miyuki 191
Taschereau, Elzéar-Alexandre 275
Taschereau, Louis-Alexandre 275
Taschereau, Thomas-Jacques 274
Thoreau, Henry David 148, 252
Tracy, Marquis of 255
Tremblay, Michel 60, 95, 192
Trent, George Norris 245
Trollope, Anthony 149, 227
Trudeau, Pierre-Elliot 185
Twiss, Ira 79
Vachon, J.-A. 275
Vanier, J.-Émile 190
Verchères, Madeleine de 204, 249
Vermare, André 265
Viger, Jacques 171
Vigneault, Gilles 92, 334
Villeneuve, Arthur 215, 323
Villeneuve, Gilles 89, 221
Vincent, known as Tehariolin, Zacharie 137
Voisine, Roch 93

Wakeham, William 303
Walker, Admiral Hovenden 255
Walker, Horatio 133, 277
Warburton, Edith 151
Ward, Artemis 150
Wellington, Duke of 199
Wells, John 170
Whale, Robert 215
Wolfe, General James 253, 271, 276
Worthington, G. H. 178
Wright, Philemon 226
Youville, Marguerite d' 173

A

Abbey of Oka 223
Abbey of Saint-Benoît-du-Lac 125, 213
Abénaquis, the 245
Abitibi-Témiscamingue 230
Acadians 308
Accommodation 351
Act of Union 40
Air Canada motor racing Grand Prix 352
Airplane 346, 348
Airports 350
Alcohol 351
Algonquins 38, 44
Aluminerie Alcan 321
Aluminum 72
Anse-Saint-Jean covered bridge 326
Apple growing 208
Aquarium of the Islands 314
Archipel de Berthier 221
Architecture, Canadian 109–130
Ardvarna 185
Arvida 322
Ash Inn 303
ATR (Association Tourisme Régional) 350, 369
Atwater Market 200
Auberge du Parc 308
Auberges 351
Augustines, the 268
Aurora borealis 234
Avenue des Pins 193
Avenue McGill 309

B

Baie des Chaleurs 307
Bald eagle 332
Bank of Montreal 166, 170
Banks 350
Banque du Peuple 170
Banque Royale 170
Barachois de Malbaie 303
Barnacle geese 245
Bas-du-Fleuve 292
Basilica Marie-Reine-du-Monde 120, 175
Basilica Notre-Dame (Montreal) 168
Basilica Sainte-Anne-de-Beaupré 278
Basilica St. Patrick 181
Basilica-cathedral Notre-Dame (Quebec City) 265
Bassin Louise 258

Battures du Kamouraska 291
Beauce, la 274
Beaver 242
Bed and Breakfasts 352
Beers 351
Beluga 295
Belvedere Camillien-Houde 183
Biodôme 197
Bishop University 215
Blackpoll warbler 287
Blockhouse, Lacolle 209
Bluebottles du Lac-Saint-Jean 321
Boatbuilders 91
Boats, crossings 348
Bois-Francs, les 244
Bonsecours 172
Bonsecours Market 117, 172
Boreal forest 32
Botanic garden of Montreal 196
Boulevard Morgan 197
Boulevard Saint-Laurent 188
Brézé, le 255
Buses 346, 348
Byward Market 227

C

Calvary of Varennes 123
Camping 353
Campus, McGill 179
Canada geese 245
Canadian International Paper 224
Canadian Parliament 227
Canadian-Pacific Railroad 209, 260
Canoeing 355
Canyons of the Vauréal River 332
Cap Diamant citadel 263
Cap Tourmente 282
Cap-des-Rosiers lighthouse 302
Capitole Theater 270
Caribou 232, 301, 354
Carnival, Quebec 258, 352
Carré d'Youville 270
Carré Saint-Louis 195
Carré Viger 194
Carrefour mondial de l'accordéon 91
Cars 349
Casavant organs 168, 205, 265
Cascades Inc 246

◆ INDEX

Casse-Cou steps 258
Cathedrals
– of the Assumption 239
– Holy Trinity 261
– Marie-Reine-du-Monde 175
– Sainte-Thérèse-d'Avila 230
– of Sainte-Trinité 261
– Trois-Rivières 118, 239
Catherine-de-Saint-Augustin Center 268
Cell phones 347
Cemeteries of Montreal 183
Ceramics 208
Cercle de la Garnison (Quebec City) 267
Champ-de-Mars 171
Charlevoix 276
Charlevoix Crossing 356
Château Brownies 210
Château de Ramezay 171
Château Dufresne 196
Château Frontenac 118, 260
Château Montebello 224
Château Saint-Louis 111
Chemin du Roy 248
Chic-Chocs 301
Christ Church Anglican Cathedral 180
Churches
– Chalmers-Wesley 267
– L'Islet-sur-Mer 123, 289
– Lavernière 313
– Neuville 111, 150
– Notre-Dame 192
– Notre-Dame-de-Bonsecours 289
– Notre-Dame-de-Fatima 127, 322
– Notre-Dame-de-la-Présentation 241
– Notre-Dame-des-Victoires 255
– Plymouth Trinity 117, 215
– Sainte-Amélie 330
– St Andrew's Presbyterian 264
– Sainte-Anne-de-Sorel 204
– Sainte-Cunégonde 200
– Saint-Eustache 222
– Saint-François-de-Sales 224, 250
– St George's 175
– Saint-Grégoire 244
– Saint-Hilaire 205
– St James United Mehodist 181

– Saint-Jean-Baptiste 190
– Saint-Jean-Baptiste (Quebec City) 120, 270
– St John the Evangelist 181
– Saint-Joseph-de-Beauce 275
– Saint-Michael-the-Archangel 190
– St Paul's 303
– St Stephen 115, 208
– Saint-Viateur 187
– Santa-Cruz 191
Cinema and television 96
Cinéma Impérial 181
Cipaille, la 98
Cirque du Soleil 95
Cité de l'Énergie 241
City halls
– Maisonneuve 197
– Montréal 119, 170
– Outremont 187
– Québec 264
Climate 347
Cod 47, 303
College 179
Compagnie du Nord-Ouest 49
Confédération, the 41
Conquest 39
Constitution of 1867 53
Costumes, traditional 74
Côte-de-Beaupré 280
Côte-des-Neiges 186
Côte-Sainte-Catherine 187
Craft fairs 270
Cri, the 234
Cross-country skiing 356
Customs 346
Cuthbert Chapel 221
Cycling 356

D

Dam of LG-2 234
Dams 68
Dépanneurs 353
Desjardins Complex 181
Dominion Square Building 178
Dorchester Square 174
Dorwin Falls 220
'Drive', the 77
Driving 349
Driving in winter 349
Dubleuet 100
Dufferin Terrace 260

E

Electricity 347
Embassy, Canadian 346

Embassy, US 350
Emergency numbers 357
Empress of Ireland 296
Épicerie J. A. Moisan 270
Estrie 210
Estrie Trail 356
Ex Machina 258
Exchange rate 346
EXPO 67 126, 198
Expos 197

F

Faubourg Saint-Jean (Quebec City) 270
Festivals 354
– Abitibi-Témiscamingue International Film 231
– Folklore 245
– Hang-gliding 301
– International Summer 270
– Lanaudière International 221
– Maple syrup 247
– Montreal International Jazz 194, 352
– Orford 213
Filles du roi, les 51
Fishing 28, 86, 249, 351
Food 353
Forest trappers 48
Forestry 76
Forests 32-35
Forges of Saint-Maurice 240
Forget Estate 284
Fort Chambly 208
Fort de la Martinière 274
Fort de Lévis 274
Fort Lennox 209
Fort Témiscamingue 231
Fortifications of Quebec 262
French consulate 266
French language 42, 62
Frères chasseurs, les 207
Fur trade 48
Fur traders 48, 75, 242

G

Gannets 306, 333
Gare du Palais 259
Gare Windsor 178
Gaspésie 298-309
Godbout boatbuilders 277
Golden Square Mile 184
Granby Zoo 210
Greyhound buses 346
Grosse-Île quarantine station 288
Grotto of Saguenay 326

Grotto of Saint-Elzéar 308
Guillemot 304, 307, 333 326

H

Health 347
Hiking 356
Historic sites
– of the battle of Ristigouche 309
–Forts-de-Lévis 274
–Lachine Canal 201
–Manoir-Papineau 224
–Pointe-au-Père 296
Hochelaga 47, 164
Horse riding 355
Hôtel Clarendon 264
Hôtel-Dieu de Québec 268
Hotels 351
House of Parliament 270
Hudson's Bay Company 49, 336
Hunting 84, 351
Hurons, the 271
Hydroelectric power stations 68, 70
– Beauharnois 209
– LG-2 234

I

Ice hockey 89, 100
Îles (islands)
– Anticosti 332
– aux Basques 293
– Bonaventure 306
– Brion 310
– du Cap aux Meules 313
– aux Coudres 281
– d'Entrée 310, 314
– du Havre Aubert 314
– du Havre aux Maisons 316
– Mingan (research station) 354
– de Montréal 198
– des Moulins 221
– aux Noix 209
– d'Orléans 276
– Sainte-Hélène 199
Île-Verte 293
Îles de Mingan research station 331, 354
Îles de Sorel 204
Îles-de-la-Madeleine 310-16, 348
Îlot des Palais 259
Insectarium 196
Institut canadien de Montréal 54
Insurance 346

Intendants' Palace 113, 259
Internet 347
Interpretation centers
– British heritage 308
– Cap-de-Bon-Désir 329
– development of the Côte-de-Beaupré 280
– fur trade 201
– lighthouses 301
– marine mammals 329
–Métabetchouane 319
– du patrimonie de Plaisance 224
– the port of Québec 258
–Saint-Jean-des-Piles 241
– seal 316
– the seigneurial regime 290
Inuit art 342
Inuits, the 38, 44, 335-44
Iroquois, the 38, 44

J

Jacques-Cartier Bridge 198
James Bay Agreement 337
Jean-Lesage (airport) 350
Jesuits, the 51
Joual, le 60

K

Kakouchacks 320
Kamouraska region 290
Kayaking 355
Kénogami 322
Kittiwake 305, 310, 333

L

La Grande Complex 69, 234
La Vérendrye nature reserve 230
Lachine Canal 200
Lachine Rapids 201
Lakes
– l'Anse-Pleureuse 301
– Maskinongé 220
– Massawippi 214
– Matane 300
– Matapédia 309
– Memphrémagog 212
– Saint-Jean 318
– Saint-Pierre 245, 248
– Taureau 220
– Trois-Saumons 290
Lambert School 275
Lanaudière 219

Land God Gave to Cain 334
Language, Quebecois 60
Latin Quarter (Montreal) 194
Laurentides 216
Le Massif ski resort 280
Les Palissades 287
Lobster 316
Long-distances buses 348
Loons 245
Louis Saint-Laurent Building 269
Lower North Shore 348
Loyalists, the 39

M

Magazines 357
Mail 356
Main Street (Montreal) 188
Maison
– Archambault 194
– Casavant 191, 205
– Chapais 291
– Chauvin 328
– Chevalier 255
– Cormier 185
– de l'Outre-Mont 187
– de la prune 292
– de Louis Richard 200
– Desjardins 274
– du Pirate 306
– du Calvet 172
– du citoyen 228
– du Colon 231
– Dumulon 231
– Forget 184
– Fornel 254
– Hamelin 248
– Jacquet 266
– Lamontagne 296, 300
– Louis-Jolliet 258
– nationale des Patriotes 205
– Papineau 117, 172
– Péan 266
– Riverview 229
– Ross 184
– Saint-Gabriel 200
– Shaughnessy 118
– Taschereau 275
– VLB 293
Maisonneuve 196
Maisonneuve fire station 197
Maisonneuve Market 197
Makivik 344
Malbaie Gorges 286
Manic 2 dam 71
Manic 5 dam 70, 330

Manoirs
– Boucher de Niverville 239
– de l'accordéon 289
– de Sales-Laterrière 284
– des Aulnaies 290
– du Saguenay 124, 322
– Globensky 222
– Le Boutillier 302
– Louis-Joseph-Papineau 224
– Masson 221
– Mauvide-Genest 277
– Richelieu 285
– Rouville-Campbell 205
– Trent 245
Maple syrup 36, 82, 100
Maria Micmac Reserve 308
Marie-de-l'Incarnation Center 269
Matamajaw Estate 309
Matane Reserve 300
McGill University 179
Media 357
Métis Garden 296
Métro de Montréal 176, 348-9
Micmacs, the 46, 308, 312
Migrations Center 288
Mile-End 190
Mills 66
–l'île aux Coudres 281
–Légaré 223
–Petit-Pré 280
– seigneurial of Maillou Falls 288
– seigneurial of Tonnancour 249
–Ulverton 246
Mingan Archipelago National Park Reserve 331
Minganie 331
Mohawks, the 52, 59
Monasteries
–Bon-Pasteur 121, 195
–Très-Saint-Sacrement 192
– Ursulines 269
Money 346, 350
Mont Orford 212
Mont Royal 92, 166, 182
Mont-Saint-Hilaire nature conservation center 208
Mont-Saint-Louis 195
Mont-Tremblant 218
Montagnais, the 329
Monte-à-Peine Falls 220
Montérégie 204
Montérégiennes 204
Montmorency Falls 276

Montreal Buddhist Church 190
Montreal Canadians 89
Montreal Furniture School 79
Motels 351
Museums
– of Argenteuil 223
– of Civilisation 255, 256
– Acadian of Quebec 308
– Amerindian of Mashteuiatsh 320
– Art (Montreal) 184
– Art (Sherbrooke) 215
– Bernier Maritime289
– Bombardier 212
– Bon-Pasteur 268
– Brome County 211
– Canadian Railroad 209
– David W. Stewart 199
– François-Pilote 290
– Grévin 261
– Laurier 246
– Louis-Hémon 321
– Malartic Mineralogy 230
– Marius-Barbeau 275
– McCord 180
– Mineralogical and Mining 247
– Montreal's Society of Archeology and Numismatics 171
– National Gallery of Canada (Ottawa) 228
– of Archeology of Pointe à Callière 173
– of Arts and Popular Traditions of Quebec (Trois-Rivières) 239
– of Bronze 247
– of Charlevoix 285
– of Civilisations 229
– of Contemporary Art Montreal 181
– of Decorative Arts of Maisonneuve 196
– of French Americans 265
– of Gaspésie 303
– of Guérin 231
– of Haut-Richelieu 208
– of Kamouraska 291
– of Natural Sciences 230
– of Pointe-à-Callière 128
– of Quebec 270
– of Religions 244
– of Saguenay-Lac-Saint-Jean 323
– of Skiing 218

◆ INDEX

– of the Abénaquis 245
– of the Augustines 268
– of the Fort 261
– of the History of Lake Saint-Jean 321
– of the Lower Saint Lawrence 292
– of the Military History of Saint-Jean-sur-Richelieu 208
– of the North Shore 330
– of the Sea 296, 314
– of the town of Lachine 201
– of the Ursulines 239, 269
– of Water 198
– Plein-Air 201
– Redpath 179
– Uplands 215
– Water transport 281
Music conservatory of Montréal 170

N

Nationalism 57
Native Americans 44, 46, 58
Nature watching 354
Navigation on the Saint Lawrence 281
Nelson's Column 116, 171
Neoclassicism 116
New York Life Insurance 125, 169
Newspapers 100, 357
Noranda Mines 302
North Nation Mills 224
Notman Collection 180
Notre-Dame Cathedral-basilica (Ottawa) 227
Notre-Dame community 185, 200
Notre-Dame-de-Bonsecours Chapel 172
Notre-Dame-de-Lourdes Chapel 195
Notre-Dame-du-Cap Sanctuary 249
Notre-Dame-du-Sacré-Cœur Sanctuary 267
Nunavik 344

O

Old Montreal 168
Old Port (Montreal) 172
Old Port (Quebec) 258
Old Seminary (Quebec) 265
Old Jesuit House 271
Olympic Complex of Montreal 196

Olympic stadium 196
Orford arts center 213
Ouananiche 326

P

Palais de justice (Montreal) 170
Palais de justice (Quebec City) 266
Palais de Justice (Saint-Joseph-de-Beauce) 275
Papeterie Saint-Gilles 281
Parking 349
Parks 355
– Basque Adventure in America 293
– Cavalier-du-Moulin 266
– Falls of the Little Bostonnais River 241
– Forillon 304
– La Mauricie 241
– Lafontaine 192
– Lahaie 190
– Montmorency 269
– Rockcliffe 228
– Sept-Chutes 219
–Frontenac 247
–Gaspésie 300
–Grands-Jardins 286
–Hautes-Gorges-de-la-rivière-Malbaie 286
–Miguasha 309
–Mont-Orford 212
–Mont-Royal 183
–Mont-Tremblant 218
–Plaisance 224
–Saguenay 324
–Sept-Îles 331
Parliament 270
Parliament Hill 227
Parti libéral 42
Parti québécois 42, 347
Passports 347
Pâtisserie Vachon 275
Patriots 207
Peace of Montreal 38
Petit-Champlain (Quebec) 258
Petite-Bourgogne, la 200
Phillips Square 180
Pierre-Elliott-Trudeau airport 350
Pilgrimages 123
Pioneers' route 229
Place
– d'Armes (Montreal) 169
– d'Youville (Montreal) 173

– Jacques-Cartier (Montreal) 170, 171
– Royale (Quebec) 254
– Ville-Marie (Montreal) 176, 178
Place names in Quebec 62
Plaisance nature reserve 224
Plateau Mont-Royal 190
Plymouth-Trinity United Church 215
Pointe à Callière 173
Pointe Saint-Charles 200
Porte Saint-Louis (Quebec) 266
Post office, Quebec 269
Pourvoiries 354
Price Brothers 264
Price Building 264
Prison de Québec 267
Prison, Trois-Rivières 115, 239
Public holidays 354
Puffins 331, 333
Pulp and papers exhibition center 239

Q

Quebec Literary and Historical Society 267
Quebecois specialties 100, 353
Quiet Revolution 56, 126

R

Radio 354
Rafting 218, 356
Ravenscrag 185
Rebellions of 1837–8 206
Récollets 51, 261
Regionalism 124
Religious communities 51
Restaurant 'Le 9e' 180
Rialto Theater 187
Rideau Canal 227
Rideau Falls 228
Rivers
– Chicoutimi 322
– Gatineau 229
– Jacques-Cartier 250
– Magog 215
– Malbaie 286
– Métabetchouane 319
– Outaouais 222, 226, 230
– Richelieu 204
– Ristigouche 309
– Rouge 218
– Sainte-Anne 250

– Saint-François 245
– Saint-Lawrence 22-5, 80, 281, 294
– Saint-Maurice 240
– Yamaska 211
Rock climbing 355
Roe deer 333
Route 109 234
Royal Proclamation of 1763 40
Rue Drolet (Montreal) 190
Rue Jeanne-Mance (Montreal) 119, 190
Rue Saint-Denis (Montreal) 195
Rue Saint-Jacques 170
Rue Saint-Louis (Quebec) 266
Rue Sainte-Catherine (Montreal) 194
Rue Sherbrooke (Montreal) 184, 195
Rue Sussex (Ottawa) 228

S

Saguenay Fjord 324, 326
Saguenay-Lac-Saint-Jean 318
Saint-Félicien Zoo 320
Saint-Henri-des-Tanneries 200
Saint-Hilaire Mountain 208
Saint-Jean-Baptiste (district) 190
Saint-Joseph Oratory 186
Saint Lawrence 22-25, 80, 281, 294
St Mark Chapel 215
Saint-Sulpice Library 195
Sainte-Famille Chapel 122, 277
Salmon 87
Seabirds 333, 354
Seals 305, 311, 331, 354
Seigneurial system 40, 50
Seigneurie des Aulnaies 290
Seminary of Nicolet 244
Seminary of Saint-Sulpice 110, 169
Shamans 340
Shared cars 349
Shipping on the Saint Lawrence 80
Shipyards 81
Shops 353, 364-5
Skiing, 356
Sledding 356
Snowbiking 355

Snowmobiles 89, 356
Snowshoeing 356
South Shore 288
Sports 88, 355-6
Square du 350e 195
Stadaconé 47
Statue of Edward VII 180
Statue of Notre-Dame-
  du-Saguenay 326
Storytellers 91
Subway (Montreal)
  176, 348-9
Sugar parties 82, 352
Sugar time 82, 352
Sulpiciens, the
  51, 168, 169
Sun Life 125, 178
Symmes Hotel 229
Synagogue Beth
  Schloïme 191

T

Taiga 32
Taxes 357
Telephone 347, 357
Television 354
Theater, Quebecois 94
Time difference 346
Tipping 357
Tourist associations 370
Traditions 90
Trains 346, 349
Traversiers 348
Triplex 193
Trout 87
Tundra 30

U

Underground city 176
University of Montreal
  (UQAM) 187, 195
Ursulines, the 51
Useful addresses
  346, 350

V

Valleys
– Gatineau 229
– Laurentienne 39
– Matapédia 309
– Rouge 218
Victoria Bridge199
Victoria Square 181
Vieux-Palais exhibition
  center 217
Viger Hotel 194
Villa Maria 185
Villages
– Bourlamaque mining
village 230
– Canadian 220
– Lumberjack 241

– québécois d'antan 245
Voltigeurs 245

W

Whaling 47, 354
White-tailed deer 301
Wildlife reserves 355
Windsor Hotel 178
Wine Trail 211
Wines 351
Winter camping 352
Wolfe-Montcalm
Monument 116, 252
Wood 76
World Trade Center 170

YZ

Youth hostels 352
ZEC 354